SOCIOLOGICAL
METHODOLOGY
2006

SOCIOLOGICAL METHODOLOGY ✂ 2006 ✂

VOLUME 36

EDITOR: Ross M. Stolzenberg

MANAGING EDITOR: Ray Weathers

An official publication by Blackwell Publishing for

THE AMERICAN SOCIOLOGICAL ASSOCIATION

SALLY T. HILLSMAN, *Executive Officer*

Library of Congress Catalog Card Information
Sociological Methodology, 1969–85
San Francisco, Jossey-Bass. 15 v. illus. 24 cm. annual. (Jossey-Bass behavioral science
series)
Editor: 1969, 1970: E. F. Borgatta; 1971, 1972, 1973–74: H. L. Costner;
1975, 1976, 1977: D. R. Heise; 1978, 1979, 1980: K. F. Schuessler;
1981, 1982, 1983–84: S. Leinhardt; 1985: N. B. Tuma

Sociological Methodology, 1986–88
Washington, DC, American Sociological Association. 3 v. illus. 24 cm. annual.
Editor: 1986: N. B. Tuma; 1987, 1988: C. C. Clogg

Sociological Methodology, 1989–1992
Oxford, Basil Blackwell. 4 v. illus. 24 cm. annual.
Editor: 1989, 1990: C. C. Clogg; 1991, 1992: P. V. Marsden
"An official publication of the American Sociological Association."
1. Sociology—Methodology—Year books. I. American Sociological
Association. II. Borgatta, Edgar F., 1924-ed.

HM24.S55   3010.0108   68-54940
                           rev.
Library of Congress   [r71h2]

British Cataloguing in Publication Data
Sociological Methodology. Vol. 30
1. Sociology. Methodology
301'.01'8

ISBN 1-4051-6724-6
ISSN 0081-1750

Library of Congress Cataloging-in-Publication Data is available at the Library of
Congress

REVIEWERS

Paul D. Allison
Tom DiPrete
George Farkas
Katherine Faust
Glenn Firebaugh
John D. Fox
Andrew Gelman
Rick Grannis
Guang Guo
Paul T. von Hippel

Jon Krosnick
Kenneth C. Land
Tim F. Liao
Roderick Little
John R. Logan
Robert D. Mare
Douglas Massey
Philippa E. Pattison
Pamela Paxton
Stanley Presser

Stephen W. Raudenbush
Sean S. Reardon
Fabio Rojas
John Skvoretz
Stephen M. Stigler
Judith Tanur
Jeroen K. Vermunt
Yang Yang

CONTENTS

Reviewers   v

Contributors   ix

Acknowledgment   xv

Information for Authors   xvii

Editor's Introduction   xix

Review and Renewal of Findings Past
1. Another Look at the Stratification of Educational   1
   Transitions: The Logistic Response Model with Partial
   Proportionality Constraints
          Robert M. Hauser and Megan Andrew

   Response:
   Statistical Models of Educational Stratification—Hauser   27
   and Andrew's Models for School Transitions
          Robert D. Mare

New Methods for Specific Situations: Cohort Models,
Exponential Graphs, Event Histories, Cluster Studies
and Logit Analyses
2. Bayesian Inference for Hierarchical Age-Period-Cohort   39
   Models of Repeated Cross-Section Survey Data
          Yang Yang

A Mixed Models Approach to the Age-Period-Cohort   75
Analysis of Repeated Cross-Section Surveys with an
Application to Data on Trends in Verbal Test Scores
                    Yang Yang and Kenneth C. Land

New Specifications for Exponential Random Graph   99
Models
                    Tom A. B. Snijders, Philippa E. Pattison,
                    Garry L. Robins, and Mark S. Handcock

Fixed-Effects Methods for the Analysis of Nonrepeated 155
Events
                    Paul D. Allison and Nicholas A. Christakis

Meaningful Regression and Association Models for   173
Clustered Ordinal Data
                    Jukka Jokinen, John W. McDonald,
                    and Peter W. F. Smith

Measuring and Analyzing Class Inequality with the Gini 201
Index Informed by Model-Based Clustering
                    Tim Futing Liao

Effect Displays for Multinomial and Proportional-Odds   225
Logit Models
                    John Fox and Robert Andersen

Survey Design and Analysis
 3. A Partial Independence Item Response Model for Surveys 257
    with Filter Questions
                    Sean F. Reardon and
                    Stephen W. Raudenbush

    Response Bias in a Popular Indicator of Reading   301
    to Children
                    Sandra L. Hofferth

Staying Alive and Other Practical Problems of Data Acquisition
 4. The Safety Dance: Confronting Harassment, Intimidation, 317
    and Violence in the Field
                    Gwen Sharp and Emily Kremer

CONTRIBUTORS

Paul D. Allison

Paul D. Allison is a professor of sociology at the University of Pennsylvania. He is currently doing research on missing data and fixed effects models. He also teaches summer workshops on categorical data analysis and event-history analysis.

Robert Andersen

Robert Andersen is Senator William McMaster Chair in Political Sociology in the Sociology Department at McMaster University, Canada, and Associate Member of Nuffield College, University of Oxford. He is also a member of the regular teaching staff at the ICPSR Summer Program in Quantitative Methods, University of Michigan. His research interests are in political sociology, social inequality, survey methods, and social statistics.

Megan Andrew

Megan Andrew is a doctoral student in the Department of Sociology at the University of Wisconsin–Madison. Her research interests are in social stratification, the life course, education and work transitions, quantitative methodology, and social policy.

Nicholas A. Christakis

Nicholas A. Christakis is a professor in the Department of Sociology at Harvard University and in the Department of Health Care Policy at

Harvard Medical School. He is also a Faculty Associate of the Institute for Quantitative Social Science at Harvard. His current research focuses on health externalities and on the spread of health-related phenomena within social networks.

John Fox

John Fox is a professor of sociology at McMaster University in Hamilton, Ontario. He is the author of many articles and several books on social statistics, statistical computing, and statistical graphics, including the recent book, *An R and S-PLUS Companion to Applied Regression* (Sage, 2002). In addition to social statistics, his research interests are in social inequality and social psychology.

Mark S. Handcock

Mark S. Handcock is a professor of statistics and sociology in the Department of Statistics at the University of Washington. His recent work focuses on combining population-level and individual-level information, statistical models for the analysis of social network data, spatial processes, and labor economics. He is a core faculty member of the Center for Statistics and the Social Sciences and the Center for Studies in Demography and Ecology.

Robert M. Hauser

Robert M. Hauser is Vilas Research Professor of Sociology and Director of the Center for Demography of Health and Aging at the University of Wisconsin–Madison. His research interests are in the life course and aging, social stratification, and social statistics. He was co-principal investigator (with David L. Featherman) on the 1973 Occupational Changes in a Generation Survey and currently serves as Principal Investigator of the Wisconsin Longitudinal Study.

Sandra L. Hofferth

Sandra L. Hofferth is a professor of family studies at the University of Maryland, College Park. Her research interests lie in the health consequences of family time allocation and activity for children. She is the principal investigator on an interdisciplinary project studying physical activity and obesity and on a project exploring the intergenerational consequences of paternal involvement.

Jukka Jokinen

Jukka Jokinen is a statistician at the National Public Health Institute, and a doctoral student in the Department of Mathematics and Statistics at the University of Helsinki, Finland. His main research interests are in epidemiology and computational statistics.

Emily Kremer

Emily Kremer is a lecturer in the Department of Sociology at the University of Wisconsin–Madison. Her main research interests are gender, marginalized masculinities, race and ethnicity, and adolescence.

Kenneth C. Land

Kenneth C. Land is the John Franklin Crowell Professor of Sociology and Director of the Center for Demographic Studies at Duke University. His main research interests are in the development of mathematical and statistical models and methods for substantive applications in demography, criminology, and social indicators/quality-of-life studies.

Tim Futing Liao

Tim Futing Liao is a professor of sociology and statistics in the Department of Sociology at the University of Illinois, Urbana-Champaign. In addition to measuring inequality, his current research interests include latent-variable approaches to missing data and methods for comparative and historical as well as panel analysis.

Robert D. Mare

Robert D. Mare is a professor of sociology at the University of California–Los Angeles. His research focuses on models for intergenerational social mobility, marriage markets and assortative mating, residential mobility and segregation, and the links between demographic processes and social inequality.

John W. McDonald

John W. McDonald is a professor of social statistics at the University of Southampton. His main research interests are in demography and social statistics.

Philippa E. Pattison

Philippa E. Pattison is a quantitative social scientist whose research is focused on the development of statistical models for networks and network-based social processes. She is a professor in the School of Behavioural Science at the University of Melbourne.

Stephen W. Raudenbush

Stephen W. Raudenbush joined the University of Chicago as the Lewis-Sebring Distinguished Service Professor and chair of the new Committee on Education in 2005. His research involves the development, testing, refinement, and application of statistical methods for studying individual change and the effects of social settings such as schools and neighborhoods on change. Professor Raudenbush is best known for his expertise in quantitative methodology using the advanced research technique of hierarchical linear models, which allows researchers to accurately evaluate data from school performance.

Sean F. Reardon

Sean Reardon is an associate professor of education and (by courtesy) sociology at Stanford University. His current research interests include causes, patterns, and consequences of residential and school segregation; race/ethnic and socioeconomic achievement disparities; and neighborhood influences of child development.

Garry L. Robins

Garry L. Robins is a mathematical psychologist in the School of Behavioural Science at the University of Melbourne, Australia. His research deals with quantitative models for social and relational systems, particularly exponential random graph (p^*) models for social networks.

Gwen Sharp

Gwen Sharp is an associate professor in the Department of History and Sociology at Southern Utah University. Her research interests are global food systems, minority landownership in the rural United States, immigration, and gender issues in sports.

Peter W. F. Smith

Peter W. F. Smith is a professor of social statistics in the Social Statistics Division, School of Social Sciences, at the University of Southampton. He is also a member of the Southampton Statistical Sciences Research Institute. His research interests are in statistical modeling methodology and its applications to social and medical data.

Tom A. B. Snijders

Tom A. B. Snijders is a professor of methodology and statistics at the Department of Sociology of the University of Groningen, and scientific director of the research and graduate school ICS (Interuniversity Center for Social Science Theory and Methodology). His main research interests are social network analysis and multilevel analysis.

Yang Yang

Yang Yang is an assistant professor in the Department of Sociology and affiliated with Center on the Aging and Population Research Center at NORC and the University of Chicago. Her research interests focus on demography of aging, social differentials of health across adult life course, and new models and methods for cohort analysis.

ACKNOWLEDGMENTS

Many people contributed to the publication of this volume. First, I thank those who submitted papers for consideration. Scholars benefit from having their work published, but they are scholars with or without their publications. Journals, however, cannot exist without articles to publish. So I am very grateful to all who submitted papers to *Sociological Methodology*, whether or not those papers were accepted for publication.

Second, I thank Ray Weathers for his essential contributions as managing editor of *Sociological Methodology*. I simply could not have edited this volume without the extraordinary skill, overflowing good will, and abundantly practical optimism that Ray Weathers brought to the enterprise each and every day. His expertise, efficiency, great care, marvelous good humor, and his distinctive and enjoyable personality have made it a true pleasure to work with him.

Third, I thank the reviewers who spent so much time evaluating the papers that were submitted for publication in this volume. Methodological papers are time-consuming and difficult to review. We rely upon reviewers to vet the accuracy of mathematical derivations as well as the more general features of submitted papers. Without these careful, painstaking, and insightful reviews, *Sociological Methodology* would vanish in an instant. I also thank the editorial board members and deputy editors of *Sociological Methodology* for their contributions.

I express my gratitude to Jennifer Scarano and other staff at Blackwell Publishing who produced *Sociological Methodology*. These people brought technical expertise, good business judgment, constructive attitudes, flexibility, and hard work to the production of *Sociological Methodology*. They make this journal possible in ways that I greatly appreciate but do not understand. I am also grateful to Stephanie Magean for quickly, efficiently, and cheerfully copy-editing all of the articles in this volume. Karen Edwards of the American Sociological Association has helped in numerous ways, and has smilingly conspired with Ray Weathers to work around my abundant bureaucratic failings.

For unusual reasons, editing *Sociological Methodology* has consumed much more time than I could have anticipated. I am enormously grateful to Craig Coelen, the president of NORC, for making available the resources that have permitted me to find that time among my other responsibilities.

I thank Michael Sobel for serving as a model of patience, restraint, and unflinching devotion to the values served by refereed scholarly publications. His contributions to *Sociological Methodology* preceded his term as editor (ending in 2001), and his contributions have persisted afterwards, sometimes in the pages of this journal, and sometimes in other ways too complex to describe here.

I thank Nava Stolzenberg for permitting her art to grace the covers of *Sociological Methodology* in 2002, 2003, 2004, 2005, and 2006.

Finally, I thank the American Sociological Association for its support of *Sociological Methodology*. A discipline's journals reflect the interests of its practitioners, as well as the intellectual content of the field itself. Thus, the publication of *Sociological Methodology* by the American Sociological Association confirms that sociology, sociologists, and the association itself all share a deep and abiding interest in the methods by which sociological research is done. Without that interest, our claims to scientific inquiry would be hollow, and we would be little more than a loosely-coupled collection of artisans bringing idiosyncratic methods of unknown quality to the production of disconnected projects.

Ross M. Stolzenberg
Editor

SUBMISSION INFORMATION FOR AUTHORS

Sociological Methodology is an annual compendium of advances in the methodology of social research. These articles promise to advance the quality and efficiency of sociological research, or to make accessible to sociologists recent methodological advances in related disciplines. *Sociological Methodology* is an official publication of the American Sociological Association.

Sociological Methodology seeks contributions that address the full range of problems confronted by empirical work in the contemporary social sciences, including conceptualization and modeling, research design, data collection, measurement, and data analysis. Work on the methodological problems involved in any approach to empirical social science is appropriate for *Sociological Methodology*. Chapters present original methodological contributions, expository statements on and illustrations of recently developed techniques, and critical discussions of research practice.

The content of each annual volume of *Sociological Methodology* is driven by submissions initiated by authors; the volumes do not have specific themes. Editorial decisions about manuscripts submitted are based on the advice of expert referees. Criteria include originality, breadth of interest and applicability, and expository clarity. Discussions of implications for research practice are vital, and authors are urged to include empirical illustrations of the methods they discuss.

Authors should submit five copies of manuscripts to

Ross M.Stolzenberg
Sociological Methodology
The University of Chicago
Department of Sociology
307 Social Science Building
1126 East 59th Street
Chicago, Illinois 60637

Manuscripts should include an informative abstract of not more than one double-spaced page, and should not identify the author within the text. Submission of a manuscript for review by *Sociological Methodology* implies that it has not been published previously and that it is not under review elsewhere.

Inquiries concerning the appropriateness of material and/or other aspects of editorial policies and procedures are welcome; prospective authors should correspond with the editor by E-mail at r-stolzen berg@chicago.edu.

EDITOR'S INTRODUCTION

With this volume of *Sociological Methodology*, my tenure as editor ends. My term of service was extended once beyond my original appointment. I appreciate the confidence implied by the invitation to edit the only methodology journal of the American Sociological Association, and by the extension of my term as editor. I am grateful to have had this opportunity to serve the discipline that has been so receptive to my own ideas and research efforts. I am thankful to the many individuals who have shown me so much kindness and given me so much help in my editorial tasks.

This Introduction is written with knowledge that introductions are rarely read beyond their first paragraph. Therefore, I limit myself to three topics: The Present, The Past, and The Future.

The Present

The present, of course, is this volume. In the first chapter, Hauser and Andrew re-visit a well-known contribution by Mare, on the analysis of educational transitions – or grade progressions. Mare responds. Each of these authors suggests something in the other's work that can be done better, but the exchange is a model of constructive debate, more a sequential collaboration than a dispute. The result is instructive on the form, substance, and method of social research.

Seven chapters in this volume contain a broad array of new and refined methods for addressing enduring concerns of social researchers.

Yang and Land add two chapters that extend and revise their conceptual and methodological contributions to age-period-cohort analysis of time. Papers by Snijders, Pattison, Robbins, Handcock, Allison, Christakis, Jokinen, McDonald, Smith, Liao, Fox, and Anderson contribute to the analysis of social networks, social inequality, and other topics of current intense social science interest.

Two more chapters in this book address key questions about data gathering and data production. Hofferth considers a specific measure used in studies of parents and children. Reardon and Raudenbush consider the ubiquitous filter questions that guide survey respondents through questionnaires.

The last chapter of this volume takes up a topic that few like to consider: safety. As one who has been called upon to restore breath to persons no longer breathing (once at sociological meetings), I can think of no topic more important for researchers than their own safety, and the safety of the students, collaborators, and subordinates whom they send into the field to gather data. Sharp and Kremer offer advice on preserving the lives and limbs of those who gather data from the general public.

In short, this volume of *Sociological Methodology* has something to interest nearly every practitioner and reader of contemporary social science research.

The Past

When I became editor of *Sociological Methodology*, I established some goals. First, I sought to maintain the high quality of articles published in the journal, and to protect the integrity of the editorial process that evaluated submissions, vetted revisions, and marched authors of accepted papers through the publication process. Previous editors had established an enviable and long record of accepting innovative and useful contributions of lasting impact. I wanted to maintain that record, and to improve upon it, if possible. I expected that the biggest challenges would be to attract a wide array of fine papers as submissions, and to get them evaluated by reviewers who would recognize their strengths and recommend solutions to their weaknesses.

As my second goal, I sought to publish papers that would broadly represent the full range of methods that sociological researchers use – or might productively use, if only they knew about them. If the American Sociological Association publishes only one methodological journal, I reasoned, it had better be a broad-gauge journal that would be of use to the entire discipline.

Third, I wished to bring *Sociological Methodology* to timely production. The pace of article submissions is unpredictable and good reviewers are intrinsically ungovernable. Technical papers require specialized reviewers, and their assistance is sometimes difficult to secure. So predictable scheduling seemed to be a matter of acquiring a backlog of accepted articles. I began with no backlog at all. I would need to work hard and get lucky to create one.

Finally, I sought to make the journal a prettier book. This was a selfish goal. I kept *Sociological Methodology* in my office and in my home. I looked at it frequently and wanted to enjoy the experience, even when the book was closed. Other readers would appreciate this goal, I thought, even if it lacked the priority of my other goals. Typography and page design were pleasing already. I sought to give the book a more attractive exterior.

How did I do? Readers are the only valid judges of papers published in *Sociological Methodology*. In time, they will make known their verdict. Authors of submitted papers, as well as readers and reviewers, will judge the effectiveness and efficiency of the editorial process. (Authors rarely forgive editors for rejecting their paper; I do hope for rare events of this type.) I am pleased to report that the journal now has a backlog of accepted, first-rate papers. I hope that this backlog makes it easier for the next editor to meet production deadlines. Of course, I now know that backlogs are not sufficient to get *Sociological Methodology* to press on time, or printed on time after it is in press, or bound on time after it is printed. Three of my five volumes were terribly delayed by interference in the editorial process by persons who hoped to suppress publication of papers that criticized their own work. Naïvely, it seems, I had not imagined the motivation or method to suppress or delay publication in scholarly journals.

The Future

The future is contained in papers not yet written. Some of those papers will be written by authors who neither need nor seek advice. However, many of those papers – and some of the most valuable ones, I predict – will be written by authors who need advice, seek it, follow it, and thereby bring their work into print. These authors frequently ask editors for general and specific advice. The best advice I can give to others is the advice that I try to take myself, every day that I write. Here it is:

- *Write on topics that other people care about*. And tell the readers why they should care.
- *Tell the reader why your findings are important*. Be direct. "This question is important because . . ." and "This result is important because . . ."
- *Be short and blunt*. Write short sentences. Use short words. Write short paragraphs. Complicated ideas are inevitable, but complicated-sounding ideas don't sell. If your idea is complicated, then find a simple way to explain it. Readers stop reading as soon as they lose track of the author's argument. That's true of reviewers too. The celebrated social psychologist Stanley Schachter used to say that if he could not explain his ideas to the satisfied understanding of his un-schooled grandmother, then he knew that he was not ready to write.
- *Start with a theoretical problem and draw theoretical conclusions*. Theories are very popular. Everybody wants one.
- *Write for a specific publication*. Be specific. Every decision you make about writing your paper should be made on the basis of how well it helps you get your paper into your target journal. Read copies of the journal in which you wish to publish, just to get a sense of the style that is favored by that journal. Then write in that style.
- *Identify the market for your research and then write in a style that appeals to that market*. For example, don't use complex mathematical notation when writing for a subfield that is allergic to fancy methods.
- *Never say that previous research is stupid*. First, all theories are eventually found to be wrong. This is science, not religion, so be easy on your predecessors. Second, your paper will be reviewed by the very same people who wrote the stupid previous research. At best, they are only human; but sometimes they are as stupid as you think, and vindictive and mean-spirited too. So say instead that you are filling gaps in the literature, building on previous findings, resolving unresolved problems, or similar.

- *Write a long abstract for the reviewers.* A long, well-written abstract will help the reviewers understand your paper. That helps you get a positive review. Of course, the copy editor will make you shorten the abstract before publication, but it's a happy task to satisfy the copy editor after your paper is accepted.
- *Revise and resubmit quickly.* An R&R (rejection with an invitation to revise and resubmit) is a successful outcome. Do whatever the reviewers tell you to do, right away. If the reviewers ask you to do stupid things, then you will have to do stupid things if you want your paper published. Don't argue with reviewers; you can do the stupid things in footnotes that declare, "A reviewer asked that we ..." Cancel your vacation. Kiss your family and friends goodbye temporarily; come to meetings late and leave early. Work nonstop except for exercise, food, and a little sleep, in that order. An R&R is like being called up for military duty; when you gotta go, you gotta go. And don't forget to take the advice that the reviewers give you.
- *Recognize your enemies* (perfectionism and pessimism) and have a strategy for defeating them. Try to write a mediocre paper. Then rewrite it until it is a very good paper. Make it your obligation to be an optimist. The important thing is to move forward at all times.
- *Circulate your paper for comments.* Ask for advice with an open mind. If advice sounds good, then take it. If the reader misunderstands, conclude that you did not write clearly enough. Some very successful authors in sociology are very good at taking advice, but not very good at much of anything else. I forget their names. But I know that they circulate their papers, get advice, take the advice that they get, and then publish in the leading journals.

In Conclusion

Again, I am grateful to have had the opportunity to edit *Sociological Methodology*. It was sometimes fun, it taught me much, and it was almost always satisfying. I hope that you, the readers of *Sociological Methodology*, will find that the same words are an apt description of this volume and the four that preceded it: "It was sometimes fun, it taught me much, and it was almost always satisfying."

ANOTHER LOOK AT THE STRATIFICATION OF EDUCATIONAL TRANSITIONS: THE LOGISTIC RESPONSE MODEL WITH PARTIAL PROPORTIONALITY CONSTRAINTS

Robert M. Hauser*
Megan Andrew*

In this paper we reanalyze Robert D. Mare's highly influential work on educational transitions among American men born in the first half of the 20th century. Contrary to previous belief, Mare found that the effects of socioeconomic background variables decline regularly across educational transitions in conditional logistic regression analyses. We have reconfirmed Mare's findings and tested

An earlier version of this paper was prepared for the May 2005 meetings of the Research Committee on Social Stratification, International Sociological Association in Oslo, Norway. The research reported herein was supported by the William Vilas Estate Trust and by the Graduate School of the University of Wisconsin–Madison. Computation was carried out using facilities of the Center for Demography and Ecology at the University of Wisconsin–Madison, which are supported by Center Grants from the National Institute of Child Health and Human Development and from the National Institute on Aging. We thank Maarten Buis, Jeremy Freese, Carl Frederick, Harry Ganzeboom, Michael Hout, and John A. Logan. We thank Robert D. Mare especially for correcting an error in an earlier draft of this paper and for his elegant and useful discussion of our work. The opinions expressed here are those of the authors. Address correspondence to Robert M. Hauser or Megan Andrew, Center for Demography and Ecology, University of Wisconsin–Madison, 1180 Observatory Drive, Madison, Wisconsin 53706 or e-mail to hauser@ssc.wisc.edu or mandrew@ssc.wisc.edu.

*University of Wisconsin-Madison

them by introducing a modified logistic response model that con-
strains selected social background effects to vary proportionally
across educational transitions. We refer to our preferred model
as the logistic response model with partial proportionality con-
straints (LRPPC). The model can easily be estimated in Stata or
using other standard statistical software. Partial proportionality
constraints may also prove useful in interpopulation comparisons
based on other linear models.

Robert Mare's (1979, 1980, 1981) innovative analyses of American educational transitions in the 1973 Occupational Changes in a Generation
(OCG) survey were among the most important and influential contributions to research on social stratification in the past three decades. Prior
to the introduction of Mare's model of educational transitions in 1980,
social stratification research typically employed linear probability models of school continuation and linear models of highest grade completed
(e.g., Hauser and Featherman 1976). This research uniformly empha-
sized the stability of the stratification process in general and the effects of
parental socioeconomic status on educational attainment. In his analyses, Mare applied a logistic response model to school continuation,
restricting the base population at risk for each successive transition to
those who had completed the prior educational transition. Contrary to
prior supposition, Mare's estimates suggested the effects of some socioeconomic background variables declined across six successive transitions
including completion of elementary school through entry into graduate
school. Mare's (1980) original estimates are reproduced in Table 1.

Mare's studies of educational transitions have been both influential and controversial. His work spawned theories on the transition rates
and odds ratios within educational systems, most notably the theories
of maximally maintained inequality (Raftery and Hout 1993) and effectively maintained inequality (Lucas 2001). Mare's models were also the
basis of a widely cited international comparative study of educational
attainment (Shavit and Blossfeld 1993). However, the thesis that effects
of social background decline across educational transitions has also
been attacked by prominent labor economists (Cameron and Heckman
1998). They suggested, among other things, that Mare's logistic response
model is only loosely motivated behaviorally and that the general decline of social background effects is a statistical artifact of the (logistic)
parameterization of the model. However, Stolzenberg's (1994) probit

TABLE 1
Coefficients Representing Effects of Social Background Characteristics on School Continuation

Variable	Completes Elementary (0–8)		Attends High School Given Completes Elementary (8–9)		Completes High School Given Attends High School (9–12)		Attends College and Completes High School (12–13)		Completes College Given Attends College (13–16)		Attends Post-college Given Completes College (16–17)	
	b	b/se(b)	b	b/se(b)	b	b/se(b)	b	b/se(b)	b	b/se(b)	b	b/se(b)
Intercept	0.9886	4.22	1.2410	5.40	-0.1778	-1.48	-1.7440	-15.98	-0.6434	-6.33	-0.4669	-3.42
FASEI	0.0075	1.42	0.0041	0.87	0.0154	7.82	0.0145	10.49	0.0115	9.28	0.0070	4.24
SIBS	-0.1325	-5.67	-0.1444	-6.40	-0.1335	-11.39	-0.1067	-9.53	-0.0737	-6.30	-0.0138	-0.84
FAMINC	0.1067	5.36	0.0587	3.79	0.0655	8.57	0.0444	9.24	0.0097	2.68	-0.0110	-2.44
FED	0.1188	4.79	0.0939	3.96	0.0784	6.77	0.0420	4.47	0.0071	0.84	-0.0050	-0.45
MED	0.1677	7.16	0.1243	5.56	0.0815	7.11	0.0940	9.29	0.0361	3.86	0.0383	3.11
BROKEN	-0.3163	-1.71	-0.1256	-0.64	-0.2192	-2.30	-0.0078	-0.09	-0.1567	-1.84	-0.3713	-3.08
FARM	-0.6060	-4.54	-1.0560	-7.94	0.3013	3.88	0.0107	0.14	0.1138	1.41	0.1826	1.55
SOUTH	-0.5948	-4.70	0.4182	3.03	-0.0973	-1.45	0.0309	0.53	-0.0604	-1.08	-0.2736	-3.66
"R2"	0.270		0.178		0.120		0.091		0.026		0.008	
$\chi^2(8)$	770.4		497.2		1226.4		1332.2		390.5		68.3	
N	5,368		5,009		9,301		7,732		7,674		4,185	
Subsample (%)	25		25		50		50		100		100	

Source: Mare (1980:301).

Note: Dependent variables are the log odds of continuing from one schooling level to the next. Estimates are based on a 1973 sample of the U.S. white male civilian noninstitutional population born between1907 and 1951. Independent variables are FASEI: father's occupational Duncan socioeconomic index when respondent was 16; FAMINC: annual income of family in thousands of constant (1967) dollars when respondent was 16; FED: father's grades of school completed; MED: mother's grades of school completed; BROKEN: absence of one or both parents from respondent's household most of the time to age 16; FARM: respondent lived on a farm at age 16; SOUTH: respondent born in the South census region. χ^2 tests null hypothesis that all coefficients are zero.

analysis reconfirmed Mare's finding that socioeconomic background has little or no influence on transitions from college to graduate training in an American cohort that completed college in the mid-1970s, and he explains the null finding by decay in the effects of SES on aspirations for further schooling. Sociologists have also criticized Mare's logistic response model of educational transitions. Applying multinomial logit models to longitudinal data from Sweden, Breen and Jonsson (2000) showed that class-origin effects on transition probabilities varied according to the particular choice made at a given transition point and that the probability of making a particular choice was path dependent.

Given the impact of Mare's work and the continuing controversy surrounding logistic response models of educational transitions, we return to the data originally analyzed by Mare in an appreciative effort to validate and extend his model. We introduce a modified version of his model that explicitly expresses and estimates changes in social origin effects across educational transitions. Rather than analyzing each educational transition separately as Mare did, we estimate a single model across all educational transitions. In this model, the relative effects of some (but not all) background variables are the same at each transition, and multiplicative scalars express proportional change in the effect of those variables across successive transitions.

1. MODELS OF EDUCATIONAL STRATIFICATION:
A REVIEW

Aside from linear regression and linear probability models, researchers in educational stratification have employed a number of more appropriate models to explore the effects of social background on educational transitions, including logistic response, log-linear, and multinomial models. Each model has advantages and disadvantages in the study of educational transitions. Logistic response or continuation odds models employ conditional samples across successive educational transitions and allow for the estimation of robust coefficients that are invariant to marginal changes in educational attainment. In these models, continuation probabilities are asymptotically independent; a model may be estimated separately for each transition, or multiple transitions may be analyzed within a single model (Bishop, Fienberg, and Holland 1975; Fienberg 1977). Although logistic response models have been widely used in stratification research, these models require a large number of parameters, allowing effects of covariates to fluctuate freely across transitions whether or not they vary in the population.

Erikson and Goldthorpe's (1992:91–92) model of uniform differences in parameters of social mobility, Xie's (1992) log-multiplicative layer model for comparing mobility tables, and Hout, Brooks, and Manza's (1995:812) model of trends in class voting in the United States are popular variants of log linear models used to study educational transitions and each resembles the model introduced here by imposing proportionality constraints on the coefficients of a model across multiple populations.[1] These models provide population average estimates of changes in an outcome over time or place, but they do not easily allow for the introduction of individual-level covariates. Moreover, estimation problems may occur when log-linear models are extended to higher dimensions or in instances where the analyst wishes to consider more than three or four transitions, whether they be educational transitions or transitions among occupational groups.

Multinomial models have also been used to study educational transitions, though perhaps less often than logistic response and log-linear models. Multinomial models provide the opportunity to assess horizontal stratification in tandem with vertical stratification, allowing for a richer analysis in some instances (Breen and Jonsson 2000). Anderson's (1984) well-known stereotype regression model provides a flexible means to consider proportionality of the effect of a group of covariates on ordered outcomes but has been relatively ignored in educational stratification research. This model is an important analytic tool in many respects. For example, DiPrete's exemplary paper (1990) uses stereotype regression models to introduce individual-level covariates in social mobility analyses. Yet, multinomial models are still of limited value in the analysis of educational transitions. They specify multiple and possibly ordered categorical outcomes but do not model the conditional risk of transitions. With the exception of stereotype regression models, multinomial models also include a large number of coefficients. As in the case of unrestricted logistic response models, these may add unnecessary complexity and may make it difficult to interpret findings.

---

[1]We thank Michael Hout for bringing these similarities to our attention.

Given the various weaknesses of existing models of educational transitions and in an effort to extend statistical models of educational stratification, we propose a logistic response model with partial proportionality constraints. We believe that the model proposed here provides a parsimonious and powerful description of changes in the effects of socioeconomic background on educational attainment and, equally important, that it has wide application in studies of changes and differentials in social stratification.

2. LOGISTIC RESPONSE MODELS WITH PARTIAL PROPORTIONALITY CONSTRAINTS

We begin with a logistic response model in Mare's (1980:297) original notation:

$$\log_e \left(\frac{p_{ij}}{1 - p_{ij}} \right) = \beta_{j0} + \sum_k \beta_{jk} X_{ijk}, \qquad (1)$$

where p_{ij} is the probability that the ith person will complete the jth school transition, X_{ijk} is the value of the kth explanatory variable for the ith person who is at risk of the jth transition, and the β_{jk} are parameters to be estimated. That is, a logistic response model is estimated for persons at risk of completing each transition with no constraints on any parameters across transitions. Delineated above, the logistic response model has two important properties. First, the effects in equation 1 are invariant to the marginal distribution of schooling outcomes. That is, for $k > 0$, a given set of β_{jk} is consistent with any rate of completion of a transition. Second, the continuation probabilities are asymptotically independent of one another (Fienberg 1977). Thus, the model may be estimated separately for each transition, or multiple transitions may be analyzed within a single model.

Suppose that instead of analyzing the data for each transition separately the data are converted to person-transition records. Thus, a record appears for each transition for which each individual is eligible. In each record, there is a single outcome variable—say, y_{ij}, where $y_{ij} = 1$ if the transition is completed and $y_{ij} = 0$ if it is not completed. Since the transitions are ordered and each transition is conditional on completion of prior transitions, there is at most one record for which $y_{ij} = 0$ for each individual—namely, for the last transition for which that individual is eligible; at all prior transitions, $y_{ij} = 1$. In this setup, for example, one could estimate a model that is similar to equation 1, except there is only one set of regression parameters, which apply equally to each transition:

$$\log_e \left(\frac{p_{ij}}{1 - p_{ij}} \right) = \beta_{j0} + \sum_k \beta_k X_{ijk}. \qquad (2)$$

This model, like that of equation (1), may be estimated with any software that supports logistic regression analysis.

However, the hypothesis that socioeconomic background effects decline across transitions might suggest a different and more parsimonious model than equation (1). We refer to this as the logistic response model with proportionality constraints (LRPC):

$$\log_e \left(\frac{p_{ij}}{1 - p_{ij}} \right) = \beta_{j0} + \lambda_j \sum_k \beta_k X_{ijk}, \qquad (3)$$

The first term on the right-hand side of equation (3) says there may be a different intercept at each transition. The summation represents effects of the X_{ijk} that are invariant across all transitions; notice there is no j index on β_k. However, there is a multiplicative scalar for each transition, λ_j, which rescales the β_k at each transition subject to the normalizing constraint that $\lambda_1 = 1$. That is, the λ_j introduce proportional increases or decreases in the β_k across transitions; thus equation (3) implies proportional changes in main effects across transitions. The proportionally constrained covariates determine a composite variable, which can be interpreted in reference to a theoretical construct. In this instance, the main effects of the covariates can be interpreted as the weights of these covariates in that composite. Although equation (3) may appear to have more terms than equation (1), it is actually more parsimonious because there are only as many multiplicative terms as transitions. Equation (1) has as many interaction terms as the product of the number of explanatory variables and the number of transitions.

Conceptually, the model in equation (3) is similar to the well-known MIMIC (multiple indicator, multiple cause) model of Hauser, Goldberger, and Jöreskog (Hauser and Goldberger 1971; Hauser 1973; Jöreskog and Goldberger 1975; Hauser and Goldberger 1975). However, proportionality constraints appear within a single-equation model estimated simultaneously in two or more populations whereas the

MIMIC model imposes proportionality constraints across the coefficients of two or more equations estimated within a single population.

Several readers have suggested that the model of equation (3) is the same as the stereotype model. Recall that this model imposes proportionality constraints on coefficients across response categories in a multinomial logistic model; however, the stereotype model pertains to a single population and does not account for the conditional risk of transitions from one category to the next. If there were more than two potential outcomes at each transition, one could possibly combine features of the stereotype and LRPC models.

Our argument is that one ought to estimate a model like that in equation (3) before proposing more complex explanations of change in the effects of socioeconomic background variables across educational transitions. However, one cannot simply jump from the finding that the model of equation (3) fits a set of data to the conclusion that the effects of background variables are the same across transitions up to a coefficient of proportionality. Allison (1999) shows that, if the model of equation (3) fits a set of data, one cannot distinguish empirically between the hypothesis of uniform proportionality of effects across transitions and the hypothesis that group differences between parameters of binary regressions are artifacts of heterogeneity between groups in residual variation.[2]

It is also possible to mix the features of equations (2) and (3) to permit some variables to interact freely with a given transition while others follow a model of proportional change. We refer to this model as the logistic response model with partial proportionality constraints (LRPPC):

$$\log_e \left(\frac{p_{ij}}{1 - p_{ij}} \right) = \beta_{j0} + \lambda_j \sum_{k=1}^{k'} \beta_k X_{ijk} + \sum_{k'+1}^{K} \beta_{jk} X_{ijk}. \qquad (4)$$

Equation (4) says that for some variables, X_k, where $k = 1, \ldots, k'$, there is proportional change in effects across transitions, while for other X_k, where $k = k' + 1, \ldots, K$, the effects interact freely with transition level. For example, equation (4) could apply to Mare's analysis where effects

---

[2] Ballarino and Schadee (2005) advance this argument in the context of an analysis of educational transitions in Italy and several other nations.

of socioeconomic variables appear to decline across transitions while those of farm origin, one-parent family, and Southern birth vary in other ways.

Equation (4) may be generalized to cover multiple cohorts as well as multiple transitions. For example, equation (5) is one such generalization:

$$\log_e \left(\frac{p_{ijt}}{1 - p_{ijt}} \right) = \beta_{jt0} + \lambda_j \sum_{k=1}^{k'} \beta_k X_{ijtk} + \sum_{k'+1}^{K} \beta_{jk} X_{ijtk}$$

$$+ \gamma_t \sum_{k=1}^{k''} \beta_k X_{ijtk} + \sum_{k''+1}^{K} \beta_{tk} X_{ijtk}. \tag{5}$$

Here, effects change proportionally across transition levels, j, for one set of variables; effects change proportionally across time for another (possibly overlapping) set of variables, indexed by t. The effects of the remaining sets of variables may interact freely with transition level j and with period t.

Estimation of equations (3) through (5) is not as simple as that of equations (1) and (2). The same linear expression, such as $\sum_k \beta_k X_{ijk}$, appears twice in the former equations—once with freely estimated coefficients and again as a linear composite in $\lambda_j \sum_k \beta_k X_{ijk}$. The problem is to estimate the models in a way that will yield the same estimates of the β_k in both expressions. One way to accomplish this is simply to iterate. First, estimate the β_k in a model with no interactions. Then, estimate the model again with an interaction in the composite estimated in the previous step, and continue until the fit and parameter values change very little from one iteration to the next (Allison 1999; MacLean 2005). We have used another method, writing the equations of the models and estimating them directly by maximum likelihood in Stata (see Appendix).[3] It may also be possible to estimate this model as if it were a MIMIC model (with uncorrelated outcome variables) using MPlus or other software for estimation of structural equation models.

In summary, this framework allows for the estimation of parsimonious, single equation models of educational transitions and addresses

---

[3] We thank Jeremy Freese for writing a Stata macro to estimate the model by maximum likelihood. For similar specifications in Stata and other statistical packages, see Allison (1999).

many of the shortcomings in extant models of educational transitions. The models are invariant to change in the marginal distribution, but they use fewer parameters and are characterized by ease in the introduction of individual-level covariates. The models can include uniform and/or partial proportionality constraints across model covariates and transitions of interest while freely estimating effects of other model covariates. Moreover, proportionality constraints in the models can be interpreted as indicative of a latent construct similar to that in the MIMIC model. Yet another possibility is to constrain the effects of a subset of variables to be invariant across populations. Finally, these models of educational transitions more easily allow for nuanced and powerful tests of the significance of estimated differences in the effects of model covariates across educational transitions and, thus, more informative inferences about the effects of social background on educational transitions. We next apply this framework in a replication of original work by Mare (1980, 1981) on educational transitions.

3. REPLICATING AND EXTENDING LOGISTIC RESPONSE MODELS USING THE 1973 OCG SURVEY

In replicating Mare's (1980) original analysis, we use the 1973 Occupational Changes in a Generation (OCG) survey data. The OCG survey was carried out as a supplement to the March 1973 Current Population Survey (CPS). It was carried out via mail in September 1973 after all of the households participating in the March demographic supplement had rotated out of the CPS. The response rate was 83 percent among target males. The present analysis includes 21,682 white men 21 to 65 years old in the civilian noninstitutional population who responded to all of the social background questions in the OCG supplement. We convert these individual records to 88,768 person-transition records.

Father's occupational status (FASEI) is the value of the Duncan Socioeconomic Index for Occupations (Duncan 1961); scale values were assigned using an adaptation of the original scale to codes for occupation, industry, and class of worker that were used in the 1970 Census.[4]

---

[4]Our code for the Duncan SEI differs from that used by Mare. Our code is more fine-grained than that which was available to Mare (1980, 1981), though the results are largely the same.

Number of siblings (SIBS) is based on questions about the number of older and younger siblings of each sex. The count of siblings was top-coded at 9. Family income (FAMINC) was represented by categorical responses to the question, "When you were about 16 years old, what was your family's annual income?" Pretest respondents indicated that they answered in contemporary rather than price-adjusted dollars, so we adjusted the midpoints of responses from dollars in the year that the participant turned 16 to 1967 dollars using the Consumer Price Index. We assigned reports of "no income or loss" to the lowest re-porting category ($1–499). After examining scatterplots of the relation-ship between various transformations of income and the probabilities of educational transitions, we top-coded the adjusted incomes at 2.5 standard deviations above the mean and re-expressed the variable in natural logs. Father's education (FED) and mother's education (MED) are expressed in years of regular schooling completed. Participants were coded as living in a broken family (BROKEN) if they responded "no" to the question, "Were you living with both your parents most of the time up to age 16?" A dummy variable for farm origin (FARM) was coded 1 if the participant said that he had not moved since age 16 (in the OCG survey) and currently lived on a farm (as reported in the CPS) or if he reported in the OCG survey that he had lived on a farm when he was 16 years old; otherwise, FARM was coded 0. State of birth was ascertained in the OCG survey, and a dummy variable (SOUTH) was created for men born in a Southern state as defined by the U.S. Bureau of the Census. With the exception of family in-come, all of the continuous background variables have approximately linear relationships in their original metrics with each of the educational transitions.

Educational attainment was ascertained in the March CPS. Re-spondents (who may or may not have been the OCG target male) re-ported both the highest grade in regular school that the OCG participant attended and whether or not he had completed that grade. With that protocol, it was possible to create plausible definitions of six key edu-cational transitions in populations at risk of those transitions: (1) com-pleting elementary school (grade 8); (2) attending high school (grade 9) among those who completed elementary school; (3) completing high school (grade 12) among those who attended high school; (4) attend-ing college among those who completed high school; (5) completing college among those who attended college;[5] and (6) attending some form of postgraduate education among those who graduated from college. Unfortunately, it would not be possible to carry out a comparable analysis of educational transitions with Census data after 1990, when the Bureau chose a one-question item on educational attainment (Hauser 1997).

Table 2 shows descriptive statistics for continuous variables used in the present analysis, and Table 3 displays descriptive statistics for the three discrete background variables. Without exception, each successive transition yields a more selective and successful set of students. At each transition, successful students have more highly educated parents with higher occupational status and income and come from smaller families than students who did not complete that transition. They are less likely to have been raised by a single parent, less likely to live or have lived on a farm, and less likely to have been born in a Southern state.[6]

3.1. Replicating Traditional Logistic Response Models

Table 4 reports our unconstrained estimates of the effects of social background characteristics on school continuation in the 1973 OCG data. These estimates are based on equation (1) and replicate Mare's (1980) original logistic response model. The coefficients differ somewhat from those estimated by Mare (1980) for several reasons. Either we did not use the same version of the 1973 OCG data file or our sample definition was different from Mare's in some way that we have been unable to determine. Unlike Mare (1980), we also use a more refined scheme for scaling father's occupational status and a logarithmic transformation of family income. Moreover, we used all of the available cases at every transition and defined the base population for college graduation to include those who attended college but did not complete at least one year of college.

---

[5]Based on comparisons of our sample counts with those reported by Mare (1980:301), we strongly suspect that he defined the base population for completion of college to exclude persons who entered college but did not complete at least one year of college work. We defined the base for college completion to include that group.

[6]We find substantially fewer men than Mare found with farm background or Southern birth.

TABLE 2

Means and Standard Deviations of Social Background Characteristics at Selected Levels of Schooling: 1973 Occupational Changes in a Generation Survey

Level of Schooling	Father's Occupation (FASEI)	Family Income (FAMINC)	Father's Schooling (FED)	Mother's Schooling (MED)	Number of Siblings (SIBS)	N
School entry	31.4	1.773	8.6	9.1	3.7	21682
	22.9	0.900	4.1	3.8	2.6	
Elementary school completion	32.6	1.857	9.0	9.5	3.5	20058
	23.1	0.832	3.9	3.6	2.5	
High school attendance	33.7	1.906	9.2	9.7	3.4	18725
	23.3	0.800	3.9	3.5	2.5	
High school graduation	36.0	1.987	9.7	10.1	3.1	15602
	23.8	0.764	3.8	3.4	2.4	
College attendance	42.8	2.165	10.7	11.0	2.6	8462
	25.1	0.710	3.9	3.3	2.1	
College graduation	46.6	2.226	11.1	11.3	2.4	4239
	25.3	0.698	3.9	3.3	2.0	

TABLE 3
Percentages of Men with Selected Background Characteristics by Levels of
Schooling: 1973 Occupational Changes in a Generation Survey

	Broken Family (BROKEN)	Farm Background (FARM)	Southern Birth (SOUTH)	% Continuing	% of All Men
School entry	10.4	16.6	27.0	92.5	100.0
Elementary completion	9.9	15.4	25.1	93.4	92.5
HS attendance	9.8	13.9	24.9	83.3	86.4
HS graduation	9.2	13.3	23.8	54.2	72.0
College attendance	8.2	9.9	22.4	50.1	39.0
College graduation	7.4	9.2	22.1	49.7	19.6

Despite these differences in variable definitions and case selection, the estimates in Table 4 follow the main patterns of Mare's original estimates (see Table 1). Social background explains less of the variation at each higher educational transition, and the effects of the socioeconomic background variables as defined by Mare (FASEI, FAMINC, FED, MED, and SIBS) typically decline from lower to higher educational transitions. Similarly, effects of the other background variables (BROKEN, FARM, and SOUTH) do not show the same pattern of decline across transitions.

3.2. *Extending Traditional Logistic Response Models: The Logistic Response Model with Partial Proportionality Constraints*

Table 5 describes the fit of single-equation models simultaneously estimated for all six educational transitions. Model 1 is a null baseline in which no parameters are fitted except the grand mean. The likelihood ratio test statistic under this model defines the denominator of the pseudo-R^2 statistics and can be used to measure improvements in the fit of more complex models. Model 2 fits an intercept for each transition, and it yields a substantial improvement in fit. Model 3 adds invariant effects of social background variables to Model 2. This follows the model in equation (2). Overall rates of transition vary across levels of schooling, but the effects of social background do not vary across transitions. This modification also yields a substantial improvement in fit.

TABLE 4
Coefficients Representing Effects of Social Background Characteristics on School Continuation: 1973 Occupational Changes in a Generation Survey

Variable	Completes Elementary (0–8)		Attends High School Given Completes Elementary (8–9)		Completes High School Given Attends High School (9–12)		Attends College Given Completes High School (12–13)		Completes College Given Attends College (13–16)		Attends Post-college Given Completes College (16–17)	
	b	b/se(b)	b	b/se(b)	b	b/se(b)	b	b/se(b)	b	b/se(b)	b	b/se(b)
Intercept	0.4655	4.45	0.8376	7.32	-0.1509	-1.78	-1.8544	-22.45	-0.4352	-4.04	-0.1628	-1.05
FASEI	0.1731	6.87	0.2308	9.40	0.1575	11.98	0.1650	17.56	0.1162	10.22	0.0678	4.22
SIBS	-0.1234	-10.83	-0.1397	-12.05	-0.1260	-15.21	-0.1042	-13.24	-0.0889	-8.02	-0.0048	-0.29
FAMINC	0.5690	18.29	0.4013	11.87	0.2953	10.92	0.2976	11.04	0.0213	0.59	-0.1552	-3.01
FED	0.1216	10.13	0.0627	5.22	0.0566	7.10	0.0465	7.12	-0.0114	-1.40	-0.0075	-0.67
MED	0.1496	13.15	0.1083	9.34	0.0911	11.46	0.0748	10.66	0.0225	2.52	0.0327	2.67
BROKEN	-0.3121	-3.66	-0.0554	-0.57	-0.2228	-3.38	-0.1001	-1.64	-0.1473	-1.79	-0.5010	-4.08
FARM	-0.1413	-2.08	-0.6979	-10.37	0.2811	4.80	-0.0278	-0.52	0.2306	2.92	-0.0152	-0.13
SOUTH	-0.6419	-10.57	0.3268	4.71	-0.0771	-1.63	0.0131	0.31	-0.0286	-0.54	-0.2649	-3.52
"R2"	0.313		0.191		0.134		0.120		0.025		0.011	
$\chi^2(8)$	3611.6		1868.4		2263.9		2582.1		293.6		64.8	
N	21,682		20,058		18,725		15,602		8,462		4,239	

Note: Dependent variables are the log odds of continuing from one schooling level to the next. Estimates are based on a 1973 sample of the U.S. white male civilian noninstitutional population born between 1907 and 1951. Independent variables are FASEI: father's occupational Duncan socioeconomic index when respondent was 16; SIBS: number of siblings; FAMINC: natural log of truncated annual income of family in thousands of constant (1967) dollars when respondent was 16; FED: father's grades of school completed; MED: mother's grades of school completed; BROKEN: absence of one or both parents from respondent's household most of the time to age 16; FARM: respondent lived on a farm at age 16; SOUTH: respondent born in the South census region. χ^2 tests null hypothesis that all coefficients are zero.

TABLE 5
Fit of Selected Models of Educational Transitions: 1973 Occupational Changes in a Generation Survey

Model	Description	Log-Likelihood	DF for Model	Model Chi-square	Contrast	Contrast Chi-square	Contrast BIC	Pseudo R-squared
1	Fit the grand mean	-46830.8	0	—		—	—	0
2	An intercept for each transition	-38674.3	5	16313.0	2 vs. 1	16313.0	16256.0	0.17
3	An intercept for each transition and constant social background effects	-34333.3	13	24995.0	3 vs. 2	8682.0	8590.8	0.27
4	An intercept for each transition and proportional social background effects	-33529.7	19	26602.2	4 vs. 3	1607.3	1538.9	0.28
5	An intercept for each transition, constant effects of socioeconomic variables, interactions of BROKEN, FARM, and SOUTH with transition	-34112.0	28	25437.6	5 vs. 3	442.6	271.7	0.27
6	An intercept for each transition, proportional effects of socioeconomic variables, interactions of BROKEN, FARM, and SOUTH with transition	-33399.7	34	26862.1	6 vs. 5	1424.6	1356.2	0.29
7	Saturated model: Intercepts for each transition and interactions of all social background variables with transition	-33332.2	53	26997.2	7 vs. 6	135.1	-81.4	0.29

Model 4 is based on equation (3). Rather than specifying constant effects of the eight social background variables, it says that all of the background effects vary in the same proportion across each transition. With six more degrees of freedom, the parameters of proportional change yield an improved model fit (change in the chi-square statistic of 1607.3). Evidently, substantial variation in effects of background across educational transitions is captured by the model of proportional change. However, Model 4 does not fit the data well. Model 7 fits all of the interactions between social background variables and transitions, and its fit is significantly better than that of Model 4 (chi-square of 395 with 34 degrees of freedom). Moreover, as noted above, the improvement of fit in Model 4 relative to Model 3 does not tell us whether the background effects actually vary proportionally across transitions or whether there are corresponding differences in residual variation across transitions.

Model 5 specifies constant effects of the socioeconomic background variables (FASEI, FAMINC, MED, and FED) and number of siblings (SIBS), but it permits effects of the other three background variables (BROKEN, FARM, and SOUTH) to interact freely with transition level. Note that Model 5 is a special case of equation 2—because some effects do not vary across educational transitions—and that Model 4 is not nested within Model 5. Comparing Model 5 to Model 3, we find a significant improvement in fit, but it is only about a quarter of the improvement from Model 3 to Model 4 and uses 15 degrees of freedom.

Model 6 is based on the specification of Model 5, but it adds proportional change across transitions in the effects of FASEI, FAMINC, MED, FED, and SIBS. It is an example of the model specified in equation (4). The improvement of fit in Model 6 relative to Model 5 is almost as large as in that of Model 4 relative to Model 3. That is, even after the introduction of freely estimated interaction effects between each transition level and BROKEN, FARM, and SOUTH, fit is improved substantially by the specification of proportional change in effects of socioeconomic background across educational transitions. However, because proportionality constraints apply only to a subset of the background effects in Model 6, we know that variation in coefficients across transitions is not entirely due to residual variation in transitions.

Finally, Model 7 is an example of the specification in equation (2) in which effects of all background variables are permitted to interact with educational transition levels. Although it uses 19 more parameters than Model 6, the improvement in fit is negligible by comparison with the other contrasts in Table 5. Thus, we prefer Model 6 to Model 7 and the other models listed in Table 5. This decision is confirmed by the BIC statistics for contrasts between models, which are also reported in Table 5. Excepting the contrast between Models 6 and 7, there is a substantial improvement in BIC between each successive model.

Table 6 shows the estimated parameters of Model 6. Recall that this model includes additive effects of all of the social background variables, freely estimated interactions of broken family, farm background, and Southern birth with transition level, and multiplicative effects of transition level with a linear composite of the socioeconomic variables and number of siblings.

Table 6 identifies four groups of parameters: (a) freely estimated additive effects, (b) freely estimated interaction effects, (c) multiplicative effects, and (d) additive effects and multiplicative composite. However, the first two groups are not distinct for purposes of estimation. In this instance, group (a) includes the main effects of each transition level and the main effects of broken family, farm background, and Southern birth while group (b) comprises the interaction effects of broken family, farm background, and Southern birth with each educational transition. There are no interaction effects with the first transition because the main effects of broken family, farm background, and Southern birth are defined to reference that transition. Group (c) specifies the multiplicative effects of the second through sixth transitions relative to the effects of socioeconomic background in the first transition. Finally, group (d) includes the main effects of the socioeconomic variables and number of siblings, which are also the weights of those variables in the composite that interact with educational transition level.

The estimates of direct interest in Table 6 are the main effects of the socioeconomic variables (d) and the multiplicative effects of the transition levels (c). As one should expect, the main effects of father's occupational status, family income, mother's education, and father's education are positive and highly significant, while that of number of siblings is negative and highly significant. The multiplicative effects of transition level are also highly significant, and they are increasingly negative at higher level transitions. These coefficients may appear anomalous at first sight, but increasingly negative effects are exactly what one should expect. That is, at each higher transition level, there is a larger proportional decrement in the main effects of the socioeconomic variables.

TABLE 6

Estimated Parameters of LRPPC Model (M6): 1973 Occupational Changes in a Generation Survey

Variable	Coefficient	Standard Error	t-Statistic
a. Freely Estimated Additive Effects			
Completes elementary (0-8, TRANS1)	0.7815	0.0777	10.06
Attends high school if completes elementary (8-9, TRANS2)	0.7738	0.0655	11.82
Completes high school if attends high school (9-12, TRANS3)	−0.3125	0.0670	−4.66
Attends college if completes high school (12-13, TRANS4)	−1.9488	0.0613	−31.79
Completes college if attends college (13-16, TRANS5)	−0.9565	0.0734	−13.03
Attends post-college if completes college (16-17, TRANS6)	−0.3145	0.1085	−2.90
Nonintact family (BROKEN)	−0.3453	0.0833	−4.15
Farm background (FARM)	−0.1010	0.0672	−1.50
Southern birth (SOUTH)	−0.6276	0.0612	−10.25
b. Freely Estimated Interaction Effects			
TRANS2 × BROKEN	0.2913	0.1265	2.30
TRANS2 × FARM	−0.6159	0.0929	−6.63
TRANS2 × SOUTH	0.9564	0.0914	10.47
TRANS3 × BROKEN	0.1390	0.1053	1.32
TRANS3 × FARM	0.3894	0.0885	4.40
TRANS3 × SOUTH	0.5488	0.0776	7.08
TRANS4 × BROKEN	0.2449	0.1024	2.39
TRANS4 × FARM	0.0506	0.0849	0.60
TRANS4 × SOUTH	0.6431	0.0740	8.69
TRANS5 × BROKEN	0.2326	0.1160	2.01
TRANS5 × FARM	0.2259	0.1018	2.22
TRANS5 × SOUTH	0.6058	0.0811	7.47
TRANS6 × BROKEN	−0.0866	0.1473	−0.59
TRANS6 × FARM	0.0767	0.1303	0.59
TRANS6 × SOUTH	0.3855	0.0967	3.99
c. Multiplicative Effects			
Attends high school if completes elementary (8-9, TRANS2)	−0.2257	0.0238	−9.50
Completes high school if attends high school (9-12, TRANS3)	−0.3704	0.0221	−16.76
Attends college if completes high school (12-13, TRANS4)	−0.4312	0.0180	−23.95

(Continued)

TABLE 6 (Continued)

Variable	Coefficient	Standard Error	t-Statistic
Completes college if attends college (13-16, TRANS5)	−0.7804	0.0157	−49.68
Attends post-college if completes college (16-17, TRANS6)	−0.9159	0.0214	−42.73
d. Additive Effects and Multiplicative Composite			
FASEI	0.2662	0.0123	21.55
SIBS	−0.1698	0.0072	−23.71
FAMINC	0.5233	0.0209	25.07
FED	0.0911	0.0066	13.90
MED	0.1435	0.0064	22.25

For example, the estimate of −.2257 for the transition to high school conditional upon completion of elementary school says that the total effect of each socioeconomic background variable is 20.3 percent smaller at the transition from elementary school to high school than it is at the transition from school entry to the completion of elementary school. Note that the decrements in the multiplicative effects are not equal across transitions. The largest decrement is that between college entry and college completion $(-0.7804 - (-0.4312) = -0.3492)$, and the second largest is between elementary school completion and high school entry (-0.2257).

To illustrate the implications of these estimates for the total effects of each of the social background variables, we insert the parameter estimates into the linear model (equation 4) and rearrange terms. The first panel of Table 7 displays the total effects in Model 6 that are implied by the parameter estimates. As expected, the effects of father's occupational status, number of siblings, family income, and parents' education decline regularly across transitions, while those of broken family, farm background, and Southern birth do not. In the second panel, for purposes of comparison, we show the corresponding unconstrained estimates from Model 7.[7] The latter are necessarily identical to those in Table 4 because Model 7 fits all of the background by level

---

[7] We are concerned here mainly with the deviations in the effects of social background variables, not with the intercepts.

TABLE 7
Comparison of Estimates from LRPPC Model (M6) with Estimates from Saturated Model (7)

Variable	Completes Elementary (0–8)	Attends High School Given Completes Elementary (8–9)	Completes High School Given Attends High School (9–12)	Attends College Given Completes High School (12–13)	Completes College Given Attends College (13–16)	Attends Post-college Given Completes College (16–17)
Model 6: Intercept for each transition, proportional effects of socioeconomic variables, and interactions of BROKEN, FARM, and SOUTH with each transition						
FASEI	0.266	0.206	0.168	0.151	0.058	0.022
SIBS	−0.170	−0.132	−0.107	−0.097	−0.037	−0.014
FAMINC	0.523	0.405	0.329	0.298	0.115	0.044
FED	0.091	0.071	0.057	0.052	0.020	0.008
MED	0.143	0.111	0.090	0.082	0.032	0.012
BROKEN	−0.345	−0.054	−0.206	−0.100	−0.113	−0.432
FARM	−0.101	−0.717	0.288	−0.050	0.125	−0.024
SOUTH	−0.628	0.329	−0.079	0.016	−0.022	−0.242
Intercept	0.781	0.774	−0.313	−1.949	−0.956	−0.314
Model 7: Saturated model with intercepts for each transition and interactions of all social background variables with each transition						
FASEI	0.173	0.231	0.158	0.165	0.116	0.068
SIBS	−0.123	−0.140	−0.126	−0.104	−0.089	−0.005
FAMINC	0.569	0.401	0.295	0.298	0.021	−0.155
FED	0.122	0.063	0.057	0.047	−0.011	−0.007
MED	0.150	0.108	0.091	0.075	0.023	0.033
BROKEN	−0.312	−0.055	−0.223	−0.100	−0.147	−0.501
FARM	−0.141	−0.698	0.281	−0.028	0.231	−0.015
SOUTH	−0.642	0.327	−0.077	0.013	−0.029	−0.265
Intercept	0.465	0.838	−0.151	−1.854	−0.435	−0.163

(Continued)

TABLE 7 (Continued)

Variable	Completes Elementary (0–8)	Attends High School Given Completes Elementary (8–9)	Completes High School Given Attends High School (9–12)	Attends College Given Completes High School (12–13)	Completes College Given Attends College (13–16)	Attends Post-college Given Completes College (16–17)
Deviations (Model 7–Model 6)						
FASEI	-0.093	0.025	-0.010	0.014	0.058	0.045
SIBS	0.046	-0.008	-0.019	-0.008	-0.052	0.010
FAMINC	0.046	-0.004	-0.034	0.000	-0.094	-0.199
FED	0.030	-0.008	-0.001	-0.005	-0.031	-0.015
MED	0.006	-0.003	0.001	-0.007	-0.009	0.021
BROKEN	0.033	-0.001	-0.016	0.000	-0.035	-0.069
FARM	-0.040	0.019	-0.007	0.023	0.106	0.009
SOUTH	-0.014	-0.002	0.002	-0.002	-0.007	-0.023
Intercept	-0.316	0.064	0.162	0.094	0.521	0.152

interactions. The third panel shows the deviations of the estimates in Model 6 from those in Model 7.

As we should expect from the contrast reported in Table 5 between Models 6 and 7, the deviations in the third panel are small in most cases. The largest single deviation (-0.199) pertains to the anomalously large and negative effect of family income on the transition from college to graduate school. A second large deviation is an underprediction of the salutary effect of farm background on the completion of college. One notable pattern in the deviations is that the model underestimates the effect of father's occupational status on higher-level transitions, and it overestimates the effects of the other background variables in the linear composite at those levels.[8]

Conceivably, one might argue that father's occupational status should be removed from the linear composite in the other social background variables and interacted freely with transition levels. However, such a decision—along with the inclusion of number of siblings in the linear composite—would be inconsistent with the more general finding that socioeconomic effects vary proportionally across transition levels. We should then be left with a less parsimonious and less appealing claim that some socioeconomic effects vary proportionally while others do not. In addition, because there is only one discrepant effect, we think that the evidence of nonproportionality is weak, and we have not modified the model.

4. DISCUSSION

In this analysis, we have shown that specification of interaction effects with a linear composite is a parsimonious way to represent and assess the way in which social background effects vary across educational transitions. Compared to Robert Mare's analysis of educational transitions among American men, we have shown that the more parsimonious LRPPC model reproduces most of the empirical features of his estimates. While estimation of the LRPPC model is not as straightforward as an ordinary regression analysis, it can be done easily and quickly with standard statistical software.

---

[8]This is consistent with Mare's (1980:302–3) observations about the pattern of coefficients in the unrestricted estimates.

We can think of several other ways in which models with inter-action effects with a linear composite could be useful. We have already noted earlier applications of a similar idea to comparative analysis of mobility tables (Erikson and Goldthorpe 1992; Xie 1992) and to trends in class voting (Hout et al. 1995). One obvious extension is to analyses, like those in Mare (1979) and in Shavit and Blossfeld (1993), where multiple educational transitions are observed in several cohorts.[9] Such models, we believe, would also be useful to structure and discipline international comparative analyses, such as pooled analyses of the data used by Shavit and Blossfeld (1993) or other cross-national studies that have been designed specifically to create comparable data. We hope that similar models and methods may prove useful across a wide range of research questions in the social and behavioral sciences.

APPENDIX: STATA CODE FOR PREFERRED MODEL OF EDUCATIONAL TRANSITIONS

```
**Model 6: Logistic Response Model with Partial Proportionality Constraints **
capture program drop pplogit
        program define pplogit
                tempname theta
        version 6
        args lnf theta1 theta2 theta3
        gen `theta' = `theta1' + `theta3' + (`theta2'*`theta3')
        quietly replace `lnf' = ln(exp(`theta')/(1+exp(`theta'))) if
                $ML_y1==1
        quietly replace `lnf' = ln(1/(1+exp(`theta'))) if $ML_y1==0
        end

        ml model lf pplogit (outcome = trans1 trans2 trans3 trans4 trans5
trans6 broken farm16 south trans2Xbroken trans2Xfarm16 trans2Xsouth
trans3Xbroken trans3Xfarm16 trans3Xsouth trans4Xbroken trans4Xfarm16
trans4Xsouth trans5Xbroken trans5Xfarm16 trans5Xsouth trans6Xbroken
trans6Xfarm16 trans6Xsouth, nocons) (trans2 trans3 trans4 trans5 trans6,
nocons) (dunc sibstt19 ln_inc_trunc edhifaom edhimoom, nocons)

**The following set of starting values are not essential**
**but estimation is much faster when starting values are assigned **

        ml init eq1:trans1 =.4041526 eq1:trans2 =.7751678 eq1:trans3 =-
.3116492 eq1:trans4 =-1.948527 eq1:trans5 =-.9562174 eq1:trans6 =-.3119838
eq1:trans2Xbroken =-.0519577 eq1:trans2Xfarm16 =-.7136086 eq1:trans2Xsouth
=.3302017 eq1:trans3Xbroken = -.2044395 eq1:trans3Xfarm16 = .2908632
eq1:trans3Xsouth =-.0779455 eq1:trans4Xbroken =-.0985229 eq1:trans4Xfarm16 =-
.0484765 eq1:trans4Xsouth =.0161895 eq1:trans5Xbroken =-.1119574
eq1:trans5Xfarm16 =.1257399 eq1:trans5Xsouth =-.0215616 eq1:trans6Xbroken =-
.4318161 eq1:trans6Xfarm16 =-.0246239 eq1:trans6Xsouth =-.2418691 eq2:trans2 =-
.2524217 eq2:trans3 =-.3919983 eq2:trans4 =-.4505379 eq2:trans5 =-.7878735
eq2:trans6 =-.9192267 eq3:dunc =.2752204 eq3:sibstt19 =-.1762127
eq3:ln_inc_trunc =.554373 eq3:edhifaom =.0953649 eq3:edhimoom =.1451568
        ml maximize
```

[9]Equation (5) of this paper provides a template for such analyses.

REFERENCES

Allison, Paul D. 1999. "Comparing Logit and Probit Coefficients Across Groups." *Sociological Methods Research* 28(2):186–208.

Anderson, J. A. 1984. "Regression and Ordered Categorical Variables." *Journal of the Royal Statistical Society*. Series B (Methodological) 46(1):1–30.

Ballarino, Gabriele, and Hans Schadee. 2005. "Really Persisting Inequalities?" Research Committee on Social Stratification, International Sociological Association. University of California, Los Angeles.

Bishop, Yvonne M. M., Stephen E. Fienberg, and Paul W. Holland. 1975. *Discrete Multivariate Analysis: Theory and Practice*. Cambridge, MA: MIT Press.

Breen, Richard, and Jan O. Jonsson. 2000. "Analyzing Educational Careers: A Multinomial Transition Model." *American Sociological Review* 65(5):754–72.

Cameron, Stephen V., and James J. Heckman. 1998. "Life Cycle Schooling and Dynamic Selection Bias: Models and Evidence for Five Cohorts of American Males." *Journal of Political Economy* 106(2):262–333.

DiPrete, Thomas A. 1990. "Adding Covariates to Loglinear Models for the Study of Social Mobility." *American Sociological Review* 55(5):757–73.

Duncan, Otis D. 1961. "A Socioeconomic Index for All Occupations." Pp. 109–38 in *Occupations and Social Status*, edited by Albert J. Reiss, Jr. New York: Free Press.

Erikson, Robert, and John H. Goldthorpe. 1992. *The Constant Flux: A Study of Class Mobility in Industrial Societies*. Oxford, England: Clarendon.

Fienberg, Stephen E. 1977. *The Analysis of Cross-Classified Categorical Data: Theory and Practice*. Cambridge, MA: MIT Press.

Hauser, Robert M. 1973. "Disaggregating a Social-Psychological Model of Educational Attainment." Pp. 255–84 in *Structural Equation Models in the Social Sciences*, edited by A. S. Goldberger and O. D. Duncan. New York: Seminar Press.

———. 1997. "Indicators of High School Completion and Dropout." Pp. 152–84 in *Indicators of Children's Well-Being*, edited by Robert M. Hauser, Brett V. Brown, and William R. Prosser. New York: Russell Sage Foundation.

Hauser, Robert M., and David L. Featherman. 1976. "Equality of Schooling: Trends and Prospects." *Sociology of Education* 49(2):99–120.

Hauser, Robert M., and Arthur S. Goldberger. 1971. "The Treatment of Unobservable Variables in Path Analysis." Pp. 81–117 in *Sociological Methodology*, vol. 1, edited by Herbert L. Costner. San Francisco: Jossey-Bass.

———. 1975. "Correction of 'The Treatment of Unobservable Variables in Path Analysis'." Pp. 212–13 in *Sociological Methodology*, vol. 5, edited by David R. Heise. San Francisco: Jossey-Bass.

Hout, Michael, Clem Brooks, and Jeff Manza. 1995. "The Democratic Class Struggle in the United States, 1948–1992." *American Sociological Review* 60(6):805–28.

Jöreskog, Karl G., and Arthur S. Goldberger. 1975. "Estimation of a Model with Multiple Indicators and Multiple Causes of a Single Latent Variable." *Journal of the American Statistical Association* 70:631–39.

Lucas, Samuel R. 2001. "Effectively Maintained Inequality: Education Transitions, Track Mobility, and Social Background Effects." *American Journal of Sociology* 106(6):1642–90.

Maclean, Alair. 2005. "Lessons from the Cold War: Military Service and College Education." *Sociology of Education* 78:250–66.

Mare, Robert D. 1979. "Social Background Composition and Educational Growth." *Demography* 16(1):55–71.

———. 1980. "Social Background and School Continuation Decisions." *Journal of the American Statistical Association* 75:293–305.

———. 1981. "Change and Stability in Educational Stratification." *American Sociological Review* 46(1):72–87.

Raftery, Adrian E., and Michael Hout. 1993. "Maximally Maintained Inequality: Expansion, Reform, and Opportunity in Irish Education, 1921–75." *Sociology of Education* 66(1):41–62.

Shavit, Yossi, and Hans-Peter Blossfeld. 1993. *Persistent Inequality: Changing Educational Attainment in Thirteen Countries.* Boulder, CO: Westview.

Stolzenberg, Ross M. 1994. "Educational Continuation by College Graduates." *American Journal of Sociology* 99(4):1042–77.

Xie, Yu. 1992. "The Log-Multiplicative Layer Effect Model for Comparing Mobility Tables." *American Sociological Review* 57(3):380–95.

RESPONSE: STATISTICAL MODELS OF EDUCATIONAL STRATIFICATION—HAUSER AND ANDREW'S MODELS FOR SCHOOL TRANSITIONS

Robert D. Mare*

Hauser and Andrew marry two good ideas that emerged within quantitative social science during the 1970s—namely, the multiple-indicator-multiple-cause (MIMIC) model for multivariate responses and the logistic response model for transitions between stages of educational attainment. The MIMIC model, now part of standard textbooks for structural equation models with latent variables (e. g., Bollen 1989), is a natural, rigorous, and efficient way to represent the effects of exogenous variables on multiple endogenous variables (Hauser and Goldberger 1971). It is also a tool for testing whether a set of variables "behave as a scale" in their relationship to other variables in a multivariate model and thus for avoiding *ad hoc*, unsubstantiated index construction (e. g., Hauser 1973). As Hauser and Andrew note, the logistic response model for school transitions is a widely used tool for the analysis of educational stratification, allowing investigators of family background effects on educational attainment to recognize that schooling is a sequence of events in time rather than a single status, and that the sources of inequality of educational opportunity and outcome may be different at different stages of schooling. It is gratifying to see that these ideas have continued to inspire application, discussion, and improvement approximately 30 years after they were introduced. In this comment, I place my

Direct correspondence to Robert D. Mare, Department of Sociology, UCLA, 264 Haines Hall, Box 951551, Los Angeles, CA 90095-1551; e-mail: mare@ucla.edu. This work was supported by the Russell Sage Foundation and benefited from the facilities of the California Center for Population Research, which is supported by the National Institute of Child Health and Human Development. In preparing this comment I benefited from conversations with Robert M. Hauser, Vida Maralani, William M. Mason, and Christine R. Schwartz.

*University of California, Los Angeles

contributions in the context in which they were conceived, note their continued potential for research on educational stratification, and discuss the strengths and weaknesses of Hauser and Andrew's contribution.

My studies of school transitions built upon approaches that already appeared in the literature and were motivated in part by contemporary arguments about how to interpret inequality of educational opportunities and outcomes. In a pioneering and meticulous investigation, Duncan (1965, 1967, 1968) used school progression ratios to describe trends in educational attainment, an illuminating complement to her investigations of family background effects on years of school completed. Spady (1967) analyzed the associations of father's educational attainment and son's school transitions, using published tabulations and the comparatively primitive statistical methods that were available for such data in the 1960s. Relying largely on simulated data, Boudon (1974) formulated a model for inequality of educational opportunity that treated schooling as a sequence of grade progressions. Hauser (1976) criticized Boudon's approach on several grounds but, most relevant for the present discussion, showed the vulnerability of Boudon's and Spady's interpretations of differences in school progression rates to artifactual ceiling and floor effects. I applied the logistic response model for dichotomous dependent variables to the effects of family background on progression through school and showed the connections between this approach and others that were in widespread use (Mare 1977, 1979, 1980, 1981a). This work took advantage of recent innovations in statistical methods (Cox 1970; Allison 1982), improvements in high speed computing, and the newly available Occupational Changes in a Generation II Survey (Featherman and Hauser 1975).

From a conceptual standpoint, the significance of the model for school transitions lies mainly in viewing educational attainment as a process in time and allowing for rigorous empirical examination the effects of potentially time-varying characteristics of individuals, families, and institutions as children and adolescents move through school (Mare 1981b; Lucas 2001; Mare and Chang 2006). This is true even though the influence of much of this work has been on traditional studies that gauge inequalities among persons who are classified by relatively static "social background" characteristics and who live in a homogeneous institutional environment (e. g., Shavit and Blossfeld 1993). School transition models also allow for distinct social processes to govern school progression at different stages, including the possibility that school progression results from the behavior of a multiplicity of actors who vary in importance across time, place, and institutional context. For example, Gamoran and Mare (1989) explored the effects of the competing objectives of families and schools in track placement and their consequences for students. In an independent line of work, Manski and Wise (1983) used variants of school transition models to show how college attendance and graduation result from the interdependent yet distinct actions of families, students, and college admissions officers. Breen and Jonsson (2000) very usefully generalized the school transition model to encompass a more complex institutional framework that includes multiple parallel pathways in education systems. Unlike these works, however, much of the most innovative recent research on educational attainment has adopted relatively asociological approaches in which educational stratification results from information processing and rational calculation by atomized families and individuals. This focus is shared by researchers who are both sympathetic to and critical of the school transition approach (e. g., Cameron and Heckman 1998; Breen and Goldthorpe 1997; Morgan 2005). It remains to be seen whether future researchers will return to a broader set of concerns about the multiple interdependent decision makers at various institutional levels who may be responsible for levels and variations in educational attainment.

Hauser and Andrew's family of models for proportionality restrictions is a significant contribution to the statistical analysis of school transitions within the framework of a discrete time hazard model (Allison 1982). They illustrate the value of proportionality restrictions on the coefficients of the school transition model, both as a way of achieving parsimony of parameters and also as a way of distilling the essence of a set of complex multivariate results. Although Hauser and Andrew make a strong case for their LRPC and LRPPC models, I think that they understate the power of their family of models. At the same time, in other ways, they may oversell it as well. I develop these points in the balance of this comment.

A key issue in interpreting variation in the effects of social background across school transitions is the identifiability of parameters in binary response models. As we now understand much better than when my work on school transition models first appeared, in logit and other models for dichotomous dependent variables, the variance of the latent dependent variable and thus the scale of the estimated coefficients are not identified (Long 1997; Cameron and Heckman 1998; Allison 1999).

To estimate these models, a normalizing constraint is required. In typical software for estimating binary response models, this constraint is to fix the variance of the errors of the equation at a constant, although other constraints, such as fixing the variance of the latent dependent variable itself, are also possible (Winship and Mare 1983, 1984). With either type of constraint, within a single equation for a binary response, we can identify only the relative sizes of the coefficients. Across equations for the same dependent variable estimated on different samples, or for different dependent variables estimated on the same sample, we cannot even identify the relative sizes of the coefficients for the effects of a single variable.[1] By contrast, in typical binary response models, the effects of the covariates on the binary response, as measured either by derivatives (when they exist) or the differences in predicted probabilities, *are* identified and do not depend on a normalizing constraint (Long 1997; Allison 1999). Given the nonlinearity of the effects of the covariates on the response probability in logit, probit, and other models, however, these effects, unlike the coefficients, depend upon the specific point in the distribution of the covariates where they are evaluated.

This problem of identification arises both in unrestricted versions of binary response models for school transitions and also in constrained versions such as Hauser and Andrews' LRPC and LRPPC models. Hauser and Andrew find that my informal description of the unconstrained school transition model coefficients—that is, that the coefficients for socioeconomic background factors decline across transitions—is consistent with the restrictions of their LRPPC model. Unfortunately, although the LRPPC and the unrestricted models of school transitions yield similar estimates, the coefficients of neither model confirm or disconfirm the conclusion that the effects of socioeconomic background decline across school transitions. Because the coefficients in the logistic response model are identified only up to a constant of proportionality within any given equation, true differences in effects

[1] When the error variance is fixed, it is also inappropriate to make within-sample comparisons among the coefficients for a given covariate across equations with varying subsets of covariates. In this case, the total variance of the latent dependent variable and thus the scale of the estimated coefficients vary from model to model as a function of the different regressors that are included. Fixing the variance of the latent dependent variable avoids this problem. It does not, however, avoid the problems of comparison across samples and across dependent variables.

of socioeconomic background across school transitions are empirically indistinguishable from heteroskedasticity of the conditional variances of the latent dependent variables.

The indeterminacy of the logistic regression coefficients raises the question of whether the validity of the proportionality restrictions in the LRPC or LRPPC models depends on the normalizing restrictions used to estimate the logistic coefficients. Fortunately, it is easy to show that this is *not* the case. That is, even though the logistic coefficients can only be estimated with an (arbitrary) normalizing constraint, the proportionality restrictions are independent of any specific constraint. For simplicity, in the following discussion I focus on the LRPC model and do not explicitly discuss the less restrictive LRPPC model. However, my conclusions about what we can learn from models that impose proportionality restrictions across equations in the school transition models apply equally to the LRPC and LRPPC models.[2]

If y_j denotes a binary variable that equals one if an individual makes the jth transition and zero otherwise, the J equation logit model for the effects of K fixed social background variables is, omitting subscripts for individuals,

$$\log \left[\frac{p(y_j = 1 | y_{j-1} = 1, X_1, \ldots, X_K)}{[1 - p(y_j = 1 | y_{j-1} = 1, X_1, \ldots, X_K)]} \right]$$

$$= b_{j0} + \sum_{k=1}^{K} b_{jk} X_k \quad (j = 1, \ldots, J; y_0 = 1). \tag{1}$$

For this model, the LRPC hypothesis is that

$$\frac{b_{jk}}{b_{j-1,k}} = \frac{b_{jk'}}{b_{j-1,k'}} = \lambda_j \quad (j = 2, \ldots, J). \tag{2}$$

Because the true variances of the underlying dependent variables in equation (1) are not identified, however, the true coefficients for the

---

[2]My discussion rules out the case discussed by Allison (1999), who shows that we can compare the coefficients of binary response models across samples when we assume that the coefficient for at least one regressor is invariant across samples. This identifying restriction may be defensible in many substantive investigations, but, without additional information, is hard to maintain *a priori* in studies of school transitions where one of the main analytic objectives is to describe variation in social background effects across school transitions.

effects of the X_k are not identified. Equivalently stated, the constants of proportionality, λ_j, are estimable, but their values incorporate both differences across equations in the effects of the regressors and also differences in the variances of the underlying dependent variables.

We can rewrite the logit model as a set of equations for latent continuous variables, say y_j^*, as

$$\frac{y_j^*}{\sigma_j} = \frac{\beta_{j0}}{\sigma_j} + \sum_{k=1}^{K} \left(\frac{\beta_{jk}}{\sigma_j}\right) X_k + \frac{\varepsilon_j}{\sigma_j}, \tag{3}$$

where β_{jk} denotes the true coefficient for the effect of the kth independent variable on the log odds of making the jth school transition and σ_j is the standard deviation of the random disturbance ϵ_j for the equation for the jth transition. Neither the β_{jk} nor the σ_j are estimable from the data without additional information. They are, however, linked to the estimable quantities in equation (1) because

$$b_{jk} = \frac{\beta_{jk}}{\sigma_j}. \tag{4}$$

If the LRPC constraints (2) hold for equation (1), then the LRPC model implies that

$$\frac{\left(\dfrac{\beta_{jk}}{\sigma_j}\right)}{\left(\dfrac{\beta_{j-1,k}}{\sigma_{j-1}}\right)} = \frac{\left(\dfrac{\beta_{jk'}}{\sigma_j}\right)}{\left(\dfrac{\beta_{j-1,k'}}{\sigma_{j-1}}\right)} = \lambda_j \qquad (j = 2, \ldots, J). \tag{5}$$

But this expression simplifies to

$$\frac{\beta_{jk}}{\beta_{j-1,k}} = \frac{\beta_{jk'}}{\beta_{j-1,k'}} = \lambda_j \left(\frac{\sigma_j}{\sigma_{j-1}}\right) = \lambda_j^*, \tag{6}$$

which shows that if the LRPC model holds for the estimable quantities b_{jk}, it also holds for the true underlying parameters β_{jk}. Although the constant of proportionality that links the true parameters for the different transitions for a given regressor (6) is not, in general, the same as for the estimable parameters (2), the LRPC hypothesis for the true parameters holds if and only if it holds for the estimable parameters as well.

Although this is an appealing result inasmuch as it implies that the LRPC hypothesis is not bedeviled by the identification problem that plagues the logistic response model itself, it may also be construed as a hollow one because the coefficients of proportionality (λ_j^*) that link the equations for the different transitions are not identified. Fortunately, however, it is possible to draw stronger and more useful conclusions when the LRPC or LRPPC model holds. As noted above, although the coefficients of binary response models are not identified without an arbitrary scale restriction, other functions of the data are estimable, including functions of the predicted probabilities under the models. In particular, the effects of the regressors as represented by the partial derivatives of the probabilities with respect to the regressors (when they exist) or differences in adjusted predicted probabilities between different values of the regressors are estimable. This raises the question of whether the restrictions of the LRPC model on the coefficients of the logistic response model imply similar restrictions on the estimable functions of the predicted probabilities. In fact, this is the case. To see this, consider the logistic response model in equation (1) and assume, without loss of generality, that the derivatives of the probabilities with respect to the X_k exist.[3] These derivatives are

$$\frac{\partial \left[p(y_j = 1 | y_{j-1} = 1, X_1, \ldots, X_K) \right]}{\partial X_k}$$

$$= b_{jk} p(y_j = 1 | y_{j-1} = 1, X_1, \ldots, X_K)$$

$$\times \left[1 - p(y_j = 1 | y_{j-1} = 1, X_1, \ldots, X_K) \right] = b_{jk} f_j, \quad (7)$$

where f_j, the density function of the standard logistic distribution, depends on the estimated parameters for the jth transition and a selected vector of values for $X_1, \ldots, X_K$ but not on the specific regressor X_k under consideration. Thus, the ratio of effects of a given regressor across two adjacent transitions evaluated at a common vector of values of the regressors is simply $b_{jk} f_j / b_{j-1,k} f_{j-1}$. If the LRPC restriction (2) holds

---

[3]A similar result to the one presented here for the effects of continuous X_k holds for the adjusted predicted probabilities for different values of discrete regressors.

for the estimated coefficients, then it holds for the derivatives too. That is,

$$\frac{b_{jk}f_j}{b_{j-1,k}f_{j-1}} = \frac{b_{jk'}f_j}{b_{j-1,k'}f_{j-1}} = \lambda_j \left(\frac{f_j}{f_{j-1}} \right). \tag{8}$$

Conversely, if (8) holds, (2) holds as well.

Thus the LRPC model implies a common hypothesis about the estimable coefficients, the unidentified true coefficients, and the estimable effects of the independent variables evaluated at a chosen vector of values of the regressors. This is an especially attractive property of the model, which may not be shared by other restricted versions of the model for school transitions. When a LRPC or LRPPC model fits the data, therefore, it is not only a pleasingly parsimonious model as Hauser and Andrew emphasize, but also deeply and robustly informative about the structure of association in school transition models.

Despite the great potential of the LRPC and LRPPC models, Hauser and Andrew overstate the case when they say that we ought to estimate the LRPC before proposing more complex explanations of change in the effects of socioeconomic background. Whether or not the LRPC model fits the data may or may not rule out specific explanations and, depending on which covariates obey the proportionality assumptions, the model may or may not yield an interpretable result. The LRPC and LRPPC models are elegant and sometimes adequate summaries of multivariate relationships. But explanations and interpretations of variation in the effects of social background may occur to an investigator before, during, or after fitting less or more parsimonious specifications of transition-specific effects and may be tested by a variety of alternative models. My own early efforts were influenced by the OCG educational stratification studies of Featherman and Hauser (Hauser and Featherman 1976; Featherman and Hauser 1978), which used relatively unparsimonious specifications of trends in social background effects. Within the constraints of additive, linear models, these studies described changes in the effects of specific background variables and, in yielding key descriptive statistics about trends in stratification, set the stage for subsequent thinking about the causes of these trends. When we turn to more parsimonious models, LRPC and LRPPC are just one of many possible classes of models. Another, as Hauser and Andrew indicate, is the model with no variation across transitions in the effects of some or all social background variables. The family of probability models for cumulative educational attainment is another (e. g., Breen 2005; Cameron and Heckman 1998). Yet another example is models in which any or all background effects vary systematically with the known values of macro-level covariates, such as the proportion of a cohort at risk to a given transition or characteristics of school systems and the economy (Mare 1977, 1981b; Rijken 1999). The LRPC and LRPPC models are very useful devices for studying educational stratification. But in a model-rich world, the investigator needs a flexible toolkit and some guiding substantive hypotheses to see what is going on. No single class of models or sequence of model tests is likely to do the trick.

REFERENCES

Allison, Paul D. 1982. "Discrete Time Methods for the Analysis of Event Histories." 61–98 in *Sociological Methodology,* vol. 12 edited by Samuel Leinhardt. Cambridge, MA: Blackwell Publishing.

———. 1999. "Comparing Logit and Probit Coefficients Across Groups." *Sociological Methods and Research* 28:186–208.

Bollen, Kenneth A. 1989. *Structural Equations with Latent Variables.* New York: Wiley.

Boudon, Raymond. 1974. *Education, Opportunity, and Social Inequality: Changing Prospects in Western Society.* New York: Wiley.

Breen, Richard. 2005. "Statistical Models of Educational Careers." Nuffield College, Oxford University, Unpublished manuscript.

Breen, Richard, and John H. Goldthorpe. 1997. "Exploring Educational Differentials: Towards a Formal Rational Action Theory." *Rationality and Society* 9:275–305.

Breen, Richard, and Jan O. Jonsson. 2000. "Analyzing Educational Careers: A Multinomial Transition Model." *American Sociological Review* 65:754–72.

Cameron, Stephen V., and James J. Heckman. 1998. "Life Cycle Schooling and Dynamic Selection Bias: Models and Evidence for Five Cohorts of American Males." *Journal of Political Economy* 106:262–333.

Cox, David R. 1970. *The Analysis of Binary Data.* London: Methuen.

Duncan, Beverly. 1965. *Family Factors and School Dropout: 1920–1960.* Cooperative Research Project No. 2258, Office of Education. Ann Arbor: University of Michigan.

———. 1967. "Education and Social Background." *American Journal of Sociology* 72:363–72.

———. 1968. "Trends in Output and Distribution of Schooling." Pp. 601–72 in *Indicators of Social Change,* edited by Eleanor B. Sheldon and Wilbert E. Moore. New York: Russell Sage Foundation.

Featherman, David L., and Robert M. Hauser. 1975. "Design for a Replicate Study of Social Mobility in the United States." Pp. 219–51 in *Social Indicator Models*, edited by Kenneth C. Land and Seymour Spilerman. New York: Russell Sage Foundation.

Featherman, David L., and Robert M. Hauser. 1978. *Opportunity and Change.* New York: Academic Press.

Gamoran, Adam, and Robert D. Mare. 1989. "Secondary School Tracking and Stratification: Compensation, Reinforcement, or Neutrality?" *American Journal of Sociology* 94:1146–83.

Hauser, Robert M. 1973. "Disaggregating a Social-Psychological Model of Educational Attainment." Pp. 255–84 in *Structural Equation Models in the Social Sciences*, edited by A.S. Goldberger and O. D. Duncan. New York: Seminar Press.

———. 1976. "Review Essay: On Boudon's Model of Social Mobility." *American Journal of Sociology* 81:911–28.

Hauser, Robert M., and David L. Featherman. 1976. "Equality of Schooling: Trends and Prospects." *Sociology of Education* 49(2):99–120.

Hauser, Robert M., and Arthur S. Goldberger. 1971. "The Treatment of Unobservable Variables in Path Analysis." Pp. 81–117 in *Sociological Methodology*, vol. 4, edited by Herbert L. Costner. San Francisco: Jossey-Bass.

Long, J. Scott. 1997. *Regression Models for Categorical and Limited Dependent Variables*. Thousand Oaks, CA: Sage.

Lucas, Samuel R. 2001. "Effectively Maintained Inequality: Education Transitions, Track Mobility, and Social Background Effects." *American Journal of Sociology* 106:1642–90.

Manski, Charles F., and David A. Wise. 1983. *College Choice in America.* Cambridge, MA.: Harvard University Press.

Mare, Robert D. 1977. "Growth and Distribution of Schooling in White Male American Cohorts: 1907–1952". Ph.D. dissertation, University of Michigan, Ann Arbor.

———. 1979. "Social Background Composition and Educational Growth." *Demography* 16:55–71.

———. 1980. "Social Background and School Continuation Decisions." *Journal of the American Statistical Association* 75:295–305.

———. 1981a. "Change and Stability in Educational Stratification." *American Sociological Review* 46:72–87.

———. 1981b. "Market and Institutional Sources of Educational Growth." Pp. 205–45 in *Research in Social Stratification and Mobility*, vol. 1, edited by Donald J. Treiman and Robert V. Robinson. Greenwich, Connecticut: JAI Press.

Mare, Robert D., and Huey-Chi Chang. 2006. "Family Attainment Norms and Educational Stratification in the United States and Taiwan: The Effects of Parents' School Transitions." Pp. 195–231 in *Mobility and Inequality: Frontiers of Research in Economics and Sociology*, edited by S.L. Morgan, D. B. Grusky, and G. Fields. Stanford, CA: Stanford University Press.

Morgan, Stephen L. 2005. *On the Edge of Commitment.* Stanford, CA: Stanford University Press.

Rijken, Susanne. 1999. *Educational Expansion and Status Attainment: A Cross-National and Over-Time Comparison.* Utrecht, Netherlands: Interuniversity Center for Social Science Theory and Methodology.

Shavit, Yossi, and Hans-Peter Blossfeld. 1993. *Persistent Inequality: Changing Educational Attainment in Thirteen Countries.* Boulder, CO: Westview Press.

Spady, William. 1967. "Educational Mobility and Access: Growth and Paradoxes." *American Journal of Sociology* 73:273–86.

Winship, Christopher, and Robert D. Mare. 1983. "Structural Equations and Path Analysis for Discrete Data." *American Journal of Sociology* 88:54–110.

———. 1984. "Regression Models with Ordinal Variables." *American Sociological Review* 49:512–25.

2

BAYESIAN INFERENCE FOR HIERARCHICAL AGE-PERIOD-COHORT MODELS OF REPEATED CROSS-SECTION SURVEY DATA

Yang Yang*

This study applies methods of Bayesian statistical inference to hierarchical APC models for the age-period-cohort analysis of repeated cross-section survey data. It examines the impacts of small sample sizes of birth cohorts and time periods and unbalanced data on statistical inferences based on the usual restricted maximum likelihood–empirical Bayes (REML-EB) estimators through Monte Carlo simulations. A full Bayesian analysis using Gibbs sampling and MCMC estimation is developed to assess the robustness of REML-EB inferences when this extra uncertainty is taken into account and the numbers of higher-level units are small. For a substantive illustration, it applies cross-classified random effects models to vocabulary test data from the General Social Survey (1974 to 2000). It is concluded that the decline in verbal ability for birth cohorts born after 1950 was correlated with

This is a revision of a paper that received the 2004 Student Paper Competition Award sponsored by the Social Statistics, Survey Research Methods, and Government Statistics Sections of the American Statistical Association. A previous version of this paper was also presented at the annual meeting of the American Sociological Association–Methodology Section, San Francisco, August 2004. I thank Ken Land and Alan Gelfand for valuable comments on an earlier version of the paper. Address correspondence to Yang Yang, Department of Sociology, the University of Chicago, 1126 E. 59th St., Chicago, IL 60637.

*University of Chicago

the levels of newspaper reading and television watching. Avenues for future research on mixed APC models are discussed.

1. INTRODUCTION

Recent methodological studies in demography and epidemiology have made great strides in estimation of age-period-cohort (APC) models (Robertson, Gandini, and Boyle 1999; Yang, Fu, and Land 2004). Research along this line focused on using fixed effects generalized linear models to delineate age, period, and cohort variations in event/exposure rates from aggregate population data. But the development and methodological assessment of the performance of modeling techniques for APC analysis of microlevel data such as sample surveys that are especially useful for testing explanatory hypotheses remain.

One form of individual-level survey data that has been increasingly used in sociological studies of social change is the repeated cross-section sample surveys. Taking the advantage of multilevel data and explanatory variables provided by such surveys, Yang and Land (2003) developed a hierarchical age-period-cohort (HAPC) models approach. Recognizing that individual respondents (level-1) are nested within cells created by the cross-classification of two higher-level units—that is, birth cohorts and time periods (level-2)—they introduced cross-classified random effects models (CCREM) to APC analyses in the context of repeated cross-sectional surveys. They showed how this approach can be used to shed new light on the recent debates of trends in vocabulary in the General Social Survey by estimating separate age, period, and cohort components of change.

This paper builds on work by Yang and Land (2006) and further considers situations that may affect the accuracy of the HAPC model estimates based on the restricted maximum likelihood–empirical Bayes (REML-EB thereafter) estimation. In APC analyses of finite time period social survey data, the numbers of periods and birth cohorts usually are too small to satisfy the large sample criteria required by the maximum likelihood estimation of variance components. In addition, the sample sizes within each cohort are highly unbalanced. Therefore, errors in variance components estimates may produce extra uncertainty in coefficient estimates that will not be reflected in the standard errors.

This added uncertainty may cast doubt on statistical inferences based on REML-EB estimates of model parameters (Raudenbush and Bryk 2002, chapt. 13). It also motivates the investigation of a full Bayesian alternative to account for the extra uncertainty brought about by the small sample sizes and unbalanced data. This paper continues to analyze the same data from the General Social Survey as studied by Yang and Land (2003). It shows how the HAPC models approach can be implemented via the Bayes-MCMC methods and how they improve statistical inferences for APC analyses. Although the methodological discussion takes place in the context of APC analyses of repeated cross-sectional sample survey data, it can be construed as having broad applications for comparisons of EB and full Bayesian methods for estimating hierarchical regression models.

The paper is organized as follows. It first specifies a hierarchical APC model of GSS data on verbal test scores and reports Monte Carlo simulations of REML-EB estimation of model parameters. It then introduces the full Bayesian HAPC model using Gibbs sampling. Results of the Bayes MCMC estimates are presented. This is followed by a sensitivity analysis of posterior estimates under various alternative prior distributions. The final section discusses the findings and reports conclusions from this study.

2. HIERARCHICAL APC MODELS OF GSS DATA: REML-EB ESTIMATION

2.1. *Data and Variables*

Table 1 presents descriptions and summary univariate statistics of all the variables included in the subsequent analyses. The dependent variable, verbal test score, and individual-level covariates are the same as those analyzed by Yang and Land (2003). These include age, education, gender, and race. In addition, two cohort covariates are included to measure the contextual effects of cohort: proportion of cohort members who read newspapers daily (NEWS) and mean hours of television watching per day (TV). Figure 1 shows large variations of these two cohort characteristics across the birth cohorts. Glenn (1994) suggested that both cohort characteristics were related to the decline in cohort mean verbal

TABLE 1
Summary Statistics for Verbal Ability Data from the GSS, 1974–2000

Variable Name	Description	N	Mean	S.D.	Min	Max
Outcome						
WORDSUM	Composite vocabulary test score	19500	6.02	2.15	0	10
Individual Level						
AGE	Respondent's age at survey year	19500	45.34	17.10	18	89
EDUCATION	Respondent's years of schooling	19500	12.72	3.02	0	20
FEMALE	Sex: = 1 if female; = 0 if male	19500	0.57	0.50	0	1
BLACK	Race: = 1 if black; = 0 if white	19500	0.15	0.35	0	1
Cohort Level		J	Mean	sd	Min	Max
NEWS	Proportion who read newspapers every day	19	0.34	0.13	0.11	0.50
TV	Average hours of TV watching per day	19	3.03	0.49	1.63	3.72
Period Level	15 survey years	K	Mean	S.D.	Min	Max
		15				

test scores since the early twentieth century. This study explicitly tests Glenn's proposition by examining the associations between these two cohort characteristics and trends in verbal ability in the HAPC models in the presence of controls for individual-level factors related to verbal ability.

2.2. *Cross-Classified Random Effects Model*

The data structure of repeated cross-sectional surveys implies that individuals are nested within cells created by the cross-classification of two types of social context: birth cohorts and survey years (Yang and Land 2003, table 3). Previous studies on this topic employed OLS regression analyses that included one of period and cohort effects, but not both. Yang and Land (2006) noted that the omission of period or

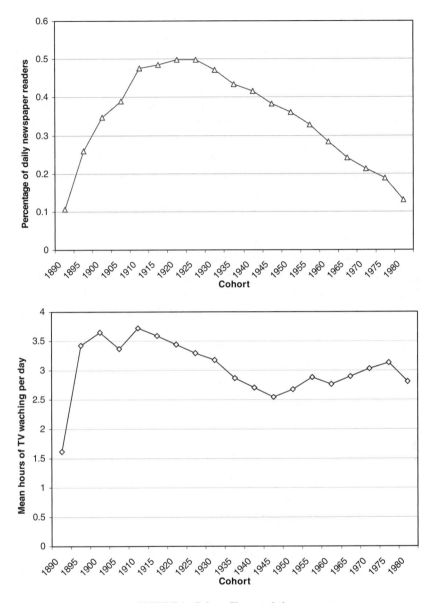

FIGURE 1. Cohort Characteristics.

cohort effects risks violating the usual independence of errors assumption of linear regression models. They also showed that the fixed effects model specification ignores the multilevel data structure that creates the possibility that the effects of cohort membership and survey year may have shared random as well as, or instead of, fixed effects on the verbal test responses. That is, it does not consider the possibility that sample respondents in the same cohort group and/or survey year may be similar in their responses to the verbal test questions due to the fact that they share random error components unique to their cohorts or periods of the survey. A failure to assess this complicated error structure adequately in APC analysis may have serious consequences for statistical inferences. The standard errors of estimated coefficients of standard regression models may be underestimated, leading to inflated t-ratios and actual alpha levels that are larger than the nominal .05 or .01 levels.

Specifically, a cross-classified random-effects model (CCREM) can be specified (1) to assess the amount and significance of the variance in the dependent variable that is associated with birth cohorts or time period while controlling for the age and other variables, and (2) to examine how much of the observed age, period, and cohort effects are explained by differences in individual characteristics, cohort characteristics, and period events (when measured). The model specifications using the GSS verbal test score data are shown below:[1]

- Level-1 or "within-cell" model:

$$
\begin{aligned}
WORDSUM_{ijk} = \beta_{0jk} &+ \beta_1 AGE_{ijk} + \beta_2 AGE_{ijk}^2 \\
&+ \beta_3 EDUCATION_{ijk} + \beta_4 FEMALE_{ijk} \\
&+ \beta_5 BLACK_{ijk} + e_{ijk}, \; e_{ijk} \sim N(0, \sigma^2) \quad (1)
\end{aligned}
$$

- Level-2 or "between-cell" model:

$$
\begin{aligned}
\beta_{0jk} &= \gamma_0 + \gamma_1 NEWS_j + \gamma_2 TV_j + u_{0j} + v_{0k}, \\
u_{0j} &\sim N(0, \tau_u), \; v_{0k} \sim N(0, \tau_v) \quad (2)
\end{aligned}
$$

---

[1]Note that this is a random-intercepts model, which is based on work by Yang and Land (2006). They found that only the intercepts, but not level 1 slopes, exhibit significant random variation across cohorts and periods in the GSS verbal test score data.

- Combined model:[2]

$$WORDSUM_{ijk} = \gamma_0 + \gamma_1 NEWS_j + \gamma_2 TV_j + \beta_1 AGE_{ijk}$$
$$+ \beta_2 AGE_{ijk}^2 + \beta_3 EDUCATION_{ijk}$$
$$+ \beta_4 FEMALE_{ijk} + \beta_5 BLACK_{ijk} + u_{0j}$$
$$+ v_{0k} + e_{ijk} \qquad (3)$$

for $i = 1, 2, \ldots, n_{jk}$ individuals within cohort j and period k; $j = 1, \ldots, 19$ birth cohorts; and $k = 1, \ldots, 15$ time periods (survey years).

In this model, β_{0jk} is the intercept or "cell mean"—that is, the mean verbal test core of individuals who belong to birth cohort j and are surveyed in year k, and $\beta_1, \ldots, \beta_5$ are the level-1 fixed effects coefficients. Note that the level-1 model is the same as that specified by Yang and Land (2006), but in the level 2 model the overall mean, β_{0jk}, is further modeled as a function of two row predictors/cohort-level variables. The model intercept, γ_0, is the expected value of β_{0jk} when all explanatory variables at level 2 are set to zero, and γ_1 and γ_2 denote cohort-level fixed effects. u_{0j} is now interpreted as the residual random effect of cohort j—that is, the contribution of cohort j averaged over all periods—on β_{0jk} after taking into account $NEWS_j$ and TV_j, assumed normally distributed with mean 0 and variance τ_u. v_{0k} is the residual random effect of period k, —that is, the contribution of period k averaged over all cohorts, assumed normally distributed with mean 0 and variance τ_v. The specifications above adopt the usual assumptions required by random effects models that the random residuals (u_{0j} and v_{0k}) are distributed independently of the explanatory/independent variables and are also orthogonal to each other (Snijders and Bosker 1999). In addition, $\beta_{0j} = \gamma_0 + \gamma_1 NEWS_j + \gamma_2 TV_j + u_{0j}$ is the cohort verbal test score averaged over all periods, and $\beta_{0k} = \gamma_0 + v_{0k}$ is the period verbal test score averaged over all cohorts.

The model identification problem induced by the linear dependency between age, period, and cohort—that is, Period = Age + Cohort—creates a major challenge for APC analysis from the point of view of conventional linear models (Mason and Fienberg 1985). The

---

[2]For simplification of the notation for the Bayesian analyses, $\beta_1, \ldots \beta_5$ will be written as $\gamma_3, \ldots \gamma_7$.

assumption of additivity, however, is only one approximation of the process of how social and demographic change occurs (Hobcraft, Menken, and Preston 1982; Smith 2004). The hierarchical APC models introduced here are one family of nonadditive models that can be extremely useful for capturing the contextual effects of cohort membership and period events on a wide range of social demographic processes. The second contribution of the hierarchical models approach to APC analysis is that it makes it possible to test explanatory hypotheses by incorporating other covariates provided by sample surveys and offers insights to substantive cohort or period phenomena that can hardly be gained from any version of the APC accounting models.

In the HAPC models shown above, the identification problem is solved by using the conventional strategy of transforming at least one variable related to age, period, or cohort so that its relationship to the others is nonlinear (Mason et al. 1973; Fienberg and Mason 1985). One key modeling assumption for the present analysis is the specification of a parametric form for the age effects. Substantive findings from previous research on U.S. verbal test scores show a curvilinear age pattern (Wilson and Gove 1999; Yang and Land 2006). Results form the exploratory data analysis of the overall age, period, and cohort trends using the Intrinsic Estimator (Yang et al. 2004) support their findings on the age pattern. Therefore equation (1) specifies the quadratic function for the age effects. The other assumption is the estimation of cohort and period variance components using hierarchical models. The innovation of this approach is that it addresses the heterogeneity problem determined by the multilevel data structure by modifying the fixed-effects specification toward a mixed fixed-random effects model that improves inference. For consistency with extant articles on trends in the GSS vocabulary test data, I use five-year birth cohorts. This also breaks the exact linear dependence from knowledge of the period of the survey and the birth cohort in which each sample respondent is a member, it is not possible to determine the exact age of each respondent. In fact, the general five-year age category of which each of these respondents is a member can be determined. But, at the level of the individual respondent, this is not an exact linear dependence. The quadratic parameterization of age effects, however, solves the identification problem regardless of whether cohorts are defined by five-year age groupings or single-year-of-age.

The conventional method of parameter estimation in such a model is based on restricted maximum likelihood (REML) estimates of variance components and empirical Bayes estimates of level-1 coefficients. I briefly review this method and consider how a Bayesian approach can add inferential strength to APC analyses of repeated cross-sectional surveys.

2.3. *REML-EB Estimation*

For any possible value of γ,[3] a likelihood of variance components τ_u, τ_v and σ^2 can be defined—say $L(\tau_u, \tau_v, \sigma^2 | \gamma, Y)$, where Y is the observed data. Averaging over all possible values of γ for the likelihood yields a likelihood of τ_u, τ_v, and σ^2 given Y alone. This is the restricted likelihood, $L(\tau_u, \tau_v, \sigma^2 | Y)$. The REML approach chooses as estimates of τ_u, τ_v and σ^2 those values that maximize the joint likelihood of these parameters given Y. Conditioning on these ML estimates, we compute generalized least squares estimates of γ and empirical Bayes estimates of the level-1 coefficients, β.

REML-EB estimates were obtained using SAS PROC MIXED (Littell et al. 1996). The modeling results are presented in the left panels of each of the three models in Table 2 in a stepwise fashion. They show that all individual covariates are significantly related to WORD-SUM, and they account for about 30 percent of the unconditional level-1 variance ($(4.526 - 3.136)/4.526$); controlling for these covariates, significant cohort effects of newspaper reading and TV watching appear; the residual variation between cohorts and between periods is close to zero, compared with the unconditional variance estimates (0.139 and 0.031). These level-2 variance components are thus substantially reduced. The AIC (Akaike Information Criterion)[4] statistics show that Model 3, which includes both the individual and cohort covariates, has the best model fit.

This approach has several strengths. First, the REML estimates of variance components are consistent and efficient in large samples—i.e., for large J and K. In addition, for large J and K, the sampling distributions of these estimators are approximately normal, provided that the REML estimates of τ_u and τ_v are positive definite. Second it follows that for large J and K, the normal distribution can be conveniently used for constructing confidence intervals and hypotheses testing. Third, since

---

[3] $\gamma = (\gamma_0, \ldots \gamma_7)^T; \beta = (\beta_0, \ldots \beta_5)^T.$
[4] $AIC = Deviance + 2DF$. The smaller the AIC, the better the model fit.

TABLE 2
Alternative Estimates of Coefficients and Summary Statistics: REML Versus Bayes Via Gibbs Under Diffuse-Normal-Gamma Priors

	Model 1 Unconditional Model				Model 2 Individual Covariates				Model 3 Cohort Covariates			
	REML		Bayes via Gibbs		REML		Bayes via Gibbs		REML		Bayes via Gibbs	
	Coeff.	S.E.	Coeff.	S.E.	Coeff.	S.E.	Coeff.	S.E.	Coeff.	S.E.	Coeff.	S.E.
(a) Fixed Effect												
Intercept, γ_0	5.851	0.082	5.851	0.113	6.167	0.059	6.159	0.064	6.198	0.052	6.196	0.055
AGE, β_1	—		—		0.030	0.017	0.032	0.018	0.016	0.019	0.017	0.019
AGE^2, β_2	—		—		−0.065	0.006	−0.065	0.006	−0.061	0.006	−0.061	0.006
EDUC, β_3	—		—		0.374	0.005	0.374	0.004	0.375	0.005	0.375	0.005
FEMALE, β_4	—		—		0.242	0.026	0.242	0.026	0.241	0.026	0.242	0.026
BLACK, β_5	—		—		−1.051	0.037	−1.051	0.037	−1.050	0.037	−1.051	0.037
NEWS$_j$, γ_1	—		—		—		—		1.403	0.467	1.387	0.488
TV$_j$, γ_2	—		—		—		—		−0.262	0.123	−0.259	0.131
(b) Variance Components												
Cohort, τ_u	0.139	0.052	0.158	0.067	0.039	0.016	0.044	0.020	0.024	0.011	0.029	0.014
Period, τ_v	0.031	0.013	0.037	0.018	0.003	0.002	0.004	0.003	0.003	0.002	0.004	0.003
Individual, σ^2	4.526	0.046	4.526	0.046	3.136	0.032	3.136	0.032	3.136	0.032	3.137	0.032
(c) Model Fit												
Deviance	84872.0		84783.3		77676.4		77627.8		77666.6		77627.9	
DF/pD[a]	4		31.5		9		30.5		11		30.3	
AIC/DIC[b]	84880.0		84814.7		77694.4		77658.3		77688.6		77658.3	
Estimation time			48.4 min				2.2 hr				2.8 hr	

[a] DF for REML and pD as the effective number of parameters for Bayes.
[b] AIC for REML and DIC for Bayes.

the EB estimates depend on REML estimates of variance components, assuming large J and K, the good large-sample properties of the REML estimates give strength to inference about β.

There are several limitations to the REML-EB approach. First, the estimates of τ_u and τ_v may be quite inaccurate in small samples. The estimates of the variances in τ_u and τ_v may not have normal distributions for small J and K. If the data are unbalanced, estimates of γ will depend on weights that are determined by REML estimates, so that random variation in these estimates will lead to uncertainty about γ that will not be reflected in standard errors. Furthermore, errors in the REML estimates will result in extra uncertainty in the EB estimates of β that will not be reflected in the standard errors. Therefore, the confidence intervals for γ and β will be shorter, and tests of significance will be more liberal than they should be. For a more detailed exposition, see Raudenbush and Bryk (2002, chapt. 13).

In the hierarchical APC analysis of interest here, the number of periods and birth cohorts are usually too small to satisfy the large sample criteria required by the REML estimations of variance components. In addition, the sample sizes within each higher-level unit—i.e., cohort and period—are highly unbalanced, especially for cohorts. There tend to be very few sample members for the oldest and youngest birth cohorts, as shown in Figure 2. In the data presented here, $J = 19$, and n_j

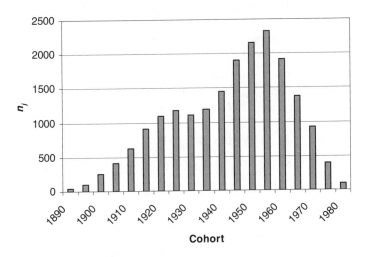

FIGURE 2. Distribution of cohort members.

vary across J with the smallest cohorts having only 38 and 100 individuals. In this case, estimates of EB coefficients will depend on weights that are functions of the maximum likelihood estimates of variance components. Therefore, errors in such estimates due to small J and K may also produce extra uncertainty in the EB estimates that will not be reflected in the standard errors. Again, tests for these point estimates may be too liberal[5] (Raudenbush and Bryk 2002:411). This problem tends to diminish when n_j or n_k is large, as in most cohorts and survey years in this example. However, for small J/K and small n_j for some cohorts, this dependence of EB estimates on REML estimates is undesirable.

2.4. *Monte Carlo Simulations*

From a Bayesian perspective, in the REML-EB approach, inferences for focal parameters depend on point estimates of other unknown auxiliary parameters, but they do not fully take into account the uncertainty about these unknowns. This may affect the inferences more when J and K are small, as is the case for the APC analysis. To address the question about the adequacy of REML estimators when J and K are small and data are unbalanced, a number of Monte Carlo simulations were conducted to examine how the HAPC model would perform under the REML assumptions. Based on the model specification in equations (1)–(3), the algorithm for simulating data sets is summarized as follows:

1. Choose the true parameter values of γ_0, γ_1, γ_2, $\beta_1, \ldots \beta_5$, τ_u, τ_v, σ^2, u_{0j}, and v_{0k} to be the REML-EB estimates.
2. Generate $u_{01}, \ldots, u_{0j}$ from $N(0, \tau_u)$.
3. Generate $v_{01}, \ldots, v_{0k}$ from $N(0, \tau_v)$.
4. Generate Y_{ijk} from $N(E(Y), \sigma^2)$, where

$$E(Y) = \gamma_0 + \gamma_1 NEWS_j + \gamma_2 TV_j + \beta_1 AGE_{ijk}$$
$$+ \beta_2 AGE_{ijk}^2 + \beta_3 EDUCATION_{ijk} + \beta_4 FEMALE_{ijk}$$
$$+ \beta_5 BLACK_{ijk} + u_{0j} + v_{0k}.$$

---

[5]This means that a test of significance would suggest rejecting the hypothesis based on the likelihood estimates, but would not suggest so based on the Bayes estimates.

These steps were used to generate 1000 data sets on verbal test scores that were fitted to the HAPC model through the REML-EB estimation. The simulations were implemented using SAS macros. The results of two sets of simulations are displayed in Table 3.

The first set of results is based on the total sample of all 19,500 respondents. The REML point estimates of the fixed effects and variance components (column 2) are quite close to the true parameter values (column 1) and thus have small biases. A good measure of performance for a point estimator is the mean squared error (MSE) that measures both the variability of the estimator and its bias,[6] and an estimator that has good MSE properties has small combined variance and bias (Casella and Berger 2002:330). The results are shown in column 4. As a test of the accuracy of the interval estimates, coverage probabilities (column 5) of the true parameters by the model estimates were calculated as the proportions of the 95 percent confidence intervals of the 1000 new estimates containing the true parameter values. Since the 1000 simulations are independent trials, the sampling distribution is *Binomial* $(1000, p)$. Hypothesis tests were conducted to determine whether the observed coverage probabilities were significantly different from $p = 0.95$. The results show that the coverage probabilities of most fixed effects interval estimates do not significantly differ from 95 percent, but the interval estimates of the *intercept* and *TV watching* cover the true parameter values significantly less than 95 percent of the time. The interval estimates of all variance components contain the population parameter values more than 95 percent of the time. The results for residual random effects show that these estimates yield larger MSEs and contain the true parameters much less often. The majority of the coverage probabilities range from 0.4 to 0.6 for cohort residuals and from 0.5 and 0.6 for period residuals.[7]

---

[6]MSE measures the average squared difference between the estimator W and the parameter θ: $\text{MSE} = E_\theta(W - \theta)^2 = Var_\theta W + (E_\theta W - \theta)^2 = Var_\theta W + (Bias_\theta W)^2$.

[7]This result is expected because it reflects the influence of small J and K on parameter estimation. The confidence intervals of cohort and period residual estimates are constructed based on their posterior variances that are in turn dependent on the variance components. The confidence intervals are exact when the variance components are known but only approximations when they are unknown. In this case, the confidence intervals are shorter than they should be unless J and K are large (Raudenbush and Bryk 2002).

TABLE 3
Monte Carlo Simulations ($n = 1,000$) of REML Estimation for the Verbal Ability Data

Parameter		(1) Par. Value	Total Sample				Thinned Sample			
			(2) Mean	(3) S.D.	(4) MSE	(5) Cov. Prob.	(6) Mean	(7) S.D.	(8) MSE	(9) Cov. Prob.
Fixed Effect										
Intercept	γ_0	6.1983	6.1977	0.1416	0.0201	0.878[a]	6.2038	1.2940	1.6744	0.899[a]
NEWS$_j$	γ_1	1.4032	1.4130	0.7953	0.6325	0.959	1.4176	1.8753	3.5170	0.914[a]
TV$_j$	γ_2	−0.2618	−0.2621	0.2494	0.0622	0.915[a]	−0.2444	1.9811	3.9250	0.914[a]
AGE	β_1	0.0159	0.0159	0.0232	0.0005	0.989	0.0194	1.2867	1.6556	0.920[a]
AGE^2	β_2	−0.0608	−0.0607	0.0060	0.0000	0.942	−0.0596	0.3975	0.1580	0.919[a]
EDUC	β_3	0.3746	0.3747	0.0046	0.0000	0.944	0.3755	0.0479	0.0023	0.936
FEMALE	β_4	0.2412	0.2406	0.0252	0.0006	0.959	0.2353	0.2302	0.0530	0.954
BLACK	β_5	−1.0502	−1.0469	0.0361	0.0013	0.947	−1.0477	0.2854	0.0815	0.951
Variance Component										
Cohort	τ_u	0.1390	0.1389	0.0519	0.0027	0.958	0.1588	0.2092	0.0442	0.651[a]
Period	τ_v	0.0313	0.0318	0.0129	0.0002	0.964	0.0471	0.0770	0.0062	0.438[a]
Individual	σ^2	3.1360	3.1327	0.0306	0.0009	0.951	3.1103	0.2735	0.0755	0.952
Random Effect										
Cohort										
1890	u_{01}	−0.0308	−0.0006	0.1842	0.0348	0.998				
1895	u_{02}	0.0089	0.0002	0.2841	0.0808	0.901[a]				
1900	u_{03}	0.1669	−0.0037	0.3083	0.1242	0.725[a]				
1905	u_{04}	−0.3074	0.0013	0.3383	0.2098	0.445[a]				
1910	u_{05}	0.0902	0.0024	0.3388	0.1225	0.666[a]				
1915	u_{06}	0.1722	−0.0031	0.3382	0.1451	0.580[a]				

TABLE 3
Continued

| Parameter | (1) Par. Value | Total Sample | | | | Thinned Sample | | | |
		(2) Mean	(3) S.D.	(4) MSE	(5) Cov. Prob.	(6) Mean	(7) S.D.	(8) MSE	(9) Cov. Prob.
u_{07}	−0.0999	0.0021	0.3424	0.1276	0.567[a]				
u_{08}	−0.0892	−0.0032	0.3561	0.1342	0.545[a]				
u_{09}	−0.0594	0.0015	0.3407	0.1198	0.565[a]				
u_{010}	−0.1285	−0.0005	0.3409	0.1326	0.546[a]				
u_{011}	−0.0333	0.0006	0.3380	0.1154	0.618[a]				
u_{012}	0.1905	0.0003	0.3231	0.1406	0.587[a]				
u_{013}	0.2090	0.0007	0.3438	0.1616	0.500[a]				
u_{014}	0.0048	0.0009	0.3580	0.1282	0.433[a]				
u_{015}	−0.0214	0.0004	0.3554	0.1268	0.480[a]	0.0018	0.1771	0.0319	0.475[a]
u_{016}	0.0027	−0.0031	0.3412	0.1165	0.571[a]	−0.0003	0.3053	0.0932	0.571[a]
u_{017}	−0.0470	0.0009	0.3303	0.1114	0.671[a]	−0.0061	0.2875	0.0843	0.668[a]
u_{018}	−0.0118	0.0055	0.3256	0.1063	0.774[a]	0.0046	0.2137	0.0459	0.731[a]
u_{019}	−0.0166	−0.0027	0.2876	0.0829	0.892[a]	0.0001	0.0195	0.0007	0.731[a]
v_{01}	0.0247	−0.0004	0.1724	0.0304	0.583[a]				
v_{02}	0.0528	0.0006	0.1655	0.0301	0.575[a]				
v_{03}	−0.0001	−0.0019	0.1663	0.0277	0.599[a]				
v_{04}	−0.0077	−0.0009	0.1678	0.0282	0.538[a]				
v_{05}	0.0181	0.0034	0.1665	0.0279	0.558[a]				
v_{06}	−0.0439	−0.0014	0.1650	0.0290	0.535[a]				
v_{07}	−0.0974	0.0021	0.1602	0.0356	0.516[a]				

continued

TABLE 3
Continued

Parameter		(1) Par. Value	Total Sample				Thinned Sample			
			(2) Mean	(3) S.D.	(4) MSE	(5) Cov. Prob.	(6) Mean	(7) S.D.	(8) MSE	(9) Cov. Prob.
1989	v_{08}	−0.0458	−0.0030	0.1626	0.0283	0.582[a]				
1990	v_{09}	0.0193	−0.0009	0.1609	0.0263	0.617[a]				
1991	v_{010}	0.0391	−0.0009	0.1623	0.0279	0.569[a]				
1993	v_{011}	0.0026	0.0700	0.0070	0.0046	0.627[a]	−0.0027	0.1322	0.0175	0.575[a]
1994	v_{012}	0.0257	0.0011	0.1643	0.0276	0.565[a]	0.0049	0.1511	0.0233	0.537[a]
1996	v_{013}	−0.0386	−0.0023	0.1643	0.0283	0.565[a]	0.0002	0.1511	0.0243	0.563[a]
1998	v_{014}	0.0449	0.0013	0.1650	0.0291	0.593[a]	−0.0004	0.1503	0.0246	0.564[a]
2000	v_{015}	0.0063	0.0024	0.1628	0.0265	0.627[a]	−0.0020	0.1541	0.0238	0.570[a]

[a] Indicates a significant difference from 95%, $p < 0.001$.

Note:

(1) True parameter values using the parameter estimates from the REML results in Table 3;

(2) Mean values of the parameter estimates for the total sample;

(3) Standard deviations of the parameter estimates for the total sample;

(4) Mean squared errors (MSE) and MSE = Variance + Bias², where Bias = Mean (2) − true parameter values (1), total sample;

(5) Coverage probability, i.e., the proportion of 95 percent confidence intervals that include the true parameter values, total sample;

(6)–(9) corresponding statistics for the thinned sample (respondents in the last five years and recent five cohorts).

To determine the effects of smaller numbers of surveys and birth cohorts that are more typical of demographic data on the performance of REML estimators, I replicated the above analysis for a subset of the total sample where only the last five periods (1993 to 2000) and five recent cohorts (1960–1980) are included. Columns 6 to 9 of Table 3 report the second set of results based on the thinned data. These results show that when J and K are small, the point estimates of the fixed effect coefficients and variance components have much larger variances and biases and larger MSEs (columns 6–8). The interval estimates are also less accurate (column 9). For five of the fixed effects, including the *intercept, newspaper reading, TV watching, age*, and *age*^{2}, the coverage probabilities of their interval estimates are significantly lower than 0.95. The results are worse for the interval estimates of variance components. In sharp contrast with the results based on the total sample with relatively larger J and K (column 5), the coverage probabilities are only 0.65 for the *cohort variance* and 0.44 for the *period variance*. The comparison of the results for the random effect coefficients also suggests that the interval estimates based on the thinned sample have lower coverage probabilities than those based on the larger sample.

In sum, the Monte Carlo simulations show that, in large samples, the REML-EB estimators of the HAPC model generally perform well in terms of producing numeric estimates of the population parameters they are intended to measure. The interval estimates, however, should be used with caution in both large and small samples. It will be useful to have methods for producing more accurate estimates with small samples of survey years and birth cohorts and unbalanced data. And this is where Bayesian MCMC estimation fits in. In the following section, I develop a full Bayesian approach that, by definition, ensures that inference about every parameter fully takes into account the uncertainty associated with all others.

3. BAYESIAN INFERENCE FOR HIERARCHICAL APC MODELS

3.1. *Gibbs Sampling and MCMC Estimation*

In a Bayesian formulation of HAPC models applied to the repeated cross sections, we combine the likelihood based on the data with prior information about the fixed and random parameters via prior distributions. Based on equations (1)–(3), the Bayesian model for the verbal ability data can be summarized as follows:

Level-1 Model (Likelihood): $f(Y \mid \beta, \sigma^2)$
Level-2 Model (Stage-1 Prior): $p(\beta \mid \gamma, \tau_u, \tau_v)$
Stage-2 Prior: $p(\gamma, \tau_u, \tau_v, \sigma^2) = p(\gamma)p(\tau_u)p(\tau_v)p(\sigma^2)$

In this formulation, each unknown parameter is viewed as a random variable that arises from certain probability distribution. The probability distribution, p, quantifies the uncertainty about the parameter. Bayes' rule then yields the joint posterior distribution:

$$p(\beta, \gamma, \tau_u, \tau_v, \sigma^2 \mid Y) \propto f(Y \mid \beta, \sigma^2)p(\beta \mid \gamma, \tau_u, \tau_v)p(\gamma, \tau_u, \tau_v, \sigma^2).$$

Marginal posterior distribution can be derived by integration of the joint posterior with regard to each parameter. Therefore, in the Bayesian approach, the inference about every parameter fully accounts for the uncertainty of other parameters through the use of conditional and joint probabilities. Point and interval estimates can then be obtained based on the exact posterior distribution.

Gibbs sampling is used as an accurate computational approach to numerical integration. The Gibbs algorithm for the HAPC model is as follows:

$$
\begin{aligned}
p(\beta, \gamma, \tau_u, \tau_v, \sigma^2 \mid Y) &\propto p_\beta(\beta \mid \gamma, \tau_u, \tau_v, \sigma^2, Y)r_\beta(\gamma, \tau_u, \tau_v, \sigma^2 \mid Y) \\
&= p_\gamma(\gamma \mid \tau_u, \tau_v, \sigma^2, \beta, Y)r_\gamma(\tau_u, \tau_v, \sigma^2, \beta \mid Y) \\
&= p_u(\tau_u \mid \tau_v, \sigma^2, \beta, \gamma, Y)r_u(\tau_v, \sigma^2, \beta, \gamma \mid Y) \\
&= p_v(\tau_v \mid \sigma^2, \beta, \gamma, \tau_u, Y)r_v(\sigma^2, \beta, \gamma, \tau_u \mid Y) \\
&= p_{\sigma^2}(\sigma^2 \mid \gamma, \beta, \tau_u, \tau_v, Y)r_{\sigma^2}(\gamma, \beta, \tau_u, \tau_v \mid Y)
\end{aligned}
$$

Gibbs sampling is based on the fact that the posterior density of all unknowns can be approximated even though the corresponding densities r have unknown forms. Starting with initial values $\gamma^{(0)}, \tau_u^{(0)}, \tau_v^{(0)}$, and $\sigma^{2(0)}$, it repeatedly samples from the conditional distributions until stochastic convergence. The chain of values generated by this sampling procedure is known as a Monte Carlo Markov Chain (MCMC). An example of the conditional distributions needed for Gibbs sampling is shown in Appendix A. Upon convergence, m iterations are obtained, and the empirical distribution of these m values of the unknowns may be regarded as an approximation to the true joint posterior. For large m, the marginal posterior may be approximated by the empirical distribution of the m values produced by the Gibbs. For this study, $m = 20,000$ for one MCMC chain (see the description below).

The benefits of the Bayesian methods typically come at a price— that is, the required choice of *prior* distributions for model parameters. The topic of the choice of priors is a vast one (e.g., see Draper 2002). A common assumption is that diffuse priors can be used in an attempt to base information solely on the data when no prior knowledge is available for the parameters of interest. This means that a prior can be used that allows the data to dominate the determination of the posterior distribution. Furthermore, the ever-increasing usage of Bayes-MCMC methods in statistical practice has produced several classes of priors that may be viewed as sufficiently "noninformative" in fairly broad settings (Guo and Carlin 2004). In the present study, Bayesian modeling was implemented through MCMC methods via the WinBUGS (Bayes Using Gibbs Sampling running under Windows) software package.[8] Since no previous sociological studies on verbal ability informed the specification of priors, I selected, in order to facilitate comparison of the REML-EB and Bayesian analyses, noninformative proper prior distributions[9] with hyperparameter values chosen so that the priors exert minimal impact relative to the data (Gelman et al. 2000; Raudenbush and Bryk 2002). I first specified conjugate priors[10] that were comprised of normal prior

---

[8]WinBUGS 1.4 is now available without charge from http://www. mrc-bsu.cam.ac.uk/bugs/, sponsored by the MRC Biostatistics Unit, Cambridge, England.

[9]In general, a prior density $p(\theta)$ is proper if it integrates to 1. If a prior density is improper, the integral of $p(\theta)$ is infinity and violates the assumption that probabilities sum to 1. Although improper priors sometimes can lead to proper posteriors, this is not always the case. And posteriors obtained from improper priors must be interpreted with great caution—one must always check that the posteriors have finite integrals and sensible forms (Gelman et al. 2000:53).

[10]Selecting priors from a distribution family that is conjugate to the likelihood leads to a posterior distribution belonging to the same distributional family as the prior. This can be computationally convenient. Morris (1983) showed the exponential families have conjugate priors. For more details, see Gelman et al. (2000:37).

for γ and inverse gamma prior for the variance components (Gelfand et al. 1990; Carlin and Louis 2000):

$$\text{Prior (1)} : p(\gamma) \sim N(0, 1.0\text{E-6})$$
$$p(1/\tau_u) \sim Gamma(0.001, 0.001); \, p(1/\tau_v)$$
$$\sim Gamma(0.001, 0.001)$$
$$p(1/\sigma^2) \sim Gamma(0.001, 0.001)$$

Alternative priors are discussed later in this paper. The priors are chosen so that the Bayesian analysis is similar to a corresponding likelihood analysis (REML-EB). The difference is that likelihoods are now adjusted and interpreted as probability distributions on the parameters.

OLS and REML estimates provided the initial values for two parallel MCMC sampling chains of 20,000 iterations each, following a 5000-iteration "burn-in" period. The Gelman and Rubin tests were used to diagnose effective convergence. A general discussion of MCMC convergence monitoring is available in Carlin and Louis (2000). I thinned each chain by 10 to reduce autocorrelation among the parameter estimates. The summary statistics were calculated after the achievement of a less correlated sample. The final sample size for posterior inferences is 4000 with 2000 per chain. Convergence Diagnostics and Output Analysis (CODA) was implemented using the R program (Best, Cowles, and Vines 1997). Major results for selected parameter estimates are included as Appendix B and C.[11]

For the purpose of comparison, the Bayes MCMC estimates are given side by side with the REML results for each model in Table 2. Note that SAS PROC MIXED delivers solutions for the model parameters only in terms of point estimates of the posterior means and associated asymptotic standard error estimates, whereas Bayes MCMC methods provide exact posterior inference for each node that includes the posterior mean estimate, the MCMC standard deviation as the estimate for the standard error, Monte Carlo error,[12] median, and quantiles.

---

[11]There are 19 cohorts and 15 periods, and therefore 34 residual random effects. Only the first and last residual estimates within each classification are shown, and their patterns are almost identical with the rest of the nodes.

[12]This is an estimate of the difference between the mean of the sample values (which is used as the estimate of the posterior mean for each parameter) and

Table 2 shows that the fixed coefficients are very similar for the REML and MCMC estimates, with the estimated standard errors slightly larger in some cases for the MCMC results. The main difference between the REML and MCMC estimates is in the level-2 variances. The Bayes via Gibbs estimators produce larger estimates of cohort and period variances and standard errors. This is due to the Bayes estimates taking into account the uncertainty brought about by the small numbers of cohorts and periods. Similar to the REML results, Model 2 under Bayes shows that controlling for individual-level covariates reduces the cohort variance by 72.2 percent (0.158 versus 0.044) and the period variance by 89.2 percent (0.013 versus 0.004). Model 3 under Bayes also suggests that the inclusion of the two cohort-level characteristics further reduces the cohort variance by 81.6 percent (0.158 versus 0.029).

For Bayesian model selection, I used the Deviance Information Criterion (DIC) (Spiegelhalter et al. 2002) that is a hierarchical modeling generalization of the AIC and is readily available in WinBUGS. At each iteration of the chain, the current value of deviance, –2 log(likelihood), was computed for the model being fitted, where likelihood is defined as $p(z \mid \theta)$, z comprises all stochastic nodes given data, and θ comprises the stochastic parents of z.[13] Denote the posterior mean of the deviance as $\bar{D}$ and the deviance based on the mean parameter values upon convergence as D. D is a point estimate of the deviance and $D = -2 * \log(p(z|\bar{\theta}))$. Then $\bar{D} - D$ is an estimate of the "effective number of parameters" (pD) of the model. The DIC statistic is calculated as $D + 2pD$. Similar to the AIC reported for REML, DIC shows better model fits for models with explanatory variables (Models 2 and 3).

The cohort and period residual random effects estimates were also compared for REML-EB and Bayes MCMC results for all three models. Figures 3 and 4 plot the posterior means and interval estimates, based on Model 3, of the residual cohort effect u_{0j} and the residual period effect v_{0k}, respectively. Figure 3 shows that for both EB and Bayes estimates, the intervals are the widest for the youngest and oldest cohorts that have relatively small sizes (n_j). Both figures show that although the

---

the true posterior mean. As a rule of thumb, an MC error that is less than about 5 percent of the sample standard deviation indicates convergence of chains.

[13] "Stochastic parents" are the stochastic nodes upon which the distribution of z depends, when collapsing over all logical relationships (Spiegelhalter et al. 2003).

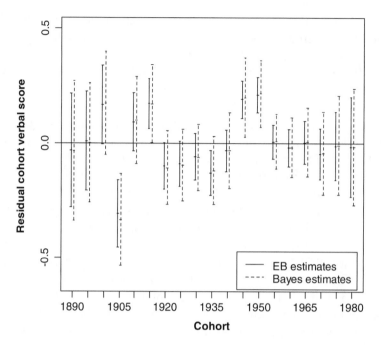

FIGURE 3. Residual cohort effect u_{0j} estimated from Model 3.

mean estimates are quite close, the Bayes credible intervals[14] are wider than the EB intervals of variance components.

3.2. *Prior Sensitivity Analysis*

With just 19 cohorts and 15 periods, I expect that the choice of priors may have some effect on posteriors that depend on these numbers (Seltzer, Wong, and Bryk 1996; Goldstein 2003). Therefore, further steps were taken to assess the sensitivity of posterior inferences to the choice of priors (Gelman et al. 2000). I formulated alternative priors to compare the results with those produced using the diffuse normal

---

[14]The Bayesian analogue of a frequentist confidence interval is referred to as a credible set or credible interval. It is defined as the following: A $100 * (1 - \alpha)\%$ credible interval for parameter θ is a subset C of Θ such that $1 - \alpha \leq p(C \mid y) = \int_C p(\theta \mid y)d\theta$ —i.e. the likelihood of θ falling in C is the probability that θ lies in C given the observed data y is at least $(1 - \alpha)$ (Carlin and Louis 2000:35). In this case, $\alpha = 0.05$; the credible and EB intervals are 95 percent intervals.

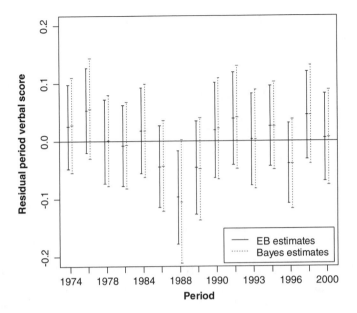

FIGURE 4. Residual period effect v_{0k} estimated from Model 3.

and inverse gamma priors. The inverse gamma prior family has been preferred by many Bayesians largely because its conditional conjugacy implies clean mathematical properties. Recent Bayesian literature on hierarchical models also suggested the utility of a uniform prior on the variance components where the inverse-gamma family of noninformative prior has problems. Gelman (2006) showed the difficulty of the inverse-gamma $(\varepsilon, \varepsilon)$ prior distribution when the limit of $\varepsilon \to 0$, in which case it yields an improper posterior density. As a result, inferences become sensitive to the choice of ε. Gelman (2006) suggested the use of a uniform prior on the variance components. For instance, a uniform prior $(0, c)$ can be considered as an alternative where c is chosen so that $(0, c)$ spans the range in which the likelihood for the parameter is non-negligible (Goldstein 2003). This prior is now offered as an alternative to the default gamma prior in the *MLwinN* software package (Rasbash and Goldstein 2000). For fixed parameters, I selected an informative normal prior with the same mean of 0 and a larger prior precision, implying more accurate prior knowledge than the diffuse normal prior (1). Different combinations of variance components priors and priors for γ produced results that can be represented by the following two priors:

Prior (2): $p(\gamma) \sim N(0, 1.0\text{E-}6)$

$\qquad p(\tau_u) \sim Uniform(0, 50);^{15} p(\tau_v) \sim Uniform(0, 50);$

$\qquad p(\sigma^2) \sim Uniform (0, 50)$

Prior (3): $p(\gamma) \sim N(0, 0.01)$

$\qquad p(1/\tau_u) \sim Gamma(0.001, 0.001); p(1/\tau_v)$

$\qquad \qquad \sim Gamma(0.001, 0.001)$

$\qquad p(1/\sigma^2) \sim Gamma(0.001, 0.001)$

Comparisons of the MCMC estimates from Model 3—including posterior means, standard deviations, MC errors, medians, and 2.5 and 97.5 percent quantiles—show similar results for three alternative sets of priors (a detailed summary is available upon request). The main difference between the three sets of estimates is in the coefficients of newspaper reading and TV watching and in the cohort and period variance components. Here the gamma priors produced results closer to each other and to the REML estimates, as is often found (Browne 1998; Goldstein 2003). The choice of priors had some effect on parameters that depend on the small numbers of level-2 units ($J = 19$ and $K = 15$). By contrast, the other parameters were based on the total sample size, so the effect of a particular diffuse prior was very small. The estimation time was the longest for the uniform prior in that it was functionally equivalent

---

[15] In the current study, the choice of the prior distributions was independent of the data. Previous literature suggests that data could be used in a limited way to choose the prior—that is, distributions can be chosen to depend on the data-level variance (Box and Tiao 1973). For instance, the individual-level random component, σ^2, will not exceed the variance of Y (4.6). Using this information as a priori leads to an upper bound on the uniform prior for σ^2. That is, instead of 0 to 50, the new bounds are from 0 to 5. These narrower bounds are consistent with the data and likely to result in faster convergence of chains. In supplemental analysis, I experimented with this alternative and found similar results using slightly shorter computing time. This data-dependent approach to selecting the prior, however, is not strictly Bayesian, so I did not present the final results using this approach.

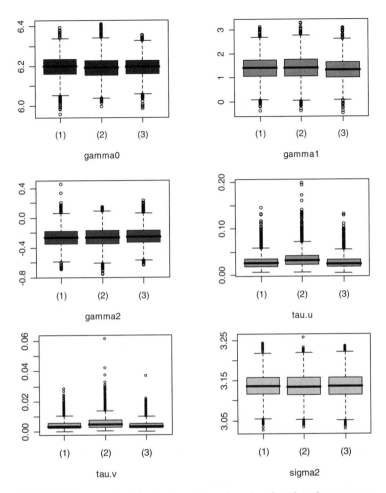

FIGURE 5. Bayes estimates using three alternative priors for selected parameters.

to an improper prior that leads to a slow convergence. The model fit was fairly close under all circumstances. A graphical summary of results under three priors is presented in Figure 5. The posterior distributions of five parameters associated with the small numbers of cohorts and periods are summarized together with σ^2. They suggest that the uniform prior on variance components produced slightly wider intervals than the gamma prior; and priors (1) and (3) do not differ much even though the latter is more informative on the fixed parameters.

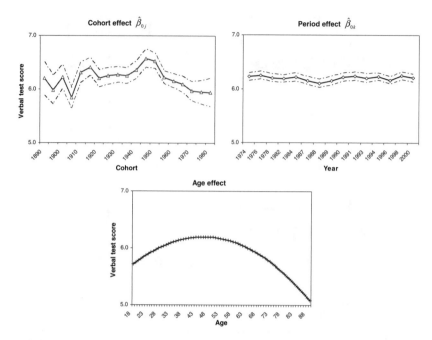

FIGURE 6. Bayes estimates of cohort, period, and age effects from model 3 under the diffuse normal and inverse gamma priors.

3.3. *Summary of Age, Period, and Cohort Effects*

Note that in the HAPC model specification each cohort j has a distinct intercept, $\hat{\beta}_{0j}$, that represents the estimated **cohort effect** net of all individual effects, and averaged across all time periods. Figure 6 shows cohort effects estimated by the Bayes method using the diffuse normal and inverse gamma priors based on the final model (Model 3).[16] Point estimates of cohort effects are nearly identical for REML estimates and Bayes estimates under each of the three priors. As shown in Figure 2, the 95 percent confidence intervals of the REML estimates of cohort effects are slightly shorter than the 95 percent credible intervals of the Bayes estimates. The general patterns of cohort variation, however, are

---

[16]Since all continuous variables are mean centered, the cohort effect is the cohort intercept at the mean age and mean education, and for the reference sex-race group, white males. The same model was estimated for three other combinations of sex and race (white females, black females, and black males). The results are similar.

not substantially different. Therefore, there indeed was a decline in verbal ability for recent cohorts born since 1950, which coincided with the continuously declining percentage of daily newspaper readers and increasing mean hours of TV viewing of those same cohorts. However, instead of a linear decline for cohort verbal ability starting in the early twentieth century as estimated by previous researchers, there was more variation for older cohorts born before 1950.

Figure 6 also exhibits the estimated **period effects** ($\hat{\beta}_{0k}$) net of all the individual effects and averaged across all birth cohorts. A similar V-shaped curve occurred across all methods of estimation. As is the case for the cohort effect estimates, the Bayes estimates for period effects have slightly wider intervals. Since the overall difference between these estimates is very small, only the Bayes estimates using the diffuse normal and inverse gamma priors are shown. There was a decrease in verbal ability from the mid-1970s to late 1980s. Then it increased to the beginning level, followed by some small fluctuations into the late 1990s.

Finally, Figure 6 displays estimates of **age effects** in a plot of the predicted WORDSUM for each age, net of all the other factors and averaged across all cohorts and periods.[17] The REML and Bayes estimates yielded the same concave quadratic pattern. The figure only shows the Bayes estimates using the diffuse normal and inverse gamma priors. Rather than a weak linear negative age effect as predicted by Glenn (1999) and Alwin and McCammon (1999), the results presented here show support for the findings of Wilson and Gove (1999) and that the age effect on vocabulary is curvilinear over the life course. Specifically, the age effect indicates that an individual's verbal ability increases from the late teens to around age 50 as a result of accumulation of vocabulary through education and other social experiences. After the age of 55, however, verbal skills gradually decline due to many reasons related with aging, such as loss of memory. This is also consistent with the theory of adult cognitive growth (Schaie 1994).

The results on explanatory factors show that all individual and cohort characteristics are significantly related to verbal test scores. Education has a strong positive association with verbal ability. Females tend to score higher on verbal tests. And whites have a large advantage over

---

[17]The estimated age effect, $\hat{Y} = \hat{\gamma}_0 + \hat{\beta}_1 \cdot Age + \hat{\beta}_2 \cdot Age^2 + \bar{u}_{0j} + \bar{v}_{0k}$, where $\bar{u}_{0j}$ and $\bar{v}_{0k}$ represent the means of estimated cohort and period residuals, respectively. No uncertainty bounds were obtained.

blacks in verbal test scores. Controlling for these covariates reduces the age coefficients, but it does not explain away all of the age effect. Two cohort characteristics examined largely account for the cohort variation in verbal test scores. As expected, cohorts with more members reading newspapers daily fare better in verbal ability. And more hours of TV watching per day impair this ability. The inclusion of these two cohort-level covariates reduces the cohort variance by over 80 percent.

4. DISCUSSION AND CONCLUSION

This study developed a Bayesian hierarchical modeling approach to APC analyses of repeated cross-sectional survey designs. I showed how Bayesian inferences can be used for cross-classified random effects models applied to the vocabulary data from the General Social Survey. I compared the empirical results obtained through two parameter estimation methods—namely, the restricted maximum likelihood–empirical Bayes method applied by Yang and Land (2006) and the full Bayes method using Gibbs sampling. The point estimates are nearly identical. However, the Bayes 95 percent credible intervals are wider in most cases than are the intervals based on REML. This increase occurs because the REML intervals do not reflect the uncertainty associated with re-gression coefficients when variance components are unknown and the REML estimates of these variance components are not accurate because of the small sample sizes at cohort and period levels. The Bayes credible intervals reflect this extra uncertainty and therefore strengthen the infer-ence. The empirical findings on fixed coefficients, variance components, and random effects are generally not highly sensitive to the imposition of alternative priors considered in the study. In sum, the analytic results shown above can be interpreted with more confidence than any previous findings of this subject and therefore help to resolve the inconsistencies across studies.

The results shed new light on the controversy concerning the age, period, and cohort components of trends in verbal ability in the United States for the past three decades. First, there are significant random variance components in the individual level, cohort level, and period level of the data. This suggests the OLS regressions employed by previous researchers are inappropriate. Second, controlling for all other variables, the age effect remains significant and is curvilinear. Therefore, it is not correct to conclude that there is no age effect when the cohort effect is considered. Third, the period effect is small, but its presence affects estimates of both the age and the cohort effects. In fact, it is the omission of controls for period effects that led to the controversy. Finally, there is evidence of a decline in cohort verbal test scores, as argued by Alwin and Glenn. The above results are consistent with those of Yang and Land (2006). The new finding that emerges from this study is that the decline of vocabulary for more recent cohorts born after 1950 was closely associated with the decreased percentage of cohort members who read the newspaper daily and increased cohort mean hours of TV watching. This cohort effect is not confounded with the aging effect.

The evaluation of the performance of REML and full Bayes estimators in the current application was restricted to well-behaved response variables in the context of hierarchical APC models of repeated cross-sectional sample surveys. Although the results based on the two methods are not drastically conflicting, the Bayesian estimators generally show improvement relative to the REML estimators. There are other cases where the divergence between the maximum likelihood and Bayes results is larger. The problem of inaccurate inference using the REML estimators can be most significant when random effects are relatively large, data are sparse and highly unbalanced, and response variables are not normally distributed.

A focus of the assessment of the comparative performance of the REML and Bayes estimates pertains to their ability to handle the relatively small sample sizes at level 2. But with 19 cohorts and 15 time periods, the GSS data have larger numbers of cohorts and periods than would be the case with many demographic and social surveys. Therefore, the results are conservative with regard to the advantage shown by the Bayes approach. The Monte Carlo experiment shows that in typical survey data where fewer than ten time periods are present (e.g., the Current Population Survey Supplements on fertility histories or National Health Interview Surveys), the REML estimators may not provide accurate point and interval estimates. In this case, analysts should consider obtaining Bayes estimates of HAPC models for statistical inferences.

The Monte Carlo simulations were conducted only for the REML-EB estimation method. If a parallel set of results can be obtained for the Bayes MCMC estimators, then a more direct model checking analysis can be carried out by comparisons of the mean squared errors (MSE) obtained through the two procedures. The one that yields the smaller MSEs is the method of choice. Such an experiment, however, was not performed due to limitations of the statistical software programs used in this study. The WinBUGS program can fit models to one data set and implement the MCMC estimation, but it does not generate the multiple hypothetical data sets that are required for the Monte Carlo procedure described in the previous section. The SAS macro program helps to generate data, but it cannot implement the MCMC estimation. The lack of one software program that integrates data generating and model fitting makes it hard to automate the simulation process and, therefore, makes it impractical for the purpose of the simulations. The exploration of Bayesian simulation methods in other programming environments such as S-Plus or C is left for future research. In addition, to reduce the computational costs, the Monte Carlo simulations could be performed with a subset of data such as a random 10 percent sample of respondents from each survey year.

Although this paper focused on one example that assumes Gaussian errors and uses a linear link, HAPC models can be placed within the Generalized Linear Mixed Effects Model (GLMM) framework that allows flexible choice of GLM and hierarchical models (McCulloch and Searle 2001). This modeling framework not only accommodates non-Gaussian outcome variables but also provides numerous possibilities of model specifications for estimating APC effects. For instance, the crossed random effects model can be reduced to a simple two-level age-cohort model if the period variance component is not statistically significant. In this case, the period variable can be treated as fixed and represented by $(K-1)$ dummy indicators in the level-1 model. Based on evidence that there are significant clustering effects by periods, we can incorporate period-level covariates to determine what may account for the period variation. Alternatively, we may specify unconditional models at level-2 when no appropriate level-2 variables are available or, if available, none are significantly related to level-2 variances. In addition, we may find that the slopes of certain covariates also have random variations across the level-2 units, and therefore, that random coefficients models need to be estimated.

The other advantage of using GLMM-based APC models is that they can be naturally extended to more sophisticated multilevel data analysis. Two improvements can be made in future research. First, we can add more levels to the hierarchical model by giving priors to the stage-2 hyperparameters that include the fixed coefficients at level 2, cohort, period, and individual variance components. The higher level models can further estimate uncertainties that may arise from probability distributions. Conjugate hyperpriors such as chi-squared distributions can be used for computational convenience. Studies can also be found in recent biostatistics literature that use autoregressive prior models (Bashir and Esteve 2001) and random walk smoothing models (Knorr-Held and Rainer 2001) for Bayesian prediction of vital rates. Second, it may be in the interest of analysts to examine effects of other social units. For example, recent reports of National Assessment of Educational Progress documented pronounced regional differences in academic test scores including reading scores in the United States (e.g., National Center for Education Statistics 1999, 2002). If state level verbal test score data are integrated into sample surveys, it is convenient to move beyond the individual-level data using the HAPC models to estimate geographic variations in academic performances.[18]

APPENDIX A

Some Conditional Distributions Needed for Gibbs Sampling

Distribution	Distribution Type	Parameters[a]
$p_\beta(\beta_{0j} \mid \gamma, \tau_u, \sigma^2, Y)$	$N(\beta_{0j}^*, V_{\beta j}^*)$	$\beta_{0j}^* = \lambda_j \hat{\beta}_{0j} + (1 - \lambda_j) W_j^T \gamma$
		$V_{\beta j}^* = \lambda_j \sigma^2 (\sum_{i=1}^{n_j} X_{ij} X_{ij}^T)^{-1}$
$p_\gamma(\gamma \mid \tau_u, \sigma^2, \beta, Y)$	$N(\gamma^*, V_\gamma^*)$	$\gamma^* = (\sum_{j=1}^{19} W_j W_j^T)^{-1} \sum W_j \hat{\beta}_{0j}$
		$V_\gamma^* = \tau_u (\sum W_j W_j^T)^{-1}$
$p_{\tau^{-1}}(\tau_u^{-1} \mid \gamma, \sigma^2, \beta, Y)$	$Gamma(a, b)$	$a = J/2 + 1$
		$b = 2/\sum_{j=1}^{19} (\beta_{0j} - W_j^T \gamma)^2$
$p_{\sigma^{-2}}(\sigma^{-2} \mid \gamma, \beta, \tau_u, Y)$	$Gamma(c, d)$	$c = N/2 + 1$
		$d = 2/\sum_{j=1}^{19} \sum_{i=1}^{n_j} (Y_{ij} - X_{ij}^T \beta)^2$

[a] $\lambda_j = \tau_u/(\tau_u + \sigma^2(\sum X_{ij} X_{ij}^T)^{-1})$ is the shrinkage.
$\hat{\beta}_{0j} = \sum X_{ij} X_{ij}^T Y_{ij} (\sum X_{ij} X_{ij}^T)^{-1}$ is the LS estimator of β_{0j}.
$W_j^T = (NEWS_j, TV_j)^T$.

[18] I thank the anonymous reviewer who suggested the above two extensions of the present study.

APPENDIX B

Gelman-Rubin Convergence Diagnostic Plots Using Model 3 with Prior (1)

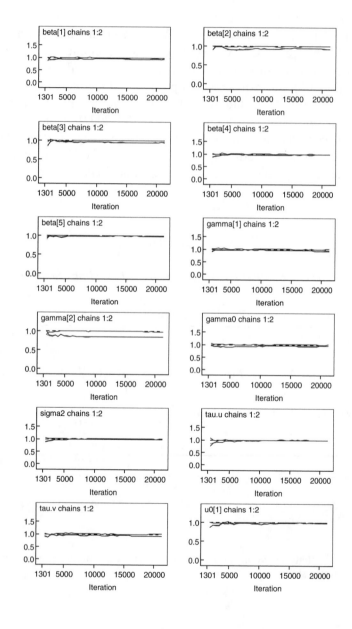

APPENDIX C

Autocorrelation Plots Using Model 3 with Prior (1)

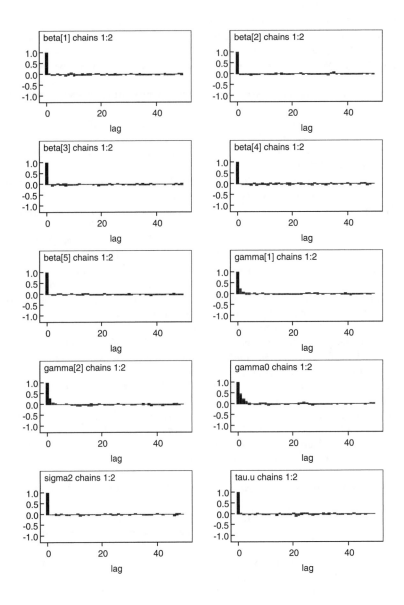

REFERENCES

Alwin, D. F., and R. J. McCammon. 1999. "Aging Versus Cohort Interpretations of Intercohort Differences in GSS Vocabulary Scores." *American Sociological Review* 64:272–86.

Bashir, S. A., and J. Esteve. 2001. "Projecting Cancer Incidence and Mortality Using Bayesian Age-Period-Cohort Models." *Journal of Epidemiology and Biostatistics* 6:287–96.

Best, N. G., M. K. Cowles, and S. K. Vines. 1997. "CODA: Convergence Diagnosis and Output Analysis Software for Gibbs Sampling Output, Version 0.4." Cambridge, MRC Biostatistics Unit (http://www.mrc-bsu.cam.ac.uk/bugs/classic/coda04/readme.shtml).

Box, G. E. P., and G. C. Tiao. 1973. *Bayesian Inference in Statistical Analysis.* Readings, MA: Addison-Wesley.

Browne, W. 1998. *Applying MCMC Methods to Multilevel Models.* Bath, England: University of Bath.

Carlin, B. P., and T. A. Louis. 2000. *Bayes and Empirical Bayes Methods for Data Analysis.* 2d ed. New York: Chapman and Hall/CRC.

Casella, G., and R. L. Berger. 2002. *Statistical Inference.* 2d ed. Duxbury Advanced Series.

Draper, D. 2002. *Bayesian Hierarchical Modeling.* New York: Springer-Verlag.

Fienberg, S. E., and W. M. Mason. 1985. "Specification and Implementation of Age, Period, and Cohort Models." Pp. 45–88 in *Cohort Analysis in Social Research,* edited by W. M. Mason and S. E. Fienberg. New York: Springer-Verlag.

Gelfand, A. E., S. E. Hills, A. Racine-Poon, and A. F. M. Smith. 1990. "Illustration of Bayesian Inference in Normal Data Models Using Gibbs Sampling." *Journal of American Statistical Association* 85:972–85.

Gelman, A. 2006. "Prior Distributions for Variance Parameters in Hierarchical Models." *Bayesian Analysis* 3:515–33 (http://www.stat.columbia.edu/~gelman/research/unpublished/tau9.pdf.).

Gelman, A., J. B. Carlin, H. S. Stern, and D. B. Rubin. 2000. *Bayesian Data Analysis.* New York: Chapman and Hall/CRC.

Glenn, N. D. 1994. "Television Watching, Newspaper Reading, and Cohort Differences in Verbal Ability." *Sociology of Education* 67:216–30.

———. 1999. "Further Discussion of the Evidence for An Intercohort Decline in Education-Adjusted Vocabulary." *American Sociological Review* 64:267–71.

Goldstein, H. 2003. *Multilevel Statistical Models.* 3rd ed. London: Oxford University Press.

Guo, X., and B. P. Carlin. 2004. "Separate and Joint Models of Longitudinal and Event Time Data Using Standard Computer Packages." *The American Statistician* 58:16–24.

Hobcraft, J., J. Menken, and S. Preston. 1982. "Age, Period, And Cohort Effects in Demography: A Review." *Population Index* 48:4–43.

Knorr-Held, L., and Evi Rainer. 2001. "Projections of Lung Cancer Mortality in West Germany: A Case Study in Bayesian Prediction." *Biostatistics* 2:109–29.

Littell, R. C., G. A. Milliken, W. W. Stroup, and R. D. Wolfinger. 1996. *SAS System for Mixed Models.* Cary, NC: SAS Institute.

Mason, K. O., W. H. Mason, H. H. Winsborough, and K. Poole. 1973. "Some Methodological Issues in Cohort Analysis of Archival Data." *American Sociological Review* 38:242–58.

Mason, W. M., and H. L. Smith. 1985. "Age-Period-Cohort Analysis and the Study of Deaths from Pulmonary Tuberculosis." Pp. 151–228 in *Cohort Analysis in Social Research*, edited by W. M. Mason and S. E. Fienberg. New York: Springer-Verlag.

McCulloch, C. E., and S. R. Searle. 2001. *Generalized, Linear, and Mixed Models.* New York: Wiley.

Morris, C. N. 1983. "Natural Exponential Families with Quadratic Variance Functions: Statistical Theory." *Annals of Statistics* 11:515–29.

National Center for Educational Statistics. 1999. *NAEP 1998 Reading Report Card for the Nations and States*, NCES 1999-500, by P. L. Donahue, K. E. Voelkl, J. R. Campbell, and J. Mazzeo. Washington, DC: NCES.

———. 2002. *The Nation's Report Card: Geography 2001*, NCES 2002-484, by A. R. Weiss, A. D. Lutkus, B. S. Hildebrant, M. S. Johnson. Washington, DC: NCES.

Rasbash, J., and H. Goldstein. 2000. *A User's Guide to MLwiN.* 2d ed. London: Institute of Education.

Raudenbush, S. W., and A. S. Bryk. 2002. *Hierarchical Linear Models: Applications and Data Analysis Methods.* Thousand Oaks, CA: Sage.

Robertson, C., S. Gandini, and P. Boyle. 1999. "Age-Period-Cohort Models: A Comparative Study of Available Methodologies." *Journal of Clinical Epidemiology* 52:569–83.

Schaie, K. Warner. 1994. "The Course of Adult Intellectual Development." *American Psychologist* 49:304–13.

Seltzer, M., W. Wong, and A. Bryk. 1996. "Bayesian Analysis in Applications of Hierarchical Models: Issues and Methods." *Journal of Educational and Behavioral Statistics* 21:131–67.

Smith, H. L. 2004. "Cohort Analysis Redux." Pp. 111–19 in *Sociological Methodology*, vol. 34, edited by Ross M. Stolzenberg. Boston: Blackwell Publishing.

Snijders, T., and R. Bosker. 1999. *Multilevel Analysis: An Introduction to Basic and Advanced Multilevel Modeling.* Thousand Oaks, CA: Sage.

Spiegelhalter, D. J., N. G. Best, B. P. Carlin, and A. van der Linde. 2002. "Bayesian Measures of Model Complexity and Fit" (with discussion and rejoinder). *Journal of the Royal Statistical Society*, Series B, 64:583–639.

Spiegelhalter, D. J., A. Thomas, N. G. Best, and D. Lunn. 2003. *WinBUGS User Manual, Version 1.4* (http://www.mrc-bsu.cam.ac.uk/bugs).

Wilson, J. A., and W. R. Gove. 1999. "The Intercohort Decline in Verbal Ability: Does it Exist?" and reply to Glenn and Alwin and McCammon. *American Sociological Review* 64:253–66, 287–302.

Yang, Y., W. J. Fu, and K. C. Land. 2004. "A Methodological Comparison of Age-Period-Cohort Models: Intrinsic Estimator and Conventional Generalized Linear Models." Pp. 75–110 in *Sociological Methodology*, vol. 34, edited by Ross M. Stolzenberg. Boston: Blackwell Publishing.

Yang, Y., and K. C. Land. 2006. "A Mixed Models Approach to Age-Period-Cohort Analysis of Repeated Cross-Section Surveys: Trends in Verbal Test Scores." In *Sociological Methodology*. Vol. 36, edited by Ross M. Stolzenberg. Boston: Blackwell Publishing.

A MIXED MODELS APPROACH TO THE AGE-PERIOD-COHORT ANALYSIS OF REPEATED CROSS-SECTION SURVEYS, WITH AN APPLICATION TO DATA ON TRENDS IN VERBAL TEST SCORES

Yang Yang*
Kenneth C. Land†

We develop a mixed (fixed and random effects) models approach to the age-period-cohort (APC) analysis of micro data sets in the form of a series of the repeated cross-section sample surveys that are increasingly available to sociologists. This approach recognizes the multilevel structure of the individual-level responses. As a substantive illustration, we apply our proposed methodology to data on verbal test scores from 15 cross-sections of the General Social Survey, 1974–2000. These data have been the subject of recent debates in the sociological literature. We show how our approach can be used to shed new light on these debates by identifying and estimating age, period, and cohort components of change.

Revision of a paper presented at the annual meeting of the American Sociological Association, August 16–19, 2003, Atlanta, Georgia. We thank Robert O'Brien and anonymous reviewers for comments. The research reported herein was supported in part by NIH/NIA Grant Numbers R01AG07198, P30AG12852, and K07AG00892. Direct correspondence to Yang Yang, Department of Sociology, University of Chicago, 1126 E. 59th St., Chicago, IL 60637; e-mail: yangy@uchicago.edu.

*University of Chicago

†Duke University

1. INTRODUCTION

For the past 80 years or so, demographers and sociologists have attempted to analyze data using *age* (A) and *time-period* (P) as explanatory variables to study phenomena that are time-specific. An analytic focus in which *cohort* (C) membership, as defined by the period and age at which an individual observation can first enter an age-by-period data array, is also important for substantive understanding (Ryder 1965). Accordingly, investigators have developed models for situations in which all three of age, period, and cohort (APC) are potentially of importance to studying a substantive phenomenon (Feinberg and Mason 1985).

One common goal of APC analysis is to assess the effects of one of the three factors on some outcomes of interest net of the influences of the other two time-related dimensions. *Age effects* represent the variation associated with different age groups brought about by physiological changes, accumulation of social experience, and/or role or status changes. *Period effects* represent variation over time periods that affect all age groups simultaneously—often resulting from shifts in social, cultural, economic, or physical environments. *Cohort effects* are associated with changes across groups of individuals who experience an initial event such as birth or marriage in the same year or years; these may reflect the effects of having different formative experiences for successive age groups in successive time periods (Robertson, Gandini, and Boyle 1999; Glenn 2003). Analysts generally agree that methodological guidance is needed to address the fundamental question of how to determine whether the phenomenon of interest is cohort-based or whether some other factors such as age or calendar year are more relevant.

The age-period-cohort (APC) accounting/multiple classification model developed by Mason and colleagues (1973) has served for over three decades as a general methodology for estimating age, period, and cohort effects in demographic and social research. This general methodology focuses on the APC analysis of data in the form of tables of percentages or occurrence/exposure rates of events such as births, deaths, disease incidence, and crimes. A major methodological challenge arises in the APC analysis of tabulated data due to the "identification problem" induced by the exact linear dependency between age, period, and cohort (Period = Age + Cohort) when the time intervals used to tabulate the data are of the same length for the age and period dimensions. This identification problem has drawn great attention in statistical studies of human populations. A number of methodological contributions to the specification and estimation of APC models have occurred in recent decades in a wide variety of disciplines, including social and demographic research (e.g., Glenn 1976, 1977; Fienberg and Mason 1978, 1985; Firebaugh 1989; Hobcraft, Menken, and Preston 1982; Wilmoth 1990; O'Brien 2000), biostatistics and epidemiology (e.g., Clayton and Shifflers 1987; Osmond and Gardner 1982; Holford 1992; Robertson and Boyle 1998; Fu 2000; Knight and Fu 2000; Yang, Fu, and Land 2004).

Most of these studies focus on aggregate population-level data. Increasingly, however, micro data sets in the form of a series of repeated cross-section sample surveys are available to social scientists. They create both new opportunities and challenges to APC analysis. The opportunities lie in the fact that these repeated cross-section survey data not only can be aggregated into population-level contingency tables for conventional multiple classification models but can also provide individual-level data on both the responses and a wide range of covariates, which can be employed for much finer-grained regression analysis. The challenge for APC analysis then becomes how social scientists can take advantage of the multilevel data structure presented in repeated cross-section surveys.

To address this challenge, we describe a methodology for APC analysis of microdata in the form of repeated cross-section surveys. In recognition of the multilevel structure of individual-level responses in repeated cross-section surveys, we propose a mixed (fixed and random) effects model approach. In particular, we introduce cross-classified hierarchical linear models (HLM) to represent variations in individual-level responses by periods (survey years) and cohorts. This leads to the identification and estimation of random effects for period and cohorts that then can become the objects of explanation. As a substantive illustration, we apply our proposed methodology to data on vocabulary test scores from 15 cross-sections of the General Social Survey (GSS), 1974–2000. These data have been the subject of recent debates in the sociological literature. We show how our approach can be used to shed light on these debates by identifying and estimating separate age, period, and cohort components of change.

2. THE VERBAL TEST SCORES CONTROVERSY AND DATA

2.1. *Questions Regarding Trends in Vocabulary Knowledge Ability*

A series of articles published in the *American Sociological Review* in 1999 center on the possible existence of an intercohort decline in verbal vocabulary knowledge in the General Social Survey, 1974 to 1996. The debate was initiated by Alwin's (1991) and Glenn's (1994) findings of a long-term intercohort decline in verbal ability beginning in the early part of the twentieth century. Wilson and Gove (1999a) took issue with this finding and argued that the Alwin and Glenn analyses confuse cohort effects with aging effects. Wilson and Gove also suggested the possibility of a curvilinear age effect and the importance of treating the collinearity between age and cohort in the GSS data. While Alwin and Glenn assumed that period effects are minimal or null, Wilson and Gove (1999a:263) found "that year of survey [time period] is negatively related to verbal score when education is controlled" and considered this as an indication of "the presence of a period effect." In response, Glenn (1999) disagreed that the decline in GSS vocabulary scores resulted solely from period influences and also argued against the Wilson and Gove claim that cohort differences actually reflected only age effects. After reexamining aging versus cohort explanations, Alwin and McCammon (1999) similarly insisted that aging explains only a tiny portion of the variation in verbal ability data and therefore is not sufficient to account for the contributions of unique cohort experiences to the decline in verbal skills. More recently, Alwin and McCammon (2001) analyzed 14 repeated cross-sections from the GSS over a 24-year period and concluded that age-related differences in cognitive abilities observed in cross-sectional samples of individuals may in part be spurious due to the effects of cohort differences in schooling and related factors. They found specifically that "the curvilinear contributions of aging to variation in verbal scores account for less than one-third of 1 percent of the variance in vocabulary knowledge, once cohort is controlled" (Alwin and McCammon 2001:151).

The above studies have employed graphical and regression analyses to suggest patterns of verbal score variations along age, period, and cohort categories. As we revisit this interesting puzzle, we find that some aspects of these studies invite further examination before definitive conclusions can be drawn. First, although the graphs presented in Wilson and Gove (1999a) are helpful in obtaining general *qualitative* impressions about age and cohort patterns, they are of limited analytic value because they are unidimensional. For example, Wilson and Gove show a plot of the mean verbal score curve adjusted for education that decreases across cohorts born from 1915 to 1975. This curve cuts across a number of periods for certain age groups. Thus, the shape of this cohort curve potentially is affected both by varying age effects and by varying period effects. Statistically, the curve represents gross age/cohort effects, which should be adjusted by controlling other relevant factors (Mason and Smith 1985; Yang et al. 2004). Furthermore, a *quantitative* assessment of how age and period effects operate to influence the shape of this cohort curve cannot be obtained by a simple visual examination of graphs like those used by Wilson and Gove (1999a, 1999b).[1]

Second, although all authors involved in this debate utilized some statistical modeling procedures, no analyses were conducted to assess the age and cohort effects simultaneously while controlling for period effects due to the APC identification problem. For instance, Wilson and Gove (1999a) estimated age-period regression models for four age groups; in reply to Wilson and Gove, Glenn (1999) reported a regression analysis of verbal scores on year (period) of the survey for five age groups. In yet another approach, Alwin and McCammon (1999) examined age effects within cohorts and vice versa, assuming minimum period effects. How tenable are the assumptions of omitting one of the three time dimensions? Given the long period of time the surveys cover (27 years), ignoring the effect of historical time period may lead to discrepant findings regarding either age or cohort effects, and the same holds for ignoring cohort effects. Whether there are substantial period or cohort effects is a question that should be addressed empirically.

In sum, the previous findings on trends in verbal scores are interesting and suggestive. But until age, period, and cohort effects are simultaneously estimated, the question of whether the trends are due to age, period, or cohort components remains incompletely resolved. When more powerful statistical modeling strategies become available to APC analysts, more systematic analyses on these verbal data can be carried out. We use this specific example to motivate the statistical methodology we present. The substantive results we present are for the

---

[1]A more detailed description of the limitations of graphical APC analysis is available by Kupper et al. (1985).

TABLE 1
Descriptive Statistics for GSS Vocabulary Test Data, 1974–2000

Variables	Definition	N	Mean	SD	Min	Max
WORDSUM	A 10-item composite vocabulary scale score	19500	6.02	2.15	0	10
AGE	Age at survey year	19500	44.81	17.40	18	89
EDUCATION	Highest levels of education completed	19500	12.72	3.03	0	20
FEMALE	Sex: 1 = female; 0 = male	19500	0.57	0.50	0	1
BLACK	Race: 1 = Black; 0 = White	19500	0.15	0.35	0	1
COHORT	Five-year birth cohorts	19			1890	1980
PERIOD	Survey years	15			1974	2000

purpose of illustrating our integrated methodology and are not construed as a systematic study of this problem. A full substantive analysis will follow in a separate paper.

2.2. General Social Survey Data and Variables

Verbal test score data are analyzed from 15 cross-sections of the General Social Survey, 1974–2000.[2] This is an extension of the 1974–1996 data on which the controversy described above is based. In these surveys, a survey respondent's vocabulary knowledge is measured by a composite scale score named WORDSUM, which is constructed by adding the correct answers to ten verbal test questions and ranges from 0 to 10. WORDSUM has a distribution that is approximately bell-shaped with a mean of about 6 and is reported in previous studies to have an internal reliability of .71 (Wilson and Gove 1999a:258).[3] The data include 19,500 respondents who had measures on WORDSUM and several covariates across all survey years. Definitions of variables included in the analyses and summary statistics are shown in Table 1. Respondents' ages in the data pooled across all surveys vary from 18 to 89. The average years of education completed is around 12.7 years. Fifty-seven percent of respondents are

[2]Survey years including verbal ability are 1974, 1976, 1978, 1982, 1984, 1987, 1988, 1989, 1990, 1991, 1993, 1994, 1996, 1998, and 2000.
[3]In an item analysis of individual words in WORDSUM, Alwin (1991:628) found that some of the words have become more difficult over time. The general conclusion in this series of articles (Alwin and McCammon 1999; Glenn 1994; Wilson and Gove 1999a), however, is that word obsolescence does not account for observed changes in the test scores over time.

TABLE 2
Two-way Cross-Classified Data Structure in the GSS: Number of Observations in Each Cohort-by-Period Cell

Cohort (J)	Year (K)															Total
	1974	1976	1978	1982	1984	1987	1988	1989	1990	1991	1993	1994	1996	1998	2000	
1890	12	18	8	0	0	0	0	0	0	0	0	0	0	0	0	38
1895	31	25	19	19	6	0	0	0	0	0	0	0	0	0	0	100
1900	62	52	49	27	18	17	13	11	5	2	0	0	0	0	0	256
1905	88	69	68	43	38	23	11	12	11	11	15	15	10	0	0	414
1910	77	89	69	75	50	48	34	27	25	29	13	31	27	18	8	620
1915	109	111	84	100	81	81	42	36	37	41	37	60	39	24	27	909
1920	115	104	112	110	73	97	60	53	40	56	55	85	59	32	37	1088
1925	113	108	106	131	99	92	52	53	53	40	50	84	81	68	52	1182
1930	129	92	90	111	81	95	47	54	43	62	43	86	72	45	64	1114
1935	130	106	108	112	80	101	39	59	44	37	58	101	100	61	64	1200
1940	119	140	130	127	100	142	49	74	49	65	58	134	117	65	78	1447
1945	179	161	184	163	133	143	98	84	85	74	85	168	161	104	85	1907
1950	179	180	197	199	170	185	101	94	95	111	99	173	169	101	111	2164
1955	89	151	180	260	162	219	102	117	106	118	127	198	213	149	145	2336
1960	0	8	59	175	186	190	109	121	102	118	103	231	208	161	147	1918
1965	0	0	0	38	75	161	101	86	76	91	111	182	188	157	111	1377
1970	0	0	0	0	0	29	32	48	55	77	81	157	188	116	145	928
1975	0	0	0	0	0	0	0	0	0	1	23	59	128	84	107	402
1980	0	0	0	0	0	0	0	0	0	0	0	0	4	34	62	100
Total	1432	1414	1463	1690	1352	1623	890	929	826	933	958	1764	1764	1219	1243	19500

female, and 15 percent are black. There are 19 five-year birth cohorts. The oldest cohort member was born in 1890 and the youngest was born in 1980.

3. A MIXED MODELS APPROACH TO APC ANALYSIS OF REPEATED CROSS-SECTION SURVEYS

3.1. *Application of Hierarchical APC Models to Multilevel Data*

The structure of the *age-period-cohort accounting/multiple classification model/fixed-effects regression model* that was articulated for demographic and social research more than 30 years ago by Mason and colleagues (1973) can be written in *linear regression form* as

$$Y = Xb + \varepsilon, \tag{1}$$

where Y is a vector of event/exposure rates or log-transformed rates from population tabular data, X is the regression design matrix consisting of "dummy variable" column vectors for the vector of model parameters b:

$$b = (\mu, \alpha_1, ... \alpha_{a-1}, \beta_1, ..., \beta_{p-1}, \gamma_1, ..., \gamma_{a+p-2})^T : \tag{2}$$

For $i = 1,....,a$ age groups $j = 1, ..., p$ periods and μ denotes the intercept or adjusted mean rate; α_i denotes the ith row age effect or the coefficient for the ith age group; β_j denotes the jth column period effect or the coefficient for the jth time period; γ_k denotes the kth diagonal cohort effect or the coefficient for the kth cohort for $k = 1,....,(a+p-1)$, with $k = a-i+j$; and ε is a vector of random errors with mean 0 and constant diagonal variance matrix $\sigma^2 I$, where I is an identity matrix. In conventional practice, one of each of the α_i, β_j, and γ_k coefficients is set to zero, thus establishing a "reference" age, period, or cohort category against which the estimated coefficients for the other categories can be compared. Then the ordinary least squares (OLS) estimator of the matrix regression model (1) is the solution $\hat{b}$ of the normal equations:

$$\hat{b} = (X^T X)^{-1} X^T Y \tag{3}$$

The key problem in APC analysis using model (1) is the *model identification problem*. This problem arises in the conventional application of model (1) to tables of percentages or occurrence/exposure rates of events such as births, deaths, disease incidence, or crimes wherein age and period are of equal interval length (for instance, five years) in the population data and the diagonal cells in the age by period arrays represent the cohorts. This results in a perfect linear relationship between the age, period, and cohort effects: Period – Age = Cohort. Therefore, it is not possible to separately estimate the effects of cohort, age, and period without assigning certain constraints to the coefficients.

There is an extensive literature on the identification and estimation of age, period, and cohort coefficients in the APC accounting model of equations (1) – (3). This literature has identified three conventional strategies for identification and estimation: (1) constraining two or more of the remaining age, period, or cohort coefficients to be equal (e.g., Mason et al. 1973; Fienberg and Mason 1978, 1985), i.e., by placing at least one additional identifying constraint on the parameter vector (3); (2) using a "proxy" variable approach that assumes the cohort or period effects are proportional to certain measured variables (Fienberg and Mason 1985; Heckman and Robb 1985; O'Brien 2000); and (3) transforming at least one of the age, period, or cohort variables so that its relationship to others is nonlinear (Mason et al. 1973; Fienberg and Mason 1985).

Noting these strategies together with the Wilson and Gove (1999a, 1999b) hypothesis that there is a curvilinear age effect on verbal vocabulary knowledge, we proceed to specify and test a model of verbal test scores in the GSS as a quadratic function of age. To illustrate how this can be used to inform the specification of an individual-level APC regression model, consider the application of the classical fixed-effects APC regression model of equation (1) to, say, the following five sample members, ages 30, 31, 32, 33, and 34, each of whom is a member of the same five-year birth cohort, the 1960–1964 birth cohort, and each of whom is a survey respondent in the 1990 GSS:

$$Y_{1,1990,1960-64} = \beta_0 + \beta_1(30) + \beta_2(30)^2 + \varepsilon_{1,1990,1960-64} \qquad (4a)$$

$$Y_{2,1990,1960-64} = \beta_0 + \beta_1(31) + \beta_2(31)^2 + \varepsilon_{2,1990,1960-64} \qquad (4b)$$

$$Y_{3,1990,1960-64} = \beta_0 + \beta_1(32) + \beta_2(32)^2 + \varepsilon_{3,1990,1960-64} \qquad (4c)$$

$$Y_{4,1990,1960-64} = \beta_0 + \beta_1(33) + \beta_2(33)^2 + \varepsilon_{4,1990,1960-64} \qquad (4d)$$

$$Y_{5,1990,1960-64} = \beta_0 + \beta_1(34) + \beta_2(34)^2 + \varepsilon_{5,1990,1960-64} \qquad (4e)$$

The five individual sample respondents are numbered from 1 through 5, respectively, their respective ages (30 through 34) have been entered into the age and age-squared terms of the model, and β_1 and β_2 denote the coefficients of the quadratic age curve. To complete the APC model specification of equations (4a–e), we have the following specification on the error terms:

$$\varepsilon_{i,1990,1960-64} = \beta_{1990} + \gamma_{1960-64} + e_{i,1990,1960-64}, \text{ for } i = 1, 2, \ldots, 5.$$
$$(4f)$$

In this fixed-effects model, it is clear that the underidentification problem of the classical APC accounting model has been resolved by the specification of the quadratic function for the age effects, and the fixed effects model could be estimated straightforwardly on the GSS microdata by using dummy variables to control for the period and cohort effects in a conventional multiple linear regression analysis. Furthermore, this statement holds true whether the analyst continues to define cohorts by five-year age groupings, as in equations (4) or by taking advantage of the single-year-of-age information in the GSS data to define single-year age cohorts.

A key point is that the error terms of equations (4) specifically include fixed-effect coefficients to measure the impact of the time period (β_{1990}) and the birth cohort ($\gamma_{1960-64}$) to which these sample respondents belong. Many extant APC regression analyses of individual-level data from repeated cross-section surveys, including some of those involved in the verbal test scores controversy reviewed above, have proceeded without including these fixed effects coefficients. This will be termed *a pooled repeated cross-section regression model*, estimates of which will be reported below as a baseline model for comparative purposes (see Table 3 below). But, without the inclusion and estimation of these

TABLE 3

Fixed-Effects Regression Models for Pooled GSS WORDSUM Data, 1974–2000, Without Controls for Period and Cohort Effects

Independent	Model				
Variable	I	II	III	IV	V
Intercept	6.018***	6.331***	6.278***	6.464***	6.204***
	(.015)	(.021)	(.027)	(.027)	(.024)
Age[a]	.018*	.110***	.109***	.087***	.192***
	(.009)	(.010)	(.010)	(.010)	(.008)
Age^{2b}		−.103***	−.104***	−.105***	−.053***
		(.005)	(.005)	(.005)	(.004)
Female			.094**	.147***	.234***
			(.031)	(.030)	(.026)
Black				−1.449***	−1.079***
				(.042)	(.036)
Education[a]					.364***
					(.004)
Adjusted R^2	.002	.022	.022	.079	.317

[a]Centered around grand means.

[b]Age squared.

Note: Standard errors are in the parentheses; *indicates $p < 0.05$; **indicates $p < 0.01$; ***indicates $p < 0.001$, two-tailed test.

coefficients for period and cohort effects, it is quite possible that the usual independence of errors assumption of linear regression analysis will be violated.

In addition, the fixed effects model of equations (4) assumes that impacts of cohort and period (survey year) on the verbal test score responses of sample members are adequately modeled as fixed. This ignores the possibility that the effects of cohort membership and survey year may have random, as well as, or instead of, fixed effects on the verbal test responses. This raises the possibility that sample respondents in the same cohort group and/or survey year may be similar in their responses to the verbal test score items due to the fact that they share random error components (i.e., through random cohort and/or period components of $e_{i,1990,1960-64}$) unique to their cohorts or periods of the survey. Note that the sharing of common elements in the error terms may result in such weak covariation among responses on the verbal test score items that there are no serious complications for estimates of APC coefficients for standard OLS regression models. But a failure to assess this potentially more complicated error structure adequately in APC analysis may have serious consequences for statistical inferences. The standard errors of estimated coefficients of conventional fixed-effects regression models like equation (1) may be underestimated, leading to inflated t-ratios and actual alpha levels that are larger than the nominal .05 or .01 levels.[4]

This heterogeneity problem can be addressed by modifying the fixed effects specification of the general APC regression model—shown in general form in equation (1) and in illustrative form for a few sample respondents in equations (4) —toward a random effects or random coefficient regression model. That is, in order to take into account the possibility that the common period and cohort elements of the error terms of equations (4) are statistically significant, we should allow for the possibility that at least some of the effect coefficients β_0, β_1, β_2, β_{1990}, and $\gamma_{1960-64}$ in equations (4) are not fixed, but instead, vary randomly by cohort and/or time period. This implies that we should modify the fixed-effects APC regression model (1) to a mixed-effects model. Toward this objective, we now move to specifying a *mixed (fixed and random) effects APC regression model*, known in the social sciences as *multilevel* or *hierarchical regression models* (Raudenbush and Bryk 2002).

3.2. Cross-Classified Random Effects APC Model

To specify a *hierarchical age-period-cohort (HAPC) regression model*, note, first, that in cross-sectional surveys such as the GSS, individuals are nested within cells created by the cross-classification of two types of social context: birth cohorts and survey years. That is, respondents are members simultaneously in cohorts and periods. This data structure is displayed in Table 2. Each row is a cohort and each column is a year. Denote the number of birth cohorts as J and the number of survey years as K. The numbers in this J by K matrix are the sample sizes, n_{jk}—the numbers of individuals who belonged to a given birth cohort and were

---

[4]See Hox and Kreft (1994) for a thorough discussion of the statistical limitations of the use of traditional statistical models for multilevel analysis. In cases involving even a small amount of covariation among the observations within groups or categories, Hox and Kreft indicate that the assumption of independence of error terms is violated and that this can lead to Type I errors that are much larger than the nominal alpha level.

surveyed in a given year. In recognition of the multilevel characteristics of this data structure, we formulate a *cross-classified random effects APC model* to assess the relative importance of the two contexts, cohort and period, in understanding individual differences in verbal test outcome.[5]

In such a model applied to the verbal test data, variability in WORDSUM associated with individuals, cohorts, and periods is specified as follows:

Level-1 or "Within-Cell" Model

$$WORDSUM_{ijk} = \beta_{0jk} + \beta_1 AGE_{ijk} + \beta_2 AGE_{ijk}^2$$
$$+ \beta_3 EDUCATION_{ijk} + \beta_4 FEMALE_{ijk}$$
$$+ \beta_5 BLACK_{ijk} + e_{ijk}, \; e_{ijk} \sim N(0, \sigma^2) \quad (5a)$$

Level-2 or "Between-Cell" Model

$$\beta_{0jk} = \gamma_0 + u_{0j} + v_{0k}, u_{0j} \sim N(0, \tau_u), \; v_{0k} \sim N(0, \tau_v) \quad (5b)$$

Combined Model

$$WORDSUM_{ijk} = \gamma_0 + \beta_1 AGE_{ijk} + \beta_2 AGE_{ijk}^2 + \beta_3 EDUCATION_{ijk}$$
$$+ \beta_4 FEMALE_{ijk} + \beta_5 BLACK_{ijk} + u_{0j} + v_{0k} + e_{ijk}$$
$$(5c)$$

for $i = 1, 2, \ldots, n_{jk}$ individuals within cohort j and period k;

$\quad j = 1, \ldots, 19$ birth cohorts;

$\quad k = 1, \ldots, 15$ time periods (survey years);

where, within each birth cohort j and survey year k, respondent i's verbal score is modeled as a function of his or her age, age-squared, educational attainment, and two covariates, gender and race, that have been found in previous research to be related to verbal ability (e.g., see Hedges and Nowell 1995; Campbell, Hombo, and Mazzeo 2000). This random-intercepts model specification allows only the level-1 intercept to vary randomly from cohort-to-cohort and period-to-period, but not the level-1 slopes. In supplemental analyses, however, we find that none of the level-1 slope coefficients exhibit significant random variation across cohorts and periods in the GSS verbal test score data.

[5]Two examples of applications of cross-classified hierarchical linear models to social data can be found in Raudenbush's (1993) study of neighborhood and school effect on children's attainment and Goldstein's (2003) study of middle school and high school effects on students' educational outcome.

In this model, β_{0jk} is the intercept or "cell mean"— that is, the mean verbal test score of individuals who belong to birth cohort j and surveyed in year k; $\beta_1, \ldots \beta_5$ are the level-1 fixed effects; e_{ijk} is the random individual effect—that is, the deviation of individual ijk's score from the cell mean, which are assumed normally distributed with mean 0 and a within-cell variance σ^2; γ_0 is the model intercept, or grand-mean verbal test score of all individuals; u_{0j} is the residual random effect of cohort j—that is, the contribution of cohort j averaged over all periods, on β_{0jk}, assumed normally distributed with mean 0 and variance τ_u; and v_{0k} is the residual random effect of period k—that is, the contribution of period k averaged over all cohorts, assumed normally distributed with mean 0 and variance τ_v. In addition, $\beta_{0j} = \gamma_0 + u_{0j}$ is the cohort verbal test score effect averaged over all periods; and $\beta_{0k} = \gamma_0 + v_{0k}$ is the period verbal test score effect averaged over all cohorts.

In hierarchical linear model analyses, an important decision pertains to "centering" or choosing the location of the individual-level explanatory variables (Raudenbush and Bryk 2002). The main choices are (1) to use the natural metric (NM) of the variables, (2) to use grand mean centering (GMC) by subtracting the complete sample or grand mean from the observed values; and (3) to center within subgroups or contexts (CWC) studied by subtracting subgroup means from observed values. When the minimum value of an explanatory variable does not include zero, as is the case of age (since the GSS sample frame is for ages 18 and over) in the model of equations (5), methodological guidelines (Raudenbush and Bryk 2002:32) indicate that one of the other options should be used. Furthermore, the literature on the effects of age on vocabulary knowledge (Wilson and Gove 1999a:257–58) cites a pure physiological age effect that does not vary by cohort context. Therefore, we applied centering on the grand mean to the individual-level age variable in equations (5). In the case of education, by contrast, Wilson and Gove (1999a: 255–56) argue that changing average levels of school years completed varies very substantially across the cohorts surveyed in the GSS. In order to take this changing cohort context of education into account, we therefore centered education on the cohort means.[6]

---

[6]For hierarchical models in which only the intercept but not the slopes are random at level-1, as is the case for the model of equation (5), Snijders and Bosker (1999:81) show that all three of the NM, GMC, and CWC approaches lead to models that are statistically equivalent in terms of the parameterizations of the

3.3. *Results*

Tables 3 and 4 report empirical estimates for regression models on the individual-level GSS data. For comparative purposes, Table 3 contains baseline ordinary least squares estimates of pooled repeated cross-section regression models without controls for period and cohort effects, as described above, applied to all 19,500 GSS respondents. Estimates of five nested regression models are given in the table. Model I contains only a linear effect of respondent's age and Model II includes a quadratic age effect. Both models show significant gross age effects, and we find the age effects are curvilinear. Models III and IV introduce the two sociodemographic regressors, respondent's sex and race, cited above. Consistent with prior research on gender and race differences in verbal ability, being female is positively associated with one's expected score on WORDSUM, whereas being black is negatively associated with the response variable. The final model reported in Table 3, Model V, contains all of the explanatory regressors of the previous models plus the respondent's education, which has previously been identified as a key explanatory variable for vocabulary knowledge (Alwin 1991; Glenn 1994; Wilson and Gove 1999a). The inclusion of respondent's education clearly raised the explained variance in WORDSUM from 8 percent in Model IV to 32 percent in Model V.

Table 4 reports the parameter estimates and model fit statistics for the crossed random effects model (equation 5) estimated on the 15 GSS repeated cross-section surveys.[7] These results are obtained using the restricted maximum-likelihood-empirical Bayes estimation method (Raudenbush and Bryk 2002, chaps. 3 and 12). Examining first the model fit statistics reported at the bottom of the table, it can be seen that the model deviance is very large compared to the degrees of freedom of the model, thus indicating a highly significant association of

combined models. In fact, we found empirically in our analyses of the WORDSUM data that there is not a great deal of difference among estimated coefficients under the three different approaches (although there are some variations in terms of variance decompositions and fit statistics). Thus, in the absence of methodological guidelines that privilege one of the three alternatives, substantive-theoretical reasoning guided the choice of centering.

[7]The model estimates reported in Table 4 were estimated by application of the SAS PROC MIXED. Cross–classified mixed models can also be obtained by using HLM 6 (Raudenbush, Bryk, and Congdon 2004).

TABLE 4
HAPC Models of the GSS WORDSUM Data: Crossed-classified Random Effects

Fixed Effects	Coefficient	se	t Ratio
INTERCEPT	6.167***	0.059	103.73
AGE	0.030#	0.017	1.75
AGE^2	−0.065***	0.005	−11.83
FEMALE	0.242***	0.025	9.40
BLACK	−1.051***	0.036	−28.74
EDUCATION	0.374***	0.004	82.95

Random Effects

Cohort	Coefficient	se	t Ratio
1890	−0.043	0.165	−0.26
1895	−0.123	0.140	−0.88
1900	0.069	0.113	0.61
1905	−0.403	0.099	−4.06
1910	0.079	0.088	0.89
1915	0.192	0.078	2.44
1920	−0.037	0.074	−0.50
1925	0.008	0.071	0.12
1930	0.030	0.071	0.46
1935	0.004	0.070	0.05
1940	0.126	0.068	1.85
1945	0.354	0.065	5.41
1950	0.326	0.065	4.99
1955	0.026	0.066	0.38
1960	−0.031	0.070	−0.44
1965	−0.079	0.076	−1.03
1970	−0.195	0.085	−2.29
1975	−0.178	0.102	−1.73
1980	−0.127	0.140	−0.91
Period			
1974	0.035	0.040	0.86
1976	0.063	0.040	1.58
1978	0.008	0.039	0.19
1982	−0.002	0.037	−0.06
1984	0.024	0.039	0.60
1987	−0.043	0.037	−1.15
1988	−0.103	0.042	−2.40
1989	−0.048	0.042	−1.13

Continued.

TABLE 4
Continued.

Random Effects	Coefficient	se	t Ratio
1990	0.020	0.043	0.47
1991	0.041	0.042	0.95
1993	0.002	0.042	0.01
1994	0.022	0.037	0.60
1996	−0.048	0.037	−1.28
1998	0.037	0.040	0.92
2000	−0.005	0.041	−0.14

Variance Components	Variance	se	p value
Cohort	0.039**	0.016	0.00
Period	0.003#	0.002	0.08
Individual	3.136***	0.032	0.00
Model Fit			

Model Fit			
Deviance (DF)	77714.4 (9)		
AIC	77732.4		

Note: #indicates $p < 0.10$;* indicates $p < .05$; ** indicates $p < .01$;
***indicates $p < .001$, two-tailed test.

the explanatory variables with the WORDSUM response variable. The variance components show that most of the variance in WORDSUM is accounted for by the individual-level regressors. Level-2 variance components results indicate that variation by cohorts is statistically significant, whereas there is little variation by time periods after controlling for age and other individual covariates. Examining further the estimated average effect coefficients for cohorts, it can be seen that the estimated effects are particularly negative for the 1905–1909 cohort and particularly positive for the 1940–1944, 1945–1949, and 1950–1954 cohorts. There also is a negative trend from the 1960–1964 cohort to the 1980–1984 cohort.

Examining next the estimated individual-level coefficients in Table 4, it can be seen that the qualitative results are similar to those reported in Table 3—a quadratic age effect, a positive effect for females, a negative effect for blacks, and a highly significant positive effect for education. Taken together, these regressors account for about 30 percent of the unconditional level-1 variance (not shown). The estimated regression coefficients and their standard errors are numerically quite similar between the two tables for the sex, race, and education variables.

Estimates for the linear component of the quadratic age curve are quite another story, however. The estimated coefficient for this term is reduced from a highly statistically significant .19 in Model V of Table 3 to a marginally significant .03 in Table 4, after cohort and time period effects are taken into account. This implies that a failure to control for the effects of cohort and period variation in vocabulary knowledge could lead to large over-estimates of the increases in verbal acuity that are due to aging from young adulthood into the middle-age years.

4. DISCUSSION AND CONCLUSION

In this paper, we have addressed what sometimes is termed the "age-period-cohort conundrum"—the fact that the classical APC accounting model is underidentified by one degree of freedom due to a linear dependency among the age, period, and cohort terms. We have described a new way of thinking about APC analysis that may prove useful in subsequent empirical analyses. Our procedure applies mixed regression models to the hierarchical analysis of the individual-level data from repeated cross-sections. In the case of the substantive analysis described here, this application is facilitated by the specification of a nonlinear parametric form for one of the age, period, or cohort dimensions that breaks the underidentification problem of the classical APC accounting model. Then hierarchical APC (HAPC) regression models in the form of cross-classified random effects models can be employed to ascertain whether or not there is significant heterogeneity in survey responses by cohort groups and/or survey years. This leads to a hierarchical regression analysis that uses covariates at the individual, cohort, and/or period levels to develop an explanatory model that accounts for the age, period, and cohort effects.

Based on this mixed models strategy, we used General Social Survey data on vocabulary knowledge to illustrate how to formulate and build cross-classified random effects APC models. These analyses are used primarily to illustrate our integrated methodology for APC analysis and are not put forward for their definitive substantive value. Nonetheless, our results lend support for some aspects of both sides of the debate on the intercohort decline in vocabulary knowledge in the United States.

First, the HAPC analyses find evidence in support of the quadratic age effect on vocabulary knowledge hypothesized by Wilson and Gove (1999a and 1999b). However, the linear effect (which indicates the extent to which the quadratic age curve of vocabulary knowledge increases with age) was reduced to statistical insignificance when controls were introduced for the random effects of time periods and cohorts. Furthermore, controlling for the effects of key individual characteristics in the HAPC analyses—namely, sex, race, and education—does not explain away all the age effects. We find that about 1 percent of variation in verbal scores at the individual level is due to the quadratic effect of aging after controlling for the random effects of cohorts and periods as well as the individual-level covariates of sex and race. This is about three times the "one-third of 1 percent" found by Alwin and McCammon (2001), as cited above, in regressions that controlled for cohort effects but not for period effects or individual-level covariates.

Second, we found only evidence of modest time period effects. This supports the contentions of Alwin and McCammon (1999) that period effects in the GSS vocabulary knowledge data are relatively minor. The presence of this effect, however, affects the estimates of age and cohort effects.

Third, the HAPC analyses find evidence in support of the contentions of Alwin (1991), Alwin and McCammon (1999), and Glenn (1994, 1999) that there has been an intercohort decline in vocabulary knowledge. In fact, we find evidence of a bimodal curve of cohort effects. There is evidence of a peak in vocabulary knowledge for cohorts born in the 1940s and perhaps the early 1950s. But our analyses also suggest a deficit for birth cohorts from the first decade of the twentieth century. Relative to this early century decline, vocabulary knowledge shows a secondary peak in the immediately following cohorts, thus yielding a bimodal cohort curve not found in previous studies.

The implications of this study are beyond the substantive results on the vocabulary knowledge controversy. The mixed regression models approach proposed here not only is methodologically relevant for APC analyses, but also enhances our ability in addressing questions that bear theoretical importance to sociological studies of social change and cohort heterogeneity (Ryder 1965). For instance, is there evidence for clustering effects of random errors, due to the fact that members of the same birth cohort may be subjected to similar unmeasured events that influence their educational outcomes? And if there is indeed significant random variability across birth cohorts, how can it be explained or what may account for the variance? The same questions may apply to the investigation of period effects. Such problems suggest the importance of explanatory factors related to birth cohort and period effects and cannot be handled by any previous version of the APC accounting framework (Smith 2004). The multilevel APC modeling approach, therefore, is obviously an improvement that offers an option for researchers interested in identifying key explanatory factors in addition to age, period, and cohort indicators. The specification and measurement of cohort-level variables, such as cohort average education, newspaper reading, and television watching identified by Alwin and McCammon (1999), Glenn (1994, 1999), and Wilson and Gove (1999a, 1999b), and their introduction into HAPC regression models in order to explain the cohort effects we have estimated is a next step in model building and assessment. Because that is a complex subject that requires detailed substantive attention, however, we defer that analysis to a subsequent paper.

Straightforward applications of HLM to APC analyses, however, may not be without limitations. In the present analyses, we adopted the conventional method of parameter estimation under a hierarchical model that is likelihood-based and considered partially Bayesian (Raudenbush and Bryk 2002). The estimates obtained through this procedure have good statistical properties when the sample sizes at level-1 and level-2 are large and the data are balanced. It should be kept in mind, however, that the numbers of years and birth cohorts in social and demographic surveys may not be large enough to ensure accurate estimation of variance components by the maximum likelihood method. In addition, the sample sizes within each cohort are highly unbalanced. Therefore, errors in variance components estimates may produce extra uncertainty in coefficient estimates that may not be reflected in the standard errors. The consequences of these complications for statistical inferences and potential solutions need further methodological exploration and will be studied in another paper.

REFERENCES

Alwin, D. F. 1991. "Family of Origin and Cohort Differences in Verbal Ability." *American Sociological Review* 56:625–38.
Alwin, D. F., and R. J. McCammon. 1999. "Aging Versus Cohort Interpretations of Intercohort Differences in GSS Vocabulary Scores." *American Sociological Review* 64:272–86.

————. 2001. "Aging, Cohorts, and Verbal Ability." *The Journals of Gerontology Series B: Psychological Sciences and Social Sciences* 56:S151–61.

Campbell, J. R., C. M. Hombo, and J. Mazzeo. 2000. *NAEP 1999—Trends in Academic Progress: Three Decades of Student Performance.* Washington, DC: National Center for Education Statistics.

Clayton, D., and E. Schifflers. 1987. "Models for Temporal Variation in Cancer Rates. II: Age-Period-Cohort Models." *Statistics in Medicine,* 6:469–81.

Fienberg, S. E., and W. M. Mason. 1978. "Identification and Estimation of Age-Period-Cohort Models in the Analysis of Discrete Archival Data." Pp.1–67 in *Sociological Methodology,* vol. 8, edited by K. F. Schuessler. San Francisco: Jossey-Bass.

————. 1985. "Specification and Implementation of Age, Period, and Cohort Models." Pp. 45–88 in *Cohort Analysis in Social Research,* edited by W. M. Mason and S. E. Fienberg. New York: Springer-Verlag.

Firebaugh, G. 1989. "Methods for Estimating Cohort Replacement Effects." Pp. 243–62 in *Sociological Methodology,* vol. 19, edited by Clifford C. Clogg. Washington, DC: Blackwell Publishers.

Fu, W. J. 2000. "Ridge Estimator in Singular Design with Application to Age-Period-Cohort Analysis of Disease Rates." *Communications in Statistics— Theory and Method* 29:263–78.

Glenn, N. D. 1976. "Cohort Analysts' Futile Quest: Statistical Attempts to Separate Age, Period, and Cohort Effects." *American Sociological Review* 41:900–904.

————. 1977. *Cohort Analysis.* Beverly Hills, CA: Sage.

————. 1994. "Television Watching, Newspaper Reading, and Cohort Differences in Verbal Ability." *Sociology of Education* 67:216–30.

————. 1999. "Further Discussion of the Evidence for an Intercohort Decline in Education-Adjusted Vocabulary." *American Sociological Review* 64:267–71.

———— 2003. "Distinguishing Age, Period, and Cohort Effects." Pp. 465–76 in *Handbook of the Life Course,* edited by J. T. Mortimer and M. J. Shanahan. New York: Kluwer Academic/Plenum.

Goldstein, H. 2003. *Multilevel Statistical Models.* 3d ed. London: Oxford University Press.

Heckman, J., and R. Robb. 1985. "Using Longitudinal Data to Estimate Age, Period, and Cohort Effects in Earnings Equations." Pp. 137–50 in *Cohort Analysis in Social Research,* edited by W. M. Mason and S. E. Fienberg. New York: Springer-Verlag.

Hedges, L. V., and A. Nowell. 1995. "Sex Differences in Mental Test Scores, Variability, and Numbers of High-Scoring Individuals." *Science* 269(July):41–5.

Hobcraft, J., J. Menken, and S. Preston. 1982. "Age, Period, and Cohort Effects in Demography: A Review." *Population Index* 48:4–43.

Holford, T. R. 1992. "Analysing the Temporal Effects of Age, Period, and Cohort." *Statistical Methods in Medical Research* 1:317–37.

Hox, J. J. and I. G. Kreft. 1994. "Multilevel Analysis Methods." *Sociological Methods and Research* 22:283–99.

Knight, K., and W. J. Fu. 2000. "Asymptotics for Lasso-Type Estimators." *The Annals of Statistics* 28:1356–78.

Kupper, L. L., J. M. Janis, A. Karmous, and B. G. Greenberg. 1985. "Statistical Age-Period-Cohort Analysis: A Review and Critique." *Journal of Chronic Disease* 38:811–30.

Kupper L.L., J. M. Janis, I. A. Salama, C. N. Yoshizawa, and B. G. Greenberg. 1983. "Age-Period-Cohort Analysis: An Illustration of the Problems in Assessing Interaction in One Observation per Cell Data." *Communications in Statistics – Theory and Method* 12:2779—807.

Mason, K. O., W. H. Mason, H. H. Winsborough, and K. Poole. 1973. "Some Methodological Issues in Cohort Analysis of Archival Data." *American Sociological Review* 38:242–58.

Mason, W. M. and H. L. Smith. 1985. "Age-Period-Cohort Analysis and the Study of Deaths from Pulmonary Tuberculosis." Pp. 151–228 in *Cohort Analysis in Social Research*, edited by W. M. Mason and S. E. Fienberg. New York: Springer-Verlag.

O'Brien, R. M. 2000. "Age Period Cohort Characteristic Models." *Social Science Research* 29:123–39.

Osmond, C., and M. J. Gardner. 1982. "Age, Period, and Cohort Models Applied to Cancer Mortality Rates." *Statistics in Medicine* 1:245–59.

Raudenbush, S. W. 1993. "A Crossed Random Effects Model for Unbalanced Data with Applications in Cross-Sectional and Longitudinal Research." *Journal of Educational Statistics* 18:321–49.

Raudenbush, S. W., and A. S. Bryk. 2002. *Hierarchical Linear Models: Applications and Data Analysis Methods*. Thousand Oaks, CA: Sage.

Raudenbush, S. W., A. S. Bryk, and R. Congdon. 2004. *HLM6: Hierarchical Linear and Nonlinear Modeling*. Lincolnwood, IL: Scientific Software International.

Robertson, C., and P. Boyle. 1998. "Age-Period-Cohort Analysis of Chronic Disease Rates I: Modeling Approach." *Statistics in Medicine* 17:1305–23.

Robertson, C., S. Gandini, and P. Boyle. 1999. "Age-Period-Cohort Models: A Comparative Study of Available Methodologies." *Journal of Clinical Epidemiology* 52:569–83.

Ryder, N. B. 1965. "The Cohort as a Concept in the Study of Social Change." *American Sociological Review* 30:843–61.

Smith, H. L. 2004. "Cohort Analysis Redux." Pp. 111–19 in *Sociological Methodology*, vol. 34, edited by Ross M. Stolzenberg. Boston, MA: Blackwell Publishing.

Snijders, T., and R. Bosker. 1999. *Multilevel Analysis: An Introduction to Basic and Advanced Multilevel Modeling*. Thousand Oaks, CA: Sage.

Tarone, R., and K. C. Chu. 2000. "Age-Period-Cohort Analysis of Breast-, Ovarian-, Endometrial- and Cervical-cancer Mortality Rates for Caucasian Women in the USA." *Journal of Epidemiology and Biostatistics* 5:221–31.

———. 1992. "Implications of Birth Cohort Patterns in Interpreting Trends in Breast Cancer Rates." *Journal of National Cancer Institute* 1992:1402–10.

Wilmoth, J. R. 1990. "Variation in Vital Rates by Age, Period, and Cohort." Pp. 295–335 in *Sociological Methodology*, vol. 20, edited by Clifford C. Clogg. Washington, DC: Blackwell Publishing.

Wilson, J. A., and W. R. Gove. 1999a. "The Intercohort Decline in Verbal Ability: Does it Exist?" *American Sociological Review* 64:253–66.

———. 1999b. "The Age-Period-Cohort Conundrum and Verbal Ability: Empirical Relationships and Their Interpretation. Reply to Glenn and to Alwin and McCammon." *American Sociological Review* 64:287–302.

Yang, Y., W. J. Fu, and K. C. Land. 2004. "A Methodological Comparison of Age-Period-Cohort Models: The Intrinsic Estimator and Conventional Generalized Linear Models." Pp. 75–110 in *Sociological Methodology*, vol. 34, edited by Ross M. Stolzenberg. Boston: Blackwell Publishing.

NEW SPECIFICATIONS FOR EXPONENTIAL RANDOM GRAPH MODELS

Tom A. B. Snijders*
Philippa E. Pattison[†]
Garry L. Robins[†]
Mark S. Handcock[‡]

The most promising class of statistical models for expressing structural properties of social networks observed at one moment in time is the class of exponential random graph models (ERGMs), also known as p^* models. The strong point of these models is that they can represent a variety of structural tendencies, such as transitivity, that define complicated dependence patterns not easily modeled by more basic probability models. Recently, Markov chain Monte Carlo (MCMC) algorithms have been developed that produce approximate maximum likelihood estimators. Applying these models in their traditional specification to observed network data often has led to problems, however, which can be traced back to the fact that important parts of the parameter space correspond to nearly degenerate distributions, which may lead to convergence problems of estimation algorithms, and a poor fit to empirical data.

This paper proposes new specifications of exponential random graph models. These specifications represent structural properties

We thank Emmanuel Lazega for permission to use data collected by him. A portion of this paper was written in part while the first author was an honorary senior fellow at the University of Melbourne.

*University of Groningen
[†]University of Melbourne
[‡]University of Washington

99

such as transitivity and heterogeneity of degrees by more compli-
cated graph statistics than the traditional star and triangle counts.
Three kinds of statistics are proposed: geometrically weighted de-
gree distributions, alternating k-triangles, and alternating indepen-
dent two-paths. Examples are presented both of modeling graphs
and digraphs, in which the new specifications lead to much better
results than the earlier existing specifications of the ERGM. It is
concluded that the new specifications increase the range and appli-
cability of the ERGM as a tool for the statistical analysis of social
networks.

1. INTRODUCTION

Transitivity of relations—expressed for friendship by the adage "friends of my friends are my friends"—has resisted attempts to be expressed in network models in such a way as to be amenable for statistical inference. Davis (1970) found in an extensive empirical study on relations of positive interpersonal affect that transitivity is the outstanding feature that differentiates observed data from a pattern of random ties. Transitivity is expressed by triad closure: if i and j are tied, and so are j and h, then closure of the triad i, j, h would mean that i and h are also tied. The preceding description is for nondirected relations, and it applies in modified form to directed relations. Davis found that triads in data on positive interpersonal affect tend to be transitively closed much more often than could be accounted for by chance, and that this occurs consistently over a large collection of data sets. Of course, in empirically observed social networks transitivity is usually far from perfect, so the tendency towards transitivity is stochastic rather than deterministic.

Davis's finding was based on comparing data with a nontransitive null model. More sophisticated methods along these lines were developed by Holland and Leinhardt (1976), but they remained restricted to the testing of structural characteristics such as transitivity against null models expressing randomness or, in the case of directed graphs, expressing only the tendency toward reciprocation of ties. A next step in modeling is to formulate a stochastic model for networks that expresses transitivity and could be used for statistical analysis of data. Such models have to include one or more parameters indicating the strength of transitivity, and these parameters have to be estimated and tested, controlling for other effects—such as covariate and node-level effects. Then, of course, it would be interesting to model other network effects in addition to transitivity.

The importance of controlling for node-level effects, such as actor attributes, arises because there are several distinct localized social processes that may give rise to transitivity. In the first, social ties may "self-organize" to produce triangular structures, as indicated by the process noted above, that the friends of my friends are likely to become my friends (i.e., a structural balance effect). In other words, the presence of certain ties may induce other ties to form, in this case with the triangulation occurring explicitly as the result of a social process involving three people. Alternatively, certain actors may be very popular, and hence attract ties, including from other popular actors. This process may result in a core-periphery network structure with popular actors in the core. Many triangles are likely to occur in the core as an outcome of tie formation based on popularity. Both of these triangulation effects are structural in outcome, but one represents an explicit social transitivity process whereas the other is the outcome of a popularity process. In the second case, the number of triangles could be accounted for on the basis of the distribution of the actors' degrees without referring to transitivity. In a separate third possibility, however, ties may arise because actors select partners based on attribute homophily, as reviewed in McPherson, Smith-Lovin, and Cook (2001), or some other process of social selection, in which case triangles of similar actors may be a by-product of homophilous dyadic selection processes. An often important question is whether, once accounting for homophily, there are still structural processes present. This would indicate the presence of organizing principles within the network that go beyond dyadic selection. In that case, can we determine whether this self-organization is based within triads, or whether triangulation is the outcome of some other organizing principle? Given the diversity of processes that may lead to transitivity, the complexity of statistical models for transitivity is not surprising.

It can be concluded that transitivity is widely observed in networks. For a full understanding of the processes that give rise to and sustain the network, it is crucial to model transitivity adequately, particularly in the presence of—and controlling for—attributes. In a wide-ranging review, Newman (2003) deplores the inadequacy of existing general network models in this regard. When the requirement is made that the model is tractable for the statistical analysis of empirical data, exponential random graph (or p^*) models offer the most promising framework within which such models can be developed. These models are described in the next section; it will be explained, however, that current specifications of these models often do not provide adequate accounts of empirical data. It is the aim of this paper to present some new specifications for exponential random graph models that considerably extend our capacity to model observed social networks.

1.1. *Exponential Random Graph Models*

The following terms and notation will be used. A *graph* is the mathematical representation of a relation, or a binary network. The number of nodes in the graph is denoted by n. The random variable Y_{ij} indicates whether there exists a tie between nodes i and j ($Y_{ij} = 1$) or not ($Y_{ij} = 0$). We use the convention that there are no self-ties—i.e., $Y_{ii} = 0$ for all i. A random graph is represented by its adjacency matrix Y with elements Y_{ij}. Graphs are by default nondirected (i.e., $Y_{ij} = Y_{ji}$ holds for all i, j), but much attention is given also to directed relations, represented by directed graphs, for which Y_{ij} indicates the existence of a tie *from i to j*, and where Y_{ij} is allowed to differ from Y_{ji}. Denote the set of all adjacency matrices by $\mathcal{Y}$. The notational convention is followed where random variables are denoted by capitals and their outcomes by small letters. We do not consider nonbinary ties here, although they may be considered within this framework (e.g., Snijders and Kenny 1999; Hoff 2003).

A stochastic model expressing transitivity was proposed by Frank and Strauss (1986). According to their definition, a probability distribution for a graph is a Markov graph if the number of nodes is fixed at n and possible edges between disjoint pairs of nodes are independent conditional on the rest of the graph. This can be formulated less compactly, for the case of a nondirected graph: if i, j, u, v are four distinct nodes, the Markov property requires that Y_{ij} and Y_{uv} are independent, conditional on all other variables Y_{ts}. This is an appealing but quite restrictive definition, generalizing the idea of Markovian dependence for random processes with a linearly ordered time parameter and for spatial processes on a lattice (Besag 1974). The basic idea is that two possible social ties are dependent only if a common actor is involved in both. In Section 3.2 we shall discuss the limitations of this dependence assumption in modeling observed social structures.

Frank and Strauss (1986) obtained an important characterization of Markov graphs. They used the assumption of permutation invariance, stating that the distribution remains the same when the nodes are relabeled. Making this assumption and using the Hammersley-Clifford theorem (Besag 1974), they proved that a random graph is a Markov graph if and only if the probability distribution can be written as

$$P_\theta\{Y = y\} = \exp\left(\sum_{k=1}^{n-1} \theta_k \, S_k(y) + \tau \, T(y) - \psi(\theta, \tau)\right) \quad y \in \mathcal{Y} \quad (1)$$

where the statistics S_k and T are defined by

$$
\begin{aligned}
S_1(y) &= \sum_{1 \le i < j \le n} y_{ij} && \text{number of edges} \\
S_k(y) &= \sum_{1 \le i \le n} \binom{y_{i+}}{k} && \text{number of } k\text{-stars } (k \ge 2) \quad (2) \\
T(y) &= \sum_{1 \le i < j < h \le n} y_{ij} \, y_{ih} \, y_{jh} && \text{number of triangles,}
\end{aligned}
$$

the Greek letters θ_k and τ indicate parameters of the distribution, and $\psi(\theta, \tau)$ is a normalizing constant ensuring that the probabilities sum to 1. Replacing an index by the + sign denotes summation over the index, so y_{i+} is the degree of node i. A configuration $(i, j_1, \ldots, j_k)$ is called a k-star if i is tied to each of j_1, j_2, up to j_k. For all k, the number of k-stars in which node i is involved, is given by $\binom{y_{i+}}{k}$. An edge is a one-star, so $S_1(y)$ is also equal to the number of one-stars. Some of these configurations are illustrated in Figure 1.

It may be noted that this family of distributions contains for $\theta_2 = \ldots = \theta_{n-1} = \tau = 0$ the trivial case of the Bernoulli graph—i.e., the purely random graph in which all edges occur independently and have the same probability $e^{\theta_1}/(1 + e^{\theta_1})$.

Frank and Strauss (1986) elaborated mainly the three-parameter model where $\theta_3 = \ldots = \theta_{n-1} = 0$, for which the probability distribution depends on the number of edges, the number of two-stars, and the number of transitive triads. They observed that parameter estimation for this model is difficult, and they presented a simulation-based method for the maximum likelihood estimation of any one of the three parameters in this model, given that the other two are fixed at 0, which is only of theoretical value. They also proposed the so-called pseudo-likelihood

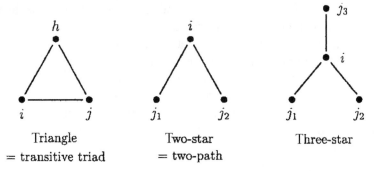

FIGURE 1. Some configurations for nondirected graphs.

estimation method for estimating the complete vector of parameters. This is based on maximizing the pseudo-loglikelihood defined by

$$\ell(\theta) = \sum_{i<j} \ln\left(P_\theta\left\{Y_{ij} = y_{ij} \mid Y_{uv} = y_{uv} \text{ for all } u < v, (u, v) \neq (i, j)\right\}\right).$$
(3)

This method can be carried out relatively easily, as the algorithm is formally equivalent to a logistic regression. However, the properties of pseudo-loglikelihood estimators have not been adequately established for social networks. In analogous situations in spatial statistics, the maximum pseudo-loglikelihood estimator has been observed to overestimate the dependence in situations where the dependence is strong and to perform adequately when the dependence is weak (Geyer and Thompson 1992). For most social networks the dependence is strong and the maximum pseudo-loglikelihood is suspect.

The paper by Frank and Strauss (1986) was seminal and led to many papers published in the 1990s. In the first place, Frank (1991) and Wasserman and Pattison (1996) proposed to use a model of this form, both for nondirected and for directed graphs, with arbitrary statistics $u(y)$ in the exponent. This yields the probability functions

$$P_\theta\{Y = y\} = \exp\left(\theta'u(y) - \psi(\theta)\right) \quad y \in \mathcal{Y}$$
(4)

where y is the adjacency matrix of a graph or digraph and $u(y)$ is any vector of statistics of the graph. Wasserman and Pattison called this family of distributions the p^* model. As this is an example of what statisticians call an exponential family of distributions (e.g., Lehmann 1983) with $u(Y)$ as the sufficient statistic, the family also is called an exponential random graph model (ERGM).

Various extensions of this model to valued and multivariate relations were published (among others, Pattison and Wasserman 1999; Robins, Pattison, and Wasserman 1999), focusing mainly on subgraph counts as the statistics included in $u(y)$, motivated by the Hammersley-Clifford theorem (Besag 1974). To estimate the parameters, the pseudo-likelihood method continued to be used, although it was acknowledged that the usual chi-squared likelihood ratio tests were not warranted here, and there remained uncertainty about the qualities and meaning of the pseudo-likelihood estimator. The concept of Markovian dependence as defined by Frank and Strauss was extended by Pattison and Robins (2002) to partial conditional independence, meaning that whether edges Y_{ij} and Y_{uv} are independent conditionally on the rest of the graph depends not only on whether they share nodes but also on the pattern of ties in the rest of the graph. This concept will be used later in this paper.

Recent developments in general statistical theory suggested Markov chain Monte Carlo (MCMC) procedures both for obtaining simulated draws from ERGMs, and for parameter estimation. MCMC algorithms for maximum likelihood (ML) estimation of the parameters in ERGMs were proposed by Snijders (2002) and Handcock (2003). This method uses a general property of maximum likelihood estimates in exponential families of distributions such as (4). That is to say, the ML estimate is the value $\hat{\theta}$ for which the expected value of the statistics $u(Y)$ is precisely equal to the observed value $u(y)$:

$$E_{\hat{\theta}} u(Y) = u(y). \tag{5}$$

In other words, the parameter estimates require the model to reproduce exactly the observed values of the sufficient statistics $u(y)$.

The MCMC simulation procedure, however, brought to light serious problems in the definition of the model given by (1) and (2). These were discussed by Snijders (2002), Handcock (2002a, 2002b, 2003), and Robins, Pattison, and Woolcock (2005), and they go back to a type of model degeneracy discussed in a more general sense by Strauss (1986). A probability distribution can be termed degenerate if it is concentrated on a small subset of the sample space, and for exponential families this term is used more generally for distributions defined by parameters on the boundary of the parameter space; near degeneracy here is defined by the distribution placing disproportionate probability on a small set of outcomes (Handcock 2003).

A simple instance of the basic problem with these models occurs as follows. If model (1) is specified with only an edge parameter θ_1 and a transitivity parameter τ, while θ_1 has a moderate and τ a sufficiently positive value, then the exponent in (1) is extremely large when y is the complete graph (where all edges are present—i.e., $y_{ij} = 1$ for all i, j) and much smaller for all other graphs that are not almost complete. This difference is so extreme that for positive values of τ—except for quite small positive values—and moderate values of θ_1, the probability is almost 1 that the density of the random graph Y is very close to 1. On the other hand, if τ is fixed at a positive value and the edge parameter θ_1 is decreased to a sufficient extent, a point will be reached where the probability mass moves dramatically from nearly complete graphs to predominantly low density graphs. This model has been studied asymptotically by Jonasson (1999) and Handcock (2002a). If τ is nonnegative, Jonasson shows that asymptotically the model produces only three types of distributions: (1) complete graphs, (2) Bernoulli graphs, and (3) mixture distributions with a probability p of complete graphs and a probability $1 - p$ of Bernoulli graphs. These distributions are not interesting in terms of transitivity. This near-degeneracy is related to the phase transitions known for the Ising and some other models (e.g., Besag 1974; Newman and Barkema 1999). The phase transition was studied for the triangle model by Häggström and Jonasson (1999) and Burda, Jurkiewicz, and Krzywicki (2004), and for the two-star model by Park and Newman (2004).

Some examples of more complex models are given in Sections 4 and 5 below. The phase transition occurs in such models as a near discontinuity of the expected value $E_\theta u(Y)$ as a function of θ—i.e., as the existence of a value of θ where a plot of coordinates $E_\theta u_k(Y)$ graphed as a function of the coordinate θ_k (or of other coordinates $\theta_{k'}$) shows a sudden and big increase, or jump (e.g., see, the Figure 16 a). Mathematically, the function still is continuous, but the derivative is extremely large. In many network data sets this increase of $E_\theta u_k(Y)$ jumps right over the observed value $u_k(y)$; and for the parameter value where the jump occurs—which has to be the parameter estimate satisfying the likelihood equation (5)—the probability distribution of $u_k(y)$ has a bimodal shape, reflecting that here the random graph distribution is a mixture of the low-density graphs produced to the left of the jump, and the almost complete graphs produced to its right. Hence, although the parameter estimate does reproduce the observation $u(y)$ as the fitted *expected* value, this expected value is far from the two modes of the fitted distribution. This fitted model does not give a satisfactory representation of the data. Illustrations are given in later sections.

One potential way out of these problems might be to condition on the total number of ties—i.e., to consider only graphs having the observed number of edges. However, Snijders (2002) showed that although conditioning on the total number of ties does sometimes lead to improved parameter estimation, the mentioned problems still occur in more subtle forms, and there still are many data sets for which satisfactory parameter estimates cannot be obtained.

A question, then, must be answered: To what extent does model (1) when applied to empirical data produce parameter estimates that are in, or too close to, the nearly degenerate area, resulting in the impossibility of obtaining satisfactory parameter estimates. A next question is whether a model such as (1) will provide a good fit. Our overall experience is that, although sometimes it is possible to attain parameter estimates that work well, even though they are close to the nearly degenerate area, there are many empirically observed graphs having a moderate or large degree of transitivity and a low to moderate density, which cannot be well represented by a model such as (1), either because no satisfactory parameter estimates can be obtained or because the fitted model does not give a satisfactory representation of the observed network. This model offers little medium ground between a very slight tendency toward transitivity and a distribution that is for all practical purposes concentrated on the complete graph or on more complex "crystalline" structures as demonstrated in Robins, Pattison, and Woolcock (2005).

The present paper aims to extend the scope of modeling social networks using ERGMs by representing transitivity not only by the number of transitive triads but in other ways that are in accordance with the concept of partial conditional independence of Pattison and Robins (2002). We have couched this introduction in terms of the important issue of transitivity, but the modeling of transitivity also requires attention to star parameters, or equivalently, aspects of the degree distribution. New representations for transitivity and the degree distribution in the case of nondirected graphs are presented in Section 3, preceded by a further explanation of simulation methods for the ERGM in Section 2.

After the technical details in Section 3, we present in Section 4 some new modeling possibilities made possible by these specifications, based on simulations, showing that these new specifications push back some of the problems of degeneracy discussed above. In Section 5 the new models are applied to data sets that hitherto have not been amenable to convergent parameter estimation for the ERGM. A similar development for directed relations is given in Section 6.

2. GIBBS SAMPLING AND CHANGE STATISTICS

Exponential random graph distributions can be simulated, and the parameters can be estimated, by MCMC methods as discussed by Snijders (2002) and Handcock (2003). This is implemented in the computer programs SIENA (Snijders et al. 2005) and statnet (Handcock et al. 2005). A straightforward way to generate random samples from such distributions is to use the Gibbs sampler (Geman and Geman 1983): cycle through the set of all random variables Y_{ij} $(i \neq j)$ and simulate each in turn according to the conditional distribution

$$P_\theta\{Y_{ij} = y_{ij} \mid Y_{uv} = y_{uv} \quad \text{for all } (u, v) \neq (i, j)\}. \tag{6}$$

Continuing this procedure a large number of times defines a Markov chain on the space of all adjacency matrices that converges to the desired distribution. Instead of cycling systematically through all elements of the adjacency matrix, another possibility is to select one pair (i, j) randomly under the condition $i \neq j$, and then generate a random value of Y_{ij} according to the conditional distribution (6); this procedure is called mixing (Tierney 1994). Instead of Gibbs steps for stochastically updating the values Y_{ij}, another possibility is to use Metropolis-Hastings steps. These and some other procedures are discussed in Snijders (2002).

For the exponential model (4), the conditional distributions (6) can be obtained as follows, as discussed by Frank (1991) and Wasserman and Pattison (1996). For a given adjacency matrix y, define by $\tilde{y}^{(1)}(i, j)$ and $\tilde{y}^{(0)}(i, j)$, respectively, the adjacency matrices obtained by defining the (i, j) element as $\tilde{y}_{ij}^{(1)}(i, j) = 1$ and $\tilde{y}_{ij}^{(0)}(i, j) = 0$ and leaving all other elements as they are in y, and define the *change statistic* with (i, j) element by

$$z_{ij} = u(\tilde{y}^{(1)}(i, j)) - u(\tilde{y}^{(0)}(i, j)). \tag{7}$$

The conditional distribution (6) is formally given by the logistic regression with the change statistics in the role of independent variables,

$$\text{logit}\left(P_\theta\left\{Y_{ij} = 1 \mid Y_{uv} = y_{uv} \text{ for all } (u, v) \neq (i, j)\right\}\right) = \theta' z_{ij}. \tag{8}$$

This is also the form used in the pseudo-likelihood estimation procedure, shown in (3).

The change statistic for a particular parameter has an interpretation that is helpful in understanding the implications of the model. When multiplied by the parameter value, it represents the change in log-odds for the presence of the tie due to the effect in question. For instance, in model (1), if an edge being present on (i, j) would thereby form three new triangles, then according to the model the log-odds of that tie being observed would increase by 3τ due to the transitivity effect.

The problems with the exponential random graph distribution discussed in the preceding section reside in the fact that for specifications of the statistic $u(y)$ containing the number of k-stars for $k \geq 2$ or the number of transitive triads, if these statistics have positive parameters, changing some value y_{ij} can lead to large increases in the change statistic for other variables y_{uv}. The change in y_{uv} suggested by these change statistics will even further increase values of other change statistics, and so on, leading to an avalanche of changes which ultimately leads to a complete graph from which the probability of escape is negligible—hence the near degeneracy. Note that this is not intrinsically an algorithmic issue—the algorithm merely reflects the full-conditional probability distributions of the model. The cause is that the underlying model places significant mass on complete (or near complete) graphs. A theoretical analysis of these issues is given by Handcock (2003).

This can be illustrated more specifically by the special case of the Markov model defined by (1) and (2) for nondirected graphs where only edge, two-star, and triangle parameters are present. The change statistic is

$$\begin{pmatrix} z_{1ij} \\ z_{2ij} \\ z_{3ij} \end{pmatrix} = \begin{pmatrix} 1 \\ \tilde{y}^{(0)}_{i+}(i, j) + \tilde{y}^{(0)}_{j+}(i, j) \\ L_{2ij} \end{pmatrix} = \begin{pmatrix} 1 \\ y_{i+} + y_{j+} - 2\,y_{ij} \\ L_{2ij} \end{pmatrix} \tag{9}$$

where $\tilde{y}^{(0)}(i, j)$ denotes, as above, the adjacency matrix obtained from y by letting $\tilde{y}_{ij}^{(0)}(i, j) = 0$ and leaving all other y_{uv} unaffected, and $\tilde{y}_{i+}^{(0)}(i, j)$ and $\tilde{y}_{j+}^{(0)}(i, j)$ are for this reduced graph the degrees of nodes i and j; while L_{2ij} is the number of two-paths connecting i and j,

$$L_{2ij} = \sum_{h \neq i, j} y_{ih} \, y_{hj}. \tag{10}$$

The corresponding parameters are θ_1, θ_2, and τ. The avalanche effect, occurring for positive values of the two-star parameter θ_2 and the transitivity parameter τ, can be understood as follows.

All the change statistics are elementwise nondecreasing functions of the adjacency matrix y. Therefore, given that θ_2 and τ are positive, increasing some element y_{ij} from 0 to 1 will increase many of the change statistics and thereby the logits (8). In successive simulation steps of the Gibbs sampling algorithm, an accidental increase of one element y_{ij} will therefore increase the odds that a next variable y_{uv} will also obtain the value 1, which in the next simulation steps will further increase many of the change statistics, etc., leading to the avalanche effect. Note that the maximum value of z_2 is $2(n - 2)$ and the maximum of z_3 is $(n - 2)$, both of which increase indefinitely as the number of nodes of the graph increases, and this large maximum value is one of the reasons for the problematic behavior of this model. It may be tempting to reduce this effect by choosing the edge parameter θ_1 strongly negative. However, this forces the model toward the empty graph. If the two forces are balanced, the combined effect is a mixture of (near) empty and (near) full graphs with a paucity of the intermediate graphs that are closer to realistic observations. If the Markov random graph model contains a balanced mixture of positive and negative star parameter values, this avalanche effect can be smaller or even absent. This property is exploited and elaborated in the following section.

3. PROPOSALS FOR NEW SPECIFICATIONS FOR STAR AND TRANSITIVITY EFFECTS

We begin this section by considering proposals that will model all k-star parameters as a function of a single parameter. Since the number of stars is a function of the degrees, this is equivalent to modeling the degree distribution. Suitable functions will ensure that the avalanche effect referred to in the previous section will not occur, or will at least be constrained. These steps can be taken within the framework of the Markov dependence assumption.

We then turn to transitivity, which is more important from a theoretical point of view but is treated after the models for k-stars and the degree distribution because of the greater complexity of the graph structures involved. The model for transitivity uses a new graph configuration that we term a k-triangle. We model k-triangles in similar ways to the stars, in that all k-triangle parameters are modeled as a function of a single parameter. But these new parameters are not encompassed by Markov dependence, and we need to relax the dependence assumption to partial conditional dependence. The discussion is principally for nondirected graphs; the case of directed graphs is presented more briefly in a later section.

3.1. *Geometrically Weighted Degrees and Related Functions*

Expression (1)–(2) shows that the exponent of a Markov graph model can contain an arbitrary linear function of the k-star counts S_k, $k = 1, \ldots, n - 1$. These counts S_k are given by binomial coefficients, which are independent polynomials of the node degrees y_{i+}, S_k being a polynomial of degree k. But it is known that every function of the numbers 1 through $n - 1$ can be expressed as a linear combination of polynomials of degrees $1, \ldots, n - 1$. Therefore, any function of the degree distribution (i.e., any function of the degrees that does not depend on the node labels) can be represented as a linear combination of the k-star counts $S_1, \ldots, S_{n-1}$. In other words, we have complete liberty to include any function of the degree distribution in the exponent of (4) and still remain within the family of Markov graphs.

Saturated models for the degree sequence were discussed by Snijders (1991) and by Snijders and van Duijn (2002). These models have the virtue of giving a perfect fit to the degree distribution and controlling perfectly for the degrees when estimating and testing other parameters, but at the expense of an exceedingly high number of parameters and the impossibility to do more with the degree distribution than describe it. Therefore we do not discuss these models here.

3.1.1. *Geometrically Weighted Degree Counts*

A specification that has been traditional since the original paper by Frank and Strauss (1986) is to use the *k*-star counts themselves. Such subgraph counts, however, if they have positive weights θ_k in the exponent in (4), are precisely among the villains responsible for the degeneracy that has been plaguing ERGMs, as noted above. One primary difficulty is that the model places high probability on graphs with large degrees. A natural solution is to use a statistic that places decreasing weights on the higher degrees.

An elegant way is to use degree counts with geometrically decreasing weights, as in the definition

$$u_\alpha^{(d)}(y) = \sum_{k=0}^{n-1} e^{-\alpha k} d_k(y) = \sum_{i=1}^{n} e^{-\alpha y_{i+}}, \tag{11}$$

where $d_k(y)$ is the number of nodes with degree k and $\alpha > 0$ is a parameter controlling the geometric rate of decrease in the weights. We refer to α as the *degree weighting parameter*. For large values of α, the contribution of the higher degree nodes is greatly decreased. As $\alpha \to 0$ the statistic places increasing weight on the high degree graphs. This model is clearly a subclass of the model (4) where the vector of statistics is $u(y) = d(y) \equiv (d_0(y), \ldots, d_{n-1}(y))$ but with a parametric constraint on the natural parameters,

$$\theta_k = e^{-\alpha k} \quad k = 1, \ldots, n - 1, \tag{12}$$

which may be called the *geometrically decreasing degree distribution assumption*. This model is hence a curved exponential family (Efron 1975). The statistic (11) will be called the geometrically weighted degrees with parameter α.

As the degree distribution is a one-to-one function of the number of *k*-stars, some additional insight can be gained by considering the equivalent model in terms of *k*-stars. Define

$$\begin{aligned} u_\lambda^{(s)}(y) &= S_2 - \frac{S_3}{\lambda} + \frac{S_4}{\lambda^2} - \cdots + (-1)^{n-2} \frac{S_{n-1}}{\lambda^{n-3}} \\ &= \sum_{k=2}^{n-1} (-1)^k \frac{S_k}{\lambda^{k-2}}. \end{aligned} \tag{13}$$

Here the weights have alternating signs, so that positive weights of some k-star counts are balanced by negative weights of other k-star counts. This implies that, when considering graphs with increasingly high degrees, the contribution from extra k-stars is kept in check by the contribution from extra $(k + 1)$-stars. Using expression (2) for the number of k-stars and the binomial theorem, we obtain that

$$u_\lambda^{(s)}(y) = \lambda^2 u_\alpha^{(d)}(y) + 2\lambda S_1 - n\lambda^2 \tag{14}$$

for $\lambda = e^\alpha/(e^\alpha - 1) \geq 1$; the parameters α and λ are decreasing functions of one another. This shows that the two statistics form the same model in the presence of an edges or 1-star term. This model is also a curved exponential family based on (1), and the constraints on the star parameters can be expressed in terms of the parameter λ as

$$\theta_k = -\theta_{k-1}/\lambda. \tag{15}$$

This equation is equivalent to the geometrically decreasing degree distribution assumption and can, alternatively, be called the *geometric alternating k-star assumption*. Statistic (13) will be called an alternating k-star with parameter λ.

As $\alpha \to \infty$, it follows that $\lambda \to 1$, and (11) approaches

$$u_\infty^{(d)}(y) = d_0(y). \tag{16}$$

Thus the boundary case $\alpha = \infty(\lambda = 1)$ implies that the number of isolated nodes is modeled distinctly from other terms in the model. This can be meaningful for two reasons. First, social processes leading to the isolation of some actors in a group may be quite different from the social processes that determine which ties the nonisolated actors have. Second, it is not uncommon that isolated actors are perceived as not being part of the network and are therefore left out of the data analysis. This is usually unfortunate practice. From a dynamic perspective, isolated actors may become connected and other actors may become isolated. To exclude isolated actors in a single network study is to make the implausible presupposition that such effects are not present.

The change statistic associated to statistic (11) is

$$z_{ij} = -\left(1 - e^{-\alpha}\right)\left(e^{-\alpha \tilde{y}_{i+}} + e^{-\alpha \tilde{y}_{j+}}\right) \tag{17}$$

where $\tilde{y} = \tilde{y}^{(0)}(i, j)$ is the reduced graph as defined above. This change statistic is an elementwise nondecreasing function of the adjacency matrix, but the change becomes smaller as the degrees $\tilde{y}_{i+}$ become larger, and for $\alpha > 0$ the change statistic is negative and bounded below by $2(e^{-\alpha} - 1)$. Thus, according to the criterion in Handcock (2003), a full-conditional MCMC for this model will mix close to uniformly. This should help protect such models from the inferential degeneracy that has hindered unconstrained models.

As discussed above, the change statistic aids interpretation. If the parameter value is positive, then we see that the conditional log-odds of a tie on (i, j) is greater among high-degree actors. In a loose sense, this expresses a version of preferential attachment (Albert and Barabási 2002) with ties from low degree to high degree actors being more probable than ties among low degree actors. However, preference for high degree actors is not linear in degree: the marginal gain in log-odds for connections to increasingly higher degree partners is geometrically decreasing with degree.

For instance, if $\alpha = \ln(2)$ (i.e., $\lambda = 2$) in equation (17), for a fixed degree of i, a connection to a partner j_1 who has two other partners is more probable than a connection to j_2 with only one other partner, the difference in the change statistics being 0.25. But if j_1 and j_2 have degrees 5 and 6 respectively (from their ties to others than i), the difference in the change statistics is less than 0.02. So, nodes with degree 5 and higher are treated almost equivalently. Given these two effects – a preference for connection to high degree nodes, and little differentiation among high degree nodes beyond a certain point, we expect to see two differences in outcomes from models with this specification compared to Bernoulli graphs with the same value for θ_1: a tendency for somewhat higher degree nodes, and a tendency for a core-periphery structure.

3.1.2. *Other Functions of Degrees*

Other functions of the node degrees could also be considered. It has been argued recently (for an overview, see Albert and Barabási 2002) that for many phenomena degree frequencies tend to 0 more slowly than exponential functions—for example, as a negative power of the degrees. This suggests sums of reciprocals of degrees, or higher negative powers of degrees, instead of exponential functions such as (14). An alternative specification of a slowly decreasing function that exploits the fact that factorials are recurrent in the combinatorial properties of graphs and that is in line with recent applications of the Yule distribution to degree distributions (see Handcock and Jones 2004), is a sum of ascending factorials of degrees,

$$u(y) = \sum_{i=1}^{n} \frac{1}{(y_{i+} + c)_r} \tag{18}$$

where $(d)_r$ for integers d is Pochhammer's symbol denoting the rising factorial,

$$(d)_r = d(d+1)\ldots(d+r-1),$$

and the parameters c and r are natural numbers $(1, 2, \ldots)$. The associated change statistic is

$$z_{ij}(y) = \frac{-r}{(\tilde{y}_{i+} + c)_{r+1}} + \frac{-r}{(\tilde{y}_{+j} + c)_{r+1}}. \tag{19}$$

The choice between this statistic and (13), and the choice of the parameters α or λ, c, and r, will depend on considerations of fit to the observed network. Since these statistics are linearly independent for different parameter values, several of them could in principle be included in the model simultaneously (although this will sometimes lead to collinearity-type problems and change the interpretation of the parameters).

3.2. Modeling Transitivity by Alternating k-Triangles

The issues of degeneracy discussed above suggest that in many empirical circumstances the Markov random graph model of Frank and Strauss (1986) is too restrictive. Our experience in fitting data suggests that problems particularly occur with Markov models when the observed network includes not just triangles but larger "clique-like" structures that are not complete but do contain many triangles. Each of the three processes discussed in the introduction are likely to result in networks with such denser "clumps." These are indeed the subject of much attention in network analysis (cohesive subset techniques), and the transitivity parameter in Markov models (and perhaps the transitivity concept more generally) can be regarded as the simplest way to examine such clique-like sections of the network because the triangle is the simplest clique that is not just a tie. But the linearity of the triangle count within the exponential is a source of the near-degeneracy problem in Markov models, when observed incomplete cliques are somewhat large and hence contain many triangles. What is needed to capture these "clique-ish" structures is a transitivity-like concept that expresses triangulation also within subsets of nodes larger than three, and with a statistic that is not linear in the triangle count but gives smaller probabilities to large cliquelike structures. Such a concept is proposed in this section.

From the problems associated with degeneracy, given the equivalence between the Markov conditional independence assumption and model (1), we draw two conclusions: (1) edges that do not share a tie may still be conditionally dependent (i.e., the Markov dependence assumption may be too restrictive); (2) the representation of the social phenomenon of transitivity by the total number of triangles is often too simplistic, because the conditional log-odds of a tie between two social actors often will not be simply a linear function of the total number of transitive triangles to which this tie would contribute.

A more general type of dependence is the *partial conditional independence* introduced by Pattison and Robins (2002), a definition that takes into account not only *which nodes* are being potentially tied, but also *the other ties that exist* in the graph—i.e., the dependence model is realization-dependent. We propose a model that satisfies the more general independence concept denoted here as [CD] for "Conditional Dependence."

Assumption [CD]: Two edge indicators Y_{iv} and Y_{uj} are conditionally dependent, given the rest of the graph, only if one of the two following conditions is satisfied:

1. They share a vertex—i.e., $\{i, v\} \cap \{u, j\} \neq \emptyset$ (the usual Markov condition).
2. $y_{iu} = y_{vj} = 1$, i.e., if the edges existed they would be part of a four-cycle (see Figure 2).

This assumption can be phrased equivalently in terms of *in*dependence: If neither of the two conditions is satisfied, then Y_{iv} and Y_{uj} are conditionally independent, given the rest of the graph.

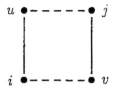

FIGURE 2. Partial conditional dependence when four-cycle is created.

One substantive interpretation of the partial conditional dependence assumption (2) is that the possibility of a four-cycle establishes the structural basis for a "social setting" among four individuals (Pattison and Robins 2002), and that the probability of a dyadic tie between two nodes (here, i and v) is affected not just by the other ties of these nodes but also by other ties within such a social setting, even if they do not directly involve i and v. A four-cycle assumption is a natural extension of modeling based on triangles (three-cycles) and was first used by Lazega and Pattison (1999) in an examination of whether such larger cycles could be observed in an empirical setting to a greater extent than could be accounted for by parameters for configurations involving at most three nodes.

We now seek subgraph counts that can be included among the sufficient statistics $u(y)$ in (4), expressing types of transitivity—therefore including triangles—and leading to graph distributions conforming to assumption [CD]. Under the Markov assumption (1), Y_{iv} is conditionally dependent on each of Y_{iu}, Y_{ij}, and Y_{jv}, because these edge indicators share a node. If $y_{iu} = y_{jv} = 1$, the precondition in the four-cycle partial conditional dependence (2), then Y_{iv} is conditionally dependent also on Y_{uj}, and hence (cf. Pattison and Robins 2002) the Hammersley-Clifford theorem implies that the exponential model (4) could contain the statistic defined as the count of such configurations. We term this configuration, given by

$$y_{iv} = y_{iu} = y_{ij} = y_{uj} = y_{jv} = 1,$$

a two-triangle (see Figure 3). It represents the edge $y_{ij} = 1$ as part of the triadic setting $y_{ij} = y_{iv} = y_{jv} = 1$ as well as the setting $y_{ij} = y_{iu} = y_{ju} = 1$.

Elaborating this approach, we propose a model that satisfies assumption [CD] and is based on a generalization of triadic structures in the form of graph configurations that we term *k-triangles*. It should be

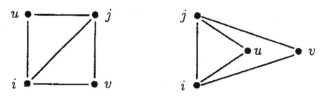

FIGURE 3. Two examples of a two-triangle.

noted that this model implies, but it is not implied by, assumption [CD]: It is a further specification.

For a nondirected graph, a k-triangle with base (i, j) is defined by the presence of a base edge $i - j$ together with the presence of at least k other nodes adjacent to both i and j. We denote a "side" of a k-triangle as any edge that is not the base. The integer k is called the *order of the k-triangle*. Thus a k-triangle is a combination of k individual triangles, each sharing the same edge $i - j$, as shown in Figure 4. The concept of a k-triangle can be seen as a triadic analogue of a k-star. If k_{max} denotes the highest value of k for which there is a k-triangle on a given base edge (i, j), then the larger k_{max}, the greater the extent to which i and j are adjacent to the same nodes, or alternatively to which i and j share network partners. Because the notion of k-triangles incorporates that of an ordinary triangle ($k = 1$), k-triangle statistics have the potential for a more granulated description of transitivity in social networks. It should be noted that there are inclusion relations between the k-triangles for different k. A three-triangle configuration, for instance, necessarily comprises three two-triangles, so the number of three-triangles cannot be less than thrice the number of two-triangles.

A summary of how dependence structures relate to conditional independence models is given by Robins and Pattison (2005). Here we use the characterization, obtained by Pattison and Robins (2002),

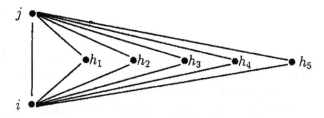

FIGURE 4. A k-triangle for $k = 5$, which is also called a five-triangle.

of the sufficient statistics $u(y)$ in (4) of partial conditionally independent graph models. In the model proposed below, the statistics $u(y)$ contain, in addition to those of the Markov model, parameters for all k-triangles. Such a model satisfies assumption [CD], which can be seen as follows. It was shown already above that this holds for two-triangles. Assuming appropriate graph realizations, [CD] implies that every possible edge in a three-triangle configuration can be conditionally dependent on every other possible edge through one or the other of the two-triangles, and hence as all possible edges are conditionally dependent, it follows from the characterization by Pattison and Robins (2002) that there is a parameter pertaining to the three-triangle in the model. Induction on k shows that the Markovian conditional dependence (1) with the four-cycle partial conditional dependence (2) implies that there can be a parameter in the model for each possible k-triangle configuration.

Our proposed model contains the k-triangle counts, but including these all as separate statistics in the exponent of (4) would lead to a large number of of statistical parameters. Therefore we propose a more parsimonious model specifying relations between their coefficients in this exponent, in much the same way as for alternating k-stars. The model expresses transitivity as the tendency toward a comparatively high number of triangles, without too many high-order k-triangles because this would lead to a (nearly) complete graph. Analogous to the alternating k-stars model, the k-triangle model described below implies a possibly substantial increase in probability for an edge to appear in the graph if it is involved in only one triangle, with further *but smaller* increases in probability as the number of triangles that would be created increases (i.e., as the edge would form k-triangles of higher and higher order). Thus, the increase in probability for creation of a k-triangle is a decreasing function of k. There is a substantively appealing interpretation: If a social tie is not present despite many shared social partners, then there is likely to be a serious impediment to that tie being formed at all (e.g., impediments such as limitations to degrees and to the number of nodes connected together in a very dense cluster, mutual antipathy, or geographic distance, depending on the empirical context). In that case, the addition of even more shared partners is not likely to increase the probability of the tie greatly.

This is expressed mathematically as follows. The number of k-triangles is given by the formula

$$T_k = \sharp\{(\{i, j\}, \{h_1, h_2, \ldots, h_k\}) \mid \{i, j\} \subset V, \{h_1, h_2, \ldots, h_k\} \subset V,$$

$$y_{ij} = 1 \text{ and } y_{ih_\ell} = y_{h_\ell j} = 1 \text{ for } \ell = 1, \ldots, k\}$$

$$= \sum_{i<j} y_{ij}\binom{L_{2ij}}{k} \quad \text{(for } k \geq 2\text{)}, \tag{20a}$$

where L_{2ij}, defined in (10), is the number of two-paths connecting i and j. (Note that for nondirected graphs, two-paths and two-stars refer to the same configuration $y_{ih} = y_{hj} = 1$; the name "star" points attention to the middle vertex h, the name "path" to the end vertices i and j.) If there exists a tie $i - j$, the value $k = L_{2ij}$ is the maximal order k for which a k-triangle exists on the base (i, j). The formula for the number of triangles, which can be called 1-triangles, is different, due to the symmetry of these configurations:

$$T_1 = \frac{1}{3}\sum_{i<j} y_{ij} L_{2ij}. \tag{20b}$$

We propose a model where these k-triangle counts occur as sufficient statistics in (4), but with weights for the k-triangle counts T_k that have alternating signs and are geometrically decreasing, like those in the alternating k-stars. We start with the 1-triangles—in contrast to (13)—these being the standard type of triangles on which the others are based, with a weight of 3 aimed at obtaining a simple expression in terms of the numbers of shared partners L_{2ij}. This leads to the following statistic. Analogous to the geometrically weighted degree count, an equivalent expression is given using (20) and the binomial formula,

$$u_\lambda^{(t)}(y) = 3T_1 - \frac{T_2}{\lambda} + \frac{T_3}{\lambda^2} - \ldots + (-1)^{n-3}\frac{T_{n-2}}{\lambda^{n-3}}$$

$$= \sum_{i<j} y_{ij} \sum_{k=1}^{n-2}\left(\frac{-1}{\lambda}\right)^{k-1}\binom{L_{2ij}}{k} \tag{21a}$$

$$= \lambda \sum_{i<j} y_{ij}\left\{1 - \left(1 - \frac{1}{\lambda}\right)^{L_{2ij}}\right\}$$

$$= \lambda S_1 - \lambda \sum_{i<j} y_{ij}e^{-\alpha L_{2ij}}, \tag{21b}$$

where again $\lambda = e^\alpha/(e^\alpha - 1)$.

Expression (21a) shows that this is a linear function of the k-triangle counts, which is basic to the proof that this statistic satisfies assumption [CD]. As in the case of k-stars, the statistic imposes the constraint $\tau_k = -\tau_{k-1}/\lambda$ $(k \geq 3)$, where τ_k is the parameter pertaining to T_k. The alternating negative weights counteract the tendency to forming big cliquelike clusters that would be inherent in a model with only positive weights for k-triangle counts. Expression (21b) is (for $\alpha > 0$) an increasing function of the numbers L_{2ij} for which there is an edge $i - j$, but it increases very slowly as L_{2ij} gets large. This expresses that the tie $i - j$ has a higher probability accordingly as i and j have more shared partners, but this increase in probability is very small for higher numbers of shared partners.

We propose to use this statistic as a component in the exponential model (4) to express transitivity, with the purpose of providing a model that will be better able than the Markov graph model to represent empirically observed networks. In some cases, this statistic can be used alongside $T = T_1$ in the vector of sufficient statistics, in other cases only (21a) (or, perhaps, only T_1) will be used—depending on how the best fit to the empirical data is achieved and on the possibility of obtaining a nondegenerate model and satisfactory convergence of the estimation algorithm.

The associated change statistic is

$$
z_{ij} = \lambda \left\{ 1 - \left(1 - \frac{1}{\lambda} \right)^{\tilde{L}_{2ij}} \right\}
$$
$$
+ \sum_h \left\{ y_{ih} y_{jh} \left(1 - \frac{1}{\lambda} \right)^{\tilde{L}_{2ih}} + y_{hi} y_{hj} \left(1 - \frac{1}{\lambda} \right)^{\tilde{L}_{2hj}} \right\}, \quad (22)
$$

where $\tilde{L}_{2uv}$ is the number of two-paths connecting nodes u and v in the reduced graph $\tilde{y}$ (where $\tilde{y}_{ij}$ is forced to be 0) for the various nodes u and v.

The change statistic gives a more specific insight into the alternating k-triangle model. Suppose $\lambda = 2$ and the edge $i - j$ is at the base of a k-triangle and consider the first term in the expression above. Then, similarly to the alternating k-stars, the conditional log-odds of the edge being observed does not increase strongly as a function of k for values of k above 4 or 5 (unless perhaps the parameter value is rather large compared to other effects in the model). The model expresses the notion that it is the first one to three shared partners that principally influence transitive closure, with additional partners not substantially increasing the chances of the tie being formed. The second and third terms of the change statistic relate to situations where the tie completes a k-triangle as a side rather than as the base. For example, for the second term, the edge $i - h$ is the base and h is a partner shared with j; the change statistic decreases as a function of the number of two-paths from i to h. This might be interpreted as actor i, already sharing many partners with h, feeling little impetus to establish a new shared partnership with j who is also a partner to h.

As was the case for the alternating k-stars, this statistic is considered for $\lambda \geq 1$, and the downweighting of higher-order k-triangles is greater accordingly as λ is larger. Again, the boundary case $\lambda = 1$ has a special interpretation. For $\lambda = 1$ the statistic is equal to

$$u_1^{(t)}(y) = \sum_{i<j} y_{ij} I\{L_{2ij} \geq 1\}, \qquad (23)$$

the number of pairs (i, j) that are directly linked ($y_{ij} = 1$) but also indirectly linked ($y_{ih} = y_{hj} = 1$ for at least one other node h). In this case the change statistic is

$$z_{ij} = I\{\tilde{L}_{2ij} \geq 1\} + \sum_{h} \{y_{ih} y_{jh} I\{\tilde{L}_{2ih} = 0\} + y_{hi} y_{hj} I\{\tilde{L}_{2hj} = 0\}\}. \qquad (24)$$

3.3. *Alternating Independent Two-Paths*

It is tempting to interpret the effect of the alternating k-triangles as an effect for a tie to form on a base, emergent from the various two-paths that constitute the sides. But the change statistic makes clear that formation of alternating k-triangles involves not only the formation of new bases of k-triangles but also new sides of k-triangles, which should be interpreted as contributing to prerequisites for transitive closure rather than as establishing transitive closure. In order to differentiate between these two interpretations, it is necessary to control for the prerequisites for transitive closure—i.e., the number of configurations that would be

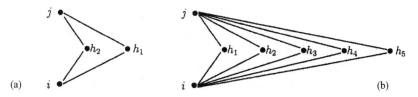

FIGURE 5. Two-independent two-paths (a) and five-independent two-paths (b).

the sides of k-triangles if there would exist a base edge. This means that we consider in addition the effect of connections by two-paths, irrespective of whether the base is present or not. This is precisely analogous in a Markov model to considering both preconditions for triangles— i.e., two-stars or two-paths—and actual triangles. For Markov models, the presence of the two-path effect permits the triangle parameter to be interpreted simply as transitivity rather than a combination of both transitivity and a chance agglomeration of many two-paths. Including the following configuration implies that the same interpretation is valid in our new model.

We introduced k-triangles as an outcome of a four-cycle dependence structure. A four-cycle is a combination of two two-paths. The sides of a k-triangle can be viewed as combinations of four-cycles. More simply, we construe them as independent (the graph-theoretical term for nonintersecting) two-paths connecting two nodes.

Thus, we define k-independent two-paths, illustrated in Figure 5, as configurations $(i, j, h_1, \ldots, h_k)$ where all nodes h_1 to h_k are adjacent to both i and j, irrespective of whether i and j are tied. Their number is expressed by the formula

$$U_k = \#\big(\{i, j\}, \{h_1, h_2, \ldots, h_k\}\big) \mid \{i, j\} \subset V, \{h_1, h_2, \ldots, h_k\} \subset V,$$
$$i \neq j, y_{ih_\ell} = y_{h_\ell j} = 1 \quad \text{for } \ell = 1, \ldots, k\}$$

$$= \sum_{i<j} \binom{L_{2ij}}{k} \qquad (\text{for } k \neq 2) \qquad (25a)$$

$$U_2 = \frac{1}{2} \sum_{i<j} \binom{L_{2ij}}{2} \qquad (\text{number of four-cycles}); \qquad (25b)$$

the specific expression for $k = 2$ is required because of the symmetries involved. The corresponding statistic, given as two equivalent expressions, of which the first one has alternating weights for the counts of independent two-paths while the second has geometrically decreasing weights for the counts of pairs with given numbers of shared partners, is

$$u_\lambda^P(y) = U_1 - \frac{2}{\lambda}U_2 + \sum_{k=3}^{n-2} \left(\frac{-1}{\lambda}\right)^{k-1} U_k \qquad (26a)$$

$$= \lambda \sum_{i<j} \left\{1 - \left(1 - \frac{1}{\lambda}\right)^{L_{2ij}}\right\},$$

$$= \lambda \binom{n}{2} - \sum_{i<j} e^{-\alpha L_{2ij}} \qquad (26b)$$

where, in analogy to the statistic for the k-triangles, the extra factor 2 is used for U_2 in (26a) in order for the binomial formula to yield the expression (26b). As before, $\lambda = e^\alpha/(e^\alpha - 1)$.

This is called the *alternating independent two-paths statistic*. The change statistic is

$$z_{ij} = \sum_{h \neq i,j} \left\{ y_{jh}\left(1 - \frac{1}{\lambda}\right)^{\tilde{L}_{2ih}} + y_{hi}\left(1 - \frac{1}{\lambda}\right)^{\tilde{L}_{2hj}} \right\}. \qquad (27)$$

As for the alternating k-star and k-triangle statistics, the alternating independent two-paths statistic can be generated by imposing the constraint $v_k = -v_{k-1}/\lambda$, where v_k is the parameter corresponding to U_k.

For $\lambda = 1$ the statistic reduces to

$$u_1^P(y) = \sum_{i<j} I\{L_{2ij} \geq 1\}, \qquad (28)$$

the number of pairs (i, j) that are indirectly connected by at least one two-path. This statistic is counterpart to statistic (23), the number of pairs both directly and indirectly linked. Taken together they assess effects for transitivity in precise analogy with triangles and two-stars for Markov graphs. Since two nodes i and j are at a geodesic distance of two if they are indirectly but not directly linked, the number of nodes at a geodesic distance two is equal to (28) minus (23). The change statistic for $\lambda = 1$ is

$$z_{ij} = \sum_{h \neq i,j} \{ y_{jh} I\{\tilde{L}_{2ih} = 0\} + y_{hi} I\{\tilde{L}_{2hj} = 0\}\}. \tag{29}$$

3.4. Summarizing the Proposed Statistics

Summarizing the preceding discussion, we propose to model transitivity in networks by exponential random graph models that could contain in the exponent $u(y)$ the following statistics:

1. The total number of edges $S_1(y)$, to reflect the density of the graph; this is superfluous if the analysis is conditional on the total number of edges—and this indeed is our advice.
2. The geometrically weighted degree distributions defined by (11), or equivalently the alternating k-stars (13), for a given suitable value of α or λ, to reflect the distribution of the degrees.
3. Next to, or instead of the alternating k-stars: the number of two-stars $S_2(y)$ or sums of reciprocals or ascending factorials (18); the choice between these degree-dependent statistics will be determined by the resulting fit to the data and the possibility of obtaining satisfactory parameter estimates.
4. The alternating k-triangles (21a) and the alternating independent two-paths (26a), again for a suitable value of λ (which should be the same for the k-triangles and the alternating independent two-paths but may differ from the value used for the alternating k-stars), to reflect transitivity and the preconditions for transitivity.
5. Next to, or instead of, the alternating k-triangles: the triad count $T(y) = T_1(y)$, if a satisfactory estimate can be obtained for the corresponding parameter, and if this yields a better fit as shown from the t-statistic for this parameter.

Of course, actor and dyadic covariate effects can also be added. The choice of suitable values of α and λ depends on the data set. Fitting this model to a few data sets, we had good experience with $\lambda = 2$ or 3 and the corresponding $\alpha = \ln (2)$ or $\ln (1.5)$. In some cases it may be useful to include the statistics for more than one value of λ—for example, $\lambda = 1$ (with the specific interpretations as discussed above) together with $\lambda = 3$. Instead of being determined by trial and error, the parameters λ (or α) can also be estimated from the data, as discussed in Hunter and Handcock (2005).

This specification of the ERGM satisfies the conditional dependence condition [CD]. This dependence extends the classical Markovian dependence in a meaningful way to a dependence within social settings. It should be noted, however, that this type of partial conditional dependence is satisfied by a much wider class of stochastic graph models than the transitivity-based models proposed here. Parsimony of modeling leads to restricting attention primarily to the statistics proposed here. Further modeling experience and theoretical elaboration will have to show to what extent it is desirable to continue modeling by including counts of other higher-order subgraphs, representing more complicated group structures.

4. NEW MODELING POSSIBILITIES WITH THESE SPECIFICATIONS

In this section, we present some results from simulation studies of these new model specifications. This section is far from a complete exploration of the parameter space. It only provides examples of the types of network structures that may emerge from the new specifications. More particularly, it illustrates how the new alternating k-triangle parameterization avoids certain problems with degeneracy that were noted above in regard to Markov random graph models.

We present results for distributions of nondirected graphs of 30 nodes. The simulation procedure is similar to that used in Robins et al. (2005). In summary, we simulate graph distributions using the Metropolis-Hastings algorithm from an arbitrary starting graph, choosing parameter values judiciously to illustrate certain points. Typically we have simulation runs of 50,000, with a burn-in of 10,000, although when MCMC diagnostics indicate that burn-in may not have been achieved we carry out a longer run, sometimes up to half a million iterations.

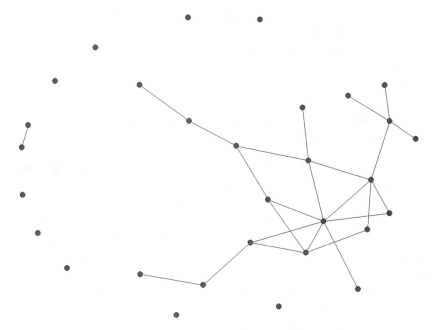

FIGURE 6. A graph from an alternating *k*-star distribution.

We sample every 100th graph from the simulation, examining graph statistics and geodesic and degree distributions.

4.1. *Geometrically Weighted Degree Distribution*

The graph in Figure 6 is from a distribution obtained by simulating with an edge parameter of -1.7 and a degree weighting parameter (for $\alpha = \ln (2) = 0.693$, corresponding to $\lambda = 2$) of 2.6. This is a low-density graph with 25 edges and a density of 0.06, and in terms of graph statistics is quite typical of graphs in the distribution. Even despite the low density, the graph shows elements of a core-periphery structure, with some relatively high degree nodes (one with degree 7), several isolated nodes, and some low degree nodes with connections into the higher degree "core." What particularly differentiates the graph from a comparable Bernoulli graph distribution with a mean of 25 edges is the number of stars, especially higher order stars. For instance, the number of four-stars in the graph is 3.5 standard deviations above that from the Bernoulli distribution. This is the result of a longer tail on the degree distribution, compensated by larger numbers of low degree nodes. (For instance, less than 2 percent of corresponding Bernoulli graphs have the combination expressed in this graph of 18 or more nodes isolated or of degree 1, and of at least one node with degree 6 or above.) Because of the core-periphery elements, the triangle count in the graph, albeit low, is still 3.7 standard deviations above the mean from the Bernoulli distribution. Monte Carlo maximum likelihood estimates using the procedure of Snijders (2002) as implemented in the SIENA program (Snijders et al. 2005) reassuringly reproduced the original parameter values, with an estimated edge parameter of −1.59 (standard error 0.35) and a significant estimated geometrically weighted degree parameter of 2.87 (S.E. 0.86).

It is useful to compare the geometrically weighted degree distribution, or alternatively alternating k-star graph distribution, of which the graph in Figure 6 is an example, against the Bernoulli distribution with the same expected number of edges. Figure 7 is a scatterplot comparing the number of edges against the alternating k-stars statistic for both distributions. The figure demonstrates a small but discernible difference between the two distributions in terms of the number of k-stars for a given number of edges. There is also a tendency here for greater dispersion of edges and alternating k-stars in the k-star distribution. As with our example graph, in the alternating k-star distributions there are more graphs with high degree nodes, as well as graphs with more low degree nodes.

Finally, in Figure 8, we illustrate the behavior of the model as the alternating k-star parameter increases. The figure plots the mean number of edges for models with an edge parameter of −4.3 and varying alternating k-star parameters, keeping $\lambda = 2$. Equation (13) implies that, as a graph becomes denser, the change statistic for alternating k-stars becomes closer to its constant maximum, so that high-density distributions are very similar to Bernoulli graphs. For an alternating k-star parameter of 1.0 or above, the properties of individual graphs generated within these distributions are difficult to differentiate from realizations of Bernoulli graphs. Even so, the distributions themselves (except those that are extremely dense) tend to exhibit much greater dispersion in graph statistics, including in the number of edges. An important point to note in Figure 8 is that there is a relatively smooth transition from low-density to high-density graphs as the parameter increases,

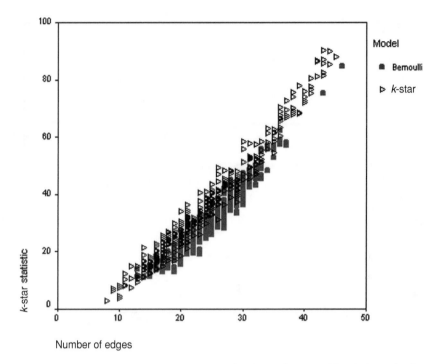

FIGURE 7. Scatterplot of edges against alternating *k*-stars for Bernoulli and alternating *k*-star graph distributions.

without the almost discontinuous jumps that betoken degeneracy and are often exhibited in Markov random graph models with positive star parameters.

4.2. *Alternating k-Triangles*

The degeneracy issue for transitivity models and the advance presented by the alternating *k*-triangle specification are illustrated in Figure 9. This figure depicts the mean number of edges for three transitivity models for various values of a transitivity-related parameter. Each of these models contains a fixed edge parameter, set at –3.0, plus certain other parameters.

The first model (labeled "triangle without star parameters" in the figure) is a Markov model with simply the edge parameter and a triangle parameter. For low values of the triangle parameter, only very

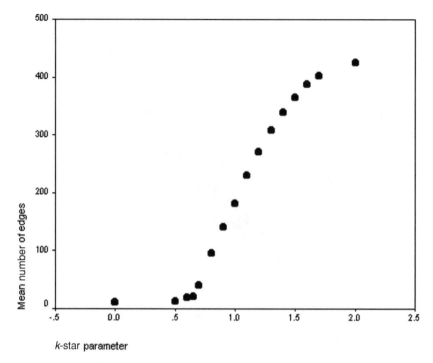

FIGURE 8. Mean number of edges in alternating k-star distributions with different values of the alternating k-star parameter.

low-density graphs are observed; for high values only complete graphs are observed. There is a small region, with a triangle parameter between 0.8 and 0.9, where either a low-density or a complete graph may be the outcome of a particular simulation. This bimodal graph distribution for certain triangle parameter values corresponds to the findings of Jonasson (1999) and Snijders (2002). Clearly, this simple two-parameter model is quite inadequate to model realistic social networks that exhibit transitivity effects.

The second model (labeled "triangle with negative star parameters" in Figure 9) is a Markov model with the inclusion of two- and three-star parameters as recommended by Robins et al. (2005), in particular a positive two-star parameter value (0.5) and a negative three-star parameter value (–0.2), and a triangle parameter with various values. The negative three-star parameter widens the nondegenerate region of the parameter space, by preventing the explosion of edges that leads

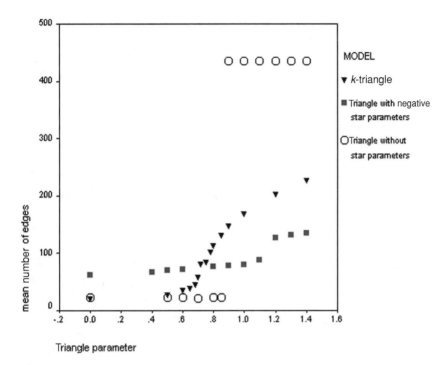

FIGURE 9. Mean number of edges in various graph distributions with different values of a triangle parameter.

to complete graphs. In this example, this works well until the triangle parameter reaches about 1.1. Below this value, the graph distributions are stochastic and of relatively low density, and they tend to have high clustering relative to the number of edges (in comparison to Bernoulli graph distributions). With a triangle parameter above 1.1, however, the graph distribution tends to be "frozen," not on the empty or full graph but on disconnected cliques akin to the caveman graphs of Watts (1999). This area of near degeneracy was observed by Robins et al. (2005).

The third model (labeled "ktriangle" in Figure 9), on the other hand, does not seem to suffer the discontinuous jump, nor the caveman area of near degeneracy, of the first and second models. It is a two-parameter model with an edge parameter and an alternating k-triangles parameter, and the expected density increases smoothly as a function of the latter parameter.

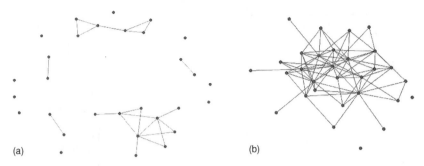

FIGURE 10. A low-density and a higher-density k-triangle graph.
Note: Edge parameter $= -3.7$ for both; alternating k-triangles parameter $= 1.0$ for (a) and 1.1 for (b).

Figure 10 contains two examples of graphs from alternating k-triangles distributions. The higher alternating k-triangles parameter shown in panel (b) of the figure results understandably in a denser graph, but the transitive effects are quite apparent from the diagrams. Both distributions have significantly more triangles than Bernoulli graphs with the same density. This is illustrated in Figure 11, which represents features of three graph distributions: the alternating k-triangles distribution of which Figure 10 (b) is a representative (edge parameter $= -3.7$; alternating k-triangle parameter $= 1.1$); the Bernoulli graph distribution with mean number of edges identical to this alternating k-triangle distribution (edge parameter $= -1.35$, resulting in a mean 89.5 edges); and a Markov random graph model with positive two-star, negative three-star, and positive triangle parameters, with parameter values chosen to produce the same mean number of edges (edge parameter $= -2.7$; two-star parameter $= 0.5$; three-star parameter $= -0.2$; triangle parameter $= 1.0$; mean number of edges $= 88.8$). We can see from the figure that for the same number of edges the alternating k-triangle distribution is clearly differentiated both from its comparable Bernoulli model as well as the Markov model in having higher numbers of triangles. The Markov model also tends to have more triangles than the Bernoulli model, reflecting its positive triangle parameter.

For an edge-plus-alternating-k-triangle model applied to the graph Figure 10 (a), SIENA produced Monte Carlo maximum likelihood estimates that converged satisfactorily and were consistent with the original parameter values: edge -3.74 (S.E. 0.30), alternating k-triangles 1.06 (S.E. 0.20).

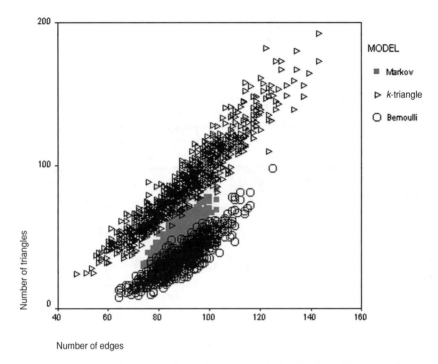

FIGURE 11. Number of triangles against number of edges for three different graph distributions.

Estimates for a Markov model with two-star, three-star, and triangle parameters do exist for this graph (as can be shown using results in Handcock 2003). However it is very difficult to obtain them using SIENA or statnet as the dense core of triangulation produced in graphs from this distribution take us into nearly degenerate regions of the parameter space of Markov models.

4.3. *Independent Two-Paths*

Some of the distinctive features of independent two-path distributions are as follows. A simple way to achieve many independent two-paths is to have cycles through two high-degree nodes. This is what we see in Figure 12, which is a graph from a distribution with edge parameter −3.7 and independent two-paths parameter 0.5. Compared to a Bernoulli graph distribution with the same mean number of edges, this

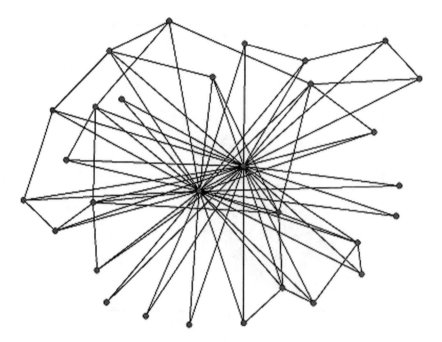

FIGURE 12. A graph from an independent two-path distribution.

graph distribution has substantially more stars, triangles, k-stars, k-triangles, and of course independent two-paths. The graph in Figure 12 is dramatically different from graphs generated under a Bernoulli distribution.

With increasing independent two-paths parameters, the resulting graphs tend to have two centralized nodes, but with more edges among the noncentral nodes. For lower (but positive) independent two-paths parameters, however, only one centralized node appears, resulting in a single starlike structure, with several isolates. We know of no set of Markov graph parameters that can produce such large starlike structures, without conditioning on degrees.

5. EXAMPLE: COLLABORATION BETWEEN LAZEGA'S LAWYERS

Several examples will be presented based on a data collection by Lazega, described extensively in Lazega (2001), on relations between lawyers in a New England law firm (also see Lazega and Pattison 1999). As a first example, the symmetrized collaboration relation was used between the 36 partners in the firm, where a tie is defined to be present if both partners indicate that they collaborate with the other. The average degree is 6.4, the density is 0.18, and degrees range from 0 to 13. Several actor covariates were considered: seniority (rank number of entry in the firm), gender, office (there were three offices in different cities), years in the firm, age, practice (litigation or corporate law), and law school attended (Yale, other Ivy League, or non–Ivy League).

The analysis was meant to determine how this collaboration relation could be explained on the basis of the three structural statistics introduced above (alternating combinations of two-stars, alternating k-stars, and alternating independent two-paths), the more traditional other structural statistics (counts of k-stars and triangles), and the covariates. For the covariates X with values x_i, two types of effect were considered as components of the statistic $u(y)$ in the exponent of the probability function. The first is the main effect, represented by the statistic

$$\sum_i x_i y_{i+}.$$

A positive parameter for this model component indicates that actors i high on X have a higher tendency to make ties to others, which will contribute to a positive correlation between X and the degrees. This main effect was considered for the numerical and dichotomous covariates. The second is the similarity effect. For numerical covariates such as age and seniority, this was represented by the statistic

$$\sum_{i,j} \text{sim}_{ij} y_{ij} \tag{30}$$

where the dyadic similarity variable sim_{ij} is defined as

$$\text{sim}_{ij} = 1 - \frac{|x_i - x_j|}{d_x^{\max}},$$

with $d_x^{\max} = \max_{i,j} |x_i - x_j|$ being the maximal difference on variable X. The similarity effect for the categorical covariates, office and law school, was represented similarly using for sim_{ij} the indicator function $I\{x_i = x_j\}$ defined as 1 if $x_i = x_j$ and 0 otherwise. A positive parameter for the similarity effect reflects that actors who are similar on X have a higher tendency to be collaborating, which will contribute to a positive network autocorrelation of X.

The estimations were carried out using the SIENA program (Snijders et al. 2005), version 2.1, implementing the Metropolis-Hastings algorithm for generating draws from the exponential random graph distribution, and the stochastic approximation algorithm described in Snijders (2002). Since this is a stochastic algorithm, as is any MCMC algorithm, the results will be slightly different, depending on the starting values of the estimates and the random number streams of the algorithm. Checks were made for the stability of the algorithm by making independent restarts, and these yielded practically the same outcomes. The program contains a convergence check (indicated in the program as "Phase 3"): after the estimates have been obtained, a large number of Metropolis-Hastings steps is made with these parameter values, and it is checked if the average of the statistics $u(Y)$ calculated for the generated graphs (with much thinning to obtain approximately independent draws) is indeed very close to the observed values of the statistics. Only results are reported for which this stochastic algorithm converged well, as reflected by t-statistics less than 0.1 in absolute value for the deviations between all components of the observed $u(y)$ and the average of the simulations, which are the estimated expected values $E_{\hat{\theta}}u(Y)$ (cf. (5) and also equation (34) in Snijders 2002).

The estimation kept the total number of ties fixed at the observed value, which implies that there is a not a separate parameter for this statistic. This conditioning on the observed number of ties is helpful for the convergence of the algorithm (for the example reported here, however, good convergence was obtained also without this conditioning). Effects were tested using the t-ratios defined as parameter estimate divided by standard error, and referring these to an approximating standard normal distribution as the null distribution. The effects are considered to be significant at approximately the level of $\alpha = 0.05$ when the absolute value of the t-ratio exceeds 2.

Some explorative model fits were carried out, and it turned out that of the covariates, the important effects are the main effects of seniority and practice, and the similarity effects of gender, office, and practice. In Model 1 of Table 1, estimation results are presented for a model that contains the three structural effects: (1) geometrically weighted degrees for $\alpha = \ln(1.5) = 0.405$ (corresponding to alternating combinations of

TABLE 1

MCMC Parameter Estimates for the Symmetrized Collaboration Relation Among Lazega's Lawyers

Parameter	Model 1		Model 2	
	Est.	S.E.	Est.	S.E.
Geometrically weighted degrees, $\alpha = \ln(1.5)$	−0.711	2.986	—	—
Alternating k-triangles, $\lambda = 3$	0.588	0.184	0.610	0.094
Alternating independent two-paths, $\lambda = 3$	−0.030	0.155	—	—
Number of pairs directly and indirectly connected	0.430	0.512	—	—
Number of pairs indirectly connected	−0.014	0.184	—	—
Seniority main effect	0.023	0.006	0.024	0.006
Practice (corporate law) main effect	0.383	0.111	0.373	0.109
Same practice	0.377	0.103	0.382	0.095
Same gender	0.336	0.124	0.354	0.116
Same office	0.569	0.105	0.567	0.103

two-stars for $\lambda = 3$), (2) alternating k-stars and (3) alternating independent two-paths, both for parameter $\lambda = 3$ and in addition, the last two of these effects for parameter $\lambda = 1$; as indicated above, the latter effects are equal to the number of pairs of nodes both directly and indirectly connected, and the number of pairs indirectly connected.

The results show that none of the structural effects except the alternating k-triangles has a t-ratio greater than 2. There is quite some collinearity between these effects. For example, the estimated correlation between the estimate for the alternating independent two-paths and that for the number of pairs indirectly connected is –0.94. All of the retained covariate effects have t-ratios larger than 2. With a backward selection procedure, nonsignificant effects were stepwise deleted from the model. The result is presented as Model 2 in Table 1. The only remaining structural effect is the alternating k-triangles effect ($\hat{\theta}_j = 0.610$, $t = 6.5$). This indicates that there is strong evidence for transitivity, as represented by the k-triangles effect, and not for any other structural effects except what is already represented by the covariates.

It appears that this model is successful in also representing other structural characteristics of this network, such as the numbers of two-, three-, and four-stars and the number of triangles. The observed number of triangles is 120, while simulations of the ERGM (carried out also using the SIENA program) show that the expected number of triangles under Model 2 is 128.5 with standard deviation 13.2. So the difference is less than 1 standard deviation. Fitting the model extended with the number of triangles did indeed lead to a nonsignificant effect for the number of triangles. The observed number of four-stars is 6091, and under Model 2 the expected number of four-stars is equal to 6635 and the standard deviation is 1042; so here also the difference between observed and expected value is less than 1 standard deviation. Thus, even though these statistics are not directly fitted, the representation of the network structure by the alternating k-triangles together with the covariate effects also gives an adequate representation of these graph statistics.

The estimates for the covariates are hardly different from those in Model 1. Note that these can be interpreted as estimates of the covariate effects on a log-odds scale, similar to effects in logistic regression models, except that they are controlled for the structural effects. This implies that exp $(\theta_j d)$ is the multiplicative effect that a difference d on variable j has on the estimated odds of a tie. Seniority ranges from 1 to 36, so the more senior partners collaborate more with others, the odds ratio for the greatest difference of 35 being exp $(0.024 \times 35) = 2.32$. Corporate lawyers have an odds of collaboration that is exp $(0.373) = 1.45$ higher than those doing litigation, and having the same specialty makes collaboration exp $(0.382) = 1.47$ more likely. The odds ratio related to having the same gender is exp $(0.354) = 1.42$, and that related to working in the same office is exp $(0.567) = 1.76$. All these odds ratios are controlled for the structural transitivity effect. Summarizing, there are especially large effects of seniority and of working in the same office, and slightly smaller but still large effects of doing corporate law, having the same specialty, and having the same gender; in addition, there is a strong transitivity effect.

The latter effect, represented by the alternating k-triangles, can be interpreted as evidence that there are organizing principles in this network that go beyond homophilous selection in creating triangles. The nonsignificance of the weighted degrees effect suggests that there are no other important effects distinguishing the partners in their level of collaborative activity beside the effects of seniority and specialty; and the significance of the k-triangle effect while controlling for the weighted degrees effect indicates that the transitivity is not the result of popularity selection effects alone. In this law firm, it seems that collaborative structures arise not just because of lawyers' personal backgrounds; nor do they arise because of popular collaborators attracting less popular followers; rather, next to the covariate effects, there is a distinct balance effect of self-organizing team formation, resulting in close-knit transitive structures. This conclusion is in line with the conclusions obtained in earlier analyses of this data set (see Lazega 2001), but the results are not directly comparable because analyses including effects of covariates as well as structural transitivity effects were not published before.

The good fit in the sense of good reproduction of a variety of other network statistics is not strongly dependent on the value of the parameter λ. Values $\lambda = 2, 4$, and 5 also yielded good results. The values $\lambda = 1$ and 6 were not satisfactory in this sense.

Model specifications containing the number of two-stars and of transitive triangles also yielded convergence of the estimation algorithm, but it did not succeed well in reproducing the observed number of pairs of nodes tied directly and indirectly; this implies that the number of pairs at a geodesic distance equal to two was not reproduced adequately. Thus, we can conclude that this example is a case where the traditional Markov random graph model for transitivity can be practically applied but that our new model specification yields a better fit to the data.

5.1. *Parameter Sensitivity in Various Models*

To illustrate the differences between the various model specifications and the difficulties of some specifications, we present some simulation results where a parameter is varied in fitted models. We contrast the specification based on the number of triangles to the one using the alternating k-triangles. In addition, we compare models with and without conditioning on the total number of edges.

A model similar to Model 2 in Table 1 was fitted to this data set, and then a long sequence of graphs was simulated by the MCMC procedure, starting with the empty graph, where all parameters except one kept their fixed value, and one designated parameter slowly increased from a low to a high value, and then decreased again to the low value, with 40,000 MCMC iteration steps for each value of this parameter. The designated parameter was the one representing transitivity, being the number of triangles, or the alternating k-triangles. The figures present the generated values of the associated statistic after the 40,000 iterations for each single parameter value.

Figure 13 gives the generated values for the model without conditioning on the number of edges (which for the number of triangles

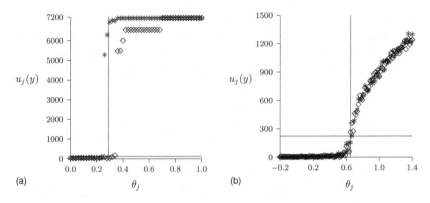

FIGURE 13.   Generated statistics $u_j(y)$ for unconditional models, as a function of triangle parameter (a) and alternating k-triangles parameter (b). (Symbol $\diamond$ indicates simulated values generated for increasing parameter values, $*$ those generated for decreasing values.)

did not lead to satisfactory convergence in the algorithm for parameter estimation but was used anyhow). A vertical line is plotted at the estimated parameter value, and a horizontal line at the observed value of the statistic. This implies that the curve of expected values should exactly go through the intersection of these two lines.

For the number of triangles, an almost discontinuous jump is observed, exactly at the intersection point that was the target for the estimation procedure. In Figure 13 (a), for the increasing parameter values, the jump up is made at a somewhat higher parameter value than the jump down for the decreasing parameter values. This path-dependence, or hysteresis, was also observed in Snijders (2002, p. 9), and it is well-known for Ising models (Newman and Barkema 1999), which show a similar kind of degeneracy. In a small interval of parameter values where this jump occurs, the distribution of the statistic (and of the graph density) has a bimodal shape. The suddenness of the jump, and the fact that the observed statistic is in the region of the jump, is associated with the large practical difficulties in fitting this model to realistic data.

For the alternating k-triangles in Figure 13 (b), a smoother sequence of values is obtained, but the slope is still quite large, especially near the parameter value of about 0.6 where the simulated values "take off" from their starting values close to 0. This is similar to what is shown for the expected values of the density in Figures 8 and 9.

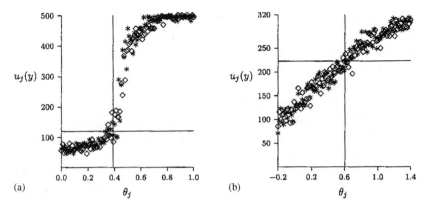

FIGURE 14. Generated statistics $u_j(y)$ for conditional models, as a function of triangle parameter (a) and alternating k-triangles parameter (b).
(Symbol $\diamond$ indicates values generated for increasing parameter values, $*$ those generated for decreasing values.)

Analogous simulated values, but for models conditioning on the observed number of edges, are given in Figure 14. Here we see in both cases a much smoother process. The hysteresis effect for the number of triangles is not observed any more, suggesting good mixing of the MCMC procedure, but this model still has quite a strong slope near the observed value of the statistic. In Figure 14 (b), which combines conditional estimation with the alternating k-triangles statistic, the generated values form a smooth pattern that confirms that estimation can proceed smoothly for this model. The figures together illustrate that both working with the newly proposed statistics rather than with the number of triangles and conditioning on the number of edges contribute to better possibilities for parameter estimation. Combining both elements yields especially good results.

6. DIRECTED RELATIONS

Directed relations are perhaps more frequent in social network research than nondirected relations. For directed relations, the requirement $Y_{ij} = Y_{ji}$ for the adjacency matrix is dropped, and the oriented nature of ties is reflected by using the term "arcs" rather than "edges." Except for the number of ties, all statistics discussed above have multiple analogues for the directed case, depending on the orientation of the ties. Rather than listing and discussing all the different analogues that can occur depending on the possible tie orientations for the statistics proposed above, we give in this section a brief list of what we think are the most important versions of these statistics for directed graphs. Since an elaborate discussion would mainly repeat much of what has been said above, we refrain from giving an extensive motivation. (It may be noted that in the formulas given above for the nondirected case, we have chosen the order of the subscripts indicating the nodes in such a way that many of the formulas are also valid for the directed case.)

For directed relations, we propose to use exponential random graph models with the following statistics for the structural part of the model.

1. The total number of arcs

$$\sum_{i \neq j} Y_{ij} \,;$$

   this is a superfluous element of the sufficient statistics if the analysis is done (as advised) conditional on the number of arcs.

2. The number of mutual dyads

$$\sum_{i < j} Y_{ij} Y_{ji}.$$

3. Geometrically weighted out-degrees

$$u_\alpha^{(od)}(y) = \sum_{k=0}^{n-1} e^{-\alpha k} d_k^{(out)}(y) = \sum_{i=1}^{n} e^{-\alpha y_{i+}}, \qquad (31)$$

   and geometrically weighted in-degrees

$$u_\alpha^{(id)}(y) = \sum_{k=0}^{n-1} e^{-\alpha k} d_k^{(in)}(y) = \sum_{i=1}^{n} e^{-\alpha y_{+i}}, \qquad (32)$$

   where $d_k^{(out)}(y)$ and $d_k^{(in)}(y)$, respectively, are the numbers of nodes with out-degrees or in-degrees equal to k. Similar to (14), these statistics can also be expressed as alternating out-k-star combinations and alternating in-k-star combinations.

4. Next to, or instead of, the alternating k-star combinations: the number of in-two-stars and the number of out-two-stars, reflecting the in-degree and out-degree variances.
5. The alternating transitive k-triangles defined by

$$\lambda \sum_{i,j} y_{ij} \left\{ 1 - \left(1 - \frac{1}{\lambda}\right)^{L_{2ij}} \right\} \tag{33}$$

and the alternating independent two-paths defined by

$$\lambda \sum_{i,j} \left\{ 1 - \left(1 - \frac{1}{\lambda}\right)^{L_{2ij}} \right\}, \tag{34}$$

where L_{2ij} is still the number of two-paths defined by (10); the orientations implied by these formulas are illustrated in Figure 15.
6. Next to, or instead of the alternating transitive k-triangles: the count of transitive triads

$$\sum_{i,j,h} Y_{ij} Y_{jh} Y_{ih}$$

and the number of two-paths, the latter reflecting the covariance between in-degrees and out-degrees.

The change statistic for the geometrically weighted out-degrees is

$$z_{ij} = -\left(1 - e^{-\alpha}\right) e^{-\alpha \tilde{y}_{i+}}. \tag{35}$$

The change statistic is still given for the alternating transitive k-triangles by (22), and for the alternating independent two-paths by (27).

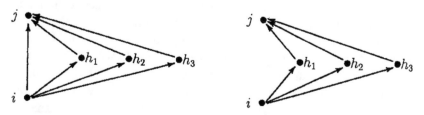

FIGURE 15. Transitive three-triangle (a) and three-independent two-paths (b).

6.1. *Example: Friendship Between Lazega's Lawyers*

As an example of modeling a directed relation, we use the friendship relation between the 36 partners in the law firm studied by Lazega (2001). This is a network with density 0.21 and average degree 7.4. In-degrees vary from 2 to 16, out-degrees from 0 to 21. The larger variability of the degrees and skewness of the distribution of the out-degrees indicates that here it may be more difficult to obtain a well-fitting model than in the preceding example. The same covariates are used as in the earlier example. For effects of actor-level covariates X on directed relations, instead of the main effect we distinguish between (1) the activity effect, represented in $u(y)$ by the statistic

$$\sum_i x_i y_{i+},$$

for which a positive parameter will tend to increase the correlation between the covariate and the out-degrees; and (2) the popularity effect, represented by

$$\sum_i x_i y_{+i},$$

which contributes to the correlation between the covariate and the in-degrees. The similarity effect connected to an actor-level covariate is defined as for the undirected case.

Preliminary analyses showed that the most important effects of covariates are the similarity effect of working in the same office, and the effects associated with seniority (rank number of entry in the firm) and practice (litigation versus corporate law). The same procedure for estimation was used as in the preceding example. A forward selection procedure using the effects listed above, with estimation conditional on the total number of ties, led to the results presented in Table 2. Model 1 contains, next to various covariate effects, the four structural effects proposed above. This appeared not to give a good fit with respect to the number of out-k-stars for $k = 2, 3, 4$. Therefore the model was extended with the the numbers of in-two-stars, out-two-stars, and two-paths. This means that the observed covariance matrix of the in- and out-degrees is fitted exactly. The results are presented in Table 2 as Model 2.

TABLE 2

MCMC Parameter Estimates for the Friendship Relation Between Lazega's Lawyers

Parameter	Model 1 Est.	Model 1 S.E.	Model 2 Est.	Model 2 S.E.
Mutual dyads	1.659	0.241	2.217	0.303
Out-two-stars	—	—	0.129	0.016
In-two-stars	—	—	0.147	0.026
Two-paths	—	—	−0.089	0.020
Geometrically weighted out-degrees, $\alpha = \ln(2)$	0.956	1.185	−1.364	1.361
Geometrically weighted in-degrees, $\alpha = \ln(2)$	−4.550	2.249	−8.367	3.893
Alternating transitive k-triangles, $\lambda = 2$	0.665	0.136	0.709	0.146
Alternating independent two-paths, $\lambda = 2$	−0.139	0.031	−0.068	0.036
Same office	0.570	0.121	0.839	0.180
Seniority popularity	−0.003	0.008	0.001	0.007
Seniority activity	0.013	0.007	0.010	0.006
Seniority similarity	0.038	0.008	0.041	0.008
Practice (corporate law) popularity	−0.049	0.159	0.066	0.122
Practice (corporate law) activity	0.320	0.134	0.205	0.104
Same practice	0.283	0.130	0.291	0.125

The estimation procedure for both models presented in this table converged well, but these results were obtained only after repeated runs of the estimation algorithm, always using the previously obtained results as the initial values for the new estimation. In this case, without conditioning on the total number of ties it was not possible to obtain convergence of the estimation algorithm. Model specifications including the total number of transitive triplets as a separate statistic did not lead to converging estimates. The strong correlations between the structural statistics lead to very strongly correlated parameter estimates, so that for a good reproduction of the model actually more decimal places for the parameter estimates are required than given in Table 2 (cf. Snijders 2002, p. 32). The parameter estimates for the geometrically weighted out-degrees and in-degrees, and the alternating independent two-paths effects differ strongly in Models 1 and 2, due to the inclusion in Model 2 of the out-two-stars, in-two-stars, and two-paths effects. There is a strong transitivity effect, represented by alternating transitive k-triangles with $\lambda = 2$ ($t = 0.709/0.146 = 4.8$ in Model 2). Further, there is evidence that—controlling for these structural effects—friendship is more likely between partners working in the same office, between those similar in seniority (this can be interpreted in part as a cohort effect), and those with the same practice. Those doing corporate law mention more friends than those doing litigation. The other covariate effects are not significant. Other effects, such as the number of transitive triplets and the numbers of three-stars and four-stars, also are represented adequately, each with a difference between observed and estimated expected value of less than 1.5 standard deviation.

A positive effect of alternating k-triangles in the presence of a negative independent two-paths effect suggests that the friendship network tends to be cliquelike, with possibly several different denser clusters of friends. Because the geometrically weighted in-degree parameters are negative, high in-degrees and high order in-stars are less likely in this network, unless of course they are implied by the transitive structure and therefore are involved in cliques of friends. So popular friends tend to be popular within clusters of dense friendships rather than between clusters.

Compared with the collaboration relation, modeling the friendship relation requires a much more complicated structural model. This network is an example where modeling transitivity by the number of transitive triplets by itself is not successful, whereas modeling transitivity by the alternating transitive k-triangles is successful and also does provide a good fit for the number of transitive triplets.

6.2. *Parameter Sensitivity in Two Models*

For this model also, the sensitivity of generated statistics to the parameter representing transitivity can yield insights in the possibility of modeling by using a particular model specification. Two models were considered, both with conditioning on the observed number of ties: the model in Table 2 and the corresponding model with the four new statistics replaced by the number of transitive triplets. For the latter model the parameter estimation did not converge satisfactorily, but the obtained parameter values were used anyway. Figure 16 gives simulated statistics for a continuous MCMC chain of graphs, where all parameter values were fixed at these estimated values, except for the number of transitive triplets (Figure 16 a) and the alternating k-triangles (Figure 16 b), which started at a very low value, increased in little steps to a very high value, and then decreased again to the low value. Again, 40,000 iteration steps

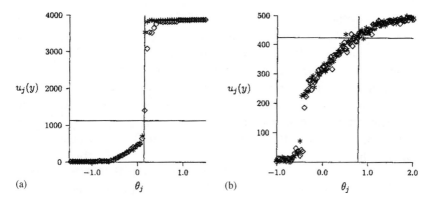

FIGURE 16. Generated statistics $u_j(y)$ for two models, as a function of a transitive triplets parameter (a) and an alternating k-triangles para-meter (b).
(Symbol ⋄ indicates values generated for increasing parameter values, ∗ those generated for decreasing values.)

of the MCMC algorithm were made for each parameter value and the resulting value of the statistic corresponding to the changing parameter is represented in the figure.

For the transitive triplets model, there is a very strong jump that occurs right at the observed value of the statistic, indicating the impossibility to adequately model this data set using this particular model—even when conditioning on the observed number of ties. A hysteresis effect can again be discerned (for iteration runs of more than 40,000, this would decrease and eventually disappear). For the alternating k-triangles model Figure 16 (b), there is a jump but it occurs in a region representing antitransitivity (at a negative parameter value of about −0.5), and does not invalidate the application of this model for this data set. The generated statistics for this model vary stochastically about a smooth function of this parameter in a wide region comprising the observed value of the statistic, which corresponds to the possibility to indeed obtain adequate parameter estimates for this specification.

7. DISCUSSION

The methodology based on exponential random graph models, also called p^* models, of which the principles were introduced and elaborated by (among others) Frank and Strauss (1986), Frank (1991), Wasserman and Pattison (1996), Pattison and Wasserman (1999), Robins, Pattison, and Wasserman (1999), Snijders (2002), and Handcock (2002b), and reviewed in Wasserman and Robins (2005), currently is the only statistical methodology for representing transitivity and other structural features in nonlongitudinal network data. Its use has been hampered by problems that now can be diagnosed—at least in part—as deficiencies in the specification of the sufficient statistics defining the exponential model. The traditional specification, where transitivity is represented by the number of transitive triangles or triplets as implied by the Markov assumption of Frank and Strauss (1986), does not allow a good representation of the quite strong but far from complete tendency to transitivity that is commonly observed in social networks. A symptom of these problems is the difficulty to find maximum likelihood estimates, but the near degeneracy and poor fit of the implied model is the more fundamental issue.

In this paper we have proposed a new specification of network statistics defining the exponential random graph model. The new statistics are geometrically weighted degrees to represent degree heterogeneity; alternating k-triangles to represent transitivity; and alternating independent two-paths to represent the preconditions for transitive configurations. Section 3.4 summarizes for nondirected graphs the resulting approach to model specification, and Section 6 gives the similar approach for directed graphs. The new statistics are defined in such a way that the model specification based on them does not imply, for moderately positive values of the parameter representing transitivity, the drive toward complete graphs that is inherent in the traditional specification. Therefore the new specification may be expected to avoid the large degeneracy problems associated with the traditional specification. This is related to the fact that the new specification does not satisfy the Markov conditional independence assumption of Frank and Strauss (1986), which often is too stringent. The new specification satisfies only a weaker type of partial conditional independence defined here as assumption [CD], a specification of dependence concepts discussed in Pattison and Robins (2002). However, the new statistics are not a panacea: in the new models phase changes occur less often but they are not completely excluded, as shown in the near discontinuity in Figure 16 (b). In this figure, however, the near discontinuity occurs at a negative value of the transitivity parameter, which in sociological applications is a relatively unimportant part of the parameter space. Our experience up to now, illustrated by examples presented above, suggests that the models defined by these statistics can be used to give a good representation of the transitivity and degree heterogeneity in many observed social networks, also for data sets in which modeling on the basis of the traditional specification, using only stars and the number of transitive triplets or triangles, was not feasible. Further work is in progress that confirms the wider modeling possibilities opened up by the new specifications. Obtaining maximum likelihood estimates under these specifications by MCMC algorithms is relatively uncomplicated for many data sets. The readily available computer programs SIENA (Snijders et al. 2005) and statnet (Handcock et al. 2005) can be used for this purpose.

The statistics proposed here may look rather contrived at first reading, but they are nevertheless a means to express that regions of incomplete cliquelike structures will occur in social networks, but that these cannot be expressed merely by noting that the network contains many triangles. The k-triangle parameters should therefore be interpreted somewhat differently from the traditional transitivity parameters based on only the triangle count; in our first example we argued that the estimates give evidence for the emergence of close-knit transitive structures that might be interpretable as self-organizing team formation. Such a "higher order" interpretation is not really available in models containing only Markov transitivity based completely on the prevalence of single triangles in the network. The greater difficulty in interpretation of the new statistics, as compared to the traditional specification, seems unavoidable to us, given the complexity of empirically observed social networks. Further experience with this model will be conducive to enhancing the interpretability of the parameters.

Other network statistics might also be possible to achieve these modeling possibilities. We do think that any statistics that achieve this will have some arbitrary elements, or seem contrived to some degree. This may have to do with the fact that network structure, as observed at one given moment, in most cases is the result of many different forces and mechanisms that operated in a period—often of long duration—before the observation of the network, precluding a simple representation of the dependencies within the network. One of the arguments supporting the statistics proposed here is that they lead to a model satisfying the comparatively simple conditional dependence assumption [CD].

The statistics contain parameters (α or λ) that are supposed to be fixed in the treatment given here, and they can be estimated in practice by trying out some reasonable values. In the examples discussed earlier, the sensitivity of the conclusions for the precise value of this parameter was small. However, it is preferable to estimate this parameter statistically. The methods to do this are presented in Hunter and Handcock (2005).

Depending on the observed data set, it is still possible that degeneracy problems occur even with these new specifications. More experience with these models, and the further development of new models, is required before a satisfactory and well-balanced methodology for the statistical modeling of networks will be attained. We think that the representation of social settings in particulars (Pattison and Robins 2002) will need more attention and will be possible by incorporating extra model elements. In some cases such extra model elements will be individual and dyadic covariates, or interactions of covariates with the structures proposed above, which is easy to carry out as it remains within the framework of the exponential random graph model. In other cases the model would have to be compounded with additional elements, such as latent structure models like the Euclidean models of Hoff, Raftery, and Handcock (2002), the ultrametric models of Schweinberger and Snijders (2003), or the model-based clustering version of Tantrum, Handcock, and Raftery (2005); in still other cases, in the exponential model one could include other complicated statistics in addition to those proposed here, along the lines of Pattison and Robins (2002).

REFERENCES

Albert, Réka, and Albert-László Barabási. 2002. "Statistical Mechanics of Complex Networks." *Review of Modern Physics* 74:47–97.

Besag, Julian. 1974. "Spatial Interaction and the Statistical Analysis of Lattice Systems." *Journal of the Royal Statistical Society*, Series B 36:192–225.

Boer, Peter, Mark Huisman, Tom A. B. Snijders, and Evelien P. H. Zeggelink. 2003. *StOCNET: An Open Software System for the Advanced Statistical Analysis of Social Networks. Version 1.4.* Groningen: ProGAMMA/ICS.

Burda, Zdzislaw, Jerzy Jurkiewicz, and André Krzywicki. 2004." Network Transitivity and Matrix Models." *Physical Review* E69, 026106.

Davis, James A. 1970. "Clustering and Hierarchy in Interpersonal Relations: Testing Two Theoretical Models on 742 Sociograms." *American Sociological Review* 35:843–52.

Davis, James A., and Samuel Leinhardt. 1972. "The Structure of Positive Interpersonal Relations in Small Groups." Pp. 218–51 in *Sociological Theories in Progress*, vol. 2., edited by Joseph Berger. Boston: Houghton-Mifflin.

Efron, Bradley. 1975. "Defining the Curvature of a Statistical Problem (with Applications to Second Order Efficiency)," *Annals of Statistics* 3:1189–242.

Frank, Ove. 1991. "Statistical Analysis of Change in Networks." *Statistica Neerlandica* 45:283–93.

Frank, Ove, and David Strauss. 1986. "Markov Graphs." *Journal of the American Statistical Association* 81:832–42.

Geman, Stuart, and Donald Geman. 1983. "Stochastic Relaxation, gibbs Distributions, and the Bayesian Restoration of Images." *IEEE Transaction on Pattern Analysis and Machine Intelligence* 6:721–41.

Geyer, Charles J., and Elizabeth A. Thompson. 1992. "Constrained Monte Carlo maximum likelihood calculations (with discussion)." *Journal of the Royal Statistical Society,* Series C, 54:657–99.

Häggström, Olle, and Johan Jonasson. 1999. "Phase Transition in the Random Triangle Model." *Journal of Applied Probability* 36:1101–15.

Handcock, Mark S. 2002a. "Specifying Models for Social Networks." Presented at Contact Networks and Transmission Dynamics of STDs, Centers for Disease Control and Prevention, National Center for HIV, STD, and TB Prevention Meeting, April 17–20, Washington, DC.

———. 2002b. "Statistical Models for Social Networks: Inference and Degeneracy." Pp. 229–40 in *Dynamic Social Network Modeling and Analysis: Workshop Summary and Papers*, edited by Ronald Breiger, Kathleen Carley, and Philippa E. Pattison. Washington, DC: National Academies Press/National Research Council of the National Academies.

———. 2003. "Assessing Degeneracy in Statistical Models of Social Networks." Working Paper No. 39, Center for Statistics and the Social Sciences, University of Washington, Seattle.

Handcock, Mark S., and James H. Jones. 2004. "Likelihood-Based Inference for Stochastic Models of Sexual Network Formation." *Theoretical Population Biology* 65:413–22.

Handcock, Mark S., David R. Hunter, Carter T. Butts, Steven M. Goodreau, and Martina Morris. 2005. statnet: *An R package for the Statistical Analysis and Simulation of Social Networks*. Manual, version 1.0. Center for Statistics and the Social Sciences, University of Washington, Seattle.

Hoff, Peter D. 2003. "Bilinear Mixed Effects Models for Dyadic Data." Working Paper No. 32, Center for Statistics and the Social Sciences, University of Washington, Seattle.

Hoff, Peter D., Adrian E. Raftery, and Mark S. Handcock. 2002. "Latent Space Approaches to Social Network Analysis." *Journal of the American Statistical Association* 97:1090–98.

Holland, Paul W., and Samuel Leinhardt. 1975. "Local Structure in Social Net-
works." Pp. 1–45 in *Sociololgical Methodology*, vol. 6, edited by David R. Heise,
Boston, MA: Blackwell Publishing.
Hunter, David R., and Mark S. Handcock. (Forthcoming). "Inference in Curved
Exponential Family Models for Networks." *Journal of Graphical and Computa-
tional Statistics.*
Jonasson, Johan. 1999. "The Random Triangle Model." *Journal of Applied Proba-
bility* 36:852–67.
Lazega, Emmanuel. 2001. *The Collegial Phenomenon: The Social Mechanisms of
Cooperation Among Peers in a Corporate Law Partnership.* Oxford, England:
Oxford University Press.
Lazega, Emmanuel, and Philippa E. Pattison. 1999. "Multiplexity, Generalized
Exchange and Cooperation in Organizations: A Case Study." *Social Networks*
21:67–90.
Lehmann, Erich L. 1983. *Theory of Point Estimation.* New York: Wiley.
McPherson, Miller, Lynn Smith-Lovin, and James M. Cook. 2001. "Birds of a
Feather: Homophily in Social Networks." *Annual Review of Sociology* 27:415–
44.
Newman, Mark E. J. 2003. "The Structure and Function of Complex Networks."
SIAM Review 45:167–256.
Newman, Mark E. J., and Gerard T. Barkema. 1999. *Monte Carlo Methods in
Statistical Physics.* Oxford, England: Clarendon Press.
Park, Juyong, and Mark E. J. Newman. 2004. "Solution of the 2-star Model of a
Network." *Condensed Matter Abstracts*, cond-mat/0405457.
Pattison, Philippa E., and Garry L. Robins. 2002. "Neighbourhood Based Models
for Social Networks." Pp. 301–37 in *Sociological Methodology*, vol. 22, edited
by Ross M. Stolzenberg. Boston, MA: Blackwell Publishing.
Pattison, Philippa E., and Stanley Wasserman. 1999. "Logit Models and Logistic
Regressions for Social Networks: II. Multivariate Relations." *British Journal of
Mathematical and Statistical Psychology* 52:169–93.
Robins, Garry L., Philippa E. Pattison, and Stanley Wasserman. 1999. "Logit Mod-
els and Logistic Regressions for Social Networks: III. Valued Relations." *Psy-
chometrika* 64:371–94.
Robins, Garry L., and Philippa E. Pattison. 2005. "Interdependencies and So-
cial Processes: Generalized Dependence Structures." Pp. 192–214 in *Models
and Methods in Social Network Analysis*, edited by Peter Carrington, John
Scott, and Stanley Wasserman. Cambridge, England: Cambridge University
Press.
Robins, Garry L., Philippa E. Pattison, and Jodie Woolcock. 2005. "Small and Other
Worlds: Global Network Structures from Local Processes." *American Journal of
Sociology* 110:894–936.
Schweinberger, Michael, and Tom A. B. Snijders. 2003. "Settings in Social Net-
works: A Measurement Model." Pp. 307–41 in *Sociological Methodology*, vol.
23, edited by Ross M. Stolzenberg. Boston, MA: Blackwell Publishing.
Snijders, Tom A. B. 1991. "Enumeration and Simulation Methods for 0-1 Matrices
with Given Marginals." *Psychometrika* 56:397–417.

————. 2002. "Markov Chain Monte Carlo Estimation of Exponential Random Graph Models." *Journal of Social Structure*, 3.2. Web journal available from http://www2.heinz.cmu.edu/project/INSNA/joss/index1.html.

Snijders, Tom A. B., Christian E. G. Steglich, Michael Schweinberger, and Mark Huisman. 2005. *Manual for SIENA version 2.1*. Groningen, Netherlands: ICS.

Snijders, Tom A. B., and David A. Kenny. 1999. "The Social Relations Model for Family Data: A Multilevel Approach." *Personal Relations* 6:471–86.

Snijders, Tom A. B., and Marijtje A. J. van Duijn. 2002. "Conditional Maximum Likelihood Estimation under Various Specifications of Exponential Random Graph Models." Pp. 117–34 in *Contributions to Social Network Analysis, Information Theory, and Other Topics in Statistics; A Festschrift in honour of Ove Frank*, edited by Jan Hagberg. Stockholm, Sweden: University of Stockholm, Department of Statistics.

Strauss, David. 1986. "On a General Class of Models for Interaction." *SIAM Review* 28:513–27.

Tantrum, Jeremy, Mark S. Handcock, and Adrian E. Raftery. 2005. "Model Based Clustering for Social Networks." Working Paper No. 46, Center for Statistics and the Social Sciences, University of Washington, Seattle.

Tierney, Luke. 1994. "Markov Chains for Exploring Posterior Distributions" (with discussion). *Annals of Statistics* 22:1701–62.

Wasserman, Stanley, and Philippa E. Pattison. 1996. "Logit Models and Logistic Regression for Social Networks: I. An Introduction to Markov Graphs and p^*." *Psychometrika* 61:401–25.

Wasserman, Stanley, and Garry L. Robins. 2005. "An Introduction to Random Graphs, Dependence Graphs, and p^*." Pp. 148–61 in *Models and Methods in Social Network Analysis*, edited by Peter Carrington, John Scott, and Stanley Wasserman. Cambridge, England: Cambridge University Press.

Watts, Duncan J. 1999. "Networks, Dynamics, and the Small-World Phenomenon." *American Journal of Sociology* 105:493–527.

FIXED-EFFECTS METHODS FOR THE ANALYSIS OF NONREPEATED EVENTS

Paul D. Allison*
Nicholas A. Christakis[†]

For repeated events, fixed-effects regression methods—which control for all stable covariates—can be implemented by doing Cox regression with stratification on individuals. For nonrepeated events, we consider the use of conditional logistic regression to estimate fixed-effects models with discrete-time data. Known in the epidemiological literature as the case-crossover design, this method fails when any covariate is a monotonic function of time. Hence, no control for time itself can be included, leading to potentially spurious estimates. As an alternative, we consider the case-time-control method for estimating the effect of a dichotomous predictor. This method allows for the introduction of a control for time by reversing the role of the dependent and independent variables. In contrast to earlier work, we show that the method can be applied to data that contain only uncensored cases, and that it is possible to control for additional covariates, both categorical and quantitative. Simulation studies indicate that the case-time-control method is substantially superior to the case-crossover method and to conventional logistic regression. The methods are illustrated by estimating the effect of a wife's death on the hazard of death for her husband.

Direct correspondence to Paul D. Allison at Sociology Department, University of Pennsylvania, 3718 Locust Walk, Philadelphia, PA 19104 (e-mail: allison@soc.upenn.edu).

*University of Pennsylvania
[†]Harvard University

155

1. INTRODUCTION

Fixed-effects methods have become increasingly popular in the analysis of longitudinal data for one compelling reason: They make it possible to control for *all* stable characteristics of the individual, even if those characteristics cannot be measured (Halaby 2004; Allison 2005). Using widely available software, fixed-effects methods can be applied to linear models (Greene 1990), logistic regression models (Chamberlain 1980), and Poisson regression models (Cameron and Trivedi 1998). For event-history analysis, a fixed-effects version of Cox regression (partial likelihood) is available for data with repeated events for each individual (Chamberlain 1985; Yamaguchi 1986; Allison 1996). But fixed-effects Cox regression is not feasible when no more than one event is observed for each individual.

In this paper, we explore fixed-effects methods for nonrepeated events using conditional logistic regression with discrete-time data. There are several peculiar features of nonrepeated event data that make a conventional fixed-effects approach problematic. As we shall see, none of the available methods works well for covariates that change monotonically with time (unless they are transformed into nonmonotonic functions). For covariates that are not monotonic with time, one approach works well when those covariates are uncorrelated with time but may be badly biased otherwise. Another method works well for covariates that are correlated with time, but only when the covariate is dichotomous, a situation that may still find many applications.

2. AN EXAMPLE

To make things concrete, we shall consider these issues in the context of an empirical example. Consider the following question: Does the death of a wife increase the hazard for the death of her husband? We have data on 49,990 married couples in which both spouses were alive and at least 68 years old on January 1, 1993.[1] Death dates for both spouses are

---

[1]To assemble a population-based sample of elderly couples, we linked Medicare claims data and other files at an individual level (using individual identifiers). We began with the 1993 Denominator File which includes 32,180,588 people 65 years of age or older. Based on Census data, we estimate that 13.2 million of these

available through May 30, 1994. During that 17-month interval, there were 5769 deaths of the husband and 1918 deaths of the wife.

Given data such as these, how can we answer our question? One straightforward approach is to do a Cox regression for husband's death with wife's vital status as a time-varying covariate. More specifically, let t_i be the husband's time of death for couple i, in days since the origin (January 1, 1993). If a death is not observed, then t_i is the censoring time (515 days). Let $W_i(t)$ be a time-varying covariate coded 1 if the wife is alive at time t and 0 otherwise. We postulate a proportional hazards model

$$\log h_i(t) = \alpha(t) + \beta W_i(t) + \delta X_i \qquad (1)$$

where $h_i(t)$ is the hazard for husband's death at time t for couple i, $\alpha(t)$ is an unspecified function of time, and X_i is a vector of time-invariant covariates for couple i. This model may be estimated with standard partial likelihood software.

Estimates for one such model are shown in the first two columns of Table 1. "Black" is a dummy variable coded 1 for black race, otherwise 0. "Age" is the age in years on January 1, 1993. "Illness burden" is a scale based on medical records for the three years prior to the start of observation, with observed values ranging from 0 to 15. We see that the hazard of death for blacks is approximately 7 percent higher than for other races, but the effect is not statistically significant. On the other

people were in marriages where both spouses were 65 or older. From this file, we identified husband/wife pairs using a method described by Iwashyna et al. (1998, 2000). The method exploits Medicare's complex system of identification codes to find spousal pairs, and it has a sensitivity of up to 80 percent. While representing a majority of married people, these couples are somewhat more likely to be those in which the husband had been employed and the wife had either never earned money or earned less than her husband. However, in the current generation of elderly, this is the modal pattern. The application of this method resulted in the identification of 4,313,221 couples, 65 percent of the total population. Of this group, 3,247,729 are couples in which both members were older than 68. Out of this group, we took a simple random sample of 50,000. We subsequently deleted ten cases due to data inconsistencies, leaving 49,990 for analysis. For these couples, we have detailed hospitalization information for three years prior to 1993 and mortality and hospitalization information for both members of each couple until mid-1994. Using established methods of quantifying illness burden, we assigned each individual a morbidity burden based on their medical records for the three years preceding cohort inception (Zhang et al. 1999).

TABLE 1
Cox Regression Estimates for Models Predicting the Hazard of Husband's Death

Covariate	Hazard Ratio	p-Value	Hazard Ratio	p-Value
Black	1.07	.22	1.07	.23
Age	1.08	<.0001	1.08	<.0001
Illness burden	1.35	<.0001	1.35	<.0001
Wife dead	1.02	.86	—	—
Wife died within 30 days	—	—	1.47	.07

hand, there is a highly significant coefficient for age, with each year of age being associated with an 8 percent increase in the hazard. Each 1-point increase in illness burden is associated with a 35 percent increase in the hazard. There is, however, no evidence for an effect of wife's death on husband's hazard of death.

One possible explanation for the null effect of wife's death is that any such effect may last for only a limited period of time. To investigate this possibility, we estimated a second model in which the time-dependent covariate for wife's vital status was coded 1 if the wife had died within the previous 30 days, otherwise 0. Results in the last two columns of Table 1 offer modest support for this hypothesis. The hazard for husband's death is about 47 percent higher during the 30-day period after wife's death, with a p-value of .07.

Would we be justified in interpreting the hazard ratio for wife's death within 30 days as representing a causal relationship? An obvious objection is that these models omit many variables that are common to husbands and wives, or at least highly correlated, and which also have an impact on mortality. Possibilities include income, education, dietary habits, exercise patterns, smoking behavior, and drinking behavior. The omission of these variables could produce a spurious relationship between wife's death and husband's death. So it would be desirable to find a way to reduce or eliminate such biases. Putting additional appropriate variables into the model would be helpful, but such variables are not always available.

3. THE CASE-CROSSOVER METHOD

In the absence of additional measured control variables, we consider a fixed-effects approach in which each couple is compared with itself at different points in time, thereby controlling for all time-invariant variables. One way of doing this is the case-crossover method, which has been widely used in the epidemiological literature (Maclure 1991; Marshall and Jackson 1993; Greenland 1996). According to the basic form of the case-crossover design, we must choose a sample of individuals who have experienced events and record the values of their covariates at the time of the event. We then choose some previous point in time when the event did not occur (a "control" period), and record the values of the covariates for the same individuals at that time. The data are analyzed by doing a matched-pair conditional logistic regression predicting whether or not the event occurred. A critical issue is how to choose the "control period" in order to minimize bias. More complicated forms of the design involve drawing more than one control period for each event. Although this can improve statistical efficiency, it is unclear how to do this in an optimal fashion (Mittleman, Maclure, and Robins 1995).

For our mortality data, we extend the case-crossover design by using information from *all* observed periods prior to the husband's death. Taking a discrete-time approach (Allison 1982), we treat each day as a distinct unit of analysis. Suppose that a husband died on day 78. We then ask the question: Given that he died, why did he die on this day and not on one of the preceding 77 days? Was there something different about those days compared with the day on which he died? As in the usual case-crossover design, we answer this question by way of conditional logistic regression.

Let p_{it} be the probability that the husband in couple i dies on day t, given that he is still alive at the beginning of that day. Let W_{it} be an indicator of wife's vital status on day t. For example, we could let W_{it} be 1 if the wife was dead on day t, otherwise 0. Alternatively, we could let W_{it} be 1 if her death occurred within, say, 60 days prior to day t, otherwise 0. We postulate the following logistic regression model

$$\log\left(\frac{p_{it}}{1 - p_{it}}\right) = \alpha_i + \gamma_t + \beta W_{it} \tag{2}$$

where γ_t represents an unspecified dependence on time and α_i represents the effects of all unmeasured variables that are specific to each couple but constant over time. Note that no time-invariant covariates are included in the model as their effects are absorbed into the α_i term.

We estimate the model by conditional maximum likelihood, thereby eliminating the α_is from the estimating equations. The mechanics are as follows. For couples in which the husband died, a separate observation is created for each day that he is observed, from the origin until the day of death. For each day, the dependent variable Y_{it} is coded 0 if the husband remains alive on that day, and coded 1 if the husband died on that day. Thus, a man who died on June 1, 1993, would contribute 152 person-days; 151 of those would have a value of 0 on Y_{it}, while the last would have a value of 1. The wife's vital status is coded 1 if she was dead on the given day, otherwise 0. For a different representation of wife's vital status, the variable is coded 1 if her death occurred within, say, 60 days prior to the given day, otherwise 0.

All couples in which the husband did not die are effectively deleted from the sample. If the husband is alive on every day of observation, there is no within-couple variation on the dependent variable, and hence no information is contributed to the likelihood function. After deleting couples with no husband deaths, the likelihood function has the following form:

$$L = \prod_i \left(\frac{\exp(\gamma_T + \beta W_{iT})}{\sum_{t=1}^{T} \exp(\gamma_t + \beta W_{it})} \right) \tag{3}$$

In this equation, i runs over all couples whose husband died, and T represents the final day of observation—that is, the day on which the husband died. Notice that α_i has been factored out of likelihood.

Most comprehensive statistical packages have routines to maximize this likelihood, usually under the name "conditional logistic regression." The likelihood function is also identical in form to the stratified partial likelihood for a Cox proportional hazards model. Hence, the model may be estimated by any Cox regression program that allows for stratification.

With a separate parameter for every day of observation, the model in equation (2) is rather complex for estimation. We thus consider only models which impose some restrictions on γ_t. We begin by setting $\gamma_t = 0$—that is, no variation over time in the likelihood of a death. Because the observation period covers only 17 months, this is not an unreasonable assumption.

It so happens that couples who have no variation on the covariates over time can also be deleted from the sample because they contribute

TABLE 2
Cross-Classification of Husband Dead by Wife Dead, 39,942 Couple-Days

	Wife Alive	Wife Dead
Husband Dead	0	126
Husband Alive	19344	20472

nothing to the likelihood.[2] In our case of a single dichotomous covariate (wife's death), we delete any couple whose wife did not die before the husband. Of the 5769 couples in which the husband died, there were only 126 cases in which the wife's death preceded the husband's in this 17-month interval. So our usable set of couples declines from 49,990 to 126, a rather drastic reduction by any standard. These 126 couples contributed a total of 39,942 couple-days.

4. RESULTS FOR COUPLE MORTALITY DATA

We first attempted to estimate a conditional logistic regression model in which W_{it} was coded 1 for wife dead on day t, otherwise 0. However, this model did not converge. The reason is quasi-complete separation, which can be seen in Table 2. If the husband is dead (on the final day of the sequence), the wife is necessarily dead, yielding a 0 frequency count in one cell of the contingency table. (Remember that conditional likelihood necessarily restricts the sample to couples where the husband dies and the wife dies before the husband.) This will also be true in every couple-specific subtable. As is well known, the log-odds ratio for a 2 × 2 table is not defined when there is a zero in the any of the cells.

In general, quasi-complete separation arises whenever the time-varying covariate can only change monotonically with time. In our case, the dummy variable for wife dead can change from 0 to 1 over time but stays at 1 until the end of the series. The problem does not occur, however, if we estimate a model in which the covariate is an indicator of whether the wife died within, say, the previous 60 days. This covariate increases from 0 to 1 when the wife dies, but then goes back to 0 after 60 days (if the husband is still alive). Estimating the model with varying windows

[2]When $\gamma_t = 0$ and W_{it} constant for all t, the expression in parentheses in equation (3) is identically equal to 1.

TABLE 3
Odds Ratios for Predicting Husband's Death from Wife's Death Within Varying
Intervals of Time, Case-Crossover Method

	Wife Died Within				
	15 Days	30 Days	60 Days	90 Days	120 Days
Odds-ratio	1.26	1.96	1.61	1.27	1.26
p-value	.54	.006	.03	.24	.25

of time can give useful information about how the effect of wife's death starts, peaks, and stops.

Table 3 gives estimated odds ratios for several different intervals of time, using conditional logistic regression. In all cases, the odds ratios exceed 1.0 and are statistically significant for the 60-day interval and the 30-day interval. For the latter, the odds of husband's death on a day in which the wife died during the previous 30 days is about double the odds if the wife did not die during that interval. It is worth keeping in mind, however, that in this data set there were only 22 couples in which the husband died within 30 days after the wife's death.

A major limitation of these analyses is that they assume no dependence on time itself, that is, $\gamma_t = 0$. Unfortunately, it has been shown that case-crossover designs can be extremely sensitive to violations of this assumption (Suissa 1995; Greenland 1996). For our example, if there is *any* tendency for the incidence of wife death to increase over the period of observation, this can produce a spurious relationship between wife's death (however coded) and husband's death. Intuitively, the reason is that husband's death always occurs at the end of the sequence of observations for each couple so any variable that tends to increase over time will appear to increase the hazard of husband's death.

Fortunately, there is little evidence for such a trend in these data. Going back to the original data set of 49,990 couples, a Weibull model for *wife's* death shows that the hazard of a death actually declines slightly with time. Similarly, in our sample of 39,942 person-days (from 126 couples) the correlation between wife's death within 30 days and time since the origin was −.04. So we seem to be in good shape for this analysis.

But what if there *were* a correlation between time and wife's death? How could the model be adapted to adjust for time dependence? A natural approach is to relax the assumption that $\gamma_t = 0$ and include some function of time in the model. Unfortunately, this strategy will not generally work for this kind of data. If the covariates include any monotonic function of time with coefficients to be estimated, the maximum likelihood estimates for those coefficients do not exist and the model will not converge. Again, the problem is that any covariate that may increase with time but never decrease (or that may decrease but never increase) will be a "perfect" predictor of husband's death because a death always occurs at the last point in time.

It is possible, however, to include nonmonotonic functions of time. For example, to allow for cyclic annual variation in the hazard of husband's death, we fit a conditional logistic regression model with three covariates: wife death within 30 days, $\sin(2\pi t/365)$, and $\cos(2\pi t/365)$ where t is the number of days since the origin. All three covariates were highly significant, and the odds ratio for wife's death remained at about 2.0.

While such a model provides useful information, it still does not solve our problem of needing to control for monotonic functions of time. As one possible solution, we estimated models with increasing functions of time in which the coefficients of time were fixed rather than estimated. These models converged, and the estimated hazard ratios were similar to those in Table 3. Since the results could depend on the fixed values of the coefficients, we performed a sensitivity analysis in which the time coefficients were systematically varied over a range of plausible values. Although the empirical application seemed to work well, results of simulation studies (not shown) convinced us that this approach is not valid. In particular, the coefficient for wife's death was badly biased unless the coefficients for time were ridiculously large, and there was no apparent way to determine the correct values for the time coefficients.

5. THE CASE-TIME-CONTROL METHOD

We now consider an alternative fixed-effects method that appears to solve the problems that arise when the distribution of the covariate is not in fact stable over time. Introduced by Suissa (1995), who called it the "case-time-control" design, this approach uses the computational device of reversing the dependent and independent variables in the estimation of the conditional logistic regression model. This makes it possible to introduce a control for time, something that cannot be done with the case-crossover method.

As is well known, when both the dependent and independent variables are dichotomous, the odds-ratio is symmetric—reversing the dependent and independent variables yields the same result, even when there are other covariates in the model.[3] In the case-time-control method, the working dependent variable is the dichotomous covariate— in our case whether or not the wife died during the preceding specified number of days. Independent variables are the dummy variable for the occurrence of the event (husband's death) on a given day and some appropriate representation of time—for example, a linear function. As in the case-crossover method, a conditional logistic regression is estimated with each couple treated as a separate stratum. Under this formulation, there is no problem including time as a covariate because the working dependent variable is not a monotonic function of time.

In Suissa's formulation of the case-time-control method, it is essential to include data from all individuals, both those who experienced the event and those who did not (the censored cases). However, his model was developed for data with only two points in time for each individual, an event period and a control period. In that scenario, the covariate effect and the time effect are perfectly confounded if the sample is restricted to those who experienced events. On the other hand, censored individuals provide information about the dependence of the covariate on time, information that is not confounded with the occurrence of the event.

By contrast, our data set (and presumably many others) has multiple "controls" at different points in time for each individual. That eliminates the complete confounding of time with the occurrence of the event (husband death), making it possible to apply the case-time-control method to uncensored cases only. That is a real advantage in situations where it is difficult or impossible to get information for those who did not experience the event. The only restriction is that when the model is estimated without the censored cases, we cannot estimate a model with a completely unrestricted dependence on time—that is, with dummy variables for every point in time.

---

[3]This symmetry is exact when the model is "saturated" in the control covariates but only approximate for unsaturated models (Breslow and Powers 1978).

Of course, if the censored cases are available (as in our data set), it may be possible to get more precise estimates by including them. But even if censored cases are available, there is a potential advantage to limiting the analysis to those who experienced the event. Suissa's version of the case-time-control method has been criticized for assuming that the dependence of the covariate on time is the same among those who did and did not experience the event (Greenland 1996). This criticism has no force if the data are limited to those with events.

For our mortality data, the working data set can be constructed as before, with one record for each day of observation, from the origin until the time of husband's death or censoring. Unlike the case-crossover analysis, we now include both censored cases (couples in which the husband did not die) and uncensored cases. However, because conditional logistic regression requires variation on the dependent variable for each conditioning stratum, we can eliminate couples whose wife did not die before the husband, with no loss of information. This restriction gives us 1743 couples who contributed a total of 872,697 couple-days.

We estimated the following model. Let H_{it} be a dummy variable for the death of husband i on day t, and let P_{it} be the probability that wife's death occurred within a specified number of days prior to day t. Our working logistic regression model is

$$\log\left(\frac{P_{it}}{1 - P_{it}}\right) = \alpha_i + \beta H_{it} + \gamma t. \qquad (4)$$

Again, we estimate the model by conditional logistic regression with each couple as a stratum.[4]

Table 4 gives estimates for the 1743 couples in which the wife died, and for the more restricted sample of 126 couples in which both the husband died and the wife died before the husband. The estimates and p-values for the two subsamples are very close and also quite similar

---

[4]We used SAS PROC LOGISTIC with the STRATA statement. Estimation of the conditional logistic regression could also be done by way of a Cox regression program, but that would be more complicated in the case-time-control method than in the case-crossover method because a couple may have more than one day on which wife had died within the preceding specified number of days. Consequently, a conventional Cox partial likelihood is not appropriate. However, a Cox regression program that can estimate a discrete model for tied data (available in SAS or Stata) can produce the correct likelihood function.

TABLE 4

Odds Ratios for Predicting Husband's Death from Wife's Death Within Varying
Intervals of Time, Case-Time-Control Method

		Wife Died Within				
		15 Days	30 Days	60 Days	90 Days	120 Days
Wife died	Odds-ratio	1.36	2.03	1.51	1.09	.97
(1743 couples)						
	p-value	.41	.004	.05	.69	.88
Both died	Odds-ratio	1.30	1.99	1.50	1.01	.80
(126 couples)						
	p-value	.48	.005	.06	.95	.27

to those in Table 3 for the case-crossover method. Again, the evidence
suggests that the effects of wife's death are limited in time, with considerable fading after about two months. The standard errors (not shown)
are virtually identical for the sample of 1743 and the sample of 126, so
little was gained here by including the censored cases.

Although our working dependent variable is wife's death, the
odds ratios should be interpreted as the effect of wife's death on the
odds of husband's death. That is because of the time ordering of
the observations—wife's death always precedes husband's death. If our
goal was to estimate the effect of husband's death on wife's mortality, we would have to construct a different data set that would sample
couple-days prior to the wife's death, but not thereafter.

5. SIMULATION RESULTS

Although the case-time-control method seems like a promising approach for fixed-effects analysis, the method has seen only a few applications in the epidemiological literature and is still considered somewhat
experimental (Greenland 1996; Schneeweiss et al. 1997; Suissa 1998;
Greenland 1999; Donnan and Wang 2001; Hernandez-Diaz et al. 2003;
Schneider et al. 2005). To verify the appropriateness of this method for
the kind of data considered here, we undertook a simulation study that
investigated the performance of the estimators under several scenarios.
For each scenario, we constructed 100 samples, each with 500 "couples"
who were followed for a maximum of 20 "months." At each month, the
husband could die or not die, with a probability determined by a logistic

regression equation. Also at each month, a "treatment" variable could take on a value of 1 or 0, again with probability determined by a logistic regression equation.

Model 1. We first tested to see whether the case-time-control method avoids the key flaw of the case-crossover method: a tendency to detect nonexistent effects when the treatment is correlated with time. The model used to generate the data had the form

$$\text{Logit}[\Pr(H_{it} = 1)] = -4 + .10t + .50u_i$$

$$\text{Logit}[\Pr(T_{it} = 1)] = -1 + .10t + .50u_i,$$

where H_{it} is a dummy variable for husband's death in couple i at time t, T_{it} is a dummy variable for treatment for couple i at time t, and u_i is a random draw from a standard normal distribution that is specific to couple i but which does not vary over time. Thus, the model does not allow for an effect of treatment on death but does assume substantial effects of time on both treatment and death (approximately a 10 percent increase in the odds at each succeeding month). Furthermore, there is substantial unmeasured heterogeneity (u_i) that is common to both death and treatment. Application of this model produced samples that averaged 6868 couple-months and 323 husband deaths. The treatment dummy was equal to 1 in 45 percent of the couple-months.

Table 5 shows the results for three different estimation methods. For each method, the table gives the true parameter value (for the effect of treatment on the log-odds of death), the mean of the 100 parameter estimates, the mean of the 100 estimated standard errors, the standard deviation of the 100 parameter estimates (which, ideally, should be the same as the mean of the standard errors), and the proportion of nominal 95 percent confidence intervals that actually include the true value ("coverage"). The case-time-control method performed about as well as could be hoped for—the mean parameter estimate is close to 0, the two estimates of the standard error are identical, and 94 percent of the nominal 95 percent confidence intervals contain the parameter value.

By contrast, the case-crossover method did poorly. The average coefficient estimate was .549 (corresponding to an odds ratio of 1.7) and only 1 percent of the confidence intervals included the true value.

TABLE 5
Estimates from Simulated Data Using Three Methods

Model	Method[a]	Parameter[b]	Estimate[c]	Average SE[d]	Standard Deviation[e]	Coverage[f]
1	CTC	.00	−.025	.132	.132	.94
1	CC	.00	.549	.126	.125	.01
1	LR	.00	.192	.118	.116	.67
2	CTC	.69	.721	.168	.168	.96
2	CC	.69	1.311	.164	.160	.00
2	LR	.69	.930	.151	.166	.48
3	CTC	.69	.687	.166	.165	.96
3	CTC(-X)	.69	1.018	.163	.166	.47
3	CC	.69	1.253	.163	.159	.06
3	LR	.69	.918	.150	.145	.49

[a] CTC = case-time-control, CC = case-crossover, LR = conventional logistic regression, CTC(-X) = case-time-control without covariate X.
[b] True value of the coefficient in the model producing the data.
[c] Mean of 100 parameter estimates.
[d] Mean of 100 standard error estimates.
[e] Standard deviation of 100 parameter estimates.
[f] Percentage of nominal 95 percent confidence intervals that include the true value.

Conventional logistic regression did a little better but was still unsatisfactory. The average coefficient estimate was .192, and only 67 percent of the confidence intervals contained the true value.

In other variations of this model (not shown), we set the coefficient for t to 0 in either the first or second equation. The case-time-control method performed well in either variation. As expected, the case-crossover method did well when there was no effect of time on treatment, but not otherwise.

Model 2. The second model modified the equation for death to allow for a nonzero effect of treatment. The equation for T was the same as before. The equation for H was

$$\text{Logit}[\Pr(H_{it} = 1)] = -3.5 + .10t + .69T_{it} + .50u_i.$$

The coefficient of .69 corresponds to an odds ratio of 2.0. This model produced samples that averaged 7987 couple-months and 217 husband deaths.

Again, as seen in Table 5, the case-time-control method does well, with a mean coefficient estimate of .721 (corresponding to an odds ratio of 2.06), with 96 percent of the confidence intervals containing the true value. By contrast, the case-crossover method greatly overestimates the coefficient, and not a single confidence interval contains the true value. As before, conventional logistic regression gives intermediate results with a 30 percent overestimate of the coefficient and nominal 95 percent confidence intervals that contain the true value in only 48 percent of the samples.

Model 3. To our knowledge, the case-time-control method has never been considered as a method to control for other time-varying covariates. Model 3 introduces a covariate that varies with time and affects both treatment and death. The equations are

$$\text{Logit}[\text{Pr}(H_{it} = 1)] = -3 + .10t + .69T_{it} + .8X_{it} + .50u_i$$
$$\text{Logit}[\text{Pr}(T_{it} = 1)] = -1 + .10t + .5X_{it} + .50u_i.$$

Since X and T are correlated, we expect that omitting X from the estimated model will bias the estimated coefficient of T in the equation for husband's death. To control for X in the case-time-control method, we shall include it as a covariate in the conditional logistic regression predicting T. The model produced samples that averaged 7409 couplemonths and 279 husband deaths.

As shown in Table 5, the case-time-control method does just as well here as with the previous scenarios. However, when the model is estimated without the covariate X, the parameter estimate is much too high (odds ratio of 2.77 rather than 2) and only 47 percent of the confidence intervals contained the true value. Even with the inclusion of X, the case-crossover method does poorly, with an odds ratio of 3.5 and only 6 percent coverage. As before, conventional logistic regression (with X included) produces estimates that are a bit too high and coverage of only 49 percent.

6. DISCUSSION AND CONCLUSION

Fundamental problems can arise when attempting to apply fixed-effects logistic regression to discrete-time event history data with nonrepeated events (the case-crossover method). In particular, the conditional likelihood estimates will not converge if the model includes any covariate that is a monotonic function of time. This includes linear, polynomial, or logarithmic functions of time itself, as well as any covariate, such as a dummy for spouse alive or dead, that can only change in one direction with time. Since time dependence cannot be controlled, the method can also produce highly spurious estimates of the effects of any covariates that happen to be correlated with time. Of course conventional Cox models could still be estimated, but that would lose the advantage of the fixed-effects approach.

The case-time-control method provides a solution to the inability to control for time. This method also relies on conditional logistic regression, but reverses the role of the dichotomous event and a dichotomous covariate. Simulations suggest that the case-time-control method produces approximately unbiased estimates of the odds ratio of interest, even in cases where both the event hazard and the dichotomous covariate are strongly dependent on time. We have extended this method in two ways. First, we argue that the inclusion of individuals who did not experience events—previously thought to be an essential feature of this method—is unnecessary if multiple control times are available for those who do experience events and the dependence on time is not left unrestricted. Second, our simulation results suggest that additional time-varying covariates can be included as controls in the regression model.

Application of both the case-crossover method and the case-time-control method to mortality data of elderly couples provides evidence that there is indeed an effect of wife's death on husband's odds of death, even when all stable covariates are controlled, but that the effect is of limited duration.

At this point, the case-time-control method is still restricted to situations in which the aim is to estimate the effect of a dichotomous covariate on an outcome event, while controlling for other covariates, either dichotomous or continuous. In principle, one ought to be able to estimate effects of multiple dichotomous covariates by estimating a separate model for each covariate as the "dependent" variable. It may also be possible to handle polytomous covariates by estimating a conditional multinomial logit model (although commercial software for estimating such models is not widely available at present). At this point, however, we are unable to use the case-time-control approach to estimate the effect of a continuous covariate. And there is little hope for estimating the effects of covariates that are monotonic with time. Still, as we saw here, many such variables can be reformulated in ways that eliminate the monotonicity.

The methods described here would be appropriate for events like deaths or loss of virginity that are, in principle, not repeatable. They may also be appropriate for events like arrests or promotions which, although repeatable in principle, may be sufficiently rare that they are observed no more than once for any individual in the sample. However, in the case of rare but repeatable events, the case-time-control method should be necessary only if observation ceases at the occurrence of the first observed event. When observation continues and the covariates continue to be measured after the occurrence of the event, we can use a conventional conditional logistic regression predicting the event, with a control for time or any other covariate that increases monotonically with time. That is because, in that observational setting, the event does not always occur at the end of the sequence of observations, and hence there is no problem of quasi-complete separation.

REFERENCES

Allison, Paul D. 1982. "Discrete-Time Methods for the Analysis of Event Histories." Pp. 61–98 in *Sociological Methodology*, vol. 13, edited by Samuel Leinhardt. San Francisco: Jossey-Bass.

———. 1996. "Fixed Effects Partial Likelihood for Repeated Events." *Sociological Methods & Research* 25:207–22.

———. 2005. *Fixed Effects Regression Methods for Longitudinal Data Using SAS*. Cary, NC: SAS Institute.

Breslow, N., and W. Powers. 1978. "Are There Two Logistic Regressions for Retrospective Studies?" *Biometrics* 34:100–105.

Cameron, A. Colin, and Pravin K. Trivedi. 1998. *Regression Analysis of Count Data*. Cambridge, England: Cambridge University Press.

Chamberlain, Gary A. 1980. "Analysis of Covariance with Qualitative Data." *Review of Economic Studies* 47:225–38.

———. 1985. "Heterogeneity, Omitted Variable Bias, and Duration Dependence." Pp. 3–38 in *Longitudinal Analysis of Labor Market Data*, edited by James J. Heckman and Burton Singer. Cambridge, England: Cambridge University Press.

Donnan, Peter T., and Jixian Wang. 2001. "The Case-Crossover and Case-Time-Control Designs in Pharmacoepidemiology." *Pharmacoepidemiology and Drug Safety* 10:259–62.

Greene, William T. 1990. *Econometric Analysis*. New York: Macmillan.

Greenland, Sander. 1996. "Confounding and Exposure Trends in Case-Crossover and Case-Time-Control Designs." *Epidemiology* 7:231–39.

———. 1999. "A Unified Approach to the Analysis of Case-Distribution (Case Only) Studies." *Statistics in Medicine* 18:1–15.

Halaby, Charles N. 2004. "Panel Models in Sociological Research: Theory into Practice." *Annual Review of Sociology* 30:507–44.

Hernandez-Diaz, Sonia, Miguel A. Hernan, Katie Meyer, Martha M. Werler, and Allen A. Mitchell. 2003. "Case-Crossover and Case-Time-Control Designs in Birth Defects Epidemiology." *American Journal of Epidemiology* 158:385–91.

Iwashyna, T. J., J. Zhang, D. Lauderdale, and N. A. Christakis. 1998. "A Methodology for Identifying Married Couples in Medicare Data: Mortality, Morbidity, and Health Care Use Among the Married Elderly." *Demography* 35:413–19.

———. 2000. "Refinements of a Methodology for Detecting Married Couples in the Medicare Data." *Demography* 37(2):251–52.

Maclure, Malcolm. 1991. "The Case-Crossover Design: A Method for Studying Transient Effects on the Risk of Acute Events." *American Journal of Epidemiology* 133:144–53.

Marshall, Roger J., and Rodney J. Jackson. 1993. "Analysis of Case-Crossover Designs." *Statistics in Medicine* 12:2333–41.

Mittleman, Murray A., Malcolm Maclure, and James M. Robins. 1995. "Control Sampling Strategies for Case-Crossover Studies: An Assessment of Relative Efficiency." *American Journal of Epidemiology* 142:91–98.

Schneeweiss, Sebastian, Til Sturmer, and Malcom Maclure. 1997. "Case-Crossover and Case-Time-Control Designs as Alternatives in Pharmacoepidemiologic Research." *Pharmacoepidemiology and Drug Safety* 6 suppl. 3:S51–59.

Schneider, M. F., S. J. Gange, J. B. Margolick, R. Detels, J. S. Chmiel, C. Rinaldo, and H. K. Armenian. 2005. "Application of Case-Crossover and Case-Time-Control Study Designs in Analyses of Time-Varying Predictors of T-Cell Homeostasis Failure." *Annals of Epidemiology* 15:137–44.

Suissa, Samy. 1995. "The Case-Time-Control Design." *Epidemiology* 6:248–53.

———. 1998. "The Case-Time-Control Design: Further Assumptions and Conditions." *Epidemiology* 9:441–45.

Yamaguchi, Kazuo. 1986. "Alternative Approaches to Unobserved Heterogeneity in the Analysis of Repeatable Events." Pp. 213–49 in *Sociological Methodology*, vol. 16, edited by Nancy Brandon Tuma. Washington, DC: American Sociological Association.

Zhang, J., T. J. Iwashyna, and N. A. Christakis. 1999. "The Performance of Different Lookback Periods and Sources of Information for Charlson Comorbidity Adjustment in Medicare Claims." *Medical Care* 37:1128–39.

MEANINGFUL REGRESSION AND ASSOCIATION MODELS FOR CLUSTERED ORDINAL DATA

Jukka Jokinen[*]
John W. McDonald[†]
Peter W. F. Smith[†]

Many proposed methods for analyzing clustered ordinal data focus on the regression model and consider the association structure within a cluster as a nuisance. However, the association structure is often of equal interest—for example, temporal association in longitudinal studies and association between responses to similar questions in a survey. We discuss the use, appropriateness, and interpretability of various latent variable and Markov models for the association structure and propose a new structure that exploits the ordinality of the response. The models are illustrated with a study concerning opinions regarding government spending and an analysis of stability and change in teenage marijuana use over time, where we reveal different behavioral patterns for boys and girls through a comprehensive investigation of individual response profiles.

Financial support from the United Kingdom Economic and Social Research Council (award number H333250026), Southampton Statistical Sciences Research Institute, and the Yrjö Jahnsson Foundation is gratefully acknowledged. We thank Anders Ekholm and the anonymous referees for helpful comments.

[*]University of Helsinki

[†]University of Southampton

173

1. INTRODUCTION

In sociological applications, the response variables of interest are often measured on an ordinal scale, such as opinions or attitudes toward sociological issues (e.g., strongly disagree, . . ., strongly agree). The research hypothesis typically addresses the question whether these responses differ in various subgroups of the population of interest. There are well-established methods for the regression analysis of ordinal responses (e.g., see Agresti 1999). However, further complication to the modeling process arises when the ordered responses are clustered in some way, such as responses to similar questions by the same individual, or repeated responses to the same question in longitudinal studies. In order to obtain correct inferences, the association between responses within a cluster has to be taken into account in the analysis. Compared to simple cross-sectional studies with independent observations, further insights can also be gained by investigating the structure of this association.

Agresti and Natarajan (2001) surveyed various strategies for analyzing these types of clustered ordinal categorical data, focusing on marginal models and cluster-specific models. Our aim here is to present a method for analyzing clustered ordinal data that combines a marginal regression model with a meaningful model for the association structure, and to relate it to methods surveyed in Agresti and Natarajan (2001).

Lang, McDonald, and Smith (1999) and Vermunt and Hagenaars (2004) analyzed a data set from the U.S. National Youth Survey, where 237 teenagers (117 boys and 120 girls), aged 13 at the beginning of the study, filled in a questionnaire yearly for five consecutive years. At the end of each year they were asked about their marijuana use during that year. The response is ordinal, with values 1 = never (nonuser), 2 = less than once a month (occasional user), and 3 = more than once a month (frequent user). Obvious substantive research questions involve comparisons of the prevalences of marijuana use by age and sex of the respondent. However, investigation of the entire response profiles of teenagers may reveal other forms of dissimilarities rather than just prevalence differences.

Lang and Agresti (1994) analyzed a data set from the 1989 U.S. General Social Survey, where 607 adults, aged over 18 years, were asked their opinion concerning government spending on (a) Environment, (b) Health, (c) Assistance to Big Cities, and (d) Law Enforcement. Each response is ordinal with levels 1 = too little, 2 = about right, 3 = too much. Lang and Agresti (1994) did not consider any covariates. In order to illustrate the potential of our method, we include the covariates age, sex, race, and political party affiliation. In addition, we include three more questions concerning government spending with the same ordinal response: (e) National Defense, (f) Education, and (g) Assistance to the Poor. An interesting regression task is to compare how the marginal distributions of these seven targets of government spending differ by political party affiliation, after adjusting for age, sex, and race of the respondent. It is also equally interesting to study whether individuals have different tendencies when answering questions concerning government spending in general. In order to achieve both goals, the joint probability of a response profile needs to be parametrized in terms of univariate probabilities and suitable dependence measures that facilitate comprehensive modeling of the association structure.

For a multivariate binary response, Ekholm, Smith, and Mc-Donald (1995) parametrized the joint probability with univariate probabilities and dependence ratios. The dependence ratio was extended to the ordinal case by Ekholm et al. (2003), who also demonstrated how meaningful association structures can easily be specified using dependence ratios. We present the dependence ratio parametrization for a multivariate ordinal response in Section 2. In Section 3, we analyze the data set from the 1989 U.S. General Social Survey, regarding opinions about government spending, and discuss the appropriateness of various exchangeable association structures presented in Ekholm et al. (2003). In Section 4, a model for temporal association is fitted to the data set concerning teenage marijuana use, and exchangeable association structures are extended further by exploiting the ordinality of the response. In Section 5 we consider maximum likelihood estimation and computational aspects. In Section 6 our approach is related to methods surveyed in Agresti and Natarajan (2001).

2. MEAN PARAMETRIZATION AND DEPENDENCE RATIOS

To formally present the connection between the joint probability of a response profile and our parameters of interest, some notation is necessary. For a simple illustration of the parametrization, see Section 2.1, and for a comprehensive representation of the relationship, see Ekholm et al. (2003). Consider a response profile of length q in cluster i, $Y_i = (Y_{i1}, \ldots, Y_{iq})$, for $i = 1, \ldots, n$, where the realizations of Y_{ik}, denoted

a_k, are ordered, $a_k = 1, \ldots, f$ and $k = 1, \ldots, q$. There are f^q possible realizations of the profile with $\mathrm{pr}(Y_i = \{a_1, \ldots, a_q\}) = \pi_i(a_1, \ldots, a_q)$, and when there is a time ordering, we refer to the response profiles as paths. To specify the probability distribution of Y_i, denote the $1 \times f^q$ vector of profile or path probabilities by π_i, with $\pi_i \mathbf{1}^T = 1$. Furthermore, define dummy variables $Y_{ik}^{(a_k)} = 1$ if $Y_{ik} = a_k$, else 0, for $a_k = 2, \ldots, f$, and $Y_{ik}^{(1)} = 1 - Y_{ik}^{(2)} - - Y_{ik}^{(f)}$. The $1 \times (f^q - 1)$ vector of mean parameters is given by

$$\boldsymbol{\mu}_i = (\mu_{i1}^{(2)}, \ldots, \mu_{iq}^{(f)}, \mu_{i12}^{(2,2)}, \ldots, \mu_{i1\ldots q}^{(f,\ldots,f)}), \tag{1}$$

where $\mu_{ik}^{(a_k)} = E(Y_{ik}^{(a_k)})$ and $\mu_{i1\ldots k}^{(a_1,\ldots,a_k)} = E(Y_{i1}^{(a_1)} \cdots Y_{ik}^{(a_k)})$. Ekholm et al. (2003) showed that there exists a one-to-one correspondence $\boldsymbol{\mu}_i \rightarrow \boldsymbol{\pi}_i$ for specifying the joint distribution in terms of these mean parameters.

Second- and higher-order means capture the information about the association between the responses within a cluster. For a more interpretable measure of association, we replace these by the corresponding dependence ratios. For example, the second-order dependence ratio is

$$\tau_{kl}^{(a_k,a_l)} = \frac{\mathrm{pr}(Y_{ik} = a_k, Y_{il} = a_l)}{\mathrm{pr}(Y_{ik} = a_k)\,\mathrm{pr}(Y_{il} = a_l)} = \frac{\mu_{ikl}^{(a_k,a_l)}}{\mu_{ik}^{(a_k)}\mu_{il}^{(a_l)}}, \tag{2}$$

for $a_k, a_l = 2, \ldots, f$ and $k, l = 1, \ldots, q, k \neq l$, that is, the joint probability divided by the joint probability assuming independence. Here we assume that the dependence ratios are the same across clusters.

To specify the joint distribution through the mean parameters in (1), the second-order means can be expressed as a simple transformation of the marginal probabilities and the second-order dependence ratios: $\mu_{ikl}^{(a_k,a_l)} = \mu_{ik}^{(a_k)}\mu_{il}^{(a_l)}\tau_{kl}^{(a_k,a_l)}$. Higher-order transformations can be expressed similarly. In what follows, we regress, using the most appropriate link function, the univariate marginal or cumulative probabilities on explanatory variables with intercept parameters θ and regression coefficients β. In order to find an underlying association model generating dependence within a cluster, we impose a structure on the $f^q - q(f - 1) - 1$ dependence ratios $\tau = (\tau_{12}^{(2,2)}, \ldots, \tau_{1\ldots q}^{(f,\ldots,f)})$ through association parameters

$$\tau = g(\alpha). \tag{3}$$

TABLE 1
Responses of Married Couples: "Sex is Fun for Me and My Partner"

Husband	Wife				
	Always Fun	Very Often	Fairly Often	Never Fun	Total
Always fun	14	9	8	2	33
Very often	9	4	5	1	19
Fairly often	7	3	8	2	20
Never fun	3	2	7	7	19
Total	33	18	28	12	91

Note that an explicit expression $\pi_i = f(\theta, \beta, \alpha)$ now exists for maximum likelihood (ML) estimation of the combined regression and association model.

2.1. Illustration of the Parametrization

Consider a bivariate ordinal data set, previously analyzed by Hout, Duncan, and Sobel (1987), concerning responses of married couples to the questionnaire item: "Sex is fun for me and my partner." The response is ordinal with levels 1 = Almost Always, 2 = Very Often, 3 = Fairly Often, 4 = Never or Occasionally. Responses of 91 couples are summarized in Table 1. It is of interest whether husbands and wives differ in the way they are distributed into these four categories. In addition, it is presumed that the married couples are in some (imperfect) way associated in their responses. Hout, Duncan, and Sobel (1987) called the former marginal dissimilarity and the latter structural dissimilarity.

Altogether $2(4 - 1) = 6$ univariate marginal probabilities, that measure marginal dissimilarity, and $4^2 - 2(4 - 1) - 1 = 9$ dependence ratios, that measure structural dissimilarity, are required to specify the joint distribution of this bivariate ordinal response. Table 2 summarizes the estimates for the saturated model with 15 parameters. The marginal distributions do not notably differ between husbands and wives. It also seems that there is little association in the joint responses of the married couples: Most of the dependence ratios are close to one, which implies near independence. However, the estimated joint probability that both of the couples respond "Never or Occasionally" is rather high, $7/91 = 0.077$, compared with the joint probability assuming independence: $(12/91) \times (19/91) = 0.0275$. This results in a dependence ratio estimate of $\hat{\tau}^{(4,4)} = 0.077/0.0275 = 2.79$.

TABLE 2
Estimates of the Saturated Model: "Sex is Fun for Me and My Partner"

			Wife		
Husband	Always Fun	Very Often	Fairly Often	Never Fun	Marginal
Always fun					
Very often	$\hat{\tau}^{(2,2)} = 1.06$	$\hat{\tau}^{(2,3)} = 0.86$	$\hat{\tau}^{(2,4)} = 0.40$	$\hat{\mu}^{(2)} = 0.21$	
Fairly often	$\hat{\tau}^{(3,2)} = 0.76$	$\hat{\tau}^{(3,3)} = 1.30$	$\hat{\tau}^{(3,4)} = 0.76$	$\hat{\mu}^{(3)} = 0.22$	
Never fun	$\hat{\tau}^{(4,2)} = 0.53$	$\hat{\tau}^{(4,3)} = 1.20$	$\hat{\tau}^{(4,4)} = 2.79$	$\hat{\mu}^{(4)} = 0.21$	
Marginal	$\hat{\mu}^{(2)} = 0.20$	$\hat{\mu}^{(3)} = 0.31$	$\hat{\mu}^{(4)} = 0.13$	1	

In order to explore the underlying mechanisms of marginal dissimilarity, restrictions can be imposed for the univariate probabilities in a regression model, using explanatory variables and various choices of link functions. In addition, structural dissimilarity can be explored by imposing a structure on the dependence ratios. This example is revisited in Section 6, where a marginal regression model is combined with a meaningful model for the association that explains the dependence between the responses of the married couples.

2.2. Properties of the Dependence Ratio

The odds ratio is the most commonly used measure of association for a multivariate categorical response; for example, see Fitzmaurice and Laird (1993), Glonek and McCullagh (1995), and Lang and Agresti (1994). To elaborate the dependence ratio measure and to relate it to the odds ratio and the relative risk in the context of one of our main examples, consider the second-order dependence ratio $\tau_{12}^{(2,3)}$ at ages 13 and 14 in the teenage marijuana use example.

1. *Interpretation:* $\tau_{12}^{(2,3)}$ compares how many times more probable than under independence it is that the teenager is first an occasional user and the next year a frequent user. The construction and the interpretation of a higher-order dependence ratio is a straightforward generalization. For example, the fifth-order dependence ratio $\tau_{12345}^{(3,3,3,3,3)}$ measures the probability of a teenager being a frequent user every year between the ages of 13 and 17 compared with the probability assuming independence.

2. *Relationship with the relative risk:* Like the relative risk (risk ratio), $\tau_{12}^{(2,3)}$ is a ratio of probabilities. Several authors favor the relative risk over the odds ratio (Greenland 1987; Sackett, Deeks, and Altman 1996; Davies, Crombie, and Tavakoli 1998), especially because risks and relative risks are easier to interpret than ratios of odds. In reply to Deeks et al. (1998), Davies, Crombie, and Tavakoli go as far as saying this: "On one thing we are in clear agreement: Odds ratios can lead to confusion and alternative measures should be used when these are available."

3. *Invariance:* Similar to the relative risk, $\tau_{12}^{(2,3)}$ is not invariant to the coding chosen. This means that using a reverse coding for the response results in a different set of association measures. However, one advantage of this asymmetry is that $\tau_{12}^{(2,3)}$ measures only the association of a teenager being first an occasional user and then a frequent user. Therefore, if the association of marijuana use, rather than nonuse, is of interest, the dependence ratio is focused on the association of interest.

4. *Range:* While the odds ratio takes values between zero and infinity, the range of the dependence ratio depends on the marginal probabilities (Ekholm 2003). The upper bound of $\tau_{12}^{(2,3)}$ is $\min(1/\mu_1^{(2)}, 1/\mu_2^{(3)})$. This is again similar to the properties of the relative risk: For example, if the baseline risk is 0.8, the maximum relative risk is $1/0.8 = 1.25$. However, if the proportion of marijuana users was really excessive, say 0.8, it is reasonable to argue that it would be of more interest to model nonuse rather than use of marijuana. Therefore, to exploit fully the preciseness of the dependence ratio as a measure of the association (see point 3 above), it is advisable to use as the baseline the category that contains the higher observed frequency out of the first and last categories.

5. *Connection with the transition probability:* When the responses within a cluster have a natural ordering, such as age in the teenage marijuana use example, the transition probabilities between the states may be of interest. A simple connection exists:

$$\tau_{12}^{(2,3)} = \frac{\mathrm{pr}(Y_{i2} = 3 | Y_{i1} = 2)}{\mathrm{pr}(Y_{i2} = 3)}. \tag{4}$$

Thus an alternative interpretation of $\tau_{12}^{(2,3)}$ is, in terms of conditional probability, given the teenager was an occasional user at the age of

13, how many times more probable it is that she or he is a frequent user at the age of 14, compared with the marginal probability.

Regardless of the above-mentioned differences between the odds ratio and the dependence ratio, we find that one of the most important advantages in using dependence ratios is a convenient formulation of various plausible association mechanisms. We illustrate this in the following two sections in the context of our two main examples.

3. OPINIONS CONCERNING GOVERNMENT SPENDING

We set ourselves a regression task to compare whether opinions concerning government spending on each of the seven targets differ according to political party affiliation. In order to adjust for possible confounders, age (in years), sex (male, female), and race (white, black, other) were also included as explanatory variables in the regression model, denoted by $\mathcal{R}$. There were four missing values for party affiliation, and two for age. These missing values were imputed using regression imputation (Little and Rubin 2002). A total of 23 missing values in the responses were assumed to be missing at random (MAR; Little and Rubin 2002) and handled accordingly; see Section 5. The marginal regression model, for $i = 1, \ldots, 607$, $k = 1, \ldots, 7$ and $a = 1, 2$, is of form

$$\eta_{ik}(a) = \theta_a + \beta_a x_{ik}^T, \tag{5}$$

where β_a is a vector of regression coefficients, constant with respect to i and k, x_{ik} is a vector of explanatory variables, and θ_1, θ_2 are the intercepts. For ordinal variables, the link function η is usually a logit, probit, or complementary log-log function of the cumulative probabilities $\text{pr}(Y_{ik} \leq a)$. In this case it is often plausible to assume $\beta_a = \beta$. However, other link functions that operate on marginal reponse categories may be useful in some situations, such as adjacent category logit and baseline category logit links (Hartzel, Agresti, and Caffo 2001). For the government spending data set, we use the logit function for cumulative probabilities, more commonly known as the proportional odds model.

In addition to marginal probabilities, altogether $3^7 - 7(3 - 1) - 1 = 2172$ dependence ratios are required to specify the profile probabilities. Consequently, a strong structure needs to be imposed on these measures. Ekholm et al. (2003) presented a set of exchangeable association models where the association is parametrized in terms of dependence ratios. We discuss the appropriateness of these models in the context of our analysis of the government spending data set. In what follows, full independence of the responses within a cluster is referred to as the null association model, denoted by $\mathcal{I}$. For the technical details of these structures, we refer the reader to Ekholm et al. (2003).

3.1. *Necessary Factor* $\mathcal{N}$

Suppose that there is a subgroup of people that, regardless of the question at hand, always answers that the government is spending too little. This kind of association can be captured by imposing a latent structure, denoted by $\mathcal{N}$, where all responses of a subject either do or do not carry a factor necessary for the response to be greater than one—that is, $a_{ik} > 1$. Conversely, if there is a subgroup that always answers "too much" regardless of the question, this can be captured similarly by using the same association structure but with reverse coding of the response; see also Section 2, point 4.

Denote the absence and presence of this kind of necessary factor by, respectively, $\{N_i = 0\}$ and $\{N_i = 1\}$ and suppose that $\mathrm{pr}(N_i = 1) = v_1$, for $i = 1, \ldots, 607$. Furthermore, suppose that the responses within a cluster are conditionally independent given N_i. If $N_i = 0$, an individual i will always answer "too little," irrespective of her or his covariate values. Therefore it is usually more appropriate to regress the effect of the covariates on the univariate probability conditional on the presence of the necessary factor. Using the conditional univariate probabilities, the profile probabilities can now be expressed, for $a_k = 1, 2, 3$, as

$$\pi_i(a_1, \ldots, a_7) = v_1\{\mathrm{pr}(Y_{i1} = a_1 | N_i = 1) \cdots \mathrm{pr}(Y_{i7} = a_7 | N_i = 1)\} \\ + \mathbf{1}_{\{a=1\}}(1 - v_1), \tag{6}$$

where $\mathbf{1}_{\{a=1\}} = 1$ if $\{a_1 = \cdots = a_7 = 1\}$, else 0. The association model has a single parameter v_1, and $1 - v_1$ quantifies the proportion of people that will always answer that the government is spending too little. To elaborate further the association model, other structures can be imposed on the conditional probabilities in (6). Note also from (6) that the probability of the profile $\{a_1 = \ldots = a_7 = 1\}$ is a sum of probabilities with and without the necessary factor. In other words, a subject may answer "too little" to all questions but still be capable of answering otherwise.

When fitted to the government spending data, $\mathcal{N}$ combined with a regression model R, gives $\hat{v}_1 = 0.99$. In other words, there is little evidence that there exists a notably large subgroup that always answers "too little."

3.2. Latent Binary Factor $\mathcal{L}$

Suppose that the population is divided into two groups with different response category probabilities. This may happen if an important dichotomous covariate has not been recorded. Suppose that each subject i has a realization of a latent factor $L_i = 1$ or 0, and that all seven responses are conditionally independent given L_i. This association model, called $\mathcal{L}$, has three parameters $\alpha = (v_2, \kappa^{(2)}, \kappa^{(3)})$, where $v_2 = \mathrm{pr}(L_i = 1)$ and $\{\kappa^{(a_k)} = \mathrm{pr}(Y_{ik} = a_k | L_i = 0)/\mathrm{pr}(Y_{ik} = a_k | L_i = 1)$, $a_k = 2, 3$. In other words, v_2 quantifies the proportion of subjects in the latent group 1, and the κ-parameters are ratios of conditional univariate probabilities for those in the latent groups 0 and 1 respectively. For $w = 2, \ldots, 7$, equation (3) is now defined using the following connection:

$$\tau^{(a_1,\ldots,a_w)} = \frac{v_2 + (1 - v_2)\kappa^{(a_1)} \cdots \kappa^{(a_w)}}{\{v_2 + (1 - v_2)\kappa^{(a_1)}\} \cdots \{v_2 + (1 - v_2)\kappa^{(a_w)}\}}. \tag{7}$$

Estimates for the combined model $\{R; \mathcal{L}\}$, fitted to the government spending data set, are reported in Table 3 and discussed in Section 3.4.

3.3. Latent Dirichlet-Distributed Propensities $\mathcal{D}$

Suppose that there is continuous variability in the way individuals respond to questions regarding government spending. This may be caused by an unobserved continuous explanatory variable, or a combination of unobserved variables, resulting in different underlying propensities for each individual. This kind of association structure can be captured by utilizing a continuous Dirichlet distribution which is an extension of the Beta distribution to more than two categories.

TABLE 3
Estimates of a Model $\{\mathcal{R}; \mathcal{L}\}$ Concerning Government Spending

Effects		Estimate	Standard Error
Sex	Female	−0.214	0.067
Race	Black	−0.437	0.119
	Other	0.431	0.192
Age	(in years)	0.0038	0.0019
Democrat	National Defense	—	—
	Assistance to Big Cities	−0.564	0.174
	Law Enforcement	−2.471	0.189
	Education	−2.919	0.201
	Enviromnent	−2.625	0.194
	Assistance to Poor	−2.904	0.204
	Health	−3.170	0.213
Independent	National Defense	−0.047	0.193
(Contrasted	Assistance to Big Cities	0.278	0.191
to Democrat)	Law Enforcement	0.264	0.207
	Education	−0.024	0.239
	Enviromnent	−0.426	0.236
	Assistance to Poor	0.191	0.235
	Health	0.525	0.240
Republican	National Defense	−0.506	0.175
(Contrasted	Assistance to Big Cities	0.503	0.191
to Democrat)	Law Enforcement	0.348	0.196
	Education	0.398	0.214
	Enviromnent	−0.017	0.210
	Assistance to Poor	1.126	0.209
	Health	0.931	0.220
Association	ν_2	0.596	0.103
	κ_2	0.362	0.057
	κ_3	1.541	0.138

Denote the propensities of subject i by $\boldsymbol{P}_i = (P_i^{(2)}, P_i^{(3)})$, $P_i^{(2)}, P_i^{(3)} \geq 0$, $P_i^{(2)} + P_i^{(3)} \leq 1$, and suppose that $\boldsymbol{P}_i$, $i = 1, \ldots, 607$, follow independently the same Dirichlet distribution with parameters $\xi_1, \xi_2, \xi_3 > 0$. In other words, each subject has an individual realization of propensities $\{1 - (p_i^{(2)} + p_i^{(3)}), p_i^{(2)}, p_i^{(3)}\}$ for, respectively, categories $1 = $ "too little," $2 = $ "about right," and $3 = $ "too much." Further suppose that all seven responses concerning government spending are conditionally independent given the propensities. We call this association model $\mathcal{D}$. For $a_k = 2, 3$, equation (3) can now be expressed with $\boldsymbol{\alpha} = (\xi_1, \xi_2, \xi_3)$ using the following connection:

$$\tau^{(a_1,\dots,a_w)} = \frac{E(P^{(a_1)}\cdots P^{(a_w)})}{E(P^{(a_1)})\cdots E(P^{(a_w)})}. \tag{8}$$

It follows from (8) that, for example, $\tau^{(2,2,2)} > \tau^{(2,2)} > 1$ and $\tau^{(2,3)} < 1$, regardless of the values of $\xi > 0$. This model, arising from the properties of a Dirichlet distribution, is therefore appropriate for studies where it is assumed that repetition of certain response categories is more probable than under independence. When fitted to the government spending data set, the estimates of the association parameters for the model $\{R; D\}$ are $\hat{\xi}_1 = 0.467, \hat{\xi}_2 = 3.010, \hat{\xi}_3 = 4.804$, which translate to, e.g., $\hat{\tau}^{(2,2)} = 1.19, \hat{\tau}^{(2,2,2)} = 1.59, \hat{\tau}^{(2,3)} = 0.89$ and $\hat{\tau}^{(2,2,3)} = 0.96$.

3.4. Results for the Combined Regression and Association Model

The results of the regression model are summarized in Table 3. The parameter estimates for the government spending targets of the Democrats are contrasted with National Defense. The view of the Democrats is that the government should spend more on all other targets than on National Defense, with the greatest emphasis on Health.

The parameter estimates for the Independents and the Republicans are contrasted with the estimates for the Democrats. In other words, 0 indicates no difference with the views of the Democrats on that specific target. People who call themselves Independent have opinions somewhere in between those of Democrats and Republicans, with views generally slightly closer to Democrats than to Republicans. The greatest differences in the viewpoints of the Democrats and the Republicans are in government spending regarding Assistance to the Poor and Health. For both these targets the Democrats expect stronger financial involvement. In contrast, for National Defense, Republicans expect the government to spend more.

Since the association models presented in Sections 3.1 to 3.3 are not nested, we use Akaike's information criteria (AIC) to compare which of the models fit the data best. AIC for models $\{R; I\}$, $\{R; N\}$, $\{R; L\}$, and $\{R; D\}$ are, respectively, 7039.9, 7029.8, 6971.9, and 6972.2. In terms of the model fit, there is virtually no difference between the fit assuming a latent binary variable and the fit assuming a latent continuous, Dirichlet-distributed variable. We would need to resort to subject-matter judgment in order to distinguish which one of the two is the more plausible mechanism. In Table 3, we report the regression model combined with a model assuming a latent binary factor for the association.

The interpretation of the association model $\mathcal{L}$ is that the population is divided into two groups, denoted by 0 and 1, with different response category probabilities concerning government spending. The percentage of subjects in group 0 is $100 \times (1 - \hat{v}_2) \approx 40$ percent, and for those in that group, the probability of answering "about right" is approximately one-third (0.362) of the probability in group 1. However, answering "too much" is 1.541 times more probable than in group 1. In searching for an explanation for the latent variable, we would need to look for a subgroup that constitutes 40 percent of the target population and is more prone to a view that the government is spending too much, compared with their counterparts.

4. STABILITY AND CHANGE IN TEENAGE MARIJUANA USE

Marginal frequencies and percentages of marijuana use for boys and girls at ages 13 to 17 are reported in Table 4. These show a monotone increase in marijuana use for both girls and boys with age, with use being consistently more frequent for boys at each age. None of the link functions described in Section 3 are superior over the others, so a proportional odds model is used for estimation of the effect of age in the regression model.

Since the clustering of the responses now occurs in time, we present a model for temporal association (Ekholm et al. 2003) and extend further the exchangeable structures by introducing a new hierarchical latent structure that exploits the ordinality of the response.

4.1. Markov Structures $\mathcal{M}$

Consider a path containing five consecutive annual responses for teenager i, $(Y_{i1}, Y_{i2}, Y_{i3}, Y_{i4}, Y_{i5})$, and suppose that these satisfy the first-order Markov assumption. For $i = 1, \ldots, 237$ and $k = 1, \ldots, 4$,

$$\mathrm{pr}(Y_{i(k+1)} = a \,|\, Y_{i1}, \ldots, Y_{ik}) = \mathrm{pr}(Y_{i(k+1)} = a \,|\, Y_{ik}). \tag{9}$$

Equation (9) implies that this association structure, denoted by $\mathcal{M}$, has $(5 - 1)(3 - 1)^2 = 16$ adjacent second-order dependence ratio parameters:

TABLE 4

Marginal Frequencies (Percentages) of Marijuana Use for Girls and Boys at Ages
13 to 17

	Girls			Boys		
Age	Never	Less than Once a Month	More than Once a Month	Never	Less than Once a Month	More than Once a Month
13	114 (95.0)	5 (4.2)	1 (0.8)	104 (88.9)	9 (7.7)	4 (3.4)
14	106 (88.3)	10 (8.3)	4 (3.3)	89 (76.1)	17 (14.5)	11 (9.4)
15	91 (75.8)	21 (17.5)	8 (6.7)	76 (65.0)	20 (17.1)	21 (17.9)
16	85 (70.8)	21 (17.5)	14 (11.7)	71 (60.7)	20 (17.1)	26 (22.2)
17	75 (62.5)	30 (25.0)	15 (12.5)	63 (53.8)	22 (18.8)	32 (27.4)

$\tau_{k\,k+1}^{(a_k,a_{k+1})}$, $a_k = 2, 3$ and $k = 1, \ldots, 4$. For such large-dimensional problems, this still leads to an unneccesarily complicated association structure. For clearer interpretability, it is advisable to strengthen the $\mathcal{M}$ assumption by further restrictions, such as functional forms for the adjacent dependence ratios, and equality of parameters for certain pairs of categories or time points. The set of association models can also be further elaborated by assuming that the $\mathcal{M}$-structures operate, independently, within the latent classes of the exchangeable structures $\mathcal{N}$ and $\mathcal{L}$.

4.2. Hierarchical Necessary Factors $\mathcal{N}2$

Consider the structure $\mathcal{N}$ presented in Section 3.1 for the teenage marijuana example, dividing the teenage population into those who would never use marijuana and those who are susceptible to marijuana use. Further suppose that there is another subpopulation among the susceptibles who might try marijuana or use it occasionally but categorically refuse to become frequent users. We can capture this kind of behavior in the population by nesting the latent structures $\mathcal{L}$ and $\mathcal{N}$.

Suppose that $\mathcal{L}$ is defined conditionally on $\{N_i = 1\}$, with $\nu_2 = \text{pr}(L_i = 1 \mid N_i = 1)$ and $\kappa^{(a_k)} = \text{pr}(Y_{ik} = a_k \mid L_i = 0, N_i = 1)/\text{pr}(Y_{ik} = a_k \mid L_i = 1, N_i = 1)$, for $a_k = 2, 3$. Furthermore, impose a restriction $\kappa^{(3)} = 0$. We denote our extension of the $\mathcal{N}$ association model by $\mathcal{N}2$. There are three latent classes and two necessary factors that operate in a hierarchical manner. The profile probabilities follow from equations (6) and (7) where $\mathcal{L}$ is imposed on the product of conditional probabilities, with $\kappa^{(3)} = 0$. Note that $\tau^{(a_1,...,a_w)}$ is here defined conditionally on $\{N_i = 1\}$ and thus ν_2 quantifies the proportion of potential frequent users within the susceptibles. This association model has three parameters, $\alpha = (\nu_1, \nu_2, \kappa^{(2)})$, but can be further simplified by assuming $\kappa^{(2)} = 1$, which implies that the susceptibles and potential frequent users have the same probability for occasional marijuana use.

4.3. Results of the Combined Regression and Association Model

Regardless of similar shape of the marginal probablilities, the observed paths show quite different patterns for boys and girls. This stresses the importance of modeling the whole path probability instead of only the marginal probabilities. The observed paths for boys are more dispersed than for girls, with the majority of girls staying as nonusers throughout the follow-up. This suggests that the association structures, although temporal, are different for boys and girls. In fact, modeling girls and boys together would require seven interaction terms with sex. Therefore, we analyze girls and boys separately.

4.3.1. Model for the Marijuana Use of Boys
As was noted in Section 4.1, assuming $\mathcal{M}$, some sensible constraints need to be imposed on the 16 second-order dependence ratios, without losing the essence of the form of the association. The dashed lines in Figure 1 summarize the 16 observed adjacent second-order dependence ratios for boys with bootstrap 95 percent confidence intervals. The solid lines in Figure 1 represent the fitted values, where the dependence ratios for movers $\tau^{(2,3)}$ and $\tau^{(3,2)}$ are assumed to follow a linear relationship for the consecutive pairs of ages, and dependence ratios of the stayers $\tau^{(2,2)}$ and $\tau^{(3,3)}$ are assumed to be stationary across the pairs of ages. This proves to be a superior fit over the exchangeable structures. The parameter estimates of this model $\mathcal{M}_6$, where the subscript indicates the number of association parameters, combined with a regression model R for the age-effect, are reported in Table 5.

From the estimated regression parameters, with age 13 as the reference category, we conclude that the probability of marijuana use increases from one year to the next. The interpretation of the Markov association model is that remaining as an occasional or a frequent user at two consecutive ages is, respectively, over two (2.366) and over three

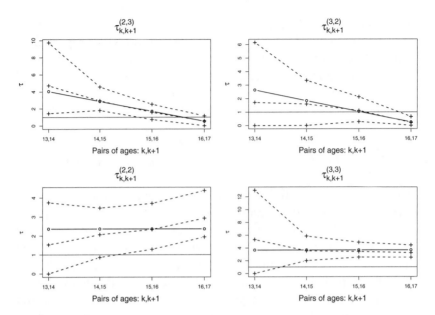

FIGURE 1. Observed second-order dependence ratios with bootstrap 95 percent confidence intervals (dashed lines) compared with the fitted dependence ratios (solid lines) for model $\{\mathcal{R}; \mathcal{M}_6\}$ for the marijuana use of boys. Horizontal line at value 1 corresponds to independence.

(3.673) times more probable than under independence. However, the dependence ratios for changing their habit from frequent use to occasional use ($\tau_{slope}^{(3,2)}$) and vice versa ($\tau_{slope}^{(2,3)}$) at two consecutive ages decrease with increasing age, change being even less probable between ages 16 and 17 than under independence (see Figure 1). This suggests that boys who use marijuana gradually develop a habit through the teenage years, which they are eventually reluctant to change.

Alternatively, if conditional dependencies are of interest, we can use equation (4) for the interpretation: given that the boy was an occasional user at age 16, the probability of being a frequent user at age 17 is only about half the marginal probability ($4.049 - 1.176 \times 3 = 0.52$). Similarly, if marijuana was used frequently at age 16, the probability of occasional marijuana use at age 17 is only a quarter the marginal probability ($2.640 - 0.798 \times 3 = 0.25$).

4.3.2. *Model for the Marijuana Use of Girls*

The observed adjacent second-order dependence ratios for girls did not reveal any clear structure. An interpretable fit assuming a Markov

TABLE 5
Model $\{\mathcal{R}; \mathcal{M}_6\}$: ML Estimates for Marijuana Use of Boys

Part of Model	Effect	Estimate	Standard Error
Regression model	age 14	0.862	0.282
	age 15	1.402	0.286
	age 16	1.649	0.295
	age 17	1.900	0.306
Association model	$\tau^{(2,2)}$	2.366	0.292
	$\tau^{(3,3)}$	3.673	0.463
	$\tau^{(2,3)}_{intercept*}$	4.049	0.814
	$\tau^{(2,3)}_{slope}$	-1.176	0.288
	$\tau^{(3,2)}_{intercept}$	2.640	0.688
	$\tau^{(3,2)}_{slope}$	-0.798	0.257

*The subscripts *intercept* and *slope* for the association parameters correspond to, respectively, intercept and slope of the fitted linear functions in Figure 1.

structure can be achieved by assuming stationarity over time for $\tau^{(a,b)}$, a, $b = 2, 3$, denoted by $\mathcal{M}_4$. The rightmost column in Table 6 summarizes the observed frequencies for girls throughout the follow-up from age 13 to 17 in three exclusive classes: (i) a nonuser at all ages, (ii) at most an occasional user at least once, and (iii) a frequent user at least once. The majority of the girls, 53 percent, fall in category (i), suggesting that the association model, assuming first-order Markov structure, could be modified to include a necessary factor. In other words, within this 53 percent, there might be a subgroup of girls not susceptible to marijuana use. Furthermore, allowing $\mathcal{M}$ to operate independently within the two latent classes of a structure $\mathcal{L}$ gives an estimate of $\kappa^{(3)}$ near zero. Imposing the restriction $\kappa^{(3)} = 0$ gives rise to an association model $\mathcal{N}2\mathcal{M}_7$, which is significantly better than $\mathcal{M}_4$ (likelihood ratio test p-value $= 0.016$). This association model implies that the population is divided into the following latent groups: the nonsusceptibles and the

TABLE 6
Observed and Fitted Counts of Models with Different Association Structures for the Marijuana Use of Girls.

Category	$\mathcal{I}$	$\mathcal{M}_4$	$\mathcal{N}2\mathcal{M}_3$	Observed
A nonuser at all ages	33.77	58.17	63.00	63
At most an occasional user at least once	49.24	40.07	36.01	36
A frequent user at least once	36.99	21.77	20.99	21

TABLE 7
Model $\{\mathcal{R}; \mathcal{N}2\mathcal{M}_3\}$ ML Estimates for Marijuana Use of Girls

Part of Model	Effect	Estimate	Standard Error
Regression model	age 14	1.063	0.505
	age 15	2.015	0.475
	age 16	2.193	0.475
	age 17	2.435	0.469
Association model	ν_1	0.629	0.087
	ν_2	0.422	0.085
	$\tau^{(2,2)} = \tau^{(3,3)}$	1.553	0.281

susceptibles. Furthermore, within the susceptibles, there is still a sub-group of potential frequent users. The plausible constraints $\tau^{(2,2)} = \tau^{(3,3)}$ and $\tau^{(2,3)} = \tau^{(3,2)} = \kappa^{(2)} = 1$ have negligible effect on the likelihood but make the interpretation of the association model, denoted by $\mathcal{N}2\mathcal{M}_3$, simpler. Table 6 presents the fitted counts of the models with associations structures $\mathcal{I}$, $\mathcal{M}_4$ and $\mathcal{N}2\mathcal{M}_3$, along with the observed counts for comparison.

Parameter estimates of the model $\mathcal{N}2\mathcal{M}_3$, combined with a regression model R for the age-effect, are reported in Table 7. The regression models for girls and boys yield similar conclusions. However, the interpretations of the association models are quite different: only 63 percent of the girls are susceptible to marijuana use from age 13 to 17, and out of these girls, only 42 percent are susceptible to frequent use. These latent structures do not, however, account for all the dependence between measurements. Temporal association still exists for the susceptibles; staying as an occasional user at two consecutive years is approximately 1.5 times more probable than under independence, as is staying as a frequent user within the latent class of potential frequent users.

5. MAXIMUM LIKELIHOOD ESTIMATION

As noted by Agresti and Natarajan (2001), methods for maximum likelihood fitting of marginal and cluster-specific models are difficult to implement or require approximate methods. This is especially complicated for large-dimensional problems, such as the government spending data with a total of seven clustered responses and several covariates. However, when applying the closed-form solution described in Section 2 instead, ML estimation is straightforward. The likelihood can be written as

$$I(\theta, \beta, \alpha) = \sum_{i=1}^{n} \log\{\pi(a_{i1}, \ldots, a_{iq})\}. \tag{10}$$

In the case where some responses are missing for subject i, such as in the government spending example, estimation is still straightforward, since only the observed values a_{ik} need to be included in equation (10). This is equivalent to assuming that the values are missing at random (MAR).

A significant computational advantage arises from the fact that when specifying π_i in terms of mean parameters, unconstrained maximization can be used, since this parametrization has a built-in unit-sum constraint (Jokinen 2006). What this effectively means is that we need to calculate only the probability of the observed profile for each i with given parameters at each iteration. In addition, as a consequence of the closed-form expression, the fitted probabilities for the unobserved profiles can also be easily calculated using the ML parameter estimates. However, when modeling sparse data sets, some of the fitted probabilities for the unobserved profiles may turn out negative. Negative probabilities can be avoided by imposing restrictions on the model parameters. However, we do not recommend this unless it implies a meaningful model. We note that estimated negative probabilities are an indication of a poorly chosen model and can be used as a diagnostic test against misspecification of the model.

An important aspect of the applicability of any novel methodology is the availability of user-friendly and versatile software. The first author has developed a package called *drm* for the statistical software R (R Development core Team 2006) for estimation of clustered and ordinal data sets using dependence ratios as measures of the association. The package is retrievable from: http://www.helsinki.fi/~jtjokine/drm. See help(drm) for the commands that will fit the models reported in Section 4. Furthermore, for longitudinal studies, *drm* allows a model for the nonresponse mechanism to be specified on top of the regression and association model; see Ekholm et al. (2003) for an example.

6. OTHER APPROACHES TO THE ANALYSIS OF CLUSTERED ORDINAL DATA

There are three main approaches to analysis of clustered categorical data: marginal models, random-effects models, and transition models. Transition models are mainly applicable if the clustering occurs in time.

A common way of specifying transition models is to include previous responses as explanatory variables into equation (5). Regression coefficients are then to be interpreted as effects conditional on previous responses; for a presentation of different specifications of such models, see Lindsey (1999: 63–67). For a more flexible approach to conditional modeling of ordinal longitudinal response, see Lindsey and Kaufmann (2004).

If the population-averaged effects of the covariates are of interest, marginal models can be applied. A third option are random-effects models, where the parameters of the regression model are to be interpreted as subject-specific effects. For a survey of these two latter approaches, see Agresti and Natarajan (2001). We review these two approaches in relation to our method, using the data in Table 1, and an example concerning reviews of 93 movies by four critics, previously analyzed by Hartzel, Agresti, and Caffo (2001).

6.1. *Marginal Models*

Consider again the example concerning responses of married couples to the questionnaire item "Sex is fun for me and my partner." A parsimonious model is achieved with a regression model without explanatory variables. Association model $\mathcal{L}$ with a parameter restriction $\kappa^{(4)} = 0$ fits the data well, yielding a likelihood ratio test statistic $L^2 = 4.92$ with 9 d.f., compared with the saturated model. This model implies that the observed weak association between couples, according to the saturated model in Table 2, may be a result of a latent binary factor. In other words, the observed association between couples is a consequence of the population of couples consisting of two groups with different response probabilities. Fitted marginals and dependence ratios of this model are summarized in Table 8.

In addition to marginal probabilities, conditional probabilities can also be easily obtained. Table 9 summarizes the probabilities of couples in the two latent groups. Note that the interpretation of $\hat{\nu}_2 = 0.41$ and restriction $\kappa^{(4)} = 0$ is that $100 \times (1 - \hat{\nu}_2) = 59$ percent of the couples would never answer "Never or Occasionally" to a question concerning sexual fun.

Marginal modeling is generally interpreted as an approach that focuses on the marginals and treats the dependence structure as a

TABLE 8

Fitted Marginals and Dependence Ratios of Model $\mathcal{L}$: "Sex is Fun for Me and My Partner"

Husband	Wife				
	Always Fun	Very Often	Fairly Often	Never Fun	Marginal
Always fun					
Very often		$\hat{\tau}^{(2,2)} = 1.21$	$\hat{\tau}^{(2,3)} = 0.90$	$\hat{\tau}^{(2,4)} = 0.45$	$\hat{\mu}^{(2)} = 0.20$
Fairly often		$\hat{\tau}^{(3,2)} = 0.90$	$\hat{\tau}^{(3,3)} = 1.05$	$\hat{\tau}^{(3,4)} = 1.27$	$\hat{\mu}^{(3)} = 0.26$
Never fun		$\hat{\tau}^{(4,2)} = 0.45$	$\hat{\tau}^{(4,3)} = 1.27$	$\hat{\tau}^{(4,4)} = 2.45$	$\hat{\mu}^{(4)} = 0.17$
Marginal		$\hat{\mu}^{(2)} = 0.20$	$\hat{\mu}^{(3)} = 0.26$	$\hat{\mu}^{(4)} = 0.17$	1

nuisance (Agresti and Natarajan 2001). A popular approach is the GEE-methodology (Liang and Zeger 1986), where models are specified only for marginal distributions and hence do not support ML estimation. Without building models for the entire response profile, a comprehensive modeling of the associations is not feasible.

For likelihood-based methods, log-linear modeling formulation is typically applied for the association. Fitzmaurice and Laird (1993) used conditional log-odds ratio parameters to specify the association, which are the canonical parameters of the log-linear model. For the sexual fun data, Hout, Duncan, and Sobel (1987) fitted log-linear models with various quasi-symmetry constraints for the association. Other forms of constraints, such as common local or global odds ratios (Lang and Agresti 1994; Glonek and McCullagh 1995) have also been suggested for clustered ordinal data. Although useful in many situations for examining the form of the association, especially in the bivariate case, these constraints can be viewed as expedient ways of handling the association when the complexity of the data increases. For example, Fitzmaurice and Laird (1993) consider the association parameters as

TABLE 9

Fitted Conditional Probabilities of Model $\mathcal{L}$: "Sex is Fun for Me and My Partner"

Latent Factor	$L_i = 1$	$L_i = 0$
Proportion in the Population	$\hat{v}_2 = 0.41$	$1 - \hat{v}_2 = 0.59$
Always fun	0.16	0.50
Very often	0.09	0.28
Fairly often	0.33	0.22
Never fun	0.42	—

pure nuisance. In our case, symmetry constraints on the fitted dependence ratio parameters in Table 8 are a result of the fit for the underlying mechanism that has generated the association. Parameter interpretation is also straightforward, since they are proportions of the population or ratios of probabilities.

6.2. Random-Effects Models

Hartzel, Agresti, and Caffo (2001) analyzed a data set from *Variety* magazine, containing reviews of 93 movies by four critics: Medved, Siskel, Ebert, and Lyons. Each review is rated as $1 =$ Pro (positive), $2 =$ Mixed (mixture of positive and negative), or $3 =$ Con (negative). An obvious regression task is to compare the distribution of the ratings for each of the critics. In addition, the investigation of the rater agreement may be considered to be equally important.

The most parsimonious fit for the regression model that compares the critics is achieved with the adjacent category logit link with differing rater effects for $a = 1$ and $a = 2$. The left panel in Table 10 compares the fits of the exchangeable association structures when the regression model for the critics effect, denoted by $\mathcal{R}$, is specified with an adjacent category logit link. According to AIC, association model $\mathcal{D}$ produces the most parsimonious fit compared with the other structures. Regression and association parameter estimates for the combined model, using $\mathcal{D}$, are reported in the right panel of Table 10.

TABLE 10

AIC of the Exchangeable Association Models (left) and ML Estimates and Standard Errors of Model $\{\mathcal{R}; \mathcal{D}\}$ (right) for Movie Critics

AIC for Five Models		ML Estimates for a Model $\{\mathcal{R}; \mathcal{D}\}$			
Model	AIC		Effect	Estimate	Standard Error
$\{\mathcal{R}; \mathcal{I}\}$	766.3	Pro Versus	Siskel	−0.104	0.311
$\{\mathcal{R}; \mathcal{N}\}$	747.1	Mixed	Ebert	−0.060	0.324
$\{\mathcal{R}; \mathcal{L}\}$	745.8		Lyons	0.792	0.371
$\{\mathcal{R}; \mathcal{N}2\}$	738.1	Mixed Versus	Siskel	0.635	0.326
$\{\mathcal{R}; \mathcal{D}\}$	734.8	Con	Ebert	1.240	0.377
			Lyons	−0.050	0.379
			ξ_1	2.148	1.772
		Association	ξ_2	0.844	0.316
			ξ_3	1.252	0.509

From the regression model, with Medved as the reference category, our conclusions are the same as Hartzel, Agresti, and Caffo (2001)—that is, the Pro Versus Mixed effect is negligible when comparing Siskel and Ebert with Medved, and the Mixed Versus Con effect is negligible when comparing Lyons with Medved. The association model suggests that there is a latent continuous variability in the quality of the movies reviewed by the critics. This can be interpreted as an indication that movies do possess certain objective criteria according to which they can be rated. One conclusion from this kind of interpretation is that judging the quality of a movie is not entirely a matter of taste.

Hartzel et al. (2001) fitted several random-effects models to account for the association of the ratings within a movie. Random-effects models take into account within subject heterogeneity in the linear predictor by imposing a mixing distribution for the mean parameter. By far the most popular choice for the mixing distribution is normal. Agresti et al. (2000) noted that this convention is possibly a controversial issue. As Lindsey (1999: 212) argued, the choice of the mixing distribution should be made on theoretical grounds in terms of how the mean is thought to vary in the population or, if necessary, empirically. As can be seen from Table 10, the exchangeable association models presented in Sections 3 and 4 provide a rich set of meaningful association structures and, in the absence of theoretical knowledge, comparison of models including and excluding within-subject heterogeneity is straightforward through likelihood ratio tests and information criteria.

The choice of a parametric or nonparametric random-effects component is usually dependent on the choice of link function relating the mean and the linear predictor; for example, see Hartzel, Agresti, and Caffo (2001). Since certain link functions may be preferable for parameter interpretation or for a more parsimonious fit, this limits the choice of random-effects models. In our case, all latent structures are imposed on the response category probabilities, which are independent of the link function used. This is a natural approach if we want to construct meaningful association models.

The parameter interpretation is the most important substantive distinction between random-effects models and regression models specified using equation (5). Regression estimates from random-effects models are cluster-specific, whereas estimates from (5) are population averaged. The merits and relevance of the effects of interest should be judged according to the problem at hand. For example, when comparing the movie critics, the question is whether the interest lies in how the critics differ when reviewing a movie, or how they differ on average across the movies. Agresti et al. (2000) noted that most of the discussion about this distinction has been related to epidemiological and clinical trial settings. However, they stressed that it is time to consider the practical implications also in social science applications. So far, latent variable models for clustered categorical data, where the regression model is of form (5), have received little attention in the social science literature.

6.3. *Combining the Three Approaches*

Vermunt and Hagenaars (2004 chap. 15) discuss the implications of marginal, transition, and random-effects approaches for ordinal longitudinal data. They fit several models, applying each of the approaches, to the data set concerning teenage marijuana use in Section 4. We can compare the overall goodness-of-fit of their models with our separate models for boys and girls by summing the AIC-values for the models fitted in Section 4.3. This sum indicates that our combined model fits substantially better than their models.

In another application of the marijuana use data, Vermunt, Rodrigo, and Ato-Garcia (2001) proposed a modification of the approach by Lang and Agresti (1994) for combining marginal, transitional, and cluster-specific approaches in a single framework. However, the application was limited to four time-points rather than all five. Our modeling approach can also be viewed as a combination of the three methods. Consider the models presented in Section 4: marginal modeling is applied for the univariate probabilities; cluster-specific models are applied using the hierarchical necessary factor; and the transitions are modeled using the Markov specification and interpreted using the relationship expressed in equation (4).

7. CONCLUDING REMARKS

A strong age effect in the prevalence of teenage cannabis use has been widely reported; for example, see Johnston, O'Malley, and Bachman (2000). Also the higher prevalence among teenage boys, compared with girls of the same age, is well-known (Hall, Johnston, and Donnelly 1999).

However, in addition to marginal prevalences, investigation of individual profiles of cannabis use has not gained similar attention. Some of this may have been because suitable tools for this joint task have not been available. We have presented a methodology that allowed us to extract valuable additional information about the different behaviors of girls and boys through a comprehensive investigation of individual response profiles. We presented in Sections 3 and 4 latent structures that provide a meaningful alternative to random-effects models for modeling the association structure. Alternatively, for longitudinal studies Markov structures in Section 4.1 can be used to describe the temporal association. Furthermore, combining some of these structures is straightforward and therefore provides an ample set of association models for multivariate categorical responses.

There exists an explicit expression for the joint probability in terms of marginal probabilities and dependence ratios. In addition, the mean parametrization facilitates maximum likelihood estimation, that is therefore straightforward and feasible even for large-dimensional problems. However, sometimes fitted probabilities for nonobserved response profiles are negative, which indicates model misspecification. Pursuing meaningful models for both the regression and association structures for a multivariate categorical response is a challenging task. Extra care is needed when fitting models to sparse data sets. Therefore, fitted response profile probabilities serve as a helpful tool for checking the plausibility of the fitted model.

Agresti (1999) stressed that with the continuing development of more complex models, an increasingly important but difficult task is communicating to nonstatisticians the interpretation of the models and their parameters. The dependence ratio is a measure of association that, for researchers used to concepts like relative risks, is easy to grasp. In addition, the parameters of the latent variable models, such as those for the hierarchical necessary factor in the model of marijuana use by girls, have a clear and simple interpretation as proportions of the population. Compared with the multivariate normal case, the association structure of a multivariate categorical response is very complex. Further development of more complex models is therefore an admirable goal. However, our view is that this should not be made at the expense of the interpretability of the model.

REFERENCES

Agresti, A. 1999. "Modelling Ordered Categorical Data: Recent Advances and Future Challenges." *Statistics in Medicine* 18:2191–207.

Agresti, A., J. G. Booth, J. P. Hobert, and B. Caffo. 2000. "Random-Effects Modeling of Categorical Response Data." Pp. 27–81 in *Sociological Methodology*, vol. 30, edited by Michael E. Sobel and Mark P. Becker. Boston, MA: Blackwell Publishing Inc.

Agresti, A., and R. Natarajan. 2001. "Modeling Clustered Ordered Categorical Data: A Survey." *International Statistical Review* 69:345–71.

Davies, H. T. O., I. K. Crombie, and M. Tavakoli. 1998. "When Can Odds Ratios Mislead?" *British Medical Journal* 316:989–91.

Deeks, J. J., M. B. Bracken, J. C Sinclair, H. T. O. Davies, M. Tavakoli, and I. K. Crombie. 1998. "Letter to the Editor: When Can Odds Ratios Mislead?" *British Medical Journal* 317:1155.

Ekholm, A., P. W. F. Smith, and J. W. McDonald. 1995. "Marginal Regression Analysis of a Multivariate Binary Response." *Biometrika* 82:847–54.

Ekholm, A., J. W. McDonald, and P. W. F. Smith. 2000. "Association Models for a Multivariate Binary Response." *Biometrics* 56:712–18.

Ekholm, A. 2003. "Comparing the Odds and the Dependence Ratios." Pp. 13–25 in *Statistics, Econometrics, and Society: Essays in Honour of Leif Nordberg*, edited by R. Höglund, M. Jäntti, and G. Rosenqvist. Helsinki: Statistics Finland.

Ekholm, A., J. Jokinen, J. W. McDonald, and P. W. F. Smith. 2003. "Joint Regression and Association Modelling for Longitudinal Ordinal Data." *Biometrics* 59:795–803.

Elliott, D. S., S. S. Ageton, D. Huizinga, B. A. Knowles, and R. J. Canter. 1983. "The Prevalence and Incidence of Delinquent Behavior: 1976–1980." *National Youth Survey*, Project Report No. 26, Boulder, CO: Behavioral Research Institute.

Fitzmaurice, G. M., and N. M. Laird. 1993. "A Likelihood-based Method for Analysing Longitudinal Binary Responses." *Biometrika* 80:141–51.

Glonek, G. F. V., and P. McCullagh. 1995. "Multivariate Logistic Models." *Journal of the Royal Statistical Society*, Series B, 57:533–46.

Greenland, S. 1987. "Interpretation and Choice of Effect Measures in Epidemiologic Analyses." *Americal Journal of Epidemiology* 125:761–68.

Hall, W., L. D. Johnston, and N. Donnelly. 1999. "Epidemiology of Cannabis Use and Its Consequences." Pp. 71–125 in *The Health Effects of Cannabis*, edited by H. Kalant, W. Corrigall, W. Hall et al. Toronto: Centre for Addiction and Mental Health.

Hartzel, J., A. Agresti, and B. Caffo. 2001. "Multinomial Logit Random Effects Models." *Statistical Modelling* 1:81–102.

Hout, M., O. D. Duncan, and M. E. Sobel. 1987. "Association and Heterogeneity: Structural Models of Similarities and Differences." Pp. 145–84 in *Sociological Methodology*, vol. 17, edited by C. C. Clogg. Washington, DC: American Sociological Association.

Jokinen, J. 2006. "Fast Estimation Algorithm for Likelihood-based Analysis of Repeated Categorical Responses." Computational Statistics & Data Analysis, in press.

Johnston, L. D., P. M. O'Malley, and J. G. Bachman. 2000. *Monitoring the Future: National Survey Results on Drug Use, 1975–1999.* Bethesda, MD: National Institute on Drug Abuse.

Lang, J. B., and A. Agresti. 1994. "Simultaneously Modeling Joint and Marginal Distributions of Multivariate Categorical Responses." *Journal of the American Statistical Association* 89:625–32.

Lang, J. B., J. W. McDonald, and P. W. F. Smith. 1999. "Association-Marginal Modeling of Multivariate Categorical Responses: A Maximum-Likelihood Approach." *Journal of the American Statistical Association* 94:1161–71.

Liang, K. Y., and S. L. Zeger. 1986. "Longitudinal Data Analysis Using Generalized Linear Models." *Biometrika* 73:13–22.

Lindsey, J. K. 1999. *Models for Repeated Measurements.* 2d ed. New York: Oxford University Press.

Lindsey, P. J., and J. Kaufmann. 2004. "Analysis of a Longitudinal Ordinal Response Clinical Trial Using Dynamic Models." *Applied Statistics* 53:523–37.

Little, R. J. A., and D. B. Rubin. 2002. *Statistical Analysis with Missing Data.* 2d ed. New York: Wiley.

R Development Core Team. 2006. "R: A Language and Environment for Statistical Computing." Vienna, Austria: R Foundation for Statistical Computing (http://www.r-project.org).

Sackett, D. L., J. J. Deeks, and D. G. Altman. 1996. "Down with Odds Ratios!" *Evidence-Based Medicine* 1:164–66.

Vermunt, J. K., M. F. Rodrigo, and M. Ato-Garcia. 2001. "Modeling Joint and Marginal Distributions in the Analysis of Categorical Panel Data." *Sociological Methods and Research* 30:170–96.

Vermunt, J. K., and J. A. Hagenaars. 2004. "Ordinal Longitudinal Data Analysis." Pp. 374–93 in *Methods in Human Growth Research*, edited by R. C. Hauspie, N. Cameron and L. Molinari. Cambridge, England: Cambridge University Press.

MEASURING AND ANALYZING CLASS INEQUALITY WITH THE GINI INDEX INFORMED BY MODEL-BASED CLUSTERING

Tim Futing Liao*

The most widely used measure for studying social, economic, and health inequality is the Gini index/ratio. Whereas other measures of inequality possess certain useful characteristics, such as the straightforward decomposability of the generalized entropy measures, the Gini index has remained the most popular, at least in part due to its ease of interpretation. However, the Gini index has a limitation in measuring inequality. It is less sensitive to how the population is stratified than how individual values differ. The twin purposes of this paper are to explain the limitation and to propose a model-based method—latent class/clustering analysis for understanding and measuring inequality. The latent cluster approach has the major advantage of being able to identify potential "classes" of individuals who share similar levels of income or one or more other attributes and to assess the fit of the model-based classes to the empirical data, based on different cluster distributional assumptions and the number of latent classes. This paper

Versions of a related paper were presented at the American Sociological Association Methodology Conference, Ann Arbor, MI, 22–24 April 2004 and at the International Conference in Memory of Two Eminent Social Scientists: C. Gini and M. O. Lorenz, Their Impact in the Twentieth-Century Development of Probability, Statistics, and Economics, Università degli Studi di Siena, 23–26 May 2005. Feedback by participants at the conferences, especially critical comments by Camilo Dagum at the 2005 conference, which established the need for a second stratification index, as well as comments by Chris Fraley, Shin-Kap Han, and two *Sociological Methodology* reviewers, are greatly appreciated. Direct correspondence to Tim F. Liao, Department of Sociology, University of Illinois, Urbana, IL 61801, USA; E-mail: tfliao@uiuc.edu.

*University of Illinois

201

*distinguishes class inequality from individual inequality, the type
that is better captured by the Gini. Once the classes are estimated,
the membership of estimated classes obtained from the best fitting
model facilitates the decomposition of the Gini index into individual and class inequality. Class inequality is then measured by two
relative stratification indices based on either the relative size of the
Gini between-class components or the relative number of stratified
individuals. Therefore, the Gini index is extended and assisted by
model-based clustering to measure class inequality, thereby real-
izing its great potential for studying inequality. Income data from
France and Hungary are used to illustrate the application of the
method.*

1. INTRODUCTION

Sociologists interested in studying social inequality often rely on measures such as the Gini index (or the Gini inequality ratio), which is
named after the Italian statistician Corrado Gini (1912). The Gini index and its associated Lorenz curve, attributed to Lorenz (1905), have
seen extremely widespread applications in the social sciences. Last year,
we passed the centennial of the original Lorenz publication. In recent
decades, there have been numerous alternative measures proposed, including the class of generalized entropy measures. Whereas the alternative measures of inequality may possess certain useful characteristics,
such as the straightforward decomposability of the generalized entropy
measures (Cowell 2000), the Gini index, which can be viewed as a special
case of the general expression for inequality indexes (Firebaugh 1999),
has remained the most popular, in large measure due to its ease of interpretation. The decomposition of the Gini, a relevant issue for this paper,
has attracted much attention in recent research (Dagum 1997a, 1997b,
1998; Milanovic and Yitzhaki 2002; Mussard, Terraza, and Seyte 2003;
Yao and Liu 1996; Yao 1999; Yitzhaki 1994).

There is no doubt that the Gini index is extremely useful for
understanding inequality, but it has a consequential limitation in measuring inequality, to be explored in this paper. It is less sensitive to
stratified differences than to individual differences. In general, a particular inequality index is only a valid measure of a undimensional concept
(Schwartz and Winship 1980). The Gini index is more a valid measure
of individual inequality than a measure of class inequality. The twin
purposes of this paper are to explain this limitation and to propose
an alternative, model-based method—latent class/clustering analysis

to extend the Gini index for understanding and measuring stratified inequality.

This paper first presents the Gini index and discusses its limitation in measuring inequality. It then focuses on a form of latent class or clustering analysis that is able to not only avoid the limitation but also capture features of stratification. A real-world example of income data from France and Hungary is examined next to illustrate the proposed method and to compare it with the Gini index in the subsequent section, where Gini decomposition is applied by using cluster classification schemes suggested by the model-based method. The decomposition results are then used to form two stratification indices for measuring the amount of class (income) inequality relative to the total amount of (income) inequality in terms of the Gini and in terms of the number of pairwise comparisons. Some concluding remarks are offered in the final section.

2. WHAT THE GINI INDEX DOES AND DOES NOT MEASURE

Let y_i designate a random distribution such as income, let $\pi = F(y_i)$ indicate the distribution for y_i, and let $\eta = F_1(y_i)$ represent the corresponding first moment distribution function. The relation between η and π, defined for $0 \leq y_i < \infty$, is the Lorenz curve (see Figure 1 for an example of the curve), and relation can be denoted by $\eta = L(\pi)$. The Gini index can then be defined accordingly:

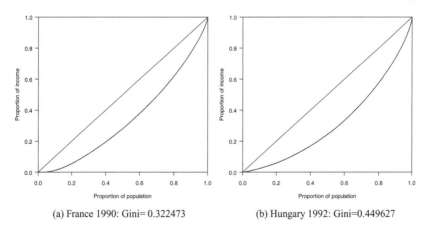

(a) France 1990: Gini= 0.322473   (b) Hungary 1992: Gini=0.449627

FIGURE 1. Gini indices and Lorenz curves for income data from France and Hungary.

$$G = 1 - 2 \int_0^1 L(\pi)d\pi. \tag{1}$$

It can also be written as

$$G = -1 + \frac{2}{\mu_y} \int_0^\infty yF(y)f(y)dy. \tag{2}$$

There are numerous computational formulas for implementing the Gini calculation. Perhaps the most revealing one is that used by Dagum (1997a, 1997b, 1998) and Mussard, Terraza, and Seyte (2003):

$$G = \frac{\sum_{i=1}^n \sum_{j=1}^n |y_i - y_j|}{2n^2\mu}. \tag{3}$$

Although all the various computation formulas will give the same results, equation (3) has the advantage of demonstrating that what is really measured by the Gini index is an average of pairwise differences between the individual cases in the sample weighted by the overall sample mean (for brevity "sample" is used in the paper through the measurement of the entire "population" may be available sometimes). It is the overall individual mean differences that matter, whether or not these individuals fall into classes or clusters. Whereas recent research has shown that Gini's mean difference is a superior measure of variability for non-normal distributions (Yitzhaki 2003), the Gini index does not capture well the clustering nature of the data, a more important point for studying social and economic stratification such as income inequality, to be illustrated below.

Let us examine a very simple simulated distribution of only six y_i data points where $i = 1 \ldots 6$. Suppose that we have a first distribution that contains the cases

$$1 : [1, 1, 1, 4, 4, 4],$$

where the values are simply certain units of income. The Gini ratio for this distribution is 0.300000, and the value of the coefficient is not affected by sample size as long as the nature of inequality remains the same. In other words, repeating the 1s and the 4s a large number of times would result in an identical Gini value of 0.300000. This remark, however, will not hold computationally for the case of complete equality—that is, if all observations have the same number of income units. For our purposes here, however, the point is irrelevant.

Next, we consider a second distribution, which is identical to Distribution 1 except for the last three cases, whose holding of income are all increased by one unit:

$$2 : [1, 1, 1, 5, 5, 5].$$

The Gini index for the distribution is 0.333333, an 11% increase over the Gini index for the first distribution. Now let us consider a third distribution:

$$3 : [1, 1, 2.5, 2.5, 4, 4].$$

This time the two middle cases have an income level that is halfway between the first two and the last two observations in Distribution 1. The third distribution has a Gini value of 0.266667, an 11% decrease from the Gini for the first distribution. A comparison of the three simple distributions reveals something rather fundamental, and rather disturbing. Either Distribution 2 or 3 represents the same amount of departure from Distribution 1 in the value of its Gini index, but for understanding their distributions and measuring inequality, do Distributions 2 and 3 differ similarly from Distribution 1? Apparently not. Distribution 2 is almost the same as Distribution 1, other than the fact that cases 4, 5, and 6 are a bit richer. Unlike Distribution 1 (or 2), which contains two (income) classes, Distribution 3 has three (income) classes and has a different shape of stratification and inequality from the first two distributions. To push the point a bit further, let us double the values of cases 4, 5, and 6 in Distribution 1, resulting in

$$4 : [1, 1, 1, 8, 8, 8].$$

The new distribution has a Gini index of 0.388889, a 30% increase over that of Distribution 1 even though the form of inequality is the same.

To further illustrate the relative insensitivity of the Gini to the shape of inequality or stratification, let us consider two more distributions:

$$5 : [1, 2.3, 3.6, 4.9, 6.2, 7.5],$$

which has a Gini coefficient of 0.297386, and

$$6 : [1, 1, 3, 3, 5, 5],$$

which has a Gini index of 0.296296. In Distribution 5, each observation after the first is 1.3 income units higher than the previous case, showing no clear patterns of class formation and only an even distribution over the scale. The distribution can be viewed as all cases belonging to one class or as if they belong to six individual classes. In Distribution 6, the cases form three distinctive classes. Interestingly, the three distributions of 1, 5, and 6 produce an almost identical Gini value. (By fine-tuning the values in Distributions 5 and 6, we can obtain an exact match for the value of 0.300000 from Distribution 1, but that is not necessary here to make the point.) However, the form of inequality is drastically different across the three distributions in question.

Why is the Gini index so insensitive to changes in the form of inequality? The Gini index is related to the Lorenz curve as twice the area between the 45-degree line and the Lorenz curve, and it can be formally written as equation (1) or (2) (see Chotikapanich and Griffiths 2001). The computational formula of equation (3) shows that it is based on the average of pairwise absolute differences. Obviously, the absolute individual values directly determine the resulting index value.

3. MODEL-BASED CLUSTERING METHOD

Cluster analysis can be viewed as a way to group similar objects with an unknown number of groups whose forms (i.e., cluster parameters) are also unknown (Kaufman and Rousseuw 1990). Similarly, Everitt (1993) viewed the purpose of cluster analysis as obtaining a useful division of objects into classes, whose numbers and properties are to be determined. These ideas convey the essence of the analysis of social inequality, where researchers seek an understanding of the lineup of the groups or social classes within which individuals are more similar than across these classes, judged by attributes such as education, income, and occupation. These attributes can be measured by educational attainment, annual household income, and occupational prestige.

A recent development takes the approach of model-based clustering, which specifies a statistical model for the population from which the sample under study is assumed to have come. Model-based clustering has a number of advantages (Vermunt and Magidson 2002): (1) the choice of the cluster criterion that is used to minimize the within-cluster variation and maximize the between-cluster variation is less arbitrary in model-based clustering than in conventional cluster analysis; (2) model-based clustering is flexible in allowing various simple and complex distributional forms for the observed variables within the clusters; (3) it is relatively simple to deal with variables of mixed measurement scales. However, this does not mean that model-based clustering is unaffected by measurement scales.

Model-based clustering also allows the observed variables to be continuous or categorical (i.e., nominal or ordinal) because clusters can be treated as latent classes; therefore, the method can be seen as latent class analysis. Here we consider only continuous observed variables in our model specifications because our empirical concern in this paper is income. The basic model-based clustering specification takes the form

$$f(\mathbf{y}_i|\theta) = \sum_{k=1}^{K} \pi_k f_k(\mathbf{y}_i|\theta_k), \tag{4}$$

where $\mathbf{y}_i$ represents an individual's scores on a set of observed variables, K denotes the number of clusters, π_k designates the prior probability that a case belongs to cluster k (or the size of cluster k), and θ defines the model parameters (Vermunt and Magidson 2002). Equation (4) specifies the distribution of $\mathbf{y}_i$ given the model parameter θ as a mixture of cluster-specific densities, $f(\mathbf{y}_i|\theta_k)$.

Equivalently, we may express the model in (4) in its likelihood form (Fraley and Raftery 2002),

$$L(\theta_k, \pi_k|\mathbf{y}_i) = \prod_{i=1}^{n} \sum_{k=1}^{K} \pi_k f_k(\mathbf{y}_i|\theta_k), \tag{5}$$

where most commonly $f(\mathbf{y}_i|\theta_k)$ is the multivariate normal (Gaussian) density ϕ_k, parameterized by its mean μ_k and covariance matrix $\sum_k$. Banfield and Raftery (1993) proposed parameterizing the cluster-specific covariance matrices $\sum_k$ by eigenvalue decomposition:

$$\sum_k = \lambda_k D_k A_k D_k^T, \tag{6}$$

where D_k is the orthogonal matrix of eigenvectors, A_k is a diagonal matrix whose elements are proportional to the eigenvalues, λ_k is an associated scalar of proportionality. More specifically, $\lambda_k = |\sum_k|^{1/d}$, where d is the number of indicators, and $A_k = \text{diag}\{\alpha_{1k}, \dots, \alpha_{pk}\}$ and $1 = \alpha_{1k} \geq \alpha_{2k} \geq \dots \geq \alpha_{pk} > 0$. The three parameters offer a nice interpretation: D_k describes the orientation of the kth cluster in the mixture, with A_k representing its shape, and λ_k its volume, which is proportional to $\lambda_k^d | A_k |$. Expressed differently, if a latent class or cluster is viewed as a group or cluster of points in a multidimensional space, the volume is the size of the cluster and the orientation and shape parameters indicate whether the cluster mixture is spherical, diagonal, or ellipsoidal. For example, the kth cluster will be roughly spherical if the largest and the smallest eigenvalues of $\sum_k$ are of the same magnitude.

The combination of these parameter specifications determines the specific statistical model to fit. For multidimensional data involving multiple variables such as education, income, and occupational prestige, the full range of models must be considered. An example of multidimensional data that involve multiple variables can be VEI, which denotes a model with clusters of varying volumes (V), shapes that are all equal (E), and an orientation that is of the identity (I). For one-dimensional data involving income distributions, however, there are only two models to estimate: E for equal variance and V for varying variance. For further details on the range of possible models, see Fraley and Raftery (1999). This paper will focus on one-dimensional data illustrated by income distributions.

3.1. Model Selection

In conventional cluster analysis, the data analyst must deal with the issue of selection of the clustering method and that of determining the number of clusters. In model-based clustering, the two issues reduce to a single concern of model selection. In the model-based clustering approach of Dasgupta and Raftery (1998) and Fraley and Raftery (1998), Bayesian model selection via Bayes factors and posterior probabilities is preferred. This in practice is evaluated by way of the Bayesian information criterion (BIC), which is implemented in the MCLUST software (Fraley and Raftery 1999, 2002).

3.2. *Density Estimation*

Estimating the number of clusters and individuals' memberships in the clusters is probably the major purpose of model-based clustering methods. However, it is also possible to obtain density estimation, in which the value of mixture likelihood is evaluated at individual points of interest. Roeder and Wasserman (1997) used normal mixtures for univariate density estimation and BIC to decide the number of components. Fraley and Raftery's method (1999, 2002) can be viewed as a multivariate extension because the parameter estimates for the best model describe a multivariate mixture density for the data.

3.3. *Uncertainty of Classification*

Fraley and Raftery (1999) described the software MCLUST, which provides iterative EM methods to implement the model-based clustering and is interfaced with both the S-Plus and R languages. The software also computes a quantity known as uncertainty, which is defined by subtracting the membership probability of the most likely group or cluster for each observation from 1. A descriptive analysis of uncertainty can indicate how well the observations are classified. Uncertainty plots can be produced for single or multidimensional data.

4. A MODEL-BASED CLUSTER ANALYSIS OF INCOME INEQUALITY

When the concern is only with the shape of (income) inequality, such analysis is relatively simple because there are only two possible models to consider—equal variance (E) or varying variance (V). For an empirical example, I apply Fraley and Raftery's (1999, 2002) model-based clustering to household income data from France and Hungary in the early 1990s. The data for France are from the 1990 French Household Panel collected among the noncollective households in Lorraine, and the data for Hungary are from the 1992 Hungarian Household Panel with noninstitutional households in the nation as the target population. The comparative samples yield 2057 valid income observations for France and 2030 valid income cases for Hungary. I analyze the two income distributions by focusing on their income inequality and how it is reflected by the Gini index. For a study of these income data by way of relative distribution methods, see Liao (2002).

First, let us analyze the income inequality in France and Hungary by using the Gini index and the Lorenz curve. During the 1980s, many social-welfare benefits were increased under the Mitterand government (Gottschalk 1993); Hungary's socialist experiment failed to erase class-based inequality (Szelenyi 1998), and inequality has increased tremendously in all postsocialist countries including Hungary. Thus, the Hungarian data should contain a greater amount of stratification than the French data, but can the Gini index reveal the difference? Figure 1 presents the Lorenz Curves for the two countries with corresponding Gini indices shown. It is rather difficult to see the difference between the two Lorenz curves, except for the barely noticeable larger area that seems to be covered by the Lorenz curve in the graph for Hungary. The Gini indices for the two sets of data suggest that the Hungarian income inequality is greater than that shown in the French data by about 0.04. For the sake of comparison, the empirical distributions of income in the two countries are presented in Figure 2. It appears that the Hungarian data are more skewed to the right with a longer tail.

However, the issue of stratification is entirely ignored by an analysis based on the Gini and Lorenz only. Next, we move on to analyzing the same data with model-based clustering by using the MCLUST program written for R. An unequal variance model with four latent classes (or clusters) fits the French income data the best, as shown in part (a) of Figure 3. Part (b) gives a graphic idea where the clusters are located in the income distribution, part (c) plots the uncertainty probabilities, with peaks located in the regions between the clusters, and part (d) presents the model-based density plot of the income distribution. The uncertainty plot clearly indicates three uncertain regions although the density plot shows only two obvious peaks and a long tail to the right.

For the Hungarian income data, however, the six-cluster unequal-variance model fits the best (Figure 4). The interpretation works the same as for Figure 3. The uncertainty plot shows five clear peaks located

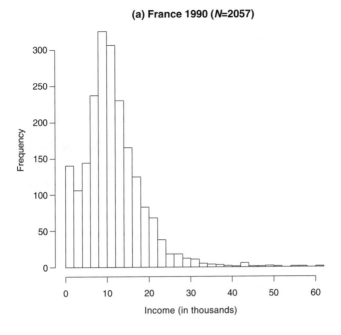

FIGURE 2. Empirical income distributions of France in 1990 and Hungary in 1992.

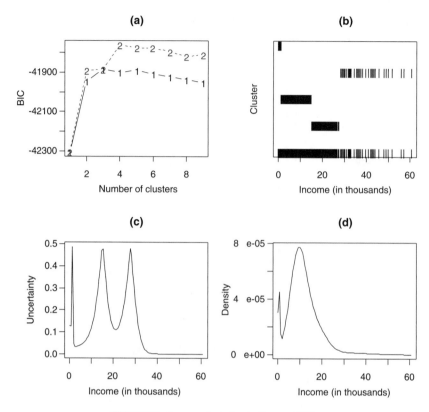

FIGURE 3. Income clustering in France, 1990.

between the clusters while the density plot gives three noticeable peaks with a slighted elevated tail skewed to the right. Figure 4(b) reveals a cluster embedded in another, a possible artifact due to the attempt to fit normal mixtures with skewed data.

Overall, the model-based clustering method allows us to see much greater detail in how the two countries differ in their patterns of stratification. Such detail is ignored by the Gini index or the Lorenz curve because these measures of inequality focus on only one kind of inequality.

Because of the right-skewed distribution for both sets of data but especially the Hungarian data, natural logarithm transformation is applied, as is commonly done on income data. The log-income distributions are presented in Figure 5.

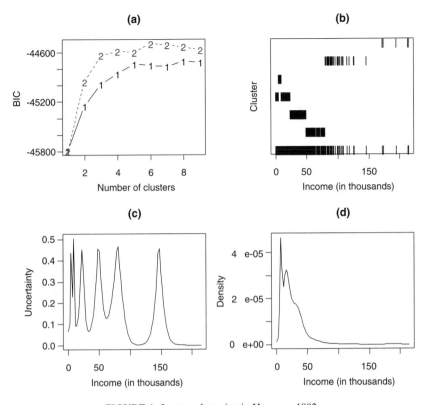

FIGURE 4. Income clustering in Hungary, 1992.

It appears that the log transformation overcompensates the skewness in the French data while the Hungarian income data distribute more normally. Such transformations may be useful when latent cluster models assume normal mixtures. Nevertheless, as we can see from Figure 5, the transformation is more appropriate when skewness is severe. If the model-based clustering method on the log-income variables is applied, the total number of latent clusters remains unchanged for the French data (Figure 6).

What has changed is the location of the focus of the clustering technique. While without log-transformation the model tends to be influenced by the higher end of the income distribution, log-income draws more scrutiny by the model to its lower end of the distribution. This is suggested by the density plot and by the uncertainty plot as

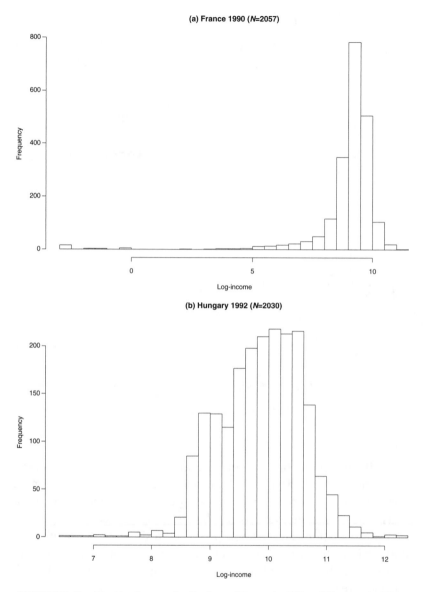

FIGURE 5. Empirical log-income distributions of France in 1990 and Hungary in 1992.

well. However, log-transformation does make a greater difference for the Hungarian data (Figure 7).

The three-cluster unequal variance model now fits the data the best. Apparently, the extreme cases at the higher end of the income

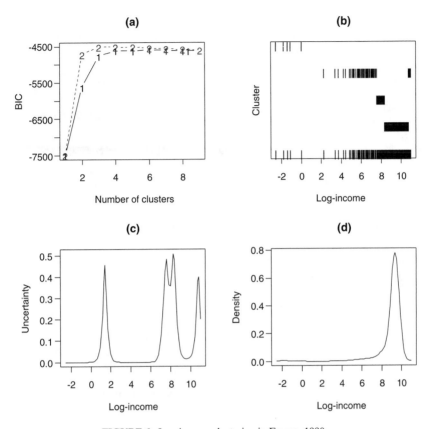

FIGURE 6. Log-income clustering in France, 1990.

distribution do not exert as much influence on the model fitting anymore. The density plot looks much more normal now, and the uncertainty plot shows two regions of high uncertainty (with three peaks) in the distribution.

5. TWO TYPES OF INEQUALITY

It has now become clear that there are two types of inequality: (1) individual inequality, which is measured by methods that include pairwise differences between individuals, and (2) class inequality, which can be broadly conceived as the degree to which there are classes or clusters of individuals in the sample (or population). The absolute

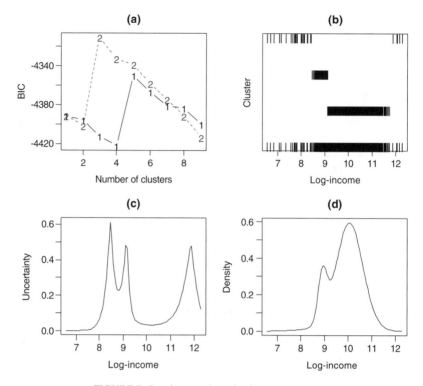

FIGURE 7. Log-income clustering in Hungary, 1992.

distances between individuals of the classes only partially reflect the distinction between classes. We may simply use the number of classes as an indicator of such inequality. However, is a population with two classes more stratified than one with three? A more informative measure is desirable. In general, the decomposition of Gini indices into the between-class and within-class components when the classes are ordered can be used as a means to partition income inequality for the purpose of measuring stratification. Here we follow the decomposition methods presented in Dagum (1997a, 1997b). (The decomposition logic is also analogous to the partitioning of world inequality into between- and within-nation inequality [Firebaugh 1999].) The overall Gini is computed as in equation (3). The within- and between-components of inequality are computed respectively as

$$G_w = \sum_{k=1}^{K} \frac{\displaystyle\sum_{i=1}^{n_k} \sum_{j=1}^{n_k} |y_i - y_j|}{2n^2 \mu}, \quad (7)$$

where n_j is the size of each j class or cluster, and K, the number of estimated classes or clusters, and

$$G_b = \sum_{k=2}^{K} \sum_{h=1}^{k-1} \frac{\displaystyle\sum_{i=1}^{n_k} \sum_{j=1}^{n_h} |y_i - y_j|}{n^2 \mu}. \quad (8)$$

Alternatively, the components of the Gini index can also be expressed as weighted averages of population shares and of income shares. For the within-group component, we have

$$G_w = \sum_{k=1}^{K} \frac{p_k s_k \displaystyle\sum_{i=1}^{n_k} \sum_{j=1}^{n_k} |y_i - y_j|}{2n^2 \mu}, \quad (9)$$

where $p_k = \frac{n_k}{n}$ and $s_k = \frac{n_k \mu_k}{n \mu}$ representing the population share and income for the kth group. Similarly, for the between-group component, we obtain

$$G_b = \sum_{k=2}^{K} \sum_{h=1}^{k-1} \frac{(p_k s_r + p_r s_k) \displaystyle\sum_{i=1}^{n_k} \sum_{j=1}^{n_h} |y_i - y_j|}{(\mu_k + \mu_r) n_k n_h}, \quad (10)$$

where income shares and population shares are again used in the weighting. However, either (7) or (9), or (8) or (10), gives rise to the same within-class or between-class components results.

The model-based latent class method is first used to estimate membership in the ordered classes in a population. For such classes, no consideration of transvariation or overlapping decomposition is necessary. Once the total amount of inequality is allocated into the individual (or within) and class (or between) components, an index of relative stratification can be simply defined as

$$S_1 = \frac{G_b}{G} = \frac{G - G_w}{G}, \tag{11}$$

where G_b is the net or total between-class component because all classes are ordered and there is no transvariation. This measure ranges from 0, where all inequality is individual-based and there is no stratification in the population, to 1, where all inequality is contributed by stratification and there is no variation within classes. The measure is relative because it is the amount of class inequality expressed as a proportion of total inequality in terms of the Gini index.

A shortcoming of equation (11) is a tendency to overemphasize the between-group differences because G_b is calculated using ordered population groups, and such groups by their very ordered nature will have greater differences between members of different groups than those within the same groups. To have a stratification index that is immune to this overemphasis, I propose another index that focuses on pairwise individual comparison ties instead of values of (income) differences. This can be expressed as

$$S_2 = \frac{\sum_{k=2}^{K} \sum_{h=1}^{k-1} \sum_{i=1}^{n_k} \sum_{j=1}^{n_h} d}{(n^2 - n)/2}, \tag{12}$$

where d is the number of unique (income) differences that exists between any pair of members i and j belonging to group k and group h, respectively, and the denominator gives the total number of (income) differences between any pair of the members in a population, simplified from the usual formula for obtaining the number of combinations by taking two members at a time out of population-sized n. For most practical considerations when membership assignments are unambiguous (and uncertainty is low), $d = 1$ because there is only one unique comparison between two members in a pair. Clearly, in the case of crisp membership probabilities (i.e., a case either belongs or does not belong to a group, with membership values of 1 or 0), the numerator of equation (12) simplifies to $\sum_{k=2}^{K} \sum_{h=1}^{k-1} n_k n_h$. For example, for Distribution 3 of [1, 1, 2.5, 2.5, 4, 4] described earlier, (12) is applied as: $S_2 = \frac{2 \times 2 + 2 \times 2 + 2 \times 2}{(6^2 - 6)/2} = 0.8$. When uncertainties are relatively high and membership is fuzzy, does the simplification still work? We set $d = m_i m_j$, where m_i is membership probability of case i, and we evaluate it below. The operation is based on fuzzy set theory where set memberships can be fuzzy instead of crisp with membership values ranging between 0 and 1 (Smithson and Verkuilen 2006). For example, we may have a simple distribution of three cases with income levels of [1, 5, 11] with memberships in two classes of [{1, 1}, {1}] when the membership function is crisp but [{1, 0.6}, {0.4, 1}] when the membership function is fuzzy. Here the curly braces indicate sets or groups, and the values in them are membership probabilities. We quickly see that $n_k n_h = 2$ when membership is crisp but $\sum_{k=2}^{K} \sum_{h=1}^{k-1} n_k n_h = 2.24$ when membership is fuzzy, and $\sum_{k=2}^{K} \sum_{h=1}^{k-1} \sum_{i=1}^{n_k} \sum_{j=1}^{n_h} d = 2.24$ for $d = m_i m_j$ too. Therefore, either the numerator of (12) or its simplification gives identical results when there is only a single fuzzy member in a group. Extending the earlier single fuzzy case example to [{1, 0.6, 0.4}, {0.4, 0.6}] where two of the three members are fuzzy, we obtain $\sum_{k=2}^{K} \sum_{h=1}^{k-1} n_k n_h = 2$ and $\sum_{k=2}^{K} \sum_{h=1}^{k-1} \sum_{i=1}^{n_k} \sum_{j=1}^{n_h} d = 2$ for $d = m_i m_j$. Thus, the simplification still works, but when membership probabilities are fuzzy, the resulting value from (12) will not in general be equal to the case when memberships are all crisp. How uncertain or fuzzy are membership estimates in the current example? I present histograms of uncertain probabilities for the French and Hungarian income data in Figure 8.

It is clear that, for the income variables in their original scale, the majority of the cases have low uncertainty levels, though the Hungarian data (mean = 0.218; median = 0.196) have a higher level of uncertainty than the French data (mean = 0.170; median = 0.125), likely due to the more severe skewness of the variable (see parts (a) and (b) in Figure 8). Once the income variables are transformed by natural logarithm, either the French (mean = 0.080; median = 0.024) or the Hungarian (mean = 0.107; median = 0.042) data present little uncertainty (see parts (c) and (d) in Figure 8). It appears that log-transformation is an effective way to reduce uncertainty in these income data and thus fuzziness in membership assignment. For the current income example, it is not necessary to rely on fuzzy membership when estimating clusters in log-income; whether or not it would be necessary can be a judgment issue for income variables in their original scale. For comparison, I present the decomposition and stratification results based on crisp membership (Table 1).

Table 1 lists three types of inequality measures—the Gini with its within- and between-class components and the indices of relative stratification, S_1 and S_2—for France and Hungary. The model-suggested

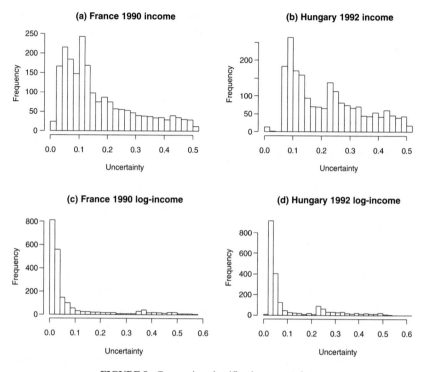

FIGURE 8. Comparing classification uncertainty.

classification schemes were used to obtain the ordering of the classes in the income distributions before computing decompositions. According to the Gini, Hungary has a slightly higher level of inequality than France (0.37 versus 0.32). However, Hungary actually had a much higher level of relative stratification according to the relative stratification indices when

TABLE 1

Comparing the Gini, Its Components, and Relative Stratification in France 1990 and Hungary 1992, Based on Crisp Group Membership

	Gini	$Gini_{within}$	$Gini_{between}$	Stratification Index 1	Stratification Index 2
French income	0.322473	0.093751	0.228722	0.709275	0.436602
Hungarian income	0.369581	0.038819	0.330762	0.894966	0.677786
French log-income	0.322473	0.210055	0.112418	0.348613	0.230252
Hungarian log-income	0.369581	0.231533	0.138048	0.373525	0.290595

compared with France (0.89 versus 0.71 and 0.68 versus 0.44) for the income variables in their original scale. The Gini between-component for the Hungarian data is higher than that for the French data (0.33 versus 0.23) while the Gini within-component for the Hungarian data is lower than that for the French data (0.04 versus 0.09); it is the difference in their proportions of the within-class components that determines the difference in the index of relative stratification of S_1, and the number of such differences, S_2. Compared with S_1, which is based on the Gini components, S_2 is based on the number of stratified members in a population. Whereas S_1 represents the proportion of the Gini index that is explained by between-group differences in (income) values, S_2 represents the proportion of the number of comparison ties or differences that exists between members of stratified groups. As for S_1, S_2 also has a minimum value of 0 and a maximum value of 1.

The bottom two rows in Table 1 presents results based on log-income. Note that log-transformed income variables are used for the estimation of latent clusters but not for the decomposition of the Gini index. That is, group membership estimates from latent cluster models of log-income are employed to decompose and construct the two stratification indices of the (not logged) income data. For an absolute measure of class inequality, the between-class component of the Gini index can be consulted with. The "absolute" (in the sense that absolute differences are computed) Gini ratios and the "relative" (in the sense that the amount of stratified differences are made relative to a total amount) indices can be used together to assess inequality in a population to offer a better, more insightful understanding. When clusters are estimated using log-income, the differences in the between-components as well as in the within-components between the French data and the Hungarian data are much smaller now (0.11 versus 0.14; 0.21 versus 0.23), and their S_1 difference is also much smaller, with a value of about 0.03 (versus about 0.19 before the transformation). Income stratification according to S_2 is also not as severe as before the log-transformation. To drive the point home, the ratio of the Hungarian Gini to the French Gini is $0.369581/0.322473 = 1.146084$ and the ratio of the Hungarian S_1 to the French S_1 is $0.894966/0.709275 = 1.261804$ in income units when their income/social stratification ratio according to S_1 is only $0.373525/0.348613 = 1.071460$ in log-income units. However, stratification measured by S_2 is still higher in Hungary because the number of stratified pairs relative to the total existing pairs is larger in Hungary than in France, or 0.290595/0.230252 = 1.262074. Thus, stratification in terms of population shares is higher in Hungary than in France.

6. CONCLUDING REMARKS

The Gini index, while very useful in the study of inequality, does have the limitation that the measure is sensitive to individual-based differences and may not be responsive to class-based stratification. I proposed a model-based latent class method to estimate order of classes within a distribution, and further utilized this information to decompose the Gini index into the within- and between-class components of inequality. The components are then used to form a Gini-based index and a comparison-based index of relative stratification.

The empirical income data from France 1990 and Hungary 1992 illustrate that the Gini may not be informative in understanding income stratification when only the overall amount of inequality is considered. Using the method proposed, we can fine-tune the measurement of inequality by separating the individual-based from the class-based inequality. The two proposed indices of relative stratification together also give us a simple and useful assessment of the amount of stratification existing in the sample, thereby extending the usefulness of the Gini index. When extended and informed by the model-based latent cluster analysis, the Gini ratio can assist in measuring the amount of not only individual-based but also class-based inequality. A logical extension of the current method is to allow fuzzy membership in the estimated latent clusters in a distribution. Another is to apply multiple indicator variables that together will form a multidimensional data space for a more accurate estimation of *social* stratification.

REFERENCES

Banfield, J. D., and A. E. Raftery. 1993. "Model-Based Gaussian and Non-Gaussian Clustering." *Biometrics* 49:803–21.

Chotikapanich, D., and W. Griffiths. 2001. "On Calculation of the Extended Gini Coefficient." *Review of Income and Wealth* 47(4):541–47.

Cowell, F. A. 2000. "Measurement of Inequality." Pp. 87–166 in *Handbook of Income Distribution*, Vol. 1 (*Handbooks in Economics* Vol. 16), edited by A. B. Atkinson and F. Bourguignon. Amsterdam: Elsevier.

Dagum, C. 1997a. "A New Approach to the Decomposition of the Gini Income Inequality Ratio." *Empirical Economics* 22(4):515–31.

————. 1997b. "Decomposition and Interpretation of Gini and the Generalized Entropy Measures." Pp. 200–205 in *Proceedings of the American Statistical Association, Business and Economic Statistics Section, 157ᵗʰ Meeting.*

————. 1998. "Fondements de bien-être social et décomposition des mesures d'inégalité dans la répartition du revenu." *Economie Appliquée* 151–202.

Dasgupta, A., and A. E. Raftery 1998. "Detecting Features in Spatial Point Processes with Clutter via Model-Based Clustering." *Journal of the American Statistical Association* 93:294–302.

Everitt, B. S. 1993. *Cluster Analysis.* London: Edward Arnold.

Firebaugh, G. 1999. "Empirics of World Income Inequality." *American Journal of Sociology* 104:1597–630.

Fraley, C., and A. E. Raftery. 1998. "How Many Clusters? Which Clustering Methods? Answers via Model-Based Clustering Analysis." *Computer Journal* 41:578–88.

————. 1999. "MCLUST: Software for Model-Based Cluster Analysis." *Journal of Classification* 16:297–306.

————. 2002. "Model-Based Clustering, Discriminant Analysis, and Density Estimation." *Journal of American Statistical Association* 97:611–31.

Gini, C. 1912. "Variabilitá e mutabilitá: Contributo allo studio delle distribuzioni e delle relazioni statistiche." *Studi Economico-giuridici della Regia Facoltà Giurisprudenza* 3(2):3–159.

Gottschalk, P. 1993. "Income and Earnings during the 1980s: The Failure of Trickledown Changes in Inequality of Family Income in Seven Industrialized Countries." *American Economic Review* 83:136–42.

Kaufman, L., and P. J. Rousseuw. 1990. *Finding Groups in Data.* New York: Wiley.

Liao, T. F. 2002. *Statistical Group Comparison.* New York: Wiley.

Lorenz, M. O. 1905. "Methods of Measuring the Concentration of Wealth." *Publications of the American Statistical Association* 9:209–19.

Milanovic, B. and S. Yitzhaki. 2002. "Decomposing World Income Distribution: Does the World Have a Middle Class?" *Review of Income and Wealth* 48:155–78.

Mussard, S., M. Terraza, and F. Seyte. 2003. "Decomposition of Gini and the Generalized Entropy Inequality Measures." *Economics Bulletin* 4:1–5.

Roeder, K., and L. Wasserman. 1997. "Practical Bayesian Density Estimation Using Mixtures of Normals." *Journal of American Statistical Association* 92:894–902.

Schwartz, J., and C. Winship. 1980. "The Welfare Approach to Measuring Inequality." Pp. 1–36 in *Sociological Methodology 1980*, Vol. II, edited by K.F.Schuessler. San Francisco: Jossey-Bass.

Smithson, M. J., and J. Verkuilen. 2006. *Fuzzy Set Theory: Applications in the Social Sciences.* Quantitative Applications in the Social Sciences, No. 147. Thousand Oaks, CA: Sage.

Szelenyi, S. 1998. *Equality by Design: The Grand Experiment in Destratification in Socialist Hungary.* Stanford, CA: Stanford University Press.

Vermunt, J., and J. Magidson. 2002. "Latent Class Cluster Analysis." Pp. 89–106 in *Applied Latent Class Analysis*, edited by J. A. Hagenaars and A. L. McCutchen. Cambridge, England: Cambridge University Press.

Yao, S. 1999. "On the Decomposition of Gini Coefficients by Population Class and Income Source: A Spreadsheet Approach and Application." *Applied Economics* 31:1249–64.

Yao, S., and J. Liu. 1996. "Decomposition of Gini Coefficients by Class: A New Approach." *Applied Economics Letters* 3:115–19.

Yitzhaki, S. 1994. "Economic Distance and Overlapping of Distributions." *Journal of Econometrics* 61:147–59.

———. 2003. "Gini's Mean Difference: A Superior Measure of Variability for Non-Normal Dsiribution." *METRO—International Journal of Statistics* 61:285–316.

EFFECT DISPLAYS FOR MULTINOMIAL AND PROPORTIONAL-ODDS LOGIT MODELS

John Fox*
Robert Andersen*

An "effect display" is a graphical or tabular summary of a statistical model based on high-order terms in the model. Effect displays have previously been defined by Fox (1987, 2003) for generalized linear models (including linear models). Such displays are especially compelling for complicated models—for example, those including interactions or polynomial terms. This paper extends effect displays to models commonly used for polytomous categorical response variables: the multinomial logit model and the proportional-odds logit model. Determining point estimates of effects for these models is a straightforward extension of results for the generalized linear model. Estimating sampling variation for effects on the probability scale in the multinomial and proportional-odds logit models is more challenging, however, and we use the delta method to derive approximate standard errors. Finally, we provide software for effect displays in the R statistical computing environment.

This is a revised version of a paper read at the ASA Methodology Conference 2004. Please address correspondence to John Fox, Department of Sociology, McMaster University, 1280 Main Street West, Hamilton, Ontario, Canada L8S 4M4; jfox@mcmaster.ca. We are grateful to Georges Monette for checking some of the derivations in this paper, and to Michael Ornstein and two anonymous reviewers for helpful suggestions.

*McMaster University

225

1. INTRODUCTION

Effect displays, in the sense of Fox (1987, 2003), are tabular or—more often—graphical summaries of statistical models. Fox (1987) introduces effect displays for generalized linear models (including linear models); Fox (2003) refines these methods and provides software for their essentially automatic implementation.

The general idea underlying effect displays—to represent a statistical model by showing carefully selected portions of its response surface—is not limited to generalized linear models, however, nor even to models that incorporate linear predictors. Moreover, the essential idea of effect displays is not wholly original with Fox (1987). For example, adjusted means in analysis of covariance (introduced by Fisher, 1936) are a precursor to more general effect displays. Goodnight and Harvey's (1978) "least-squares means" in analysis of variance and covariance, and Searle, Speed, and Milliken's (1980) "estimated population marginal means" are effect displays restricted to interactions among factors (i.e., categorical predictors) in a linear model.

King, Tomz, and Wittenberg (2000) and Tomz, Wittenberg, and King (2003) have presented similar ideas, but their approach is based on Monte-Carlo simulation of a model. In contrast, the analytical results that we give below can be computed directly. Long (1997) discusses several strategies for presenting statistical models fit to categorical response variables, including displaying estimated probabilities. Hastie, Tibshirani, and Friedman's (2001, sec. 10.13.2) "partial dependence plots" and Weisberg's (2005: 185–90) "marginal model plots" are also related to effect displays.

The primary purpose of this paper is to extend the effect displays in Fox (1987, 2003) to the multinomial logit model and to the proportional-odds logit model, statistical models that find common application in social research. As we will show, this extension is largely straightforward, although the derivation of standard errors is challenging, particularly in the proportional-odds model. We begin by reviewing effect displays for generalized linear models, using as examples a binary logit model and a linear model. We then present results for the multinomial and proportional-odds logit models. In each of these sections, we illustrate the results with examples.

We see the main contribution of this paper as twofold: First, by extending the methods in Fox (1987, 2003) to models commonly used for polytomous data, we provide a means for carefully visualizing models of this type that have complex structure, such as polynomial or spline regressors and interactions. Second, we derive standard errors for fitted probabilities in multinomial and proportional-odds logit models, permitting us to show statistical uncertainty in effect displays constructed for these models.

2. EFFECT DISPLAYS FOR GENERALIZED LINEAR MODELS: BACKGROUND AND PRELIMINARY EXAMPLES

A general principle of interpretation for statistical models containing terms that are marginal to others (in the sense of Nelder 1977) is that high-order terms should be combined with their lower-order relatives— for example, an interaction between two factors should be combined with the main effects marginal to the interaction. In conformity with this principle, Fox (1987) suggests identifying the high-order terms in a generalized linear model and computing fitted values for each such term. The lower-order "relatives" of a high-order term (e.g., main effects marginal to an interaction, or a linear and quadratic term in a third-order polynomial, which are marginal to the cubic term) are absorbed into the term, allowing the predictors appearing in the high-order term to range over their values. The values of other predictors are fixed at typical values: For example, a covariate could be fixed at its mean or median, a factor at its proportional distribution in the data, or to equal proportions in its several levels.

Some models have high-order terms that "overlap"—that is, that share a lower-order relative (other than the constant). Consider, for example, a generalized linear model that includes interactions AB, AC, and BC among the three factors A, B, and C. Although the three-way interaction ABC is not in the model, it is nevertheless illuminating to combine the three high-order terms and their lower-order relatives (see Fox 2003 and the example developed in Section 2.1).

Let us turn now to the generalized linear model (e.g., McCullagh and Nelder 1989 or Firth 1991) with linear predictor $\eta = X\beta$ and link function $g(\mu) = \eta$, where μ is the expectation of the response vector y. Here, everything falls into place very simply: We have an estimate $\hat{\beta}$ of β, along with the estimated covariance matrix $\widehat{V(\hat{\beta})}$ of $\hat{\beta}$.

Let the rows of X^* include all combinations of values of predictors appearing in a high-order term, along with typical values of the remaining predictors. The structure of X^* with respect, for example, to interactions, is the same as that of the model matrix $\mathbf{X}$. Then the fitted values $\hat{\eta}^* = \mathbf{X}^*\hat{\beta}$ represent the effect in question, and a table or graph of these values—or, alternatively, of the fitted values transformed to the scale of the response, $g^{-1}(\hat{\eta}^*)$—is an effect display. The standard errors of $\hat{\eta}^*$, available as the square-root diagonal entries of $\mathbf{X}^* \widehat{V(\hat{\beta})} \mathbf{X}^{*\prime}$, may be used to compute pointwise confidence intervals for the effects, the endpoints of which may then also be transformed to the scale of the response.

In an application, as we will illustrate presently, we prefer plotting on the scale of the linear predictor (where the structure of the model—for example, with respect to linearity—is preserved) but labeling the response axis on the scale of the response. This approach has the advantage of making the configuration of the display invariant with respect to the values at which the omitted predictors are held constant, in the sense that only the labeling of the response axis changes with a different selection of these values.[1]

2.1. *A Binary Logit Model: Toronto Arrests for Marijuana Possession*

Following Fox (2003), we construct effect displays for a binary logit model fit to data on police treatment of individuals arrested in Toronto for simple possession of small quantities of marijuana. (The data discussed here are part of a larger data set featured in a series of articles in the Toronto Star newspaper.) Under these circumstances, police have the option of releasing an arrestee with a summons to appear in court—similar to a traffic ticket—or bringing the individual to the police station for questioning and possible indictment. The principal question of interest is whether and how the probability of release is influenced by the subject's sex, race, age, employment status, and citizenship, the year in which the arrest took place, and the subject's previous police record. Most of these variables are self-explanatory, with the following exceptions:

- Race appears in the model as "color," and is coded as either "black" or "white." The original data included the additional categories

---

[1] As David Firth has pointed out to us, however, this invariance does not hold with respect to standard errors, which are affected by the fixed elements of $\mathbf{X}^*$, a fact that follows from considering effects as fitted values. Standard errors will tend to be smaller for components of $\mathbf{x}'$ near the center of the data.

"brown" and "other," but their meaning is ambiguous and their use relatively infrequent. Moreover, the motivation for collecting the data was to determine whether blacks and whites are treated differently by the police.

• The observations span the years 1997 through (part of) 2002. A few arrests in 1996 were eliminated. In the analysis reported below, year is treated as a factor (i.e., as a categorical predictor).

• When suspects are stopped by the police, their names are checked in six databases—of previous arrests, previous convictions, parole status, and so on. The variable "checks" records the number of databases on which an individual's name appeared.

Preliminary analysis of the data suggested a logit model including interactions between color and year and between color and age, and main effects of employment status, citizenship, and checks. The effects of age and checks appear to be reasonably linear on the logit scale and are modeled as such.

Estimated coefficients and their standard errors are shown in Table 1. Where predictors are represented by dummy regressors, the

TABLE 1

Maximum-Likelihood Estimates and Standard Errors for Coefficients in the Logit Model for the Toronto Marijuana-Arrests Data

Coefficient	Estimate	Standard Error
Constant	0.344	0.310
Employed (yes)	0.735	0.085
Citizen (yes)	0.586	0.114
Checks	−0.367	0.026
Color (white)	1.213	0.350
Year (1998)	−0.431	0.260
Year (1999)	−0.094	0.261
Year (2000)	−0.011	0.259
Year (2001)	0.243	0.263
Year (2002)	0.213	0.353
Age	0.029	0.009
Color (white) × Year (1998)	0.652	0.313
Color (white) × Year (1999)	0.156	0.307
Color (white) × Year (2000)	0.296	0.306
Color (white) × Year (2001)	−0.381	0.304
Color (white) × Year (2002)	−0.617	0.419
Color (white) × Age	−0.037	0.010

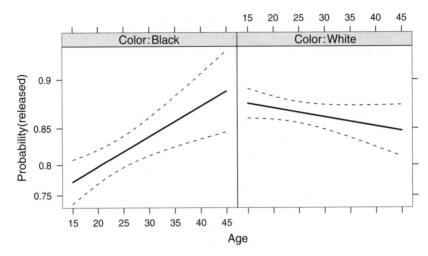

FIGURE 1. Effect display for the interaction of color and age in the logit model fit to the Toronto marijuana-arrests data. The vertical axis is labeled on the probability scale, and a 95-percent point-wise confidence envelope is drawn around the estimated effect. This graph, and those in Figures 2 and 3, are produced by the software described in Fox (2003).

category coded one is given in parentheses; for year, the baseline category is 1997. A fundamental point to be made with respect to this table is that it is difficult to tell from the coefficients alone how the predictors combine to influence the response. This difficulty is primarily a function of the complex structure of the model—that is, the interactions of color with year and age—but partly due to the fact that the coefficients are effects on the logit scale.[2] It is true that with some mental arithmetic we can draw certain conclusions from the table of coefficients. For example, the fitted probability of release declines with age for whites but increases with age for blacks. Grasping the color-by-year interaction is more difficult, however, as is discerning the combined effect of these three predictors.

Two effect displays for the model fit to the Toronto marijuana-arrests data appear in Figures 1 and 2. Figure 1 depicts the interaction between color and age. The lines in this graph are plotted on the logit

---

[2]A common device, which speaks partly to the second problem but not the first, is to exponentiate the coefficients in the logit model. The exponentiated coefficients are interpretable as multiplicative effects on the odds of the response. Interpreting interactions using exponentiated coefficients becomes even more difficult because it requires mental multiplication rather than addition.

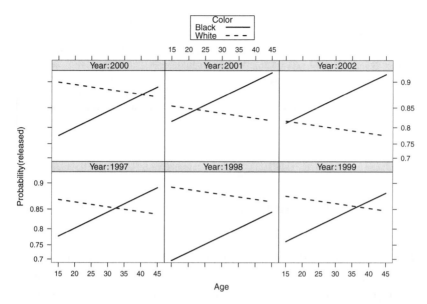

FIGURE 2. An effect display that combines the color-by-year and color-by-age interactions.

scale (i.e., the scale of the linear predictor), but the vertical axis of the graph is labeled on the probability scale (the scale of the response); the broken lines give point-wise 95-percent confidence envelopes around the fitted values. Figure 2 combines the color-by-age interaction with the color-by-year interaction. Because there is no three-way interaction (and no interaction between age and year), the lines for blacks are parallel across the six panels of the graph, as are the lines for whites. A graph such as Figure 2 effectively communicates what the model has to say about how color, age, and year combine to influence the probability of release.[3]

The $\mathbf{X}^*$ matrix for the effect display in Figure 1 has the following form:

---

[3]This and other examples in this paper include interactions between quantitative and categorical predictors, but effect displays are equally applicable to interactions between and among categorical predictors (and between and among quantitative predictors—e.g., see the example in Fox 1987). Indeed, handling categorical predictors is more straightforward because there is no need to make an arbitrary selection of values to plot, while two-dimensional plots of interactions between quantitative predictors require slicing the response surface. Effect displays for linear models containing only factors (i.e., analysis-of-variance models) are sometimes termed "least-squares means" (Goodnight and Harvey 1978) or "population marginal means" (Searle, Speed, and Milliken 1980).

$$
\begin{bmatrix}
(b_1) & (b_2) & (b_3) & (b_4) & (b_5) & (b_6) & (b_7) & (b_8) & (b_9) & (b_{10}) & (b_{11}) & (b_{12}) & (b_{13}) & (b_{14}) & (b_{15}) & (b_{16}) & (b_{17}) \\
1 & 0.79 & 0.85 & 1.64 & 0 & 0.17 & 0.21 & 0.24 & 0.23 & 0.05 & 15 & 0 & 0 & 0 & 0 & 0 & 0 \\
1 & 0.79 & 0.85 & 1.64 & 1 & 0.17 & 0.21 & 0.24 & 0.23 & 0.05 & 15 & 0.17 & 0.21 & 0.24 & 0.23 & 0.05 & 15 \\
1 & 0.79 & 0.85 & 1.64 & 0 & 0.17 & 0.21 & 0.24 & 0.23 & 0.05 & 16 & 0 & 0. & 0 & 0 & 0 & 0 \\
1 & 0.79 & 0.85 & 1.64 & 1 & 0.17 & 0.21 & 0.24 & 0.23 & 0.05 & 16 & 0.17 & 0.21 & 0.24 & 0.23 & 0.05 & 16 \\
1 & 0.79 & 0.85 & 1.64 & 0 & 0.17 & 0.21 & 0.24 & 0.23 & 0.05 & 17 & 0 & 0 & 0 & 0 & 0 & 0 \\
1 & 0.79 & 0.85 & 1.64 & 1 & 0.17 & 0.21 & 0.24 & 0.23 & 0.05 & 17 & 0.17 & 0.21 & 0.24 & 0.23 & 0.05 & 17 \\
1 & 0.79 & 0.85 & 1.64 & 0 & 0.17 & 0.21 & 0.24 & 0.23 & 0.05 & 18 & 0 & 0 & 0 & 0 & 0 & 0 \\
1 & 0.79 & 0.85 & 1.64 & 1 & 0.17 & 0.21 & 0.24 & 0.23 & 0.05 & 18 & 0.17 & 0.21 & 0.24 & 0.23 & 0.05 & 18 \\
\vdots & \vdots & \vdots & \vdots & \vdots & \vdots & \vdots & \vdots & \vdots & \vdots & \vdots & \vdots & \vdots & \vdots & \vdots & \vdots & \vdots \\
1 & 0.79 & 0.85 & 1.64 & 1 & 0.17 & 0.21 & 0.24 & 0.23 & 0.05 & 45 & 0.17 & 0.21 & 0.24 & 0.23 & 0.05 & 45 \\
\end{bmatrix}
$$

The columns in the matrix are labeled with the coefficients to which they pertain and are in the same order as in Table 1:

- The ones in the first column represent the regression constant.
- The second column contains the proportion of arrestees who were employed—that is, the mean of the dummy regressor for employment.
- The third column contains the proportion of arrestees who were Canadian citizens.
- The fourth column contains the average number of checks.
- The fifth column cycles through the two values of the dummy regressor for color.
- Columns six through ten contain the proportions of arrestees in the years 1998 through 2002; recall that 1997 is the baseline level for the dummy regressors for year.
- Column 11 cycles through the values of age, from 15 through 45. Because there are therefore $2 \times 31 = 62$ combinations of values of color and age, the $\mathbf{X}^*$ matrix has 62 rows.
- Columns 12 through 16 represent the interaction of color and year. Because year is "held constant" at its marginal distribution, this term is absorbed in the color main effect.
- Column 17 represents the color by age interaction.

2.2. A Linear Model: Canadian Occupational Prestige

The data for our second example, also adapted from Fox (2003), pertain to the rated prestige of 102 Canadian occupations. The prestige of the

TABLE 2

Coefficients for Regression of Occupational Prestige on Income and Education Levels of Occupations and on Percentage of Occupational Incumbents Who are Women

Coefficient	Estimate	Standard Error
Constant	−72.92	15.49
Log income	12.67	1.84
Education (1)	−8.20	7.8
Education (2)	25.66	5.50
Education (3)	30.42	4.59
Women (linear)	11.98	9.38
Women (quadratic)	18.47	6.83

Education is represented in the model by a three degree-of-freedom B-spline, percentage women by a second-order orthogonal polynomial.

occupations is regressed on three predictors, all derived from the 1971 Census of Canada: the average income of occupational incumbents, in dollars (represented in the model as the log of income); the average education of occupational incumbents, in years (represented by a B-spline with three degrees of freedom); and the percentage of occupational incumbents who were women (represented by an orthogonal polynomial of degree two). Estimated coefficients and standard errors for this model are shown in Table 2.

This model does a decent job of summarizing the data, but the meaning of its coefficients is relatively obscure—despite the fact that the model includes no interactions. The coefficient of log income, for example, would be more easily interpreted had we used logs to the base two rather than natural logs. The coefficients corresponding to the different elements of the B-spline basis do not have straightforward individual interpretations. Finally, although we can see from the coefficients for the orthogonal polynomial fit to the percentage of women that the linear trend in this predictor is non-significant while the quadratic trend is highly significant, these two coefficients are best interpreted in combination. It is therefore much more straightforward to apprehend these terms graphically as effect displays (Figure 3). We prefer to plot income on the natural scale rather than using a log horizontal axis, making the income effect nonlinear.

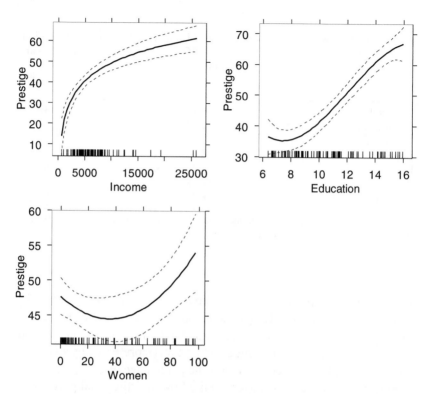

FIGURE 3. Effect plots for the predictors of prestige in the Canadian occupational prestige data. The model includes the log of income, a three-degree-of-freedom B-spline in education, and a quadratic in the percentage of occupational incumbents who are women. The "rug plot" (one-dimensional scatterplot) at the bottom of each graph shows the distribution of the corresponding predictor. The dashed lines give point-wise 95-percent confidence intervals around the fitted values.

3. EFFECT DISPLAYS FOR THE MULTINOMIAL LOGIT MODEL

3.1 *Basic Results*

The multinomial logit model is arguably the most widely used statistical model for polytomous (multicategory) response variables (e.g., McCullagh and Nelder 1989, chap. 5; Fox 1997, chap. 15; Long 1997, chap. 6; Powers and Xie 2000, chap. 7). Letting μ_{ij} denote the probability that observation i belongs to response category j of m categories, the model is given by

$$\mu_{ij} = \frac{\exp(\mathbf{x}'_i \boldsymbol{\beta}_j)}{\sum\limits_{k=1}^{m} \exp(\mathbf{x}'_{ik}\boldsymbol{\beta}_{kj})} \quad \text{for} \quad j = 1, \ldots, m, \tag{1}$$

where $\mathbf{x}'_i = (1, x_{i2}, \ldots, x_{ip})$ is the model vector for observation i and $\boldsymbol{\beta}_j = (\beta_{j1}, \beta_{j2}, \ldots, \beta_{jp})'$ is the parameter vector for response category j. Observations may represent individuals, who therefore fall into a particular category of the response, or a vector of category counts for a multinomial observation (as in a contingency table, where both the predictors and the response variables are discrete); the first situation is a special case of the second, setting all of the multinomial total counts (i.e., the "multinomial denominators") n_i to 1.

As it stands, model 1 is overparametrized because of the constraint that the probabilities for each observation sum to one: $\sum_{j=1}^{m} \mu_{ij} = 1$. The resulting indeterminacy can be handled by a normalization, placing a linear constraint on the parameters, $\sum_{j=1}^{m} a_j \boldsymbol{\beta}_j = 0$, where the a_j are constants, not all zero. The choice of constraint is inessential: Fitted probabilities, $\hat{\mu}_{ij}$, and hence the likelihood, under the model are unaffected by the constraint, and consequently the effect displays developed in this paper are invariant with respect to the specific constraint employed; indeed, this invariance is a strength of effect displays. In contrast, the meaning of specific parameters depends upon the constraint, and as we will explain, adds to the difficulty of directly interpreting coefficient estimates for the model. The most common constraint is to set one of the β_j to zero (i.e., to set one of the a_j to 1 and the rest to 0); for convenience, we will set $\beta_m = 0$, allowing us to rewrite equation (1) as

$$\mu_{ij} = \frac{\exp(\mathbf{x}'_i \boldsymbol{\beta}_j)}{1 + \sum\limits_{k=1}^{m-1} \exp(\mathbf{x}'_{ik}\boldsymbol{\beta}_{kj})} \quad \text{for} \quad j = 1, \ldots, m-1$$

$$\tag{2}$$

$$\mu_{im} = 1 - \sum_{k=1}^{m-1} \mu_{ik} \quad \text{(for category } m\text{)}.$$

Algebraic manipulation of model 2 suggests an interpretation of the coefficients of the model

$$\log \frac{\mu_{ij}}{\mu_{im}} = \mathbf{x}_i'\boldsymbol{\beta}_j \quad \text{for} \quad j = 1, \ldots, m - 1, \tag{3}$$

and thus the coefficient vector $\boldsymbol{\beta}_j$ is for the log-odds of membership in category j versus the "baseline" category m. We can, moreover, express the log-odds of membership for any pair of categories in terms of *differences* in their coefficient vectors:

$$\log \frac{\mu_{ij}}{\mu_{ij'}} = \mathbf{x}_i'(\boldsymbol{\beta}_j - \boldsymbol{\beta}_{j'}) \quad \text{for} \quad j, j' \neq m. \tag{4}$$

All this is well and good, but it does not produce intuitively easy-to-grasp coefficients, since pair-wise comparison of the categories of the response is not in itself a natural manner in which to think about a polytomous variable. This difficulty of interpretation pertains even to models in which the structure of the model vector $\mathbf{x}'$ is simple.

Our strategy for building effect displays for the multinomial logit model is essentially the same as for generalized linear models: Find fitted values—in this case, fitted probabilities—under the model for selected combinations of values of the predictors. The fitted values on the probability scale, $\hat{\mu}_{ij}$, are given by model 2, substituting estimates $\hat{\boldsymbol{\beta}}_j$ for the parameter vectors $\boldsymbol{\beta}_j$.

Finding standard errors for fitted values on the probability scale is more of a challenge, however. As is obvious from model 2, the fitted probabilities are nonlinear functions of the model parameters. We did not encounter this difficulty in the binary logit model because we could work on the scale of the linear predictor, translating the endpoints of confidence intervals to the probability scale (or equivalently, relabeling the logit axis). In the multinomial logit model, however, as noted, the linear predictor $\eta_{ij} = \mathbf{x}_i' \boldsymbol{\beta}_j$ is for the logit comparing category j to category m, not for the logit comparing category j to its complement, $\log[\mu_{ij}/(1 - \mu_{ij})]$.

Suppose that we compute the fitted value at $\mathbf{x}'_0$ (e.g., a focal point in an effect display). Differentiating μ_{0j} with respect to the model parameters yields

$$\frac{\partial \mu_{0j}}{\partial \boldsymbol{\beta}_j} = \frac{\exp(\mathbf{x}_0'\boldsymbol{\beta}_j)\left[1 + \sum_{k=1, k\neq j}^{m-1} \exp(\mathbf{x}_0'\boldsymbol{\beta}_k)\right] \mathbf{x}_0}{\left[1 + \sum_{k=1}^{m-1} \exp(\mathbf{x}_0'\boldsymbol{\beta}_k)\right]^2}$$

$$\frac{\partial \mu_{0j}}{\partial \beta_{j' \neq j}} = -\frac{\{\exp\left[\mathbf{x}_0'\left(\beta_{j'} + \beta_j\right)\right]\} \mathbf{x}_0}{\left[1 + \sum_{k=1}^{m-1} \exp(\mathbf{x}_0'\beta_k)\right]^2}$$

$$\frac{\partial \mu_{0m}}{\partial \beta_j} = -\frac{\exp(\mathbf{x}_0'\beta_j)\mathbf{x}_0}{\left[1 + \sum_{k=1}^{m-1} \exp(\mathbf{x}_0'\beta_k)\right]^2}.$$

Let the estimated asymptotic covariance matrix of the (stacked) coefficient vectors be given by

$$\hat{V}(\hat{\beta}) = \hat{V}\begin{bmatrix} \hat{\beta}_1 \\ \hat{\beta}_2 \\ \vdots \\ \hat{\beta}_{m-1} \end{bmatrix} = [v_{st}], s, t = 1, \ldots, r$$

Here, $r = p(m - 1)$ represents the total number of parameters in the combined parameter vectors. $\hat{v}(\hat{\beta})$ is typically computed along with $\hat{\beta}$ when the model is estimated. Then, by the delta method (Rao 1965: 321–27),

$$\hat{V}(\hat{\mu}_{0j}) \simeq \sum_{s=1}^{r} \sum_{t=1}^{r} \hat{v}_{st} \frac{\partial \hat{\mu}_{0j}}{\partial \hat{\beta}_s} \frac{\partial \hat{\mu}_{0j}}{\partial \hat{\beta}_t} \qquad (5)$$

(where $\simeq$ denotes approximation).

Because the $\hat{\mu}_{0j}$ are bounded by 0 and 1, confidence intervals on the probability scale are problematic, especially for values near the boundaries. We therefore suggest the following refinement: Re-express the category probabilities μ_{0j} as logits,

$$\lambda_{0j} = \log \frac{\mu_{0j}}{1 - \mu_{0j}}. \qquad (6)$$

These are *not* the paired-category (i.e., "baseline") logits (given in equations 3 and 4) to which the parameters of the multinomial logit model directly pertain but rather the log-odds of membership in each category relative to all others. Differentiating equation (6) with respect to μ_{0j} produces

$$\frac{d\lambda_{0j}}{d\mu_{0j}} = \frac{1}{\mu_{0j}(1 - \mu_{0j})}$$

and, consequently, by a second application of the delta method,

$$\hat{V}(\hat{\lambda}_{0j}) \simeq \frac{1}{\hat{\mu}_{0j}^2(1 - \hat{\mu}_{0j})^2} \hat{V}(\hat{\mu}_{0j}).$$

Using this result, we can form a confidence interval around $\hat{\lambda}_{0j}$, and translate the endpoints back to the probability scale.

This procedure applies regardless of the method used to estimate the parameters of the model and their covariances. For example, especially when the multinomial logit model is fit to aggregated data, overdispersion can be a concern. Following McCullagh and Nelder (1989, chap. 5), we can estimate the overdispersed multinomial-logit model by quasi-likelihood, producing the usual estimates of the regression coefficients, but inflating the coefficient variances (and covariances) by the estimated dispersion parameter, which is implicitly set to one in the traditional multinomial logit model. A similar remark applies to the proportional-odds logit model discussed in Section 4.[4]

3.2. *Example: Political Knowledge and Party Choice in Britain*

The example in this section is adapted from work by Andersen, Heath, and Sinnott (2002) on political knowledge and electoral choices in Britain (see also Andersen, Tilley, and Heath 2005). The data are from the 1997–2001 British Election Panel Study (BEPS). Although the same respondents were questioned at eight points in time, we use information only from the final wave of the study, which was conducted following the 2001 British election. After removing cases with missing data, the sample size is 2206.

We fit a multinomial logit model to describe how attitude toward European integration—an important issue during the 2001 British election—and knowledge of the major political parties' stances on

---

[4]As it turns out, overdispersion is not a problem for the examples developed in this and the following section: In both instances, the estimated dispersion—based, as suggested by McCullagh and Nelder (1989), on the Pearson statistic for the model—is slightly less than 1.

Europe interact in their effect on party choice. The variables in the model are as follows:

- The response variable is party choice, which has three categories: Labour, Conservative, and Liberal Democrat. Those who voted for other parties are excluded from the analysis. The Conservative platform was decidedly Eurosceptic, while both Labour and the Liberal Democrats took a clear pro-Europe position.
- "Europe" is an 11-point scale that measures respondents' attitudes toward European integration. High scores represent "Eurosceptic" sentiment.
- "Political knowledge" taps knowledge of party platforms on the European integration issue. The scale ranges from 0 (low knowledge) to 3 (high knowledge). An analysis of deviance suggests that a linear specification for knowledge is acceptable.
- The model also includes age, gender, perceptions of economic conditions over the past year (both national and household), and evaluations of the leaders of the three major parties.

Estimated coefficients and their standard errors from a final multinomial logit model fit to the data are shown in Table 3. We have already argued that interpreting coefficients in logit models is not simple, especially in the presence of interactions. Interpretation of the multinomial logit model is further complicated because the coefficients refer to contrasts of categories of the response variable with a baseline category. Nonetheless, we can see even from the coefficients that attitude toward Europe was related to party choice and that this relationship differed according to level of political knowledge. An analysis of deviance confirms that the interaction between attitude toward Europe and political knowledge is statistically significant. As was the case with the binary logit model, however, further interpretation is simplified by plotting this interaction as an effect display.

Figure 4 shows the relationship between attitude toward Europe and the fitted probability of voting for each of the three parties at the several levels of political knowledge (ranging from 0 to 3). An alternative display, with 95 percent confidence intervals around the fitted probabilities, appears in Figure 5. A third display, in Figure 6, shows the response categories in a manner similar to a stacked bar graph.[5]

[5]We are grateful to Michael Ornstein for suggesting this display.

TABLE 3

Coefficients for a Multinomial Logit Model Regressing Party Choice on Attitude Toward European Integration, Political Knowledge, and Other Explanatory Variables

Labour/Liberal Democrat		
Coefficient	Estimate	Standard Error
Constant	−0.155	0.612
Age	−0.005	0.005
Gender (male)	0.021	0.144
Perceptions of economy	0.377	0.091
Perceptions of household economic position	0.171	0.082
Evaluation of Blair (Labour leader)	0.546	0.071
Evaluation of Hague (Conservative leader)	−0.088	0.064
Evaluation of Kennedy (Liberal Democrat leader)	−0.416	0.072
Europe	−0.070	0.040
Political knowledge	−0.502	0.155
Europe × Knowledge	0.024	0.021

Conservative/Liberal Democrat		
Coefficient	Estimate	Standard Error
Constant	0.718	0.734
Age	0.015	0.006
Gender (male)	−0.091	0.178
Perceptions of economy	−0.145	0.110
Perceptions of household economic position	−0.008	0.101
Evaluation of Blair (Labour leader)	−0.278	0.079
Evaluation of Hague (Conservative leader)	0.781	0.079
Evaluation of Kennedy (Liberal Democrat leader)	−0.656	0.086
Europe	−0.068	0.049
Political knowledge	−1.160	0.0219
Europe × Knowledge	0.183	0.028

It is much easier to interpret the interaction between attitude and knowledge in these effect plots than directly from the coefficients: At the lowest level of knowledge, there is apparently no relationship between attitude toward Europe and party choice. In contrast, as knowledge increases, respondents are progressively more likely to match their votes to party platforms—that is, the more Eurosceptic votes are, the more likely they are to support the Conservative Party and the less likely they are to support Labour or the Liberal Democrats. We therefore see much

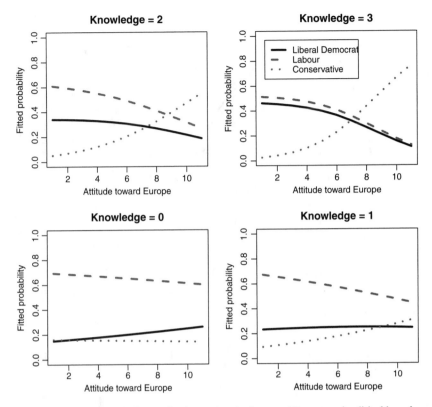

FIGURE 4. Display of the interaction between attitude toward Europe and political knowledge, showing the effects of these variables on the fitted probability of voting for each of the three major British parties in 2001.

more clearly than we could from Table 3 the importance of information to voting behavior—issues do matter in elections, but only to those who have knowledge of party platforms (a point discussed at greater length in Andersen 2003).

4. EFFECT DISPLAYS FOR THE PROPORTIONAL-ODDS LOGIT MODEL

4.1. *Basic Results*

The proportional-odds logit model is a common model for an ordinal response variable (e.g., McCullagh and Nelder 1989, chap. 5; Fox 1997,

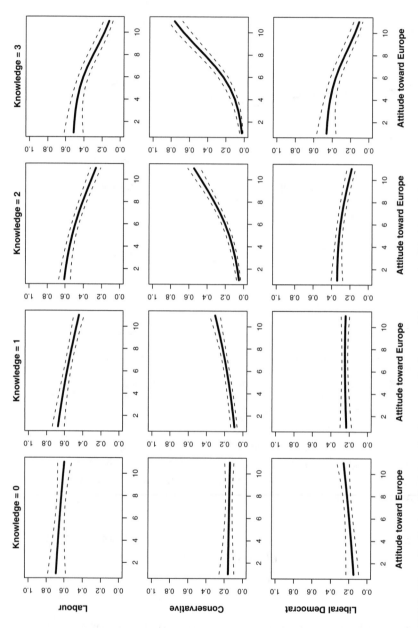

FIGURE 5. Alternative display of the interaction between attitude toward Europe and political knowledge. The dashed lines give point-wise 95-percent confidence intervals around the fitted probabilities.

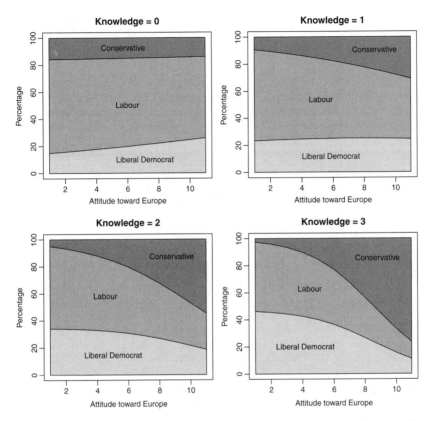

FIGURE 6. A third version of the effect display for the interaction between attitude toward Europe and political knowledge.

chap. 15; Long 1997, chap. 5; Powers and Xie 2000, chap. 6). The model is often motivated as follows: Suppose that there is a continuous, but unobservable, response variable, ξ, which is a linear function of a predictor vector $\mathbf{x}'$ plus a random error:

$$\xi_i = \boldsymbol{\beta}'\mathbf{x}_i + \varepsilon_i$$
$$= \eta_i + \varepsilon_i$$

We cannot observe ξ directly, but instead implicitly dissect its range into m class intervals at the (unknown) thresholds $\alpha_1 < \alpha_2 < \cdots < \alpha_{m-1}$, producing the observed ordinal response variable y. That is,

$$y_i = \begin{cases} 1 & \text{for} \quad \xi_i \leq \alpha_1 \\ 2 & \text{for} \quad \alpha_1 < \xi_i \leq \alpha_2 \\ \vdots & \\ m-1 & \text{for} \quad \alpha_{m-2} < \xi_i \leq \alpha_{m-1} \\ m & \text{for} \quad \alpha_{m-1} < \xi_i. \end{cases}$$

The cumulative probability distribution of y_i is given by

$$\Pr(y_i \leq j) = \Pr(\xi_i \leq \alpha_j)$$
$$= \Pr(\eta_i + \varepsilon_i \leq \alpha_j)$$
$$= \Pr(\varepsilon_i \leq \alpha_j - \eta_i)$$

for $j = 1, 2, \ldots, m - 1$. If the errors ε_i are independently distributed according to the standard logistic distribution, with distribution function

$$\Lambda(z) = \frac{1}{1 + e^{-z}},$$

then we get the proportional-odds logit model

$$\text{logit}[\Pr(y_i > j)] = \log_e \frac{\Pr(y_i > j)}{\Pr(y_i \leq j)} \tag{7}$$
$$= -\alpha_j + \boldsymbol{\beta}' \mathbf{x}_i$$

for $j = 1, 2, \ldots, m - 1$. (The similar ordered probit model is produced by assuming that the ε_i are normally distributed.)

Model 7 is overparametrized: Since the $\boldsymbol{\beta}$ vector typically includes a constant, say β_1, we have $m-1$ regression equations, the intercepts of which are expressed in terms of m (i.e., one too many) parameters. A solution is to eliminate the constant from $\boldsymbol{\beta}$. Setting $\beta_1 = 0$ in this manner in effect establishes the origin of the latent continuum ξ; we already implicitly established the scale of ξ by fixing the variance of the error to the variance of the standard logistic distribution ($\pi^2/3$). For convenience, we will absorb the negative sign into the intercept, rewriting the model as

$$\text{logit}[\text{Pr}(y_i > j)] = \alpha_j + \boldsymbol{\beta}'\mathbf{x}_i, \quad \text{for} \quad j = 1, 2, \ldots, m - 1.$$

The thresholds are then the negatives of the intercepts α_j. Because fitted probabilities under the model are unaffected by this reparametrization, effect displays are invariant as well.

The proportional-odds model is more parsimonious than the multinomial logit model (and other models for unordered polytomies): While the proportional-odds model has $m + p - 2$ independent parameters, the multinomial logit model has $p(m-1)$ independent parameters. Of course, the proportional-odds model is also less flexible, and may not adequately represent the data.

We propose two strategies for constructing effect displays for the proportional-odds model. The more straightforward strategy is to plot on the scale of the latent continuum, using the estimated thresholds, $-\hat{\alpha}_j$, to show the division of the continuum into ordered categories. There is not much more to say about this approach, since—other than marking the thresholds (as illustrated in the example in Section 4.2)— one proceeds exactly as for a linear model.

The second approach is to display fitted probabilities of category membership, as we did for the multinomial logit model. Suppose that we need the fitted probabilities at $\mathbf{x}'_0$ (where the constant regressor has been removed from the design vector $\mathbf{x}'$, and the intercept from the parameter vector $\boldsymbol{\beta}$). Let $\eta_0 = \mathbf{x}'_0\boldsymbol{\beta}$, and let $\mu_{0j} = \text{Pr}(Y_0 = j)$. Then

$$\mu_{01} = \frac{1}{1 + \exp(\alpha_1 + \eta_0)}$$

$$\mu_{0j} = \frac{\exp(\eta_0)\left[\exp(\alpha_{j-1}) - \exp(\alpha_j)\right]}{\left[1 + \exp(\alpha_{j-1} + \eta_0)\right]\left[1 + \exp(\alpha_j + \eta_0)\right]}, j = 2, \ldots, m - 1$$

$$\mu_{0m} = 1 - \sum_{j=1}^{m-1} \mu_{0j}$$

As in the case of the multinomial logit model, we derive approximate standard errors by the delta method. The necessary derivatives are messier here, however:

$$\frac{\partial \mu_{01}}{\partial \alpha_1} = -\frac{\exp(\alpha_1 + \eta_0)}{[1 + \exp(\alpha_1 + \eta_0)]^2}$$

$$\frac{\partial \mu_{01}}{\partial \alpha_j} = 0, \, j = 2, \ldots, m-1$$

$$\frac{\partial \mu_{01}}{\partial \beta} = -\frac{\exp(\alpha_1 + \eta_0)\mathbf{x}_0}{[1 + \exp(\alpha_1 + \eta_0)]^2}$$

$$\frac{\partial \mu_{0j}}{\partial \alpha_{j-1}} = \frac{\exp(\alpha_{j-1} + \eta_0)}{\left[1 + \exp(\alpha_{j-1} + \eta_0)\right]^2}$$

$$\frac{\partial \mu_{0j}}{\partial \alpha_j} = -\frac{\exp(\alpha_j + \eta_0)}{\left[1 + \exp(\alpha_j + \eta_0)\right]^2}$$

$$\frac{\partial \mu_{0j}}{\partial \alpha_{j'}} = 0, \, j' \neq j, j-1$$

$$\frac{\partial \mu_{0j}}{\partial \beta} = \frac{\exp(\eta_0) \left[\exp(\alpha_j) - \exp(\alpha_{j-1})\right] \left[\exp(\alpha_{j-1} + \alpha_j + 2\eta_0) - 1\right] \mathbf{x}_0}{\left[1 + \exp(\alpha_{j-1} + \eta_0)\right]^2 \left[1 + \exp(\alpha_j + \eta_0)\right]^2}$$

$$\frac{\partial \mu_{0m}}{\partial \alpha_{m-1}} = \frac{\exp(\alpha_{m-1} + \eta_0)}{[1 + \exp(\alpha_{m-1} + \eta_0)]^2}$$

$$\frac{\partial \mu_{0m}}{\partial \alpha_j} = 0, \, j = 1, \ldots, m-2$$

$$\frac{\partial \mu_{0m}}{\partial \beta} = \frac{\exp(\alpha_{m-1} + \eta_0)\mathbf{x}_0}{[1 + \exp(\alpha_{m-1} + \eta_0)]^2}.$$

Let us stack up all of the parameters in the vector $\gamma = (\alpha_1, \ldots, \alpha_{m-1}, \beta')'$, and let

$$\hat{V}(\hat{\gamma}) = [v_{st}], \, s, t = 1, \ldots, r,$$

where $r = m + p - 2$. Then, as for the multinomial logit model,

$$\hat{V}(\hat{\mu}_{0j}) \simeq \sum_{s=1}^{r} \sum_{t=1}^{r} v_{st} \frac{\partial \hat{\mu}_{0j}}{\partial \hat{\gamma}_s} \frac{\partial \hat{\mu}_{0j}}{\partial \hat{\gamma}_t}$$

and

$$\hat{V}(\hat{\lambda}_{0j}) \simeq \frac{1}{\hat{\mu}_{0j}^2 (1 - \hat{\mu}_{0j})^2} \hat{V}(\hat{\mu}_{0j}),$$

where

$$\lambda_{0j} = \log \frac{\mu_{0j}}{1 - \mu_{0j}}$$

are the individual-category logits—that is, the log-odds of membership in a particular category versus all others, *not* the cumulative logits modeled directly by the proportional-odds model (given in equation 7).

4.2. Example: Cross-National Differences in Attitudes Toward Government Efforts to Reduce Poverty

We now turn to an application of effect displays to a proportional-odds logit model. Data for this example are taken from the World Values Survey of 1995–1997 (Inglehart et al., 2000). We use a subset of the World Values Survey, focusing on four countries (with sample sizes in parentheses): Australia (1874), Norway (1127), Sweden (1003), and the United States (1377). Although the variables that we employ are available for more than 40 countries, we restrict attention to these four nations to simplify the example. The variables in the model are as follows:

- The response variable is produced from answers to the question, "Do you think that what the government is doing for people in poverty in this country is about the right amount, too much, or too little?" We order the responses as too little < about right < too much.
- Explanatory variables include gender, religion (coded 1 if the respondent belonged to a religion, 0 if the respondent did not), education (coded 1 if the respondent had a university degree, 0 if not), and country (dummy coded, with Sweden as the reference category).

Preliminary analysis of the data suggested modeling the effect of age as a cubic polynomial (we use an orthogonal cubic polynomial) and including an interaction between age and country.[6] The coefficients and

---

[6] As a reviewer has pointed out, because of their nonlocal character, higher-order polynomial fits can be risky. Although we generally prefer more local fits such as regression splines, we use a cubic polynomial here to make a point about interpretation—that is, that multiple-degree-of-freedom effects, particularly involving interactions, are difficult to interpret from the coefficients. This is true of

TABLE 4

Coefficients for a Proportional-Odds Logit Model Regressing Attitude Toward
Government Efforts to Help People in Poverty on Gender, Age, Religion,
Education, and Country

Coefficient	Estimate	Standard Error
Gender (male)	0.169	0.053
Religion (yes)	−0.168	0.078
University degree (yes)	0.141	0.067
Age (linear)	10.659	5.404
Age (quadratic)	7.535	6.245
Age (cubic)	8.887	6.663
Norway	0.250	0.087
Australia	0.572	0.823
USA	1.176	0.087
Norway × Age (linear)	−7.905	7.091
Australia × Age (linear)	9.264	6.312
USA × Age (linear)	10.868	6.647
Norway × Age (quadratic)	−0.625	8.027
Australia × Age (quadratic)	−17.716	7.034
USA × Age (quadratic)	−7.692	7.352
Norway × Age (cubic)	0.485	8.568
Australia × Age (cubic)	−2.762	7.385
USA × Age (cubic)	−11.163	7.587
Thresholds		
Too little | about right	0.449	0.106
About right | too much	2.262	0.111

[a] Age is represented in the model by a cubic orthogonal polynomial, and interactions
between age and country are included in the model.

their standard errors from a final model fit to the data are displayed in
Table 4.

The complexity of the nonlinear trend for age, its interaction with
country, and coefficients for cumulative logits make it extremely difficult to interpret the parameter estimates associated with age. Instead, we
construct effect displays for the interaction of age with country. Figure 7
plots fitted probabilities for each category of the response variable

orthogonal polynomials, as used here, of ordinary polynomials (which provide the
same fit to the data), and of regression splines. In fact, the cubic fit that we have
employed represents the data well, and provides results similar to a regression spline.
See Hastie and Tibshirani (1990, sec. 2.9) for a good discussion of regression splines
and their general advantages relative to polynomial regression.

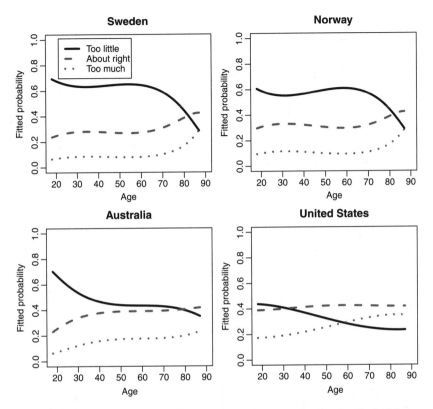

FIGURE 7. Display of the interaction between age and country, showing the effects of these variables on attitude toward government efforts to help people in poverty; the graphs indicate the fitted probability for each of the three categories of the response variable.

in the same manner as for the multinomial logit model of Section 2.2. Because country takes on only four values while age is continuous, we construct a separate plot for each country, placing age on the horizontal axis. There are three fitted lines in each plot—representing the fitted probability of choosing each response category. Figure 8 is generally similar, but with 95 percent point-wise confidence intervals around the fitted probabilities (and separate panels for each response category, so as not to clutter the plots). Figure 9 shows an alternative display with stacked response categories.

Although the graphs in Figures 7–9 are informative—we see, for example, that age differences are relatively muted in the United States

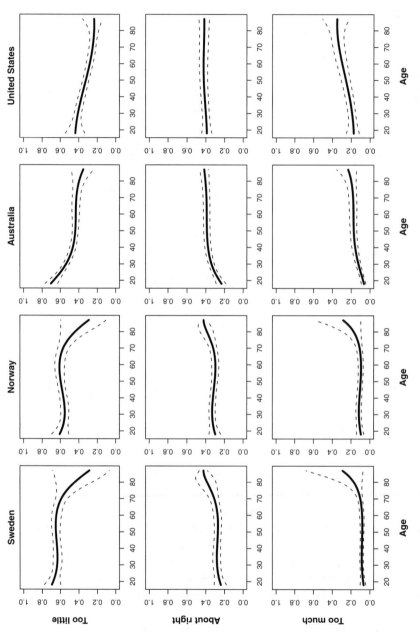

FIGURE 8. Display of the interaction between age and country, showing point-wise 95 percent confidence intervals around the fitted probabilities.

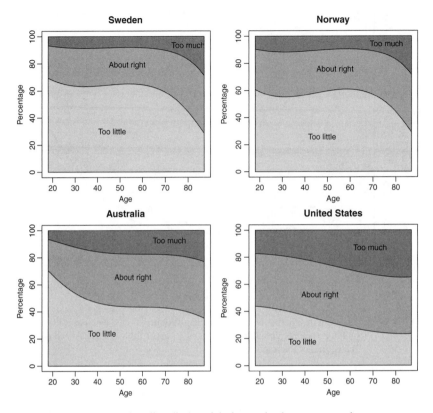

FIGURE 9. Alternative effect display of the interaction between age and country.

and that respondents there are less likely than others to feel that the government is not doing enough for the poor—the displays do not take full advantage of the parsimony of the proportional-odds model. We can capitalize on the structure of the proportional-odds model to plot the fitted response on the scale of the latent attitude continuum. We pursue this strategy in Figure 10, in which there is only one line for each country.[7] The estimated thresholds from the proportional-odds model are displayed as horizontal lines, dividing the latent continuum into three categories. Notice that none of the fitted curves exceeds the

---

[7]Abstract versions of Figure 10 are often used to explain the proportional-odds model (e.g., see Agresti 1990, fig. 9.2), but not typically to present the results of fitting the model to data and not for the kind of partial-effect plot developed in this paper.

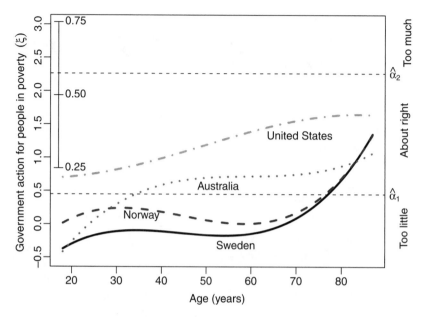

FIGURE 10. Plotting the interaction between age and country on the latent attitude continuum, ξ. The horizontal lines at $\hat{\alpha}_1$ and $\hat{\alpha}_2$ are the thresholds between adjacent categories of the response.

second cut-point, and it is therefore unnecessary to include this cut-point in the graph; we do so to show explicitly that "too much" is never the modal response. The scale at the upper left of the graph shows the range spanned by the middle half of the standardized logistic distribution (i.e., the interquartile range, approximately $2 \times 1.1 = 2.2$ on the scale of the latent response), suggesting variation around the expected response; this is not to be confused with a confidence interval around the fitted response.

The patterns revealed by the effect displays are quite interesting: Even though their countries do more than the others to help those in poverty, people in Norway and Sweden are generally more likely than those in the United States or Australia to feel that the effort is insufficient. Moreover, attitudes are relatively similar among all age groups in the Scandinavian countries, with the exception of those at the highest ages, while in the United States and Australia, there are more general age trends toward decreased sympathy with the poor.

5. DISCUSSION

Statistical models for polytomous response variables are increasingly employed in social research. Too frequently, however, the results of fitting these models are described perfunctorily. Efforts to ensure careful model specification can be largely wasted if the results are not conveyed clearly. Although it is difficult to interpret the coefficients of complex statistical models that transform response probabilities nonlinearly, simply discussing their signs and statistical significance tells us little about the structure of the data. The approach described and illustrated in this paper, in contrast, goes a long way toward clarifying the fit of multinomial logit and proportional-odds models and simplifying their interpretation.

Effect displays allow us to visualize key portions of the response surface of a statistical model, and thus to understand better how explanatory variables combine to influence the response. The computation of effect displays for models of polytomous response variables is fairly straightforward and can be implemented in most statistical software. Computations associated with standard errors and confidence intervals for these effect displays are more difficult, however. We intend to extend the `effects` package for R (described in Fox 2003) to cover multinomial and proportional-odds logit models, making the construction of effect displays for these models essentially automatic. Until that time, a program described in the appendix to this paper may be employed for computing effects, their standard errors, and confidence limits.

APPENDIX: COMPUTING

Fitted values and their standard errors for effect displays may be computed with an R function (program), `polytomousEffects`, available on the web at <http://socserv.socsci.mcmaster.ca/jfox/Papers/polytomous-effect-displays.html>. Also available are code and data for the examples in this paper. R (Ihaka and Gentleman, 1996; R Development Core Team, 2004) is a free, open-source implementation of the S statistical computing environment now in widespread use, particularly among statisticians. The `polytomousEffects` function uses the strategy for safe prediction described in Hastie (1992, sec. 7.3.3) to ensure that fitted values are computed correctly in models with terms (such as orthogonal polynomials and B-splines) whose basis depends upon the data.

REFERENCES

Agresti, A. 1990. *Categorical Data Analysis*. New York: Wiley.

Andersen, R. 2003. "Do Newspapers Enlighten Preferences? Personal Ideology, Party Choice, and the Electoral Cycle: The United Kingdom, 1992–97." *Canadian Journal of Political Science* 36:601–20.

Andersen, R., A. Heath, and R. Sinnott. 2002. "Political Knowledge and Electoral Choice." *British Elections and Parties Review* 12:11–27.

Andersen, R., J. Tilley, and A. Heath. 2005. "Political Knowledge and Enlightened Preferences." *British Journal of Political Science* 35:285–303.

Firth, D. 1991. "Generalized Linear Models." Pp. 55–82 in *Statistical Theory and Modeling: In Honour of Sir David Cox, FRS* edited by D. V. Hinkley, N. Reid, and E. J. Snell. London: Chapman and Hall.

Fisher, R. A. 1936. *Statistical Methods for Research Workers, 6th ed.* Edinburgh: Oliver and Boyd.

Fox, J. 1987. "Effect Displays for Generalized Linear Models." Pp. 347–61 in *Sociological Methodology*, vol. 17, edited by C. C. Clogg. Washington, DC: American Sociological Association.

—— 1997. *Applied Regression Analysis, Linear Models, and Related Methods*. Thousand Oaks, CA: Sage.

—— 2003. "Effect Displays in R for Generalised Linear Models." *Journal of Statistical Software* 8(15):1–27.

Goodnight, J. H., and W. R. Harvey. 1978. "Least Squares Means in the Fixed-Effect General Linear Model." Technical Report No. R-103. Cary, NC: SAS Institute.

Hastie, T. J. 1992. "Generalized Additive Models." Pp. 249–307 in *Statistical Models in S* edited by J. M. Chambers and T. J. Hastie. Pacific Grove, CA: Wadsworth.

Hastie, T. J., and R. J. Tibshirani. 1990. *Generalized Additive Models*. London: Chapman and Hall.

Hastie, T., R. Tibshirani, and J. Friedman. 2001. *The Elements of Statistical Learning: Data Mining, Inference, and Prediction*. New York: Springer.

Ihaka, R., and R. Gentleman. 1996. "R: A Language for Data Analysis and Graphics." *Journal of Computational and Graphical Statistics* 5:299–314.

Inglehart, R. E. A. 2000. *World values surveys and European value surveys, 1981–1984:1990–1993, and 1995–1997* [computer file]. Ann Arbor, MI: Institute for Social Research [producer], Inter–University Consortium for Political and Social Research [distributor].

King, G., M. Tomz, and J. Wittenberg. 2000. "Making the Most of Statistical Analyses: Improving Interpretation and Presentation." *American Journal of Political Science* 44:347–61.

Long, J. S. 1997. *Regression Models for Categorical and Limited Dependent Variables*. Thousand Oaks, CA: Sage.

McCullagh, P., and J. A. Nelder. 1989. *Generalized Linear Models*. 2d ed. London: Chapman and Hall.

Nelder, J. A. 1977. "A Reformulation of Linear Models" (with commentary). *Journal of the Royal Statistical Society*, Series A, 140:48–76.

Powers, D. A., and Y. Xie. 2000. *Statistical Methods for Categorical Data Analysis*. San Diego: Academic Press.

R Core Development Team. 2004. *R: A Language and Environment for Statistical Computing*. Vienna: R Foundation for Statistical Computing.

Rao, C. R. 1965. *Linear Statistical Inference and Its Applications*. New York: Wiley.

Searle, S. R., F. M. Speed, and G. A. Milliken. 1980. "Population Marginal Means in the Linear Model: An Alternative to Least Squares Means." *The American Statistician* 34:216–21.

Tomz, M., J. Wittenberg, and G. King. 2003. "Clarify: Software for Interpreting and Presenting Statistical Results." *Journal of Statistical Software* 8:1–29.

Weisberg, S. 2005. *Applied Linear Regression*. 3d ed. New York: Wiley.

3

A PARTIAL INDEPENDENCE ITEM RESPONSE MODEL FOR SURVEYS WITH FILTER QUESTIONS

Sean F. Reardon*
Stephen W. Raudenbush†

In many surveys, responses to earlier questions determine whether later questions are asked. The probability of an affirmative response to a given item is therefore nonzero only if the participant responded affirmatively to some set of logically prior items, known as "filter items." In such surveys, the usual conditional independence assumption of standard item response models fails. A weaker "partial independence" assumption may hold, however, if an individual's responses to different items are independent conditional on the item parameters, the individual's latent trait, and the participant's affirmative responses to each of a set of filter items. In this paper, we propose an item response model for such "partially independent" item response data. We model such item response patterns as a function of a person-specific latent trait and a set of item parameters. Our model can be seen as a generalized hybrid of a discrete-time hazard model and a Rasch model. The proposed procedure yields estimates of (1) person-specific, interval-scale measures of a latent trait (or traits), along with person-specific standard errors of measurement; (2) conditional and marginal

The research reported here was funded by grants from the National Institute of Alcohol and Alcohol Use (grant R01-AA13814) and the William T. Grant Foundation. We thank Stephen Buka and Scott Novak for helpful comments and Richard Congdon for applications programming to implement the statistical methods reported herein.

*Stanford University
†University of Chicago

item severities for each item in a protocol; (3) person-specific conditional and marginal probabilities of an affirmative response to each item in a protocol; and (4) item information and total survey information. In addition, we show here how to investigate and test alternative conceptions of the dimensionality of the latent trait(s) being measured. Finally, we compare our procedure with a simpler alternative approach to summarizing data of this type.

1. INTRODUCTION

In social surveys, it is common to inquire about whether events have occurred, and if so, to inquire about specific aspects of these events, such as their frequency and intensity. Examples include substance use (whether one has used a substance, and if so how often and how heavily); crime (whether one has been involved in a given type of crime, and if so, how often); symptoms of a disease; purchases of a given product. Protocols of this type have a conditional structure: responses to earlier questions determine whether later questions are asked. The researcher presumes that the entire ensemble of responses carries useful information about one or more underlying "latent" behavioral traits or attributes.

Unfortunately, standard latent variable models for item response data are not suited for the analysis of data having a conditional structure. Instead, such models assume local independence—that is, conditional independence of all item responses given the item parameters and the person traits being measured (Lord & Novick 1968). Such an assumption cannot hold when responses to a prior item determine whether a later item is asked. However, a weaker "partial independence" assumption may hold, where by "partial independence" we mean local independence of item responses given a participant's affirmative responses to each of a set of logically prior items.

In this paper, we propose a principled procedure for modeling response patterns to such protocols as a function of a person-specific latent trait and a set of item parameters. Our procedure yields estimates of four quantities of interest: (1) person-specific, interval-scale measures of a latent trait (or traits), along with person-specific standard errors of measurement; (2) conditional and marginal item severities for each item in a protocol; (3) person-specific conditional and marginal probabilities of an affirmative response to each item in a protocol; and (4) item information and total survey information. In addition, we show here how to investigate and test alternative conceptions of the dimensionality of the latent trait(s) being measured. Finally, we compare our procedure with a simpler alternative approach to summarizing data of this type.

We achieve these aims by formulating fixed and random effects models for item responses that may be conditional on prior responses while being independent of responses to other items. The modeling approach can be seen as a generalized hybrid of a discrete-time hazard model and a Rasch model. The conditional structure of the items enables us to define "risk sets" of individuals who possess a nonzero probability of responding affirmatively to sets of logically subsequent items; the logic of the discrete-time hazard model (Allison 1982) and the (formally equivalent) continuation ratio model for ordinal outcomes (Armstrong and Sloan 1989; Cox 1988; Fienberg 1980) provides guidance here. Unlike the discrete-time and continuation ratio models, however, our model incorporates the possibility that multiple "locally-independent" items may be asked of each individual in a risk set. The model assumes that each person possesses a latent trait or attribute that affects the probability of an affirmative response to each such locally independent item, conditional on having affirmatively answered all logically prior items. In addition, each such item may have subsequent items conditional upon it, allowing us to fit models based on complex sets of both conditional and independent items.

Although the approach we develop in this paper has application to a wide range of substantive survey domains, we focus on a single potential application—the problem of estimating latent alcohol and marijuana use from a set of survey items regarding substance use in the last year—in order to provide a concrete illustration of the method. In particular, we demonstrate the application of our model to study the alcohol and marijuana use of a large, diverse, and representative sample of children growing up in Chicago. To illustrate how our model can be used to investigate the dimensionality of latent characteristics, we then investigate whether adolescent alcohol and marijuana use can be considered aspects of a single underlying latent substance use trait, or whether they represent distinct behavioral traits.

2. BACKGROUND AND SIGNIFICANCE

Researchers interested in adolescent substance abuse—as well as in a wide range of other substantive domains—have contended with the conditional structure of survey data in a variety of ways. Each has some utility in particular circumstances, but none of the available methods used to date efficiently combines information across all item responses within the framework of latent trait analysis, which is the aim of the current paper.

2.1. *Single-Item Analysis*

A simple strategy for analyzing data having a conditional structure is to study one item at a time (Adalbjarnardottir 2002; Bailey, Flewelling, and Rachal 1992; Chassin, Pitts, and Prost 2002; Hill et al. 2000; Khoo and Muthen 2000). Suppose, for example, that the first question on a survey is "Have you had a drink during the past year?" Modeling responses to such a question as a function of covariates or exposure to prevention programs could be quite useful.

    One obvious limitation of single-item analysis is that it does not allow a pooling of information across item responses to reduce the error with which a latent trait is measured. This limitation of single-item analysis provides an important rationale for latent trait models for multiple item responses. Latent trait models also supply a basis for quantifying measurement error, a benefit that single-item analysis cannot enjoy. Moreover, if a questionnaire includes many items, single-item analysis applied to each item will give rise to a large number of hypothesis tests, increasing the risk of a Type I error. It may prove difficult to summarize evidence across the many analyses so generated.

    The limitations of single-item analysis described above apply to all multiple-item surveys, even those without a conditional structure. However, when single-item analysis is applied to survey items having a conditional structure, a subtle and potentially pernicious additional concern arises: conditioning on an error-prone response. To illustrate, consider a case in which persons who respond affirmatively to the question "Have you had a drink in the past year?" are asked "Were you drunk in the last year?" Applying single-item analysis to this second, conditional question requires that those who responded negatively to the first question be discarded. Yet, some of those cases may be discarded simply as a result of measurement error.

Consider a thought experiment in which two persons with the same propensity to drink respond differently to the first question because of differences in estimating when they last had a drink or because the timing of the last drink differed slightly. For example, one person might have had a drink 364 days ago and correctly responded "yes" to the first question while a second person with an identical propensity to drink may have had a drink 366 days ago and thus correctly responded "no" to the first question. In this case, single-item analysis for the second item would require that the second person be discarded, strictly as a result of measurement error. Selecting the sample for an analysis conditional on measurement error may then create unwanted results such as regression to the mean. The only way to avoid such a problem using single-item analysis is to restrict application to nonconditional items. But such a procedure then requires that information from all conditional items be discarded, meaning that the expense required to collect this additional information will have been wasted.

2.2. *Multiple Item Analysis*

A second strategy is to develop a transformation that combines multiple-item responses to a single variable believed to determine these multiple-item responses. This strategy is widely used. (Recent examples are found in Barnes et al. 2000; Bennett et al. 1999; Colder and Stice 1998; Duncan, Duncan, and Hops 1996; Hussong, Curran, and Chassin 1998; Scheier et al. 2000; Schulenberg et al. 1996; Silberg et al. 2003; Wills and Cleary 1999.) In this approach, item responses might be added, for example, or combined into ordered categories. In comparison to single-item analysis, such an approach has the advantage of combining more information from the survey to measure the variable of interest, in principle reducing measurement error and also allowing a more parsimonious analytic plan. A limitation of this method, however, is that it is not based on a probabilistic model for how the item responses are generated. Thus, the benefits of latent trait analysis via item response modeling are not available. These include a principled calibration of items, study of item fit, the quantification of measurement error, and the evaluation of dimensionality.

The study of dimensionality has emerged as an important topic in item response modeling (Adams, Wilson, and Wang 1997; Cheong and Raudenbush 2000; Raudenbush, Johnson, and Sampson 2003; Reckase 1985). Study of dimensionality has important implications for the assessment of construct validity. Suppose, for example, that responses to items about alcohol use and marijuana use are treated as a single dimension when in truth two separate dimensions, one for each substance, are driving the item responses. Such a unidimensional analysis would fail to reveal the different processes that predict use of the two substances. Multidimensionality takes a different form when subgroups (e.g., males and females) respond differently to particular items even holding constant the latent trait of interest. Such differential item functioning (DIF; Holland & Wainer 1993), sometimes called "item bias," can be studied in a principled way using item response modeling, but this benefit has not yet been extended to surveys having a conditional item structure.

Finally, when the items have a partially conditional structure, constructing a variable by a simple transformation of multiple-item responses may propagate measurement error. Let us again take up the example described above, in which two persons having the same propensity to use alcohol responded differently to the question "Have you used alcohol during the past year?" In this case, the person responding affirmatively, but not the person responding negatively, will be asked more questions, perhaps many more questions, increasing the opportunity for the two cases to be incorrectly differentiated when all item responses are combined.

2.3. *The Case for a Latent Trait Model for Partially Independent Item Response Data*

The foregoing discussion suggests that the advantages afforded by latent trait analysis ought to be extended to survey data having a partially conditional structure. This requires a reasonable probabilistic model to describe responses to a mixture of item types. We shall define a "gate" item as one that must be answered affirmatively if a set of logically subsequent items is to be administered to a given respondent. Individuals who answer a given "gate" item or set of items affirmatively are then in the "risk set" for logically subsequent items. Our probabilistic approach regards the marginal probability of an affirmative response to a given item as the product of the probability of responding affirmatively to its gate item(s) (i.e., being in the risk set for the given item) and the conditional probability of responding affirmatively to that item given that one responded affirmatively to its gate item(s). Our approach thus combines a hazard model of the probability of passing a gate, given that prior gates have been passed, and a Rasch model to describe variation in the probabilities of responding affirmatively to sets of items, conditional on being in the risk set for each item. To illustrate, we apply this approach to a large and representative sample of data on children growing up in Chicago.

3. SAMPLE AND DATA

For the illustrative examples in this paper, we use data on adolescent substance use from a subsample of the longitudinal cohort study of the Project on Human Development in Chicago Neighborhoods (PHDCN), an ongoing, multilevel, prospective, longitudinal study designed to investigate the effects of neighborhood demographic and social context on a wide array of developmental and behavioral outcomes. The PHDCN study consists of a representative sample of children and youth living in 80 neighborhoods of Chicago between 1995 and 1996. The sampling design and data collection procedures for PHDCN are described in detail in Sampson, Morenoff, and Raudenbush (2005).

Our sample consists of adolescents from the 12-, 15-, and 18-year-old cohorts of the PHDCN sample. Each adolescent was interviewed three times, at roughly two- to three-year intervals. For each adolescent in our subsample, we use only one of three available longitudinal observations for the analyses reported here—wave 1 interview data from the 18-year-old cohort; wave 2 interview data from the 15-year-old cohort; and wave 3 interview data from the 12-year-old cohort. We restrict the age range in our sample in order to avoid confounding measurement issues with potential age variation in the measurement model. Of the 1531 eligible subjects, we exclude 79 subjects (5%) missing data on any of the four alcohol items (70 subjects) or on any of four demographic variables—age, gender, race/ethnicity, and socioeconomic status (9 subjects). Thus our subsample consists of interview data from a representative sample of 1452 Chicago adolescents, aged 16–19 between 1995 and 2001 (mean age=17.4, S.D.=.8; 53% female; 19% white, 37% black; 44% Latino).

Adolescents in the PHDCN sample were asked a set of questions about their alcohol use in the last year. We use information from four alcohol use questions:

1. *How many times did you drink alcohol in the last year?* (possible responses were: never, 1–2 times, 3–5 times, 6–11 times, 12–24 times, 25–50 times, 51–99 times, 100–199 times, 200 or more times).
2. *How many times were you drunk in the last year?* (asked of those whose response to question 1 indicated they had a drink at least once in the last year—subjects could answer with any number; responses ranged from 0 to 300).
3. *How many times did you drink in the last month?* (asked of those whose response to question 1 indicated they had a drink at least once in the last year—possible responses were: never, 1–2 times, 3-5 times, 6–9 times, 10–14 times, 15–20 times, 21 or more times).
4. *How many times did you have more than 5 drinks in a row in the last month?* (asked of those whose response to question 3 indicated they had a drink at least once in the last month—possible responses were: never, 1 time, 2 times, 3–5 times, 6–9 times, 10 or more times).

From these four questions, we construct 11 binary items, each of which indicates whether an individual's response to a specific question is at or above a certain threshold level. For example, using thresholds of 1, 6, and 25 for the first question, we construct three items: *Did you drink at least 1 time in the last year? Did you drink at least 6 times in the last year? Did you drink at least 25 times in the last year?* For question 2 we use thresholds of 1, 6, and 25; for question 3, we use thresholds of 1, 3 and 10; and for question 4 we use thresholds of 1 and 3.

This procedure results in 11 binary items (see Table 1). Each of these items has a "risk set"—the set of persons who could have logically answered '*yes*' to the item, given their prior responses. This is the set of persons who answered *yes* to the logically prior item or items (e.g., the risk set for the '*had at least one drink in the last month*' item is the set of persons who said *yes* to the '*had at least one drink in the last year*' item). The conditional probability for an item is the probability of saying yes to the item, conditional on being in the risk set for the item.

TABLE 1
Observed Alcohol Item Response Frequencies

Item	Description	Gate Items	Marginal Probability	Risk Set	Number of *yes*	Conditional Probability
1	Alcohol in year	-none-	.554	1,452	805	.554
2	Alcohol 6x in year	1	.262	805	380	.472
3	Alcohol 25x in year	1, 2	.116	380	169	.445
4	Drunk in year	1	.341	805	495	.615
5	Drunk 6x in year	1, 4	.094	495	137	.277
6	Drunk 25x in year	1, 4, 5	.038	137	55	.401
7	Alcohol in month	1	.320	805	464	.576
8	Alcohol 3x in month	1, 7	.158	464	229	.494
9	Alcohol 10x in month	1, 7, 8	.039	229	57	.249
10	Binge in month	1, 7	.160	464	233	.502
11	Binge 3x in month	1, 7, 10	.064	233	93	.399

The marginal probability for an item is simply the probability of saying *yes* to the item.

Although we could have constructed more items or fewer items by selecting a different set of thresholds, our choice of thresholds was not arbitrary. We chose thresholds that would differentiate well across the range of responses and would give conditional probabilities far from 0 or 1, since constructing the items this way preserves most of the information in the responses while keeping the number of constructed items relatively parsimonious.[1]

4. THE MODEL

4.1. *Item Structure and the Gate Matrix*

Suppose that persons $i = 1, \ldots, n$ respond to items $k = 1, \ldots, K$, generating, for each person, the response vector $\mathbf{Y}_i = [y_{i1}, y_{i2}, \ldots, y_{iK}]$, where

[1] In additional analyses (not shown) we use 8 thresholds for questions 1 and 2 (1, 3, 6, 12, 25, 51, 100, 200), 6 thresholds for question 3 (1, 3, 6, 10, 15, 21), and 5 thresholds for question 4 (1, 2, 3, 6, 10). This uses the maximum possible information from questions 1, 3, and 4, and most of the information from question 2, and results in 27 items rather than 11. Results based on this more detailed set of conditional items are not substantially different from those based on the more parsimonious set of items, so we present the more parsimonious set here for simplicity of presentation.

$y_{ik} = 1$ if person i responded affirmatively to item k, and $y_{ik} = 0$ if person i responded negatively to item k or if person i did not respond to item k because he or she responded negatively to a gate item for item k, and so was not asked item k. We indicate the item structure as follows: we say that item j is a gate for item k if $y_j = 0$ implies that $y_k = 0$. We define the $K \times K$ gate matrix G, where element $G[k,j] = G_{kj} = 1$ if item j is a gate item for item k, and 0 otherwise (by definition, $G_{kk} = 0$, since an item cannot be a gate item for itself). The pattern of 1s in a given row k of G indicates which items are gate items for item k; the pattern of 1s in a given column j of G indicates which items are conditional on item j (items for which j is a gate item).

Next we define h_{ik}, the gate value for item k for person i, as follows: define $h_{ik} = 1$ if $y_{ij} = 1$ for all items j that are gate items for k, and $h_{ik} = 0$ if $y_{ij} = 0$ for at least one item j that is a gate item for k:

$$h_{ik} = \prod_{j=1}^{K} \left[1 - G_{kj} \left(1 - y_{ij} \right) \right]. \tag{1}$$

In other words, h_{ik} indicates whether the gate item or items for item k for person i are satisfied, and so indicates whether person i is in the risk set for item k. In a survey, h_{ik} will be 0 for items that person i is not asked because he or she did not meet the conditions necessary to be asked them (because his or her response to item k is determined by his or her negative response(s) to one or more of the gate items for item k). We denote the risk set R_k for item k as the set of all individuals i who have $h_{ik} = 1$.

To make this more concrete, consider a simple set of three items, where all individuals are asked item 1, but where items 2 and 3 are asked conditional on an affirmative response to item 1. Such an item structure can be illustrated as follows:

For this item structure, the gate matrix G would be

$$G = \begin{bmatrix} 0\ 0\ 0 \\ 1\ 0\ 0 \\ 1\ 0\ 0 \end{bmatrix}. \qquad (2)$$

If we added a fourth item that was conditional on item 3, the item structure and corresponding gate matrix would be

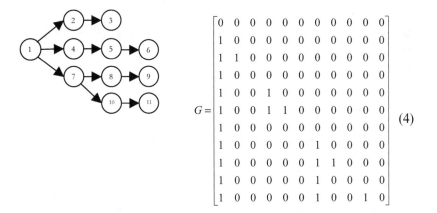

$$G = \begin{bmatrix} 0 & 0 & 0 & 0 \\ 1 & 0 & 0 & 0 \\ 1 & 0 & 0 & 0 \\ 1 & 0 & 1 & 0 \end{bmatrix}. \qquad (3)$$

For our alcohol data, the item structure and corresponding gate matrix defined by the questionnaire skip fields and the thresholds we use to define the binary items are (where the items are numbered as in Table 1):

$$G = \begin{bmatrix} 0 & 0 & 0 & 0 & 0 & 0 & 0 & 0 & 0 & 0 & 0 \\ 1 & 0 & 0 & 0 & 0 & 0 & 0 & 0 & 0 & 0 & 0 \\ 1 & 1 & 0 & 0 & 0 & 0 & 0 & 0 & 0 & 0 & 0 \\ 1 & 0 & 0 & 0 & 0 & 0 & 0 & 0 & 0 & 0 & 0 \\ 1 & 0 & 0 & 1 & 0 & 0 & 0 & 0 & 0 & 0 & 0 \\ 1 & 0 & 0 & 1 & 1 & 0 & 0 & 0 & 0 & 0 & 0 \\ 1 & 0 & 0 & 0 & 0 & 0 & 0 & 0 & 0 & 0 & 0 \\ 1 & 0 & 0 & 0 & 0 & 0 & 1 & 0 & 0 & 0 & 0 \\ 1 & 0 & 0 & 0 & 0 & 0 & 1 & 1 & 0 & 0 & 0 \\ 1 & 0 & 0 & 0 & 0 & 0 & 1 & 0 & 0 & 0 & 0 \\ 1 & 0 & 0 & 0 & 0 & 0 & 1 & 0 & 0 & 1 & 0 \end{bmatrix} \qquad (4)$$

As an aside, note that the gate matrix can be more complex than this: In our case, item 2 (*drank alcohol 6 or more times in the last year*), for example, is a logical gate for item 5 (*was drunk 6 or more times in the last year*), even though this is not reflected in the skip patterns of the survey questionnaire. If we incorporated this logical gate (and other similar ones) into the gate matrix, we would have

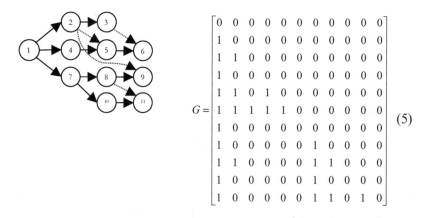

$$G = \begin{bmatrix} 0 & 0 & 0 & 0 & 0 & 0 & 0 & 0 & 0 & 0 & 0 \\ 1 & 0 & 0 & 0 & 0 & 0 & 0 & 0 & 0 & 0 & 0 \\ 1 & 1 & 0 & 0 & 0 & 0 & 0 & 0 & 0 & 0 & 0 \\ 1 & 0 & 0 & 0 & 0 & 0 & 0 & 0 & 0 & 0 & 0 \\ 1 & 1 & 0 & 1 & 0 & 0 & 0 & 0 & 0 & 0 & 0 \\ 1 & 1 & 1 & 1 & 1 & 0 & 0 & 0 & 0 & 0 & 0 \\ 1 & 0 & 0 & 0 & 0 & 0 & 0 & 0 & 0 & 0 & 0 \\ 1 & 0 & 0 & 0 & 0 & 0 & 1 & 0 & 0 & 0 & 0 \\ 1 & 1 & 0 & 0 & 0 & 0 & 1 & 1 & 0 & 0 & 0 \\ 1 & 0 & 0 & 0 & 0 & 0 & 1 & 0 & 0 & 0 & 0 \\ 1 & 0 & 0 & 0 & 0 & 0 & 1 & 1 & 0 & 1 & 0 \end{bmatrix} \quad (5)$$

In our illustrative example for this paper, we use gate matrix (4) above, though the model applies equally well to a matrix like that in (5).[2]

4.2. Model Notation

Let ϕ_{ik} denote the conditional probability of a *yes* response to item k for person i (conditional on a *yes* response to all gate items for item k). That is,

$$\phi_{ik} = \Pr(y_{ik} = 1 | h_{ik} = 1). \quad (6)$$

[2]The problem with (5) is that the data may not exactly correspond to the logical gate matrix in (5): for example, some subjects may have said they were drunk 6 or more times in the last year but also said that they had not had a drink 6 or more times in the last year. To use the logical gate matrix in (5) with such data requires us to decide that one of these two responses is incorrect and to recode it. To use the questionnaire gate matrix in (4) allows us to use the responses as provided (but erroneously assumes the responses to the two items in question are condition-ally independent, which is incorrect—item 5 is conditional on item 2). In our data, there are 22 cases (1.5% of 1452 total cases) containing logically inconsistent re-sponses to the four alcohol use questions (e.g., a subject reported drinking fewer than 6 times in the last year, but reported being drunk 6 or more times in the last year, or drinking 10 or more times in the last month).

We assume that each individual has a conditional probability of saying *yes* to each item k, even if he or she is not asked item k because he or she does not say *yes* to the necessary gate item(s). This conditional probability will be a function of θ_i, the unobserved latent trait for person i. In the fixed effects models below, θ_i is a fixed parameter, while in the random effects models, we shall assume $\theta_i \sim N(0, \tau)$.

Finally, let π_{ik} denote the marginal probability that person i responds affirmatively to item k:

$$\begin{aligned} \pi_{ik} &= \Pr(y_{ik} = 1) \\ &= \phi_{ik} \cdot \pi_{iR_k}, \end{aligned} \tag{7}$$

where π_{iR_k} is the marginal probability that person i is in the risk set for item k:

$$\begin{aligned} \pi_{iR_k} &= \Pr(h_{ik} = 1) \\ &= \prod_{j=1}^{K} \phi_{ij}^{G_{kj}}. \end{aligned} \tag{8}$$

Thus we have

$$\begin{aligned} \pi_{ik} &= \phi_{ik} \cdot \pi_{iR_k} \\ &= \phi_{ik} \prod_{j=1}^{K} \phi_{ij}^{G_{kj}} \end{aligned} \tag{9}$$

To summarize our notation:

k indexes items.

i indexes persons.

y_{ik} is the observed response to item k for person i.

Y_i is the observed response vector for person i.

h_{ik} is the observed gate value for item k for person i.

H_i is the observed vector of gate values for person i.

R_k is the risk set for item k.

G_{kj} indicates whether item k is conditional on item j.

ϕ_{ik} denotes the conditional probability of a *yes* response to item k for person i.

π_{ik} denotes the marginal probability of a *yes* response to item k for person i.

θ_i denotes the (unobserved) latent trait for person i.

γ_k denotes the conditional severity of item k.

τ denotes the variance of θ_i.

4.3. Fixed Effects Likelihood

We model the conditional probability of a positive response to item k as

$$\phi_{ik} = \left[1 + e^{-(\theta_i - \gamma_k)}\right]^{-1}. \tag{10}$$

Under the fixed effects specification, the parameters are $\gamma_1, \ldots, \gamma_K; \theta_1, \ldots, \theta_n$. The probability of observing response pattern $\mathbf{Y}_i$ for person i is then given by

$$\Pr(\mathbf{Y}_i) = \prod_{k=1}^{K} \left[\phi_{ik}^{y_{ik}} (1 - \phi_{ik})^{(1-y_{ik})}\right]^{h_{ik}} \tag{11}$$

From this, we write the fixed effects log-likelihood, l_f, of observing the response pattern $\mathbf{Y}$ found in the data, where $\gamma = (\gamma_1, \ldots, \gamma_K)$ and $\theta = (\theta_1, \ldots, \theta_n)$, as

$$
\begin{aligned}
l_f = \ln[L(\mathbf{Y}; \gamma, \theta)] &= \sum_{i=1}^{n} \sum_{k=1}^{K} h_{ik} \left[y_{ik} \ln\left(\frac{\phi_{ik}}{1 - \phi_{ik}}\right) + \ln(1 - \phi_{ik})\right] \\
&= \sum_{k=1}^{K} \sum_{i \in R_k} [y_{ik}\eta_{ik} + \ln(1 - \phi_{ik})] \\
&= \sum_{k=1}^{K} l_{fk} \\
&= \sum_{i=1}^{n} l_{fi},
\end{aligned}
\tag{12}
$$

where $l_{fk} = \sum_{i=1}^{n} h_{ik}[y_{ik}\eta_{ik} + \ln(1 - \phi_{ik})]$ is the fixed effects log-likelihood for item k, given γ_k and θ; $l_{fi} = \sum_{k=1}^{K} h_{ik}[y_{ik}\eta_{ik} + \ln(1 - \phi_{ik})]$ is the fixed effects log-likelihood for person i, given γ and θ_i; and $\eta_{ik} = \ln[\phi_{ik}/(1 - \phi_{ik})]$. Note that $y_{ik} = 0$ by definition when $h_{ik} = 0$, so l_{fk} is the log-likelihood of observing the pattern of responses to item k for all who satisfied the gate items to item k (all those in R_k). The observed (structural) 0s for item k among those who did not satisfy the gate items for k contribute no information to the log-likelihood l_{fk} since they are determined by the condition $h_{ik} = 0$.

Since l_{fk} depends only on those who can possibly have answered item k, we can drop item k for person i from the data set if $h_{ik}=0$. This is what we do in a discrete-time hazard model. In fact, equation (12) above is the log-likelihood for the hazard model in the special case where $h_{i(k+1)}=y_{ik}$ for all k—that is, where the items are strictly ordered and each item is conditional on the prior item.[3] In addition, in the case where $h_{ik} = 1$ by definition for all k (where there are no gate items; each individual responds to all questions), then (12) above is the likelihood for the fixed effects Rasch model with K items per person.

We note that γ_k is interpretable as the "conditional severity" of item k, and θ_i is the value of the latent trait of individual i. The conditional severity of item k corresponds to the value of θ_i at which a person would have a 0.5 probability of answering item k affirmatively, conditional on that person having satisfied the gate conditions for item k. Expressed differently, the conditional severity of item k is the log-odds of a negative response to item k for a person with a value of $\theta_i = 0$ (an "average" person), conditional on that person having met the gate conditions for item k.

The fixed effects model can be estimated using standard software for logistic regression under the model

$$\eta_{ik} = \theta_i + \sum_{j=1}^{K} \gamma_j D_{ij}, \tag{13}$$

where D_{ij} is a dummy variable indicating that person i is responding to item j. One limitation of the fixed effects Rasch model is that we must discard all information from individuals who either endorse all items or who fail to endorse any items. This means that we obtain estimates of θ_i for only the subset of individuals who endorse some, but not all, items.

---

[3]The discrete-time hazard model and the continuation ratio model for ordinal data are formally equivalent models, and both can be seen as a special case of our model, corresponding to a gate matrix where all entries below the diagonal are equal to 1, and all entries on or above the diagonal are 0. In the usual discrete-time and continuation ratio models, we drop θ_i from the model in equation (12), since there is no information from which to estimate it, though we keep θ_i in the case of the multilevel versions of these models (Barber et al. 2000; Reardon, Brennan, and Buka 2002).

4.4. *Random Effects Likelihood*

Under the random effects model, we assume that

$$\theta_i \sim N(0, \tau), \tau \geq 0. \tag{14}$$

The parameters to be estimated are then $(\gamma_1, \ldots, \gamma_K, \tau)$ and the random effects likelihood[4] for participant i is

$$L(\mathbf{Y}_i; \gamma, \tau) = (2\pi\tau)^{-1/2} \int e^{l_{fi} - \theta_i^2/2\tau} d\theta_i. \tag{15}$$

The integral is not available in closed form but can be approximated in several ways, including adaptive Gauss-Hermite Quadrature (Pinheiro and Bates 1995) and the Laplace method (Raudenbush, Yang, and Yosef 2000).

   Under the random effects model, person-specific inferences are readily obtained from the posterior distribution of the latent variable θ_i given the data $\mathbf{Y}_i$ and the parameter estimates $(\hat{\gamma}, \hat{\tau})$. The point estimate and uncertainty estimate for the person-specific latent trait are obtained, respectively, from the posterior mean

$$\begin{aligned}
\theta_i^* &= E\left(\theta_i | \mathbf{Y}_i, \hat{\gamma}, \hat{\tau}\right) \\
&= \int \theta_i p\left(\theta_i | \mathbf{Y}_i, \hat{\gamma}, \hat{\tau}\right) d\theta_i \\
&= [L(\mathbf{Y}_i; \hat{\gamma}, \hat{\tau})]^{-1} (2\pi\hat{\tau})^{-1/2} \int \theta_i e^{\hat{l}_{fi} - \theta_i^2/2\hat{\tau}} d\theta_i,
\end{aligned} \tag{16}$$

and the posterior variance

$$\begin{aligned}
V_i^* &= E\left[\left(\theta_i - \theta_i^*\right)^2 | \mathbf{Y}_i, \hat{\gamma}, \hat{\tau}\right] \\
&= \int \left(\theta_i - \theta_i^*\right)^2 p\left(\theta_i | \mathbf{Y}_i, \hat{\gamma}, \hat{\tau}\right) d\theta_i \\
&= [L(\mathbf{Y}_i; \hat{\gamma}, \hat{\tau})]^{-1} (2\pi\hat{\tau})^{-1/2} \int \left(\theta_i - \theta_i^*\right)^2 e^{\hat{l}_{fi} - \theta_i^2/2\hat{\tau}} d\theta_i,
\end{aligned} \tag{17}$$

where $\hat{l}_{fi} = l_{fi}$ evaluated at $\gamma = \hat{\gamma}$. These posterior means and variances are obtained from integrals approximated via the Laplace method

---

[4] Note that in the special case where $h_{ik} = 1$ by definition for all items (where none of the items are conditional on other items), the likelihood in (15) is identical to that of the random effects Rasch model with K items (Raudenbush, Johnson, and Sampson 2003).

(Raudenbush et al. 2005). They are regarded as empirical Bayes estimates because they are conditional upon point estimates of γ and τ. Unlike the fixed effects model, the random effects model allows us to retain all persons in the analysis, including those who answered all questions negatively or all questions affirmatively. Another advantage is that the random effects model summarizes heterogeneity between persons in a single parameter (τ), allowing efficient estimation even in the presence of item missing data under the comparatively mild assumption that the data are missing at random (Little & Rubin 2002). Finally, the random effects model extends naturally to the case where person traits are modeled as a function of covariates, a procedure we illustrate below.

5. AN EMPIRICAL EXAMPLE

To fit the partially conditional item-response model, we first construct a person-item data set based on the observed response patterns. We illustrate the construction of the person-item data set using hypothetical data from three observed subjects. Table 2(a) describes observed responses to the four alcohol use questions for three hypothetical subjects. Subject 1, a 17-year-old, reported that he had not had a drink in the last year, and so did not answer the remaining three questions. Subject 2, a 16-year-old, reported 3 to 5 drinking occasions in the last year. Because she reported at least one drinking occasion in the last year, she was also asked how many times she had been drunk in the last year, and how many times she had had a drink in the last month. She responded negatively to each of these, meaning that she was not asked the fourth question. Finally, subject 3, an 18-year-old, reported drinking 25 to 50 times and being drunk 5 times in the last year, and drinking 3 to 5 times and binge drinking 3 times in the last month.

The information in these four ordinal items is recoded into 11 binary items, as described above (see Table 1). Table 2(b) reports the observed item response pattern for these 11 items, with skipped items coded as (structural) zeros.

Converting the binary item response pattern in Table 2(b) to a person-item data set is analogous to constructing a person-period data set for use with a discrete-time hazard model (Singer and Willett 2003), although it requires reference to the gate matrix G in order to construct it. The person-item data set has 11 item indicator dummy variables, one for each of the 11 binary items in our data. In addition, the person-item data set includes a binary response variable y, which indicates whether a

TABLE 2(a)
Observed Responses for Three Hypothetical Subjects

ID	# Times Had a Drink, Last Year	# Times Drunk, Last Year	# Times Had a Drink, Last Month	# Times Had 5+ Drinks, Last Month	Sex	Age
1	0 times	-skip-	-skip-	-skip-	M	17
2	3–5 times	0 times	0 times	-skip-	F	16
3	25–50 times	5 times	3–5 times	3 times	M	18

TABLE 2(b)
Binary Item Response Pattern for Three Hypothetical Subjects

	Item Number												
ID	1	2	3	4	5	6	7	8	9	10	11	Sex	Age
1	0	0	0	0	0	0	0	0	0	0	0	M	17
2	1	0	0	0	0	0	0	0	0	0	0	F	16
3	1	1	1	1	0	0	1	1	0	1	1	M	18

TABLE 2(c)
Person-Item Data Set for Three Hypothetical Subjects

ID	y	D_1	D_2	D_3	D_4	D_5	D_6	D_7	D_8	D_9	D_{10}	D_{11}	Sex	Age
1	0	1	0	0	0	0	0	0	0	0	0	0	M	17
2	1	1	0	0	0	0	0	0	0	0	0	0	F	16
2	0	0	1	0	0	0	0	0	0	0	0	0	F	16
2	0	0	0	0	1	0	0	0	0	0	0	0	F	16
2	0	0	0	0	0	0	0	1	0	0	0	0	F	16
3	1	1	0	0	0	0	0	0	0	0	0	0	M	18
3	1	0	1	0	0	0	0	0	0	0	0	0	M	18
3	1	0	0	1	0	0	0	0	0	0	0	0	M	18
3	1	0	0	0	1	0	0	0	0	0	0	0	M	18
3	0	0	0	0	0	1	0	0	0	0	0	0	M	18
3	1	0	0	0	0	0	0	1	0	0	0	0	M	18
3	1	0	0	0	0	0	0	0	1	0	0	0	M	18
3	0	0	0	0	0	0	0	0	0	1	0	0	M	18
3	1	0	0	0	0	0	0	0	0	0	1	0	M	18
3	1	0	0	0	0	0	0	0	0	0	0	1	M	18

subject responded affirmatively to the item represented by each specific line of data.

In the person-item data, there is one observation for each item k for each person i where $h_{ik}=1$. Thus, in Table 2(c), there is a single line of data for subject 1, corresponding to item 1 (*had at least 1 drink in the*

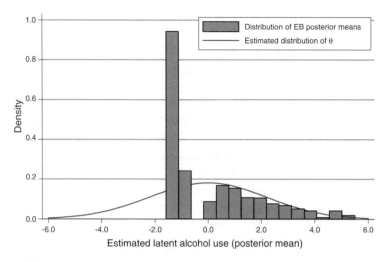

FIGURE 1. Distribution of estimated latent alcohol use (empirical Bayes estimates).

last year), since he was in the risk set for item 1 (everyone is in the risk set for item 1, because it is not conditional on any other item—it has no gate items), but not in the risk set for any other item. Likewise, there are four lines of data for subject 2, one for item 1, to which she answered affirmatively, and one each for items 2, 4, and 7. Because she responded negatively to each of these, she is in the risk set for none of the remaining items, and so none are included in the person-item data. Finally, subject 3 has 10 lines of data in the person-item data, since he was in the risk set for all but one of the questions—he responded negatively to item 5 (*was drunk at least 6 times in the last year*), and so was not in the risk set for item 6 (*was drunk at least 25 times in the last year*).

We fit a random effects model (equations 13–15) to these data using the EM algorithm with Laplace approximation to the likelihood (Raudenbush, Yang, and Yosef 2000) using the software package HLM6 (Raudenbush et al. 2005). From the fitted model we obtain four quantities of interest: (1) person-specific, interval-scale measures of a latent trait (or traits), along with person-specific standard errors of measurement; (2) estimates of conditional and marginal severities for each item in the protocol; (3) person-specific conditional and marginal probabilities of an affirmative response to each item in the protocol; and (4) measures of item information and total survey information. We describe how to obtain and interpret these quantities in the following sections.

5.1. *Person-Specific Estimates of Latent Alcohol Use*

From the fitted random effects model, we obtain empirical Bayes person-specific posterior means (θ_i^*) and variances (V_i^*) as given by equations (16) and (17). Figure 1 illustrates the distribution of θ_i^*, $i = 1, \ldots, n$. The fitted random effects model also yields an estimate of the variance τ of the latent alcohol use trait ($\hat{\tau} = 4.816$), and the solid line in Figure 1 describes this estimated distribution of the latent trait. The distribution of θ_i^* has a large spike at $\theta_i^* = -1.58$. In fact, 647 of the 1452 subjects have $\theta_i^* = -1.58$; these are those individuals who responded *no* to the first item (*ever drink in the last year*). Because these individuals were asked no other items, their estimated θ_i^* is based on a single item, and so contains much more uncertainty than does θ_i^* for individuals who were asked more questions.

Figure 2 illustrates the precision of θ_i^*, given by the posterior standard deviation $(V_i^*)^{1/2}$. The left-vertical describes the posterior standard deviation in the units of θ; the right-vertical axis describes the posterior standard deviation expressed in terms of the estimated standard deviation of θ, $(V_i^*/\hat{\tau})^{1/2}$; this conversion makes the magnitude of the posterior standard deviations more interpretable. The 647 subjects who reported never drinking in the last year have the largest posterior standard

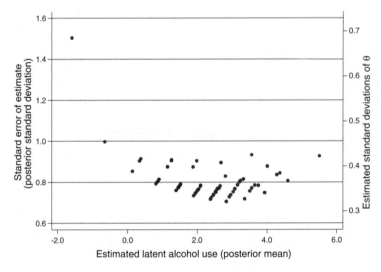

FIGURE 2. Precision of estimated latent alcohol use.

TABLE 3
Estimated Conditional and Marginal Item Severities

Item	Description	Estimated Conditional Severity		Estimated Marginal Severity
1	Alcohol in year	−0.362	(0.089)	−0.362
2	Alcohol 6x in year	1.388	(0.116)	1.656
3	Alcohol 25x in year	2.823	(0.150)	3.215
4	Drunk in year	0.481	(0.114)	1.003
5	Drunk 6x in year	3.423	(0.152)	3.557
6	Drunk 25x in year	4.195	(0.223)	4.777
7	Alcohol in month	0.729	(0.113)	1.169
8	Alcohol 3x in month	2.133	(0.144)	2.577
9	Alcohol 10x in month	4.666	(0.202)	4.846
10	Binge in month	2.081	(0.138)	2.543
11	Binge 3x in month	3.607	(0.186)	4.017

Note: Standard errors in parentheses. Conditional difficulties are estimated coefficients from fitted model; marginal difficulties are the value of θ that corresponds to a marginal probability of 0.5, given the estimated conditional item difficulties and the gate matrix.

deviations $((V_i^*)^{1/2} = 1.50 = .69\hat{\tau}^{1/2})$, reflecting the lack of information from which to estimate θ_i for these individuals. The precision is greatest for individuals with values of θ_i^* in the middle range of the estimates—corresponding to individuals whose latent use is well-differentiated by the items on the survey. We return to this point in the discussion of the survey information function below.

5.2. Estimated Item Conditional and Marginal Severity

The fitted random effects model yields the estimated parameters shown in Table 3. The estimated coefficients on the 11 item indicator variables represent the estimated item conditional severity for each of the items. As we noted above, the conditional severity of item k is interpreted as the value of θ_i at which an individual would have a 0.5 probability of answering item k affirmatively, given that he or she is in the risk set for the item.

In addition to obtaining estimates of the item conditional severities, we can also obtain estimates of the item marginal severities. The

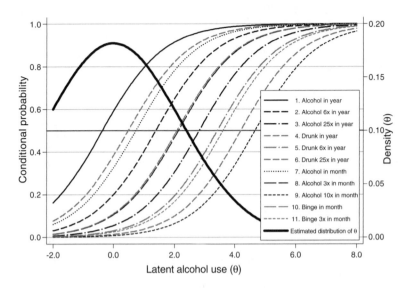

FIGURE 3. Estimated item conditional probabilities, by latent trait.

marginal severity of item k is the value of θ_i at which an individual would have a 0.5 probability of answering item k affirmatively, given the estimated item conditional severities and the gate matrix. These marginal severities are of more interest—and are more interpretable—than the conditional severities, since they correspond to estimated behavioral prevalences in the population. Given the estimated item conditional severity parameters from Table 3, we compute the item marginal severities by finding the value of θ such that $\pi_k = 0.5$, where π_k is given by

$$\pi_k = \left(1 + e^{-(\theta-\hat{\gamma}_k)}\right)^{-1} \prod_{j=1}^{K} \left(1 + e^{-(\theta-\hat{\gamma}_j)}\right)^{-G_{kj}} \quad (18)$$

Since π_k is a strictly increasing continuous function of θ, we solve $\pi_k(\theta) = 0.5$ for θ by interpolation. Table 3 reports these estimated item marginal severities.

Figures 3 and 4 illustrate the fitted conditional and marginal probability curves for each item. Figure 3 illustrates the conditional probability curve for each item, with the estimated distribution of

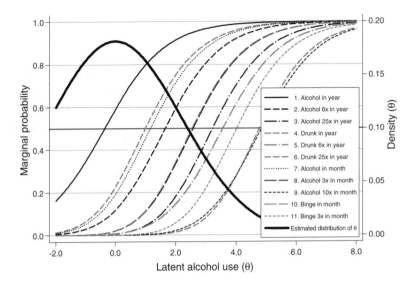

FIGURE 4. Estimated item marginal probabilities, by latent trait.

θ_i overlaid. Note that the item conditional severity parameters reported in Table 3 and illustrated in Figure 3 should not be interpreted as providing a meaningfully ordered ranking of item behavioral severity. For example, the conditional severity of item 11 (*had 5 or more drinks in a row at least 3 times in the last month*) is slightly higher than the conditional severity of item 5 (*was drunk at least 6 times in the last year*), but we cannot tell from these coefficient estimates alone whether the prevalence of binge drinking three or more times in the last month is greater or less than the prevalence of being drunk at least six times in the last year. This is because the conditional severities depend on the item structure (the gate matrix) and so are not straightforwardly interpretable. We note also that, in our example, the estimated conditional severities are all greater than 0, except that for item 1 (*ever drank in the last year*). This implies that we have little information in the data with which to discriminate individuals with low values of θ_i from one another, a point we return to below.

Figure 4 illustrates the estimated marginal probability curves, computed from equation (18). Unlike the item conditional probability curves, the marginal probability curves are not parallel, since they are the product of multiple conditional probability curves. However, the marginal probability curves do yield a meaningful ordered ranking of item severity. As we expect given the item structure, the least severe item is item 1 (*ever have a drink in the last year*); next are items 3 (*ever drunk in the last year*) and 4 (*ever have a drink in the last month*). At the other end of the ranking, the highest severity are items 9 (*had a drink 10 or more times in the last month*) and 6 (*was drunk at least 25 times in the last year*). Note that the marginal probability curves for these two items cross. Although the curves are so close in this case as to be statistically indistinguishable (particularly given the small number of individuals in the risk set for either item), the curve crossing—were it significant—would be interpreted as indicating that item 6 is the most severe item among those with values of θ_i above 4.0, while item 9 is the most severe among those with lower values of θ_i.

5.3. Estimated Person-Specific Item Conditional and Marginal Probabilities

Given the estimated item conditional severity parameters from Table 3 and the person-specific (empirical Bayes) estimates of θ_i, we can compute estimated person-specific conditional probabilities for each item. These are given by substituting the estimated conditional severity parameters and the estimated $\hat{\theta}_i^*$ from equation (16) into equation (10):

$$\hat{\phi}_{ik} = \left(1 + e^{-(\theta_i^* - \hat{\gamma}_k)}\right)^{-1}. \tag{19}$$

From these estimates, we can compute the predicted person-specific marginal probability for each item k as

$$\hat{\pi}_{ik} = \hat{\phi}_{ik} \prod_{j=1}^{K} \hat{\phi}_{ij}^{G_{kj}}. \tag{20}$$

5.4. Comparing Observed and Predicted Item Conditional and Marginal Probabilities

In addition to examining the fitted conditional and marginal probability curves, we wish to examine the fit of the model to the observed data.

One way of doing this is to assess how closely the model predictions fit the observed conditional and marginal proportions of individuals endorsing each item. We have two methods of checking this. The first relies on predicting the person-specific conditional and marginal probabilities as above, and then averaging these over those in the risk set for a given item. Specifically, we first compute each $\hat{\phi}_{ik}$ and $\hat{\pi}_{ik}$ from equations (19) and (20), and then, for each item k, we compute $\bar{\hat{\phi}}_k = \sum_i h_{ik}\hat{\phi}_{ik}$, the predicted average conditional probability of endorsing item k among those in the risk set for item k, and $\bar{\hat{\pi}}_k = \sum_i \hat{\pi}_{ik}$, the predicted average marginal probability of endorsing item k among those in the sample. We then compare these predictions with the observed conditional and marginal proportions in the data (see Table 4).

Because of shrinkage in θ_i^* as an estimate of θ_i, the predicted average conditional probabilities will be biased, though the direction of bias is not consistent. Persons with high true values of θ_i will be assigned estimates θ_i^* that are biased negatively (toward zero), thus underestimating their conditional probabilities ϕ_{ik}. In contrast, persons with low true values of θ_i will be assigned estimates θ_i^* that are biased positively (toward zero), thus overestimating their conditional probabilities ϕ_{ik}. For any given item k that is conditional on at least one other item, the risk set R_k will, in general, contain more individuals with high values of θ_i than with low values of θ_i, since those with higher values of θ_i will be more likely to respond affirmatively to the gate items for k. Thus, when we average the $\hat{\phi}_{ik}$ over those in R_k, the resulting average will tend to be a negatively biased estimate of the true average conditional probability of item k. Even if these biases are small, when these biased conditionals are multiplied to obtain marginal probabilities, the negative biases will tend to accumulate, yielding larger bias in the estimated average marginal probabilities than in the estimated marginal conditional probabilities. This pattern is evident in Table 4.

The second method of assessing the model fit relies on integrating the estimated marginal probability curve over the estimated distribution of θ in order to obtain estimated average conditional and marginal probabilities. Specifically, we compute the estimated average marginal probability for each item k as

$$\bar{\hat{\pi}}_k = (2\pi\hat{\tau})^{-1/2} \int \hat{\pi}_{k\theta} e^{-\theta^2/2\hat{\tau}} d\theta, \qquad (21)$$

TABLE 4
Observed and Predicted Conditional and Marginal Probabilities, Method 1

Item	Conditional Probability			Marginal Probability		
	Observed	Predicted	Difference	Observed	Predicted	Difference
1. Alcohol in year	.554	.518	−.036	.554	.518	−.036
2. Alcohol 6x in year	.472	.461	−.011	.262	.227	−.035
3. Alcohol 25x in year	.445	.438	−.007	.116	.097	−.019
4. Drunk in year	.615	.616	.001	.341	.296	−.045
5. Drunk 6x in year	.277	.263	−.014	.094	.083	−.011
6. Drunk 25x in year	.401	.393	−.008	.038	.030	−.008
7. Alcohol in month	.576	.573	−.003	.320	.277	−.043
8. Alcohol 3x in month	.494	.490	−.004	.158	.138	−.020
9. Alcohol 10x in month	.249	.233	−.016	.039	.031	−.008
10. Binge in month	.502	.499	−.003	.160	.141	−.019
11. Binge 3x in month	.399	.392	−.007	.064	.056	−.008

where $\hat{\bar{\pi}}_{k\theta}$ is the estimated marginal probability at θ, as defined in equation (20).[5] From (21), we compute the estimated average conditional probability of endorsing item k among those in the risk set for item k as

$$\hat{\bar{\phi}}_k = \frac{\hat{\bar{\pi}}_k}{\hat{\bar{\pi}}_{R_k}}, \tag{22}$$

where $\hat{\bar{\pi}}_{R_k}$ is the estimated average marginal probability of being in the risk set for item k. In the case where each item has at most only a single immediately prior gate item (that is, for each item k, there is at most one item j such that $y_{ij} = 1$ implies $h_{ik} = 1$), the marginal probability of being in the risk set for item k is simply the marginal probability of endorsing the single immediately prior gate item.[6] Table 5 compares the predicted average conditional and marginal probabilities with the observed conditional and marginal proportions in the data.

Note that method one (Table 4) yields very good estimates of the average conditional probabilities, while method two (Table 5) yields very good estimates of the marginal probabilities. This difference is likely due to the fact that method one is based on directly estimating the average conditional probabilities from the model estimates and then multiplying these to obtain the average marginals. Here slight biases in the estimated conditional probabilities (particularly if the biases are generally in the same direction, as they are here) will be multiplied into larger biases in the estimated marginal probabilities in this case. Method two, in contrast, is based on directly estimating the average marginal probabilities and then taking ratios of these to compute the average conditionals. Again, slight biases in the estimated marginal probabilities may be

---

[5]The integral in (21) has no closed form, so we can evaluate it numerically, or by simulating a distribution of $\theta \sim N(0,\tau)$ and averaging the value of π_{ik} over the simulated distribution of θ.

[6]In the more general case, as for example, in the gate matrix described by matrix (5), the marginal probability of being in the risk set for item k is given by

$$\pi_{R_k} = \prod_{m_1=1}^{K} \prod_{m_2=1}^{K} \cdots \prod_{m_K=1}^{K} (\pi_{m_1})^{G[k,m_1]} \left[(\pi_{m_2})^{G[m_1,m_2]} \cdots \left[(\pi_{m_K})^{G[m_{K-1},m_K]} \right]^{-1} \cdots \right]^{-1}.$$

TABLE 5
Observed and Predicted Conditional and Marginal Probabilities, Method 2

Item		Conditional Probability			Marginal Probability		
		Observed	Predicted	Difference	Observed	Predicted	Difference
1.	Alcohol in year	.554	.551	−.003	.554	.551	−.003
2.	Alcohol 6x in year	.472	.469	−.003	.262	.259	−.003
3.	Alcohol 25x in year	.445	.400	−.045	.116	.103	−.013
4.	Drunk in year	.615	.618	.003	.341	.341	.000
5.	Drunk 6x in year	.277	.260	−.017	.094	.089	−.005
6.	Drunk 25x in year	.401	.338	−.063	.038	.030	−.008
7.	Alcohol in month	.576	.578	.002	.320	.318	−.002
8.	Alcohol 3x in month	.494	.480	−.014	.158	.153	−.005
9.	Alcohol 10x in month	.249	.208	−.041	.039	.032	−.007
10.	Binge in month	.502	.489	−.013	.160	.156	−.004
11.	Binge 3x in month	.399	.363	−.036	.064	.057	−.007

compounded into larger discrepancies in the conditional probabilities through multiplication. Since the marginal probabilities are generally likely to be of greater interest, method two provides a more useful assessment of model fit.

In both cases, the discrepancies tend to be negative, meaning that the model appears to slightly underestimate the observed conditional and marginal probabilities of item endorsement. The greatest discrepancies between the observed and predicted probabilities occur for the rarest items, possibly because the upper tail of the true distribution of θ is somewhat longer than that given by the simulated normal distribution. This is also suggested by the apparent correlation between the bias in the predicted conditional probabilities and the marginal probabilities of the items—if the predicted distribution is too thin in the upper tail, this will show up most dramatically in computing the conditional probabilities for the items with the highest conditional severities. Overall, however, the model appears to fit the data rather well.

5.5. Computing Item and Survey Information

As we note above, Figures 2, 3, and 4 each provide some insight into the information content of the survey. It is evident from Figure 2 that the uncertainty in the estimated latent alcohol use trait is smallest for θ_i^* in the vicinity of 3.0. Likewise, Figures 3 and 4 suggest that the survey items will discriminate best among individuals with values of θ somewhere in the range of 1.0 to 4.0, since most of the items have conditional and marginal severities in this range. The items are not independent of one another, so—unlike in a Rasch model, where all items are independent of one another—the total information in the survey does not necessarily correspond to the density of the item severities, since more severe items will be asked of relatively few subjects.

We formalize the notion of survey information here. We consider two approaches to defining the survey information. First, we consider Fisher information based on the fixed effects model. The fixed effects model yields a simple, interpretable, and useful measure of total survey information. Second, we compute a person-specific measure of information: the inverse of the empirical Bayes posterior variance V_i^* of θ_i given the data and the estimates of γ and τ. A graph of this measure of information as a function of the person-specific empirical Bayes estimates θ_i^* provides additional insight about the values of θ for which the survey is most informative.

Under the fixed effects model, the observed Fisher information for person i is defined as the negative of the second derivative of the log-likelihood, given θ_i:

$$I_i(\theta_i) = -\frac{\partial^2 l_{fi}}{\partial \theta^2}$$

$$= -\frac{\partial^2}{\partial \theta^2} \sum_{k=1}^{K} h_{ik} \left[y_{ik} \ln \left(\frac{\phi_{ik}}{1 - \phi_{ik}} \right) + \ln(1 - \phi_{ik}) \right] \quad (23)$$

$$= \sum_{k=1}^{K} h_{ik} \phi_{ik} (1 - \phi_{ik}).$$

From this, we can derive the expected Fisher information, given θ_i, as

$$E[I_i(\theta_i)] = E\left(\sum_{k=1}^{K} h_{ik} \phi_{ik} (1 - \phi_{ik}) \right)$$

$$= \sum_{k=1}^{K} E(h_{ik}) \phi_{ik} (1 - \phi_{ik})$$

$$= \sum_{k=1}^{K} \pi_{i R_k} \phi_{ik} (1 - \phi_{ik}) \quad (24)$$

$$= \sum_{k=1}^{K} \pi_{ik} (1 - \phi_{ik}).$$

As equation (24) indicates, the expected information content of the survey protocol, given θ_i, is a sum of the expected information from each item. The information contained in each item is the product of the expected size of the risk set for the item and the expected information content of the item.[7] Items will provide the most information for values of θ such that the risk set, given θ, is large, and the conditional probability of the item, given θ, is 0.5. This is useful for considering how to construct survey protocols designed to measure latent traits.

The Fisher information is based on the fixed effects model—that is, it describes the information conditional on θ. The Bayesian information is given by the inverse of the posterior variance in equation (17).

---

[7]We note that, in the case of the Rasch model, all individuals are in the risk set for each item, so the expected Fisher information given in (24) reduces in this special case to $\sum_{k=1}^{K} \phi_{ik}(1 - \phi_{ik})$, as expected.

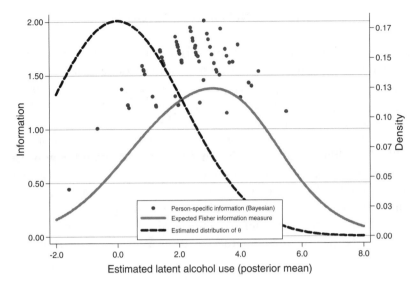

FIGURE 5. Estimated total survey information, by latent trait.

Figure 5 plots both the estimated Bayesian information ($\hat{V}_i^{*-1}$) and the expected Fisher information (equation 24) against θ_i. The figure shows that the total information based on the fixed effects model (solid curve) is highest just between 3.0 and 4.0. The graph of the empirical Bayes person-specific information (see the dots in the figure) tells a very similar story. The maximum values of this information measure are also between 3.0 and 4.0. As we might expect, the empirical Bayes information is uniformly higher than the information from the fixed effects model. The information at any θ from the fixed effects model is based only on the data for a single person, while the empirical Bayes information is the sum of that person-specific information and the information about γ and τ provided by the rest of the sample. In this way, the empirical Bayes procedure augments the information from each participant, "borrowing strength" from the sample as a whole.

It is evident from Figure 5 that the survey has little discriminatory power for individuals with $\theta_i < 0$. It may be that we are not interested in differentiating among such individuals, but if we were, Figure 5 would suggest the need to include more low severity items in the survey protocol.

6. ASSESSING DIMENSIONALITY

Dimensionality of the latent characteristic may be assessed in at least three ways. First, we may hypothesize multiple dimensions of latent alcohol use and attempt to confirm that different items correspond to different latent dimensions by examining the estimated correlation matrix among the hypothesized dimensions. Second, we may investigate whether observed covariates are similarly associated with the hypothesized dimensions, reasoning that if covariates are differently associated with the hypothesized dimensions, then they cannot be considered unidimensional (Raudenbush, Johnson, and Sampson 2003). Third, we may employ a differential item functioning test to investigate whether all the items are similarly associated with observed covariates. We describe each of these approaches to investigating dimensionality below.

6.1. *Examining the Correlation Matrix Among Hypothesized Dimensions*

Let θ^a and θ^b denote latent characteristics, and let a_k and b_k be dummy variables indicating whether item k is an indicator of latent characteristic θ^a or θ^b, respectively (we assume $a_k + b_k = 1$ for all k). Then we fit the random effects model

$$\ln\left(\frac{\phi_{ik}}{1-\phi_{ik}}\right) = a_k\theta_i^a + b_k\theta_i^b + \sum_{j=1}^{K}\gamma_j D_{ij},$$

$$\begin{bmatrix} \theta_i^a \\ \theta_i^b \end{bmatrix} \sim N\left(\begin{bmatrix} 0 \\ 0 \end{bmatrix}, \begin{bmatrix} \tau_a & \tau_{ab} \\ \tau_{ab} & \tau_b \end{bmatrix}\right), \tag{25}$$

where D_{ij} is a dummy variable indicating that a response refers to item j for person i. The estimated correlation between θ^a and θ^b is indicative of the extent to which the items measuring θ^a and θ^b represent different dimensions.

6.2. *Examining the Association of Covariates with Hypothesized Dimensions*

If θ^a and θ^b measure the same dimension, then an observed covariate X should be similarly associated with both. To test this, we fit the model

$$\ln\left(\frac{\phi_{ik}}{1-\phi_{ik}}\right) = a_k\left(u_i^a + \gamma_a X_i\right) + b_k\left(u_i^b + \gamma_b X_i\right) + \sum_{j=1}^{K} \gamma_j D_{ij},$$

$$\begin{bmatrix} u_i^a \\ u_i^b \end{bmatrix} \sim N\left(\begin{bmatrix} 0 \\ 0 \end{bmatrix}, \begin{bmatrix} \tau_a & \tau_{ab} \\ \tau_{ab} & \tau_b \end{bmatrix}\right) \qquad (26)$$

and test the hypothesis $H_0:\gamma_a=\gamma_b$. A rejection of H_0 indicates that θ^a and θ^b measure different dimensions.

6.3. *Assessing Dimensionality via Differential Item Functioning*

A third way of assessing dimensionality is to examine the model for differential item functioning (DIF). If the items all measure the same latent characteristic, then observable covariates ought to be similarly associated with each of the items. We can test for DIF by each observed covariate X by fitting the model

$$\ln\left(\frac{\phi_{ik}}{1-\phi_{ik}}\right) = \theta_i + \sum_{j=1}^{K}\left(\gamma_j + \delta_j X_i\right) D_{ij}, \quad \theta_i \sim N(0,\tau) \qquad (27)$$

and testing the null hypothesis $H_0:\delta_1=\delta_2=\ldots=\delta_K$ (We use a likelihood ratio test, comparing this model's deviance to the deviance of a model where the δ_js are constrained to be equal.)

6.4. *Empirical Assessment of Substance Use Dimensionality*

To illustrate these different approaches to assessing dimensionality, we use a slightly different example than above. Here we use the same sample of adolescents from the PHDCN sample but include information from two additional survey questions—measuring marijuana use—in the data. Specifically, we use information from two marijuana use items:

5. *How many times did you use marijuana in the last year?* (possible responses were: never, 1–2 times, 3–5 times, 6–11 times, 12–24 times, 25–50 times, 51–99 times, 100–199 times, 200 or more times).
6. *How many times did you use marijuana in the last month?* (asked of those whose response to question 5 indicated they used marijuana at least once in the last year; possible responses were: never, 1–2 times, 3–5 times, 6–9 times, 10–14 times, 15–20 times, 21 or more times).

As with the four alcohol items, from these two items we construct multiple binary items, each indicating whether an individual's response is above a certain threshold (we use thresholds of 1, 6, 25, and 100 for the first item, and thresholds of 1, 3, and 10 for the second). The full set of 18 derived alcohol and marijuana binary items and their response patterns are described in Table 6, and their item structure and corresponding gate matrix is given below (where the items are ordered as above):

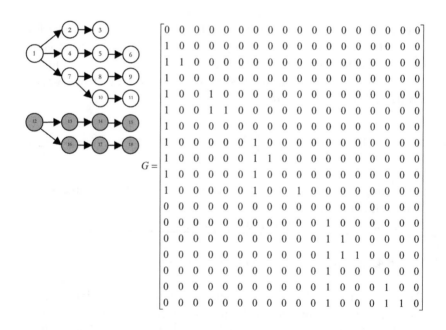

$$G = \begin{bmatrix} 0 & 0 & 0 & 0 & 0 & 0 & 0 & 0 & 0 & 0 & 0 & 0 & 0 & 0 & 0 & 0 & 0 & 0 \\ 1 & 0 & 0 & 0 & 0 & 0 & 0 & 0 & 0 & 0 & 0 & 0 & 0 & 0 & 0 & 0 & 0 & 0 \\ 1 & 1 & 0 & 0 & 0 & 0 & 0 & 0 & 0 & 0 & 0 & 0 & 0 & 0 & 0 & 0 & 0 & 0 \\ 1 & 0 & 0 & 0 & 0 & 0 & 0 & 0 & 0 & 0 & 0 & 0 & 0 & 0 & 0 & 0 & 0 & 0 \\ 1 & 0 & 0 & 1 & 0 & 0 & 0 & 0 & 0 & 0 & 0 & 0 & 0 & 0 & 0 & 0 & 0 & 0 \\ 1 & 0 & 0 & 1 & 1 & 0 & 0 & 0 & 0 & 0 & 0 & 0 & 0 & 0 & 0 & 0 & 0 & 0 \\ 1 & 0 & 0 & 0 & 0 & 0 & 0 & 0 & 0 & 0 & 0 & 0 & 0 & 0 & 0 & 0 & 0 & 0 \\ 1 & 0 & 0 & 0 & 0 & 0 & 1 & 0 & 0 & 0 & 0 & 0 & 0 & 0 & 0 & 0 & 0 & 0 \\ 1 & 0 & 0 & 0 & 0 & 0 & 1 & 1 & 0 & 0 & 0 & 0 & 0 & 0 & 0 & 0 & 0 & 0 \\ 1 & 0 & 0 & 0 & 0 & 0 & 1 & 0 & 0 & 0 & 0 & 0 & 0 & 0 & 0 & 0 & 0 & 0 \\ 1 & 0 & 0 & 0 & 0 & 0 & 1 & 0 & 0 & 1 & 0 & 0 & 0 & 0 & 0 & 0 & 0 & 0 \\ 0 & 0 & 0 & 0 & 0 & 0 & 0 & 0 & 0 & 0 & 0 & 0 & 0 & 0 & 0 & 0 & 0 & 0 \\ 0 & 0 & 0 & 0 & 0 & 0 & 0 & 0 & 0 & 0 & 0 & 1 & 0 & 0 & 0 & 0 & 0 & 0 \\ 0 & 0 & 0 & 0 & 0 & 0 & 0 & 0 & 0 & 0 & 0 & 1 & 1 & 0 & 0 & 0 & 0 & 0 \\ 0 & 0 & 0 & 0 & 0 & 0 & 0 & 0 & 0 & 0 & 0 & 1 & 1 & 1 & 0 & 0 & 0 & 0 \\ 0 & 0 & 0 & 0 & 0 & 0 & 0 & 0 & 0 & 0 & 0 & 1 & 0 & 0 & 0 & 0 & 0 & 0 \\ 0 & 0 & 0 & 0 & 0 & 0 & 0 & 0 & 0 & 0 & 0 & 1 & 0 & 0 & 0 & 1 & 0 & 0 \\ 0 & 0 & 0 & 0 & 0 & 0 & 0 & 0 & 0 & 0 & 0 & 1 & 0 & 0 & 0 & 1 & 1 & 0 \end{bmatrix}$$

(28)

TABLE 6
Observed Alcohol and Marijuana Item Response Frequencies

Item	Description	Gate Items	Marginal Probability	Risk Set	Number of *Yes*	Conditional Probability
1	Alcohol in year	-none-	.557	1,431	797	.554
2	Alcohol 6x in year	1	.261	797	374	.472
3	Alcohol 25x in year	1,2	.116	374	166	.445
4	Drunk in year	1	.342	797	489	.615
5	Drunk 6x in year	1,4	.093	489	133	.277
6	Drunk 25x in year	1,4,5	.037	133	53	.401
7	Alcohol in month	1	.319	797	457	.576
8	Alcohol 3x in month	1,7	.156	457	223	.494
9	Alcohol 10x in month	1,7,8	.040	223	57	.249
10	Binge in month	1,7	.160	457	229	.502
11	Binge 3x in month	1,7,10	.064	229	91	.399
12	Marijuana in year	-none-	.293	1,431	419	.293
13	Marijuana 6x in year	12	.164	419	235	.561
14	Marijuana 25x in year	12,13	.094	235	134	.570
15	Marijuana 100x in year	12,13,14	.046	134	66	.493
16	Marijuana in month	12	.177	419	252	.601
17	Marijuana 3x in month	12,16	.112	252	159	.631
18	Marijuana 10x in month	12,16,17	.065	159	93	.585

Note: The sample is slightly smaller here than in Table 1, due to the omission of 21 individuals who did not answer the marijuana items.

We hypothesize that alcohol and marijuana use may be separate dimensions of substance use. Under this assumption, we view the 11 alcohol items (unshaded above) as conditional indicators of a latent alcohol use dimension, and the 7 marijuana items (shaded above) as conditional indicators of a latent marijuana dimension. We might hypothesize that these two latent characteristics are distinct in the population—an individual's alcohol use may not correspond well to his or her marijuana use.

When we fit the model (25) to our data, using each of the hypothesized dimensional structures, we obtain an estimated correlation near 1.0 between the latent alcohol and marijuana use levels. This high correlation is more a result of the fact that we have very little information from which to separately estimate the two factors, rather than strong evidence that they are perfectly correlated. So this is a rather weak test of dimensionality, except in the case where we have far more items than those here.

TABLE 7
Estimated Coefficients on Selected Covariates Predicting Hypothesized Separate
Dimensions of Substance Use

	Male	SES	Age	Black	Hispanic
Main Effect[a]	0.839***	0.160**	0.816***	−0.823***	−1.025***
Dimension-Specific Effect					
Alcohol[b]	0.771***	0.183***	0.985***	−1.208***	−1.098***
Marijuana[b]	0.910***	0.137*	0.649***	−0.466*	−0.988***
p-value[c]	*0.167*	*0.289*	*<.001*	*<.001*	*0.476*
Differential Item					
Functioning (DIF) Test					
p-value[d]	*0.095*	*0.084*	*<.001*	*<.001*	*>.500*

    [a] Asterisks indicate *p*-value from deviance test of null hypothesis that the estimated coefficient is zero (*$p < .05$; **$p < .01$; ***$p < .001$). Coefficient estimates obtained from model that assumes a single substance use domain.

    [b] Asterisks indicate *p*-value from deviance test of null hypothesis that the estimated coefficient on the specified dimension is zero (*$p < .05$; **$p < .01$; ***$p < .001$).

    [c] *p*-value from deviance test of equivalence of coefficients on both dimensions.

    [d] *p*-value from deviance test of equivalence of coefficients on all 18 alcohol and marijuana items.

    Notes: Coefficient estimates are taken from models of the form shown in (18), but with the constraint $u_i^a = u_i^b$ for all i (see text), and with each covariate entered separately in a different model (except *black* and *hispanic*, which are entered in a model together).

Our second approach to assessing dimensionality derives from the insight that if θ^a and θ^b measure the same dimension of substance use, then an observed covariate X should be similarly associated with both (Raudenbush, Johnson, and Sampson 2003). We test this, using covariates *age, sex, SES*,[8] and race/ethnicity (*black* and *hispanic*, versus omitted category *white*) in models of the form shown in equation (26).[9] The resulting estimates, and the *p*-values corresponding to the tests of the hypothesis that the associations between X and each of the hypothesized dimensions are equal, are shown in Table 7.

Table 7 provides some evidence of multidimensionality. First, the relationship between age and alcohol use ($\hat{\gamma}_a = 0.985$, $p < .001$)

    [8]SES is a standardized composite indicator of socioeconomic status, derived from measures of mother and father's education levels and occupations, and family income.

    [9]The fitted model is slightly different than described in Equation (26): this model would not converge when covariates were included on the alcohol and marijuana constructs, because the alcohol and marijuana random effects u^a and u^b were too highly correlated. We constrain the two random effects to be equal to obtain the estimates shown in Table 7.

appears greater than the relationship between age and marijuana use ($\hat{\gamma}_b = 0.649$, $p < .001$). Indeed, the difference between these two coefficients (0.985-$0.649 = 0.336$) is highly statistically significant ($p < .001$). This means that, in the age range represented in our sample, use levels differ by age more for alcohol than for marijuana. In addition, the difference between blacks and whites in alcohol use ($\hat{\gamma}_a = -1.208$, $p < .001$) appears greater than the difference between blacks and whites in marijuana use ($\hat{\gamma}_b = -0.466$, $p < .05$). In fact, the difference between these two coefficients ($-1.208 - (-0.466) = -0.742$) is highly statistically significant ($p < .001$). We cannot, however, reject the null hypothesis that each of the other covariates tested (*sex*, *SES*, and *hispanic*) are similarly associated with the hypothesized alcohol and marijuana dimensions.

Our third approach to assessing dimensionality is to test the items for differential item functioning (DIF). Using the same five covariates as above, we fit models of the form shown in equation (27), and test the null hypothesis that the association of the covariate with each of the 18 alcohol and marijuana items is constant across items. Figure 6 shows the 95% confidence intervals for each coefficient for each item. The solid horizontal line in each part of the figure indicates the estimated coefficient from the model assuming a constant relationship between the covariate and each item (these are the "main effects" reported in Table 7). The two dashed lines in each part represent the estimated coefficients from the model allowing the covariate to have different associations with the latent alcohol and marijuana use traits (these are the "dimension-specific effects" reported in Table 7). Table 7 reports the *p*-values from deviance tests of the null hypothesis of constant association across items. The results of the DIF test are consistent with those of the covariate modeling approach above: both age and race (black versus white) are differentially associated with the conditional log-odds of endorsing different items.

The three approaches to assessing the dimensionality of the item responses described here have different strengths and limitations. The first approach, based on estimating the correlation among hypothesized latent characteristics indicated by different items, allows us to test the hypothesis that distinct subsets of items are indicators of separate dimensions without reference to any specific observable covariate. This test, however, generally has very low power, and so may easily result in a failure to detect existing multidimensionality unless the latent characteristics are estimated with high precision (which requires a large

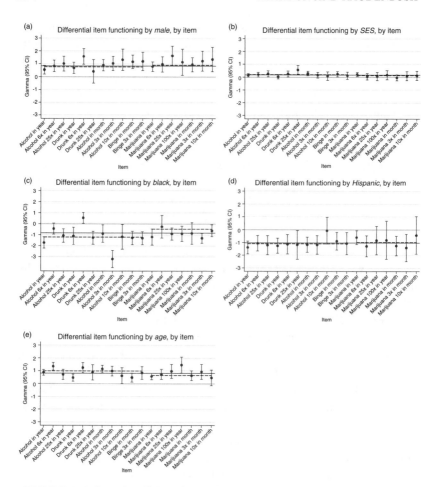

FIGURE 6. Estimated coefficients from differential item functioning tests, by covariate.

number of items to provide information across the range of the latent characteristics' distributions). The second approach, based on testing whether observed covariates are similarly associated with each hypothesized latent characteristic, has greater power to detect hypothesized multidimensionality, but only if that multidimensionality is associated with observable covariates. The third approach, based on the DIF test, has the advantage that it does not require us to specify a hypothesized dimensional structure to the items. The DIF test, however, has low power when the number of items becomes large, since the test will have degrees of freedom equal to K, the number of items. Moreover, the DIF test, like the second approach, can detect multidimensionality only if that multidimensionality is associated with observable covariates.

Under the assumption of unidimensionality, the latent trait model we propose here, like all logit models, contains an implicit set of proportional odds assumptions. In particular, the model makes assumptions analogous to the level-2 proportional odds and proportional error assumptions described in Reardon, Brennan, and Buka (2002). Applied to our model, these assumptions require that a given difference in a covariate or in the residual unobserved latent trait (that part of the latent trait not explained by the covariates in the model, if any) is associated with a proportional difference in the conditional odds of an affirmative response to each item. One way to view the dimensionality tests described here is as tests of these proportionality assumptions— our approach assumes a definition of dimensionality based on the insight that multidimensionality is evident in a violation of one or more proportional odds assumptions. Expressed differently, the proportional odds assumption is equivalent to the additivity assumption in the Rasch model. One could, in principle, relax this assumption and use a two-parameter model rather than a Rasch model to study the conditional probabilities in order to test the additivity assumption of the Rasch scale and to identify items that do not fit the Rasch scale (Raudenbush, Johnson, and Sampson, 2003).

7. CONCLUSION

We noted above that one approach used by some researchers in modeling nonindependent items like these is to create a variable reflecting the sum or average of the item responses. It is illustrative to compare our estimates of the person-specific latent trait values with those that would be obtained using this simpler sum-of-item-responses approach. Figure 7 illustrates the relationship in our data between the observed and expected sums of alcohol item responses[10] and the estimated latent alcohol use $\hat{\theta}_i^*$ (we use only the 11 alcohol items here, not the additional

---

[10]The expected sum of item responses, given θ_i^*, is simply the sum of the K marginal item probabilities at θ_i^*. We note also that the expected sum of item responses tends to underestimate the observed sum of item responses, particularly for large values of θ_i^*, as a result of shrinkage in the estimation of θ_i^*.

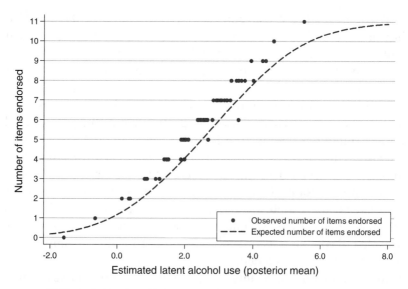

FIGURE 7. Number of items endorsed, by estimated latent alcohol use.

7 marijuana items). The correlation between the observed sum of item responses and $\hat{\theta}_i^*$ is strikingly high (r = .989), as evident in Figure 7. We might reasonably ask, then, what is the value of our modeling approach when it yields estimates that are largely indistinguishable from a simple sum of the item responses?

The latent trait model proposed here has a number of advantages over the sum-of-item-responses approach. First, the latent trait model provides estimates (and associated standard errors) of the item conditional severities, which can be used to estimate item marginal severities. These can be used to compute person-specific marginal probabilities of saying *yes* to a given item, and so provide information regarding the relative prevalence of specific behaviors at any given level of the latent trait. In conjunction with the estimate of τ, these marginal probabilities allow us to estimate the prevalence of specific behaviors in the population. The sum-of-item-responses approach yields no information on item severity or prevalence, which in many cases may be a primary goal of the analysis.

Second, our approach yields not only estimates of the distribution of the latent trait and person-specific estimates of θ_i^*, but also person-specific estimates of the uncertainty in θ_i^* (equation 17). The sum-of-item-responses approach provides no estimate of uncertainty;

it assumes no measurement error. A third advantage of our model is that it is robust to item-missing data, under missing-at-random (MAR) and coarsening-at-random assumptions; see Barber et al. (2000); Little and Rubin (2002). The sum-of-item-responses approach does not allow missing data, since an average of nonmissing items will be biased upward relative to the average of the complete set of items (because the marginal probability of missing items will generally be lower than the marginal probability of nonmissing items).

Fourth, the latent trait model and its interpretation are generally robust to different item structures, while the sum-of-item-responses approach is not. To see this, note that the expected sum of item responses shown in Figure 7 is a nonlinear function of θ_i^*. The curve describing the expected sum of item responses is steepest in that part of the distribution of θ where the marginal probability curves (Figure 4) are, on average, steepest. In general, this will be where the item marginal severities are most densely concentrated. As a result, the relationship between both the observed and expected sums of item responses and θ_i^* will be sensitive to the item structure used. Adding or removing items from the survey or the analysis will therefore alter the interpretation of the metric of the sum of item responses. It will not, however change the interpretation of the metric of θ, since θ will always be expressed in a well-defined interval-scale metric relative to the conditional log-odds of item responses.

Finally, the partial independence item response model is general enough to lend itself to a number of possible applications and extensions. It can, for example, be used to construct measurement models that use information from a combination of dichotomous and ordinal items—a situation common to many social surveys. It could, for example, be used to model a discrete-time "multiple hazard" process—for example, where an individual is exposed to multiple, partially independent events (e.g., conditional on having some medical procedure, a person might be at risk for several conditionally independent postoperative complications).

In this paper, we have extended the methodology of latent trait modeling via item response theory to the case of surveys with filter or "gate" items—items for which the responses determine whether subsequent questions are asked. Such data are common in social surveys but violate the conditional independence assumption of standard item response models. The partial independence assumption we rely on here is weaker than the standard conditional independence assumption, as it requires conditional independence of item responses only given membership in the risk set for each item. Thus, while the Rasch model, the discrete-time hazard model (including the multilevel discrete-time model), and the continuation ratio model are each special cases of our model, the partial independence item response model is more general than each of these.

REFERENCES

Adalbjarnardottir, S.. 2002. "Adolescent Psychosocial Maturity and Alcohol Use: Quantitative and Qualitative Analysis of Longitudinal Data." *Adolescence* 37(145):18–53.

Adams, R. J., M. R. Wilson, and W. C. Wang. 1997. "The Multidimensional Random Coefficients Multinomial Logit Model." *Applied Psychological Measurement* 21:1–23.

Allison, P. D.. 1982. "Discrete-Time Methods for the Analysis of Event Histories." Pp. 61–98 in *Sociological Methodology*, vol. 13. edited by Samuel Leinhardt. San Francisco, CA: Jossey-Bars.

Armstrong, B. G., and M. Sloan. 1989. "Ordinal Regression Models for Epidemiologic Data." *American Journal of Epidemiology* 129(1):191–204.

Bailey, S. L., R. L. Flewelling, and J. V. Rachal. 1992. "Predicting Continued Use of Marijuana Among Adolescents: The Relative Importance of Drug-Specific and Social Context Factors." *Journal of Health and Social Behavior* 33(March):51–66.

Barber, J. S., S. Murphy, W. G. Axinn, and J. Maples. 2000. "Discrete-Time Multilevel Hazard Analysis." Pp. 201–35 in *Sociological Methodology*, vol. 30, edited by Michael E. Sobel and Mark P. Becker. Boston, MA: Blackwell Publishing.

Barnes, G. M., A. S. Reifman, M. P. Farrell, and B. A. Dintcheff. 2000. "The Effects of Parenting on the Development of Adolescent Alcohol Misuse: A Six-Wave Latent Growth Model." *Journal of Marriage and the Family* 62:175–86.

Bennett, M. E., B. S. McCrady, V. Johnson, and R. J. Pandina. 1999. "Problem Drinking from Young Adulthood to Adulthood: Patterns, Predictors and Outcomes." *Journal of Studies on Alcohol* 60:605–14.

Chassin, L., S. C. Pitts, and J. Prost. 2002. "Binge Drinking Trajectories from Adolescence to Emerging Adulthood in a High-Risk Sample: Predictors and Substance Abuse Outcomes." *Journal of Consulting and Clinical Psychology* 70(1):67–78.

Cheong, Y. F., and S. W. Raudenbush. 2000. "Measurement and Structural Models for Children's Problem Behaviors." *Psychological Methods* 5(4):477–95.

Colder, C. R., and E. Stice. 1998. "A Longitudinal Study of the Interactive Effects of Impulsivity and Anger on Adolescent Problem Behavior." *Journal of Youth and Adolescence* 27(3):255–74.

Cox, C. 1988. "Multinomial Regression Models Based on Continuation Ratios." *Statistics in Medicine* 7(3):435–41.

Duncan, T. E., S. C. Duncan, and H. Hops. 1996. "The Role of Parents and Older Siblings in Predicting Adolescent Substance Use: Modeling Development via Structural Equation Latent Growth Methodology." *Journal of Family Psychology* 10(2):158–72.

Fienberg, S. E. 1980. *The Analysis of Cross-classified Categorical Data.* 2d ed. Cambridge, MA: MIT Press.

Hill, K. G., H. R. White, I.-J. Chung, J. D. Hawkins, and R. F. Catalano. 2000. "Early Adult Outcomes of Adolescent Binge Drinking: Person- and Variable-Centered Analyses of Binge Drinking Trajectories." *Alcoholism: Clinical and Experimental Research* 24(6):892–901.

Holland, P. W., and H. Wainer, eds. 1993. *Differential Item Functioning.* Hillsdale, NJ: Lawrence Erlbaum.

Hussong, A. M., P. J. Curran, and L. Chassin. 1998. "Pathways of Risk for Accelerated Heavy Alcohol Use Among Adolescent Children of Alcoholic Parents." *Journal of Abnormal Child Psychology* 26(6):453–66.

Khoo, S., and B. Muthen. 2000. "Longitudinal Data on Families: Growth Modeling Alternatives." Pp. 43–78 in *Multivariate Applications in Substance Use Research: New Methods for New Questions*, edited by J. S. Rose, L. Chassin, C. C. Presson, and S. J. Sherman. Mahwah, NJ: Lawrence Erlbaum.

Little, R. J. A., and D. B. Rubin. 2002. *Statistical Analysis with Missing Data.* 2nd ed. New York: Wiley.

Lord, F. M., and M. R. Novick. 1968. *Statistical Theory of Mental Test Scores.* Reading, MA: Addison-Wesley.

Pinheiro, P. C., and D. M. Bates. 1995. "Approximations to the Log-Likelihood Function in the Nonlinear Mixed Effects Model." *Journal of Computational and Graphical Statistics* 4:12–35.

Raudenbush, S. W., A. S. Bryk, Y. F. Cheong, and R. Congdon. 2005. *Hierarchical Linear and Nonlinear Modeling, Version 6: Users' Guide and Software Program.* Chicago: Scientific Software International.

Raudenbush, S. W., C. Johnson, and R. J. Sampson. 2003. "A Multivariate, Multilevel Rasch Model for Self-Reported Criminal Behavior." Pp. 169–211 in *Sociological Methodology*, vol. 33, edited by Ross M. Stolzenberg. Boston, MA: Blackwell Publishing.

Raudenbush, S. W., M.-L. Yang, and M. Yosef. 2000. "Maximum Likelihood for Generalized Linear Models with Nested Random Effects via High-Order, Multivariate Laplace Approximation." *Journal of Computational and Graphical Statistics* 9(1):141–57.

Reardon, S. F., R. T. Brennan, and S. L. Buka. 2002. "Estimating Multilevel Discrete-Time Hazard Models Using Cross-Sectional Data: Neighborhood Effects on the Onset of Adolescent Cigarette Use." *Multivariate Behavioral Research* 37(3):297–330.

Reckase, M. 1985. "The Difficulty of Items that Measure More Than One Ability." *Applied Psychological Measurement* 9:401–12.

Sampson, R. J., J. D. Morenoff, and S. W. Raudenbush. 2005. "Social Anatomy of

Racial and Ethnic Disparities in Violence." *American Journal of Public Health* 95(2):224–32.

Scheier, L. M., G. J. Botvin, K. W. Griffin, and T. Diaz. 2000. "Dynamic Growth Models of Self-Esteem and Adolescent Alcohol Use." *Journal of Early Adolescence* 20(2):178–209.

Schulenberg, J., K. N. Wadsworth, P. M. O'Malley, J. G. Bachman, and L. D. Johnston. 1996. "Adolescent Risk Factors for Binge Drinking During the Transition to Young Adulthood: Variable- and Pattern-Centered Approaches to Change." *Developmental Psychology* 32(4):659–74.

Silberg, J., M. Rutter, B. D'Onofrio, and L. Eaves. 2003. "Genetic and Environmental Risk Factors in Adolescent Substance Use." *Journal of Child Psychology and Psychiatry* 44(5):664–76.

Singer, J. D., and J. B. Willett. 2003. *Applied Longitudinal Data Analysis: Modeling Change and Event Occurrence*. New York: Oxford University Press.

Wills, T. A., and S. D. Cleary. 1999. "Peer and Adolescent Substance Use Among 6th–9th Graders: Latent Growth Analyses of Influence Versus Selection Mechanisms." *Health Psychology* 18(5):453–63.

RESPONSE BIAS IN A POPULAR INDICATOR OF READING TO CHILDREN

*Sandra L. Hofferth**

This paper examines the hypothesis that parents exaggerate their reading with children aged 3 to 5 when asked typical single-item questions and that the extent of exaggeration is greater for better-educated parents. It examines differences in parental reporting of reading to children that may result from differences in response bias. It examines whether differences in reading with children by race/ethnicity, income, and family structure hold up after controlling for maternal education and other factors. Finally, it examines whether any bias we find affects the relationship between reading and achievement test scores. Data are from the Child Development Supplement to the Panel Study of Income Dynamics, a nationally representative sample of children and their parents who were asked detailed questions about their lives and activities in 1997.

1. INTRODUCTION

Reading is a critical skill acquired early in life. In spite of its desirability and the focus on reading in the "No Child Left Behind" legislation, fewer than one-third of elementary school-age children read for pleasure on a daily basis, and the amount of time spent reading is quite modest, about 1 hour per week (Hofferth and Sandberg 2001). Reading to young children promotes their acquisition of language and literacy and correlates with achievement on verbal tests and tests of reading comprehension (Snow, Burns, and Griffin 1998; Wells 1985). Thus, a

This paper was presented at a workshop on the National Children's Study, December 10, 2004, Crystal City, Virginia.

*University of Maryland

commonly used indicator of school preparation is the proportion of young children whose parents read aloud to them on a daily basis. I argue that our national statistics overstate the extent to which parents read to their children. Incorrect information may produce increased expectations for achievement and lowered attention to the promotion of early literacy.

In 1996, 57 percent of children aged 3 to 5 were reported to have been read to aloud by a family member every day in the last week (Federal Interagency Forum, 1997). Although the majority of parents read to children regularly, the same report shows that parental reading varies substantially by the education of the mother. For example, more than three out of four children whose mothers were college graduates were read to every day, compared with only 37 percent of children whose mothers had not completed high school (Federal Interagency Forum, 1997). The report also shows that white children were more likely to be read aloud to every day than black or Hispanic children, 59 percent of white, non-Hispanic children compared with 39 percent of black, non-Hispanic children and 37 percent of Hispanic children. Children from families with incomes below the poverty line were also less likely to be read to on a regular basis, 44 percent compared with 56 percent. Similarly, only 46 percent of children living with a single parent were said to have been read to daily, compared with 61 percent of children living with two parents.

We expect better-educated parents to read more frequently to their children because of their own greater frequency of reading and greater reading facility. However, we also know that parents are aware that they should read to their children, and more educated parents are probably the most aware of the benefits of and social pressures to read to children. Therefore, it is likely that, on surveys, better-educated parents report more reading than actually occurs because they want to be viewed as good parents. In addition, faced with demand for recall over a period of a week but with relatively imprecise response categories, a stylized response could be expected. Under such conditions, parents are likely to exaggerate the frequency of positive behaviors and minimize the frequency of negative ones.

Although we might expect well-educated parents to report more reading to children, there is no clear reason why, net of education, high-income parents should report greater reading to children than low-income parents. Children's books are available at low or no cost to all families. We might expect single parents to read less than married parents because the former have no other adult with whom to share child rearing. We might also expect race/ethnic differences in reading to children. Besides different customs and beliefs and differences in literacy, race/ethnic groups exhibit different family structures, face different employment opportunities, and live under different economic and social circumstances. Variations in these circumstances may account for some of the apparent differences in reading behavior. Finally, race/ethnic minority groups may respond differently to surveys asking objective questions about socially desirable behaviors than do majority groups.

This paper examines the hypothesis that parents, in fact, exaggerate their reading to children aged 3 to 5 and that the extent of exaggeration is greater for better-educated parents. If so, more accurate reports should show lower education effects than less accurate ones. It also examines whether differences in reading with children by income, race/ethnicity, and family structure continue after controlling for education and other factors. Finally, it examines whether the measurement of reading affects the relationship between reading and achievement test scores. If reading matters, then we would expect the more accurate report to be more closely associated with children's test scores than the less accurate report. This paper examines the association between different measures of reading to children and actual scores on the Woodcock-Johnson letter-word identification test, a test of children's ability to identify and respond to letters and words, including those he or she has not seen before (Woodcock and Mather 1989).

2. DATA AND METHODS

2.1. *The Child Development Supplement to the Panel Study of Income Dynamics*

The Panel Study of Income Dynamics (PSID), a nationally representative sample of American men, women, children, and the families in which they reside, completed its thirty-third wave of data collection in 2003. Data on financial circumstances and marital and fertility behavior were collected annually from 1968 to 1997 and biennially thereafter. In 1997, the PSID added a refresher sample of immigrants to the United States (since 1968) so that the sample represented the U.S. population in 1997. When weights are used, the PSID has been found to be representative of Americans and their families (Fitzgerald, Gottschalk, and Moffitt 1998).

In 1997, the National Institute of Child Health and Human Development (NICHD) funded the collection of information on up to two randomly selected 0–12-year-old children of PSID respondents both from the primary caregivers and from the children themselves, called the PSID Child Development Supplement. The study completed interviews with 2,394 child households and about 3,600 children, a response rate of 88 percent (Hofferth et al. 1999). Poststratification weights based upon the 1997 Current Population Survey are used to make the data nationally representative but Ns represent actual sample sizes. The sample used in this analysis consists of 605 children 3 to 5 years of age in 1997 and not yet enrolled in school, the group on which parental reading was calculated in reports on indicators of preschool readiness. In addition, only children living with their mothers are included in this study. Finally, for the examination of the vocabulary achievement test, the sample consists of the subgroup of 380 children who took that test and have data for both diary days.

2.2. *Stylized Questions about Reading to Children*

The most common method used to collect time data is to ask parents directly how much time they spend in activities such as reading to their child. This type of question is called a "stylized question" because it asks the respondent to provide an estimate of time spent in an activity, often coded into categories, but generally allows considerable latitude for interpretation of the question. In the core set of questions asked of the primary caregiver, usually the mother, the CDS asked the following stylized version of the question about reading: "How often do you read to (child)? Would you say (1) never, (2) several times a year, (3) several times a month, (4) about once a week, (5) a few times a week, or (6) every day?" This is comparable to the way the question was asked in the 1996 National Household Education Survey, the most widely quoted source (Federal Interagency Forum, 1997). From this, an indicator variable "reads daily" can be created.

Although simple and widely used, this method is known to be biased. First, it is subject to social desirability bias. People report more time spent on desirable activities (such as reading) than on less desirable ones (Robinson 1985). Second, there is no comparison against which to check consistency, validity, or reliability because activities do not have to add to 24 hours in a day. Activity times asked in this manner have been shown to be quite inaccurately reported (Juster and Stafford 1985). Third, the poor design of the question or response categories may also lead to biased reporting. The question does not refer to a specific time period, suggesting that a rough average of reading frequency over recent weeks is sought. Additionally, the response categories themselves are vague, skipping from every day to a few times a week and then to once a week, leading the reader to expect some leeway in response. Thus "every day" may mean 5 to 7 days a week, "a few times a week" may mean 3 to 4 times a week, and "once" may mean 1 or 2 days a week. We don't know how respondents interpret the question. A vague question could lead more people to say "every day" than one specifying which days they read to their child.

2.3. *Time Diaries*

Substantial methodological work has established the validity and reliability of data collected in time-diary form (Juster and Stafford 1985). The instrument for assessing time use in the 1997 CDS was a "time diary," an open-ended chronological report by the child and/or the child's primary caretaker about the child's activities for one randomly selected weekday and one weekend day for each child aged 0–12 in the family in 1997. The time diary was interviewer-administered and asked several questions about children's flow of activities, such as what they were doing at that time, when the activity began and ended, who was doing it with them, and what else they were doing (if they were engaged in multiple activities).

The advantage of the time diary is that the total time in one day has to add to 24 hours. Consequently, even if individual times are slightly inaccurate, the times are consistent with one another. The disadvantage of the time diary is that it represents only a sample of children's days. Thus, although it accurately represents the activities of a sample of children on a given day, it is only a very small sample of a given child's days and, as such, has limited reliability. To improve reliability, most time-use studies obtain at least one weekend day and one weekday and many also obtain multiple samples over a period of time, such as a year. In addition, reporting is not always complete. Activities that occur only occasionally or that take a small amount of time are likely to be forgotten or ignored and activities that occur in conjunction with other activities may also be underreported. Reading to children is salient and regular enough that it should be captured in the diary. Parents could combine a number of activities, such as bathing and reading, and report that the child was "getting ready for bed." However, interviewers are trained to probe for the detailed activities that entailed.

In the coding process, children's activities were classified into ten general activity categories and further subdivided into three-digit subcategories (such as reading) that can be recombined in a variety of ways to characterize children's activities. From the diary, daily time in which a child read a book, a magazine, or other materials, or was being read to, and a parent was engaged in the activity with the focal child were summed to form the variable "time parent spent reading to child." A variable was created separately for a weekday and for a weekend day. In addition, a third variable, whether the child was read to aloud by a parent *on either a weekday or a weekend day* was created from these two separate diary days, for children with a completed diary for both weekend day and weekday. These variables are compared with data from the stylized question *also asked in the same 1997 study*, an indicator for whether the parent reported that the focal child was read to aloud by a parent on a daily basis. We expect that the closest match should be between the weekday diary day and the parent's stylized report of reading on a daily basis. That is, if the parent reports reading daily in the direct question, reading should be coded on any single diary day. However, because the reliability of one diary day is lower than two, we allow for some error and some slippage by also comparing the stylized responses with whether their child was read to by a parent on either one of the two diary days.

2.4. *Measurement of the Demographic Variables*

The demographic variables used to analyze the impact of family factors on parent time spent reading to children aged 3 to 5 include age of child, gender of child, race of child, age of head, family income, education of mother, and number of children. In order to capture the joint nature of employment and family structure, we included a seven-category variable—dual-earner family; male breadwinner, female home-maker family; female breadwinner, male nonemployed family; two parent, neither employed family; single employed female headed family; single nonemployed female-headed family; and male-headed family (most of whom were employed). The male breadwinner, female homemaker family was the omitted, comparison category.

2.5. *Analysis Plan*

We first compare the point estimates of the proportion of children read to daily by parents measured by the stylized question and by the time diary. This provides a basis for assessing the accuracy of stylized parental reports of reading to children. Second, we examine the bivariate association between education, race/ethnicity, income and family structure and reading to children to see how reporting varies by these factors. Third, we regress the stylized indicator of daily reading on the time diary measures to examine how closely the diary-estimated time is associated with the stylized indicator and the influence of other factors, even after the "true" measure is included. Finally, using structural equation models estimated by maximum likelihood in AMOS, we model the association between maternal education and the child's vocabulary test score, mediated by the stylized and time diary estimates of parental reading. This provides a test of the reliability and validity of the two measures. The structural model is

$$LW = a\,SR + b\,DR + c\,E_4$$
$$SR = d\,ME + e\,E_3$$
$$DR = f\,ME + g\,Z$$
$$WD = h\,DR + i\,E_1$$
$$WE = j\,DR + k\,E_2$$
$$\text{cov}\,(E_1, E_3)\text{ ne } 0$$
$$\text{cov}\,(E_2, E_3)\text{ ne } 0$$

where LW=letter word test score, SR = stylized reading, DR = diary reading (latent variable), ME = mother's education, WD = weekday diary measure, WE = weekend diary measure, E_1 - E_4 = errors in measured variables, Z = error in latent variable, ne = not equal to, and a - k are coefficients.

3. RESULTS

3.1. *National Estimates of Parental Reading to Children*

In 1997, 47 percent of 3–5-year-old children not yet enrolled in school were reported in the CDS stylized question to have been read to every day (Table 1, column 1). Based upon information obtained from the time diary, 29 percent of parents read to their child on a weekday (column 3) and 29 percent read on a weekend day (not shown). The difference between the measures in columns 1 and 3 is statistically significant. Although this suggests bias in the stylized question, estimates from one diary day may be unreliable. If we allow for use on *either* diary day (column 2), the results are closer; 42 percent of children were estimated to have been read to by parents on either day. The difference between this estimate and the estimate based upon the stylized question is not statistically significant.

Are there differences in reading by family characteristics? Looking at differences by mother's education, first, from the stylized question, the proportion reading to children ranges from 29 percent for those mothers who completed less than high school to 66 percent for college graduates (Table 1). In contrast, from the weekday time diary, 10 percent of mothers with less than a high school education read to their children, compared with 36 percent of mothers who graduated from college. The relationship is still highly statistically significant, but the chi-square (not shown) is smaller using the weekday diary than using the stylized measure.

Other differences are quite substantial in the stylized question but they are much reduced in the time diaries. For example, the differences within samples by family income are significant using the stylized measure of daily reading and the diary measure based upon reading on either diary day, but they are not statistically different using the weekday diary measure. The difference by race/ethnicity within samples is statistically significant for the stylized question and for the question based upon either weekday or weekend diary, but not for the single day diary. Finally, differences by family structure are not consistent with expectations using the stylized question, but they are using the diary estimate. In the stylized question, working single mothers read more than married mothers, working or not; however, in the diary, married mothers read more.

TABLE 1
Percentage of 3–5 Year Old Children Read to Daily by Parents[1]

	Child Read to Every Day, from Stylized Q	Child Read to Either Weekend or Weekday, Time Diary	Child Read to by Parent on Weekday, Time diary
All Families	46.8[b]	42.20	28.50
Mother's Education			
Less than high school	28.97[b]	21.47	10.40
High school	34.12	37.95	25.86
Some college	59.66[ab]	46.45	36.17
College grad+	65.78[b]	56.66	36.33
Within group difference	$p < .001$	$p < .001$	$p < .001$
Race/Ethnicity			
White	54.65[b]	47.22	32.31
Black	31.89[b]	26.50	23.33
Hispanic	20.87	31.26	11.48
Asian	48.49[c]	39.21	21.61
Within group difference	$p < .001$	$p < .05$	ns
Income			
<$14,000	38.78[b]	31.69	24.77
$14—27,999	41.55[b]	38.21	25.76
$28–48,999	41.81[b]	40.50	25.30
$49—69,999	56.10[b]	45.63	32.02
$70,000+	57.49[b]	54.56	36.08
Within group difference	$p < .01$	$p < .05$	ns
Family Structure			
Two breadwinners	49.75[b]	48.69	31.91
Male breadwinner	49.52[b]	47.26	32.44
Female breadwinner	30.15[c]	28.62	13.60
No breadwinner	21.70[c]	21.35	10.00
Working female head	52.88[ab]	34.98	23.93
Nonworking female head	33.30	26.10	24.39
Male head, working	26.60[c]	30.74	17.42
Within group difference	$p < .05$	$p < .05$	ns
Sample Size	604	91	503

Source: 1997 Panel Study of Income Dynamics—Child Development Supplement.
[1]Child not in kindergarten.
[a]Frequency from stylized Question significantly different from Child read to either weekend or weekday ($p < .05$).
[b]Frequency from stylized Question significantly different from Child read to on weekday time diary ($p < .05$)
[c]Sample size too small to perform test.

These results suggest that race/ethnicity, family structure, and income affect response patterns in the stylized question but do not affect the time diary measures of parental reading to children. However, this does not prove that social desirability bias exists.

3.2. *Multivariate Analysis*

To test the existence and extent of bias, the parent's stylized report of daily reading to children is regressed on the "correct" measure of reading, the measure of reading to children on the weekday diary day, controlling for the education of mother, race/ethnicity, family income, family structure, and the other variables (Table 2). (The results are similar if

TABLE 2

Logistic Regression of Stylized Daily Reading on Diary Reading and Controls

Variable	Coefficient	Standard Error
Intercept	-1.929^{***}	0.995
Read to child on weekday (diary)	1.203^{***}	0.235
Child age (year)	-0.270	0.161
Child gender (1 = female, 0 = male)	-0.046	0.212
Mother's education (years)	0.270^{***}	0.056
White	omitted	
Black	-0.679^{+}	0.353
Hispanic	-0.540	0.408
Asian	-0.399	0.693
Other race	-1.115^{+}	0.629
Mother's age (years)	-0.017	0.016
Male breadwinner	omitted	
Two earner	-2.560	0.254
Female breadwinner	-0.649	0.609
No breadwinner	-1.286^{+}	0.770
Female working head	0.382	0.341
Female nonworking head	-0.080	0.469
Income (in \$10, 000)	0.009	0.030
Number of children	-0.071	0.097
Sample size	486	
-2 log likelihood	576	
CHI SQUARE	115	
P value	0.0001	

$^{+}p \leq 10; \, ^{*}p \leq .05; \, ^{**}p \leq .01; \, ^{***}p \leq .001.$
Source: 1997 Panel Study of Income Dynamics–Child Development Supplement.

we use the diary measure for *either* weekend or weekday and, therefore, are not shown.) Whether children's parents read to them on a weekday diary day is highly significantly associated with parental report of reading on a daily basis. Those who read on that day are 3.3 times (odds ratio, not shown) as likely to report daily reading as those who did not so read.

As anticipated, the education of the mother is strongly associated with stylized reporting of daily reading by the primary caregiver, even after controlling for the "real" measure of reading. More educated mothers are significantly more likely to report the child was read to aloud on a daily basis, even controlling for the "real" extent of reading (the diary measure).

The parents of black children are marginally less likely to report that they read to their child, even after controlling for the "real" extent of reading. Thus black parents tend to underreport reading to children, compared to whites. They may engage in other literacy activities, such as storytelling. Children in two-parent no-breadwinner families are marginally less likely to be read to by a parent; such parents are likely to have a mental or physical disability limiting their ability to read to children. None of the other control variables are associated with parents' report of reading on a daily basis. Most of the variation is explained by whether parents actually read; the remainder has a substantial social desirability (education) or cultural bias (race/ethnic differences). More educated parents are aware that they should be reading to children and are more likely to report that they do even at the risk of bending the truth. There was no reason to believe that income or family structure would be related to reading to children, once education and the actual extent of reading to children were controlled, and this expectation was confirmed. We focus on maternal education in our structural models.

3.3. *Does the Measure we use Matter in Predicting Children's Verbal Achievement?*

The best test for the validity of our measures of parental reading time is whether they are associated with the child's vocabulary test score. Here we used the continuous measure of time parents read to children from the diary and the ordinal indicator from the stylized question.[1] The model fits the data well, with a GFI of .991, an AGFI of .933, and an RMSEA of .091, with a range from .033 to .159. Although mother's education is probably also related to the vocabulary test score for reasons other than reading to children, adding that path did not improve the fit of the model. Paths from the errors were set to one for identification. In addition, one of the paths from the latent diary variable to the weekday diary variable was set to one to scale the results. The results are the following (standardized estimates/unstandardized estimate, with the standard error underneath the unstandardized estimate):

$$LW = 0.23/3.24 \; SR + 0.30/30.21 \; DR + E_4$$
$$\qquad\qquad (.73) \qquad\qquad (10.52)$$
$$SR = 0.38/.17 \; ME + E_3$$
$$\qquad (.02)$$
$$DR = 0.36/.02 \; ME + Z$$
$$\qquad (.01)$$
$$WD = 0.38/1 \; DR + E_1$$
$$WE = 0.53/1.22 \; DR + E_2$$
$$\qquad\qquad (.40)$$
$$\text{cov}\,(E_1, E_3) = .19/.06$$
$$\qquad\qquad (.02)$$
$$\text{cov}\,(E_2, E_3) = .21/.05$$
$$\qquad\qquad (.01)$$

Measurement of Parental Reading Time. The variances of the errors for the two diary days, weekday and weekend day, are small (var $E_1 =$ .11 and var $E_2 = .07$). In contrast, the residual for the stylized reading measure (SR) is large (var $E_3 = .78$).[2] We permitted correlations between the errors in the diary and the stylized reading estimates, and both were significant, although small (cov $E_1, E_3) = .06$ and cov E_2,

---

[1] The structural model is based upon the following correlation matrix:

	Mother's Education	Stylized Reading	Letter-word	Week-end	Week-day	Mean	Standard Deviation
Mother's education	1.00					13.48	2.15
Stylized reading	0.365	1.00				5.26	1.00
Letter-word score	0.282	0.265	1.00			100.88	13.74
Weekend day	0.173	0.137	0.173	1.00		0.19	0.30
Weekday	0.086	0.205	0.123	0.240	1.00	0.16	0.32

[2] Variances for the other variables are the following: $ME = 4.557$, $Z = 0.016$, and $E_4 = 156$.

$E_3 = .05$). The reliability of the latent diary variable was calculated in two different ways, using RC, "reliability of the construct" (Fornell and Larcker 1981), and "Coefficient H" (Hancock and Mueller 2001). Reliability as measured by RC was .34 and as measured by Coefficient H was .36. Using measures of the two different diary days provides somewhat better reliability than using a single item, but neither of these reliabilities is particularly high. Reliability depends upon both the number of indicators and their interrelationship. Adding another diary day would improve this measure substantially. Because weekdays are more similar than weekend days, adding a weekday would give the biggest boost to reliability, whereas adding a weekend day would provide more boost to validity.

Education and Reading to Children. Examining the unstandardized paths, we see that, as hypothesized, the association of the mother's education with the time spent reading to the child in the diary (.02) is relatively weak, whereas the effect is larger for the stylized measure (.17). This is because the proportion who read at all is only 29 percent on a weekday, making the total time spent (including zeros) quite small, 12 minutes on average. The standardized estimates, however, are quite similar, .38 for the stylized measure and .36 for the diary measure. Of course, the model assumes that the distances between categories on the *stylized* measure are equal, whereas we know that this is not the case. Moving from category 4, read once a week, to category 5, read a few times a week, to category 6, read every day, does not add equivalent amounts of reading time. In contrast, the diary measure is in hours, a ratio scale variable. For this reason as well as the previous analyses, there is some support for the hypothesis that mother's education is more strongly related to the stylized measure than to the time diary measure, though it is clearly linked to both measures.

Parental Reading and Child Vocabulary. As shown above, time spent reading to children from the diary measures is very strongly linked to the child's letter word test score. One additional hour is associated with a 2 SD increase in vocabulary score (30.21). One additional number higher in stylized reading frequency, also a large increase, is associated with only a .24 SD increase in vocabulary score (3.24). The standardized coefficients also show a larger impact of the diary measure than the stylized measure (.30 versus .23, respectively).

4. DISCUSSION AND CONCLUSIONS

As hypothesized, our research showed that parents exaggerate the extent to which they read to children. Not as much reading on a daily basis is documented in the time diary as reported in the stylized single question. The stylized estimate is closest to what would be estimated as reading on either of two diary days. The second hypothesis was also confirmed. Because reading is a positively evaluated activity of which educated parents are aware, better-educated parents report more reading with children, even after adjusting for the actual level of reading they do, than less-educated parents. Because better-educated parents read to children less than they report to interviewers in stylized questions, actual educational differences in reading by education are smaller than the stylized numbers suggest. The third hypothesis was that the more reliable diary measure would be more highly associated with the letter-word test score than the less reliable stylized question. The structural equation model supported both that the diary was more reliable than the stylized question and that it was more valid in that there was a stronger link to the vocabulary test score.

On what basis do I argue that the stylized question has a greater *social desirability component* than the diary measure? Reading to children does not vary by income, family structure, or race/ethnicity, according to the time diary. The effects of maternal education in increasing reading, in contrast, are real but smaller using the diary than the stylized measure.

This study has several limitations. First, the research used a cross-section of children and their families. Second, only two diary days were available, limiting the testing of reliability in different study designs. Having two different types of questions within a large nationally representative sample has facilitated this analysis. Given that no other large data collection effort has collected time diaries, this is the only data set that could have been used.

In what ways does the over-reporting of parental reading to children matter to child achievement? Using a stylized estimate of time children are read to by parents underrepresents the effects of the reading to children because it contains substantial response bias. Thus, educators may underestimate its importance. As it stands now, we are getting an exceedingly rosy picture of parental involvement in children's reading, a picture that is inaccurate by a substantial margin due to reliance on a single stylized question. Although the resulting picture may not be harmful to children, it prevents addressing one of the root causes of children's reading problems, low levels of literacy activities at home.

REFERENCES

Federal Interagency Forum on Child and Family Statistics. 1997. *America's Children: Key National Indicators of Well-Being.* Washington, DC: Forum on Child and Family Statistics.

Fitzgerald, John, Peter Gottschalk, and Robert Moffitt. 1998. "An Analysis of Sample Attrition in Panel Data: Michigan Panel Study of Income Dynamics." *Journal of Human Resources* 33(2):251–99.

Fornell, C., and D.F. Larcker. 1981. "Evaluating Structural Equation Models with Unobservable Variables and Measurement Error." *Journal of Marketing Research* 18:39–50.

Hancock, Greg R., and Robert O. Mueller. 2001. "Rethinking Construct Reliability Within Latent Variable Systems." Pp. 195–216 in *Structural Equation Modeling: Present and Future—Festschrift in honor of Karl Jöreskog,* edited by R. Cudeck, S. du Toit, and D. Sörbom. Lincolnwood, IL: Scientific Software International.

Hofferth, Sandra L., Pamela Davis-Kean, Jean Davis, and Jonathan Finkelstein. 1999. *1997 User Guide: The Child Development Supplement to the Panel Study of Income Dynamics.* Ann Arbor, MI: Institute for Social Research, University of Michigan.

Hofferth, Sandra, and John F. Sandberg. 2001. "Changes in American Children's Use of Time, 1981–1997." Pp. 193–229 in *Children at the Millennium: Where Have We Come From, Where are we Going?* edited by S. Hofferth and T. Owens. Advances in Life Course Research Series, New York: Elsevier Science.

Juster, F. Thomas, and Frank P. Stafford. 1985. *Time, Goods, and Well-Being.* Ann Arbor, MI: Institute for Social Research, University of Michigan.

Robinson, John P. 1985. "The Validity and Reliability of Diaries Versus Alternative Time Use Measures." Pp. 33–62 in *Time, Goods, and Well-Being,* edited by F.T. Juster and F.P. Stafford. Ann Arbor, MI: Survey Research Center, Institute for Social Research.

Snow, Catherine, M. Susan Burns, and Peg Griffin. 1998. *Preventing Reading Difficulties in Young Children.* Washington, DC: National Academy Press.

Wells, Gordon. 1985. "Preschool Literacy-Related Activities and Success in School." Pp. 229–55 in *Literacy, Language and Learning,* edited by D. Olson, N. Torrance, and A. Hildyard. Cambridge, England: Cambridge University Press.

Woodcock, Robert, and Nancy Mather. 1989. *W-J-R Tests of Achievement: Examiner's Manual.* Woodcock-Johnson Psycho-Educational Battery-Revised. Allen, TX: DLM Teaching Resources.

4

THE SAFETY DANCE: CONFRONTING HARASSMENT, INTIMIDATION, AND VIOLENCE IN THE FIELD

Gwen Sharp*
Emily Kremer†

This paper discusses how gender dynamics may put female researchers at risk of harassment or even violence from participants, research assistants, or bystanders when conducting fieldwork. Based on a review of the existing literature on fieldwork safety, as well as the authors' own experiences interviewing male participants, the authors argue that attention to protecting subjects of research has led the social science community to largely ignore the possibility that in some cases, researchers themselves may be at risk. The paper concludes with suggested strategies for increasing researcher safety during data collection, as well as a call for issues of fieldwork safety to be more openly discussed by supervisors, professors, advisors, and others who guide novice researchers through the fieldwork process.

The authors would like to thank Douglas Jackson-Smith for comments on early versions of this manuscript, as well as members of the Fem-Sem brownbag at the University of Wisconsin–Madison for encouragement and suggestions. Direct all correspondence to Gwen Sharp, Department of History and Sociology, 225 Centrum Arena, 351 W. Center St., Southern Utah University, Cedar City, UT 84720; E-mail: sharpg@suu.edu.

*Southern Utah University
†University of Wisconsin–Madison

317

1. INTRODUCTION

The rise of feminist critiques of social science research methods, as well as increased regulation of researcher-subject interactions, has led to heightened awareness of the need to protect research subjects from exploitation or harm. Given past abuses of research subjects, increased scrutiny of research protocols was certainly needed. However, the increased efforts to protect subjects have obscured another safety issue: *researchers* may face dangers during fieldwork.

Certainly social scientists have addressed the issue of safety during fieldwork, especially when research involves topics that are obviously risk-prone. Jamieson (2000) and Jankowski (1991) recount the dangers they encountered during fieldwork on criminal activity and street gangs, respectively. Kovats-Bernat (2002) and Nilan (2002) discuss the dangers of working in regions characterized by guerilla warfare or terrorism.

However, less attention has been paid to safety issues that arise during fieldwork on topics or in settings that do not, in and of themselves, present obvious dangers. In some cases the characteristics of the researcher with respect to participants may create the conditions for harassment or violence in the field. Race, gender, sexual orientation, and disability status are just some of the factors that may lead a researcher to be endangered in a situation that may not pose a risk to others.

In this article, we focus on gender dynamics between female researchers and male subjects. Despite the widespread recognition of the role of gender dynamics in social life, sociologists have to a large extent ignored how these dynamics affect their own work. We review the literature on harassment and violence during fieldwork, discuss our own experiences, and provide suggestions for improving researcher safety in the field.

2. LITERATURE REVIEW

A number of scholars discuss the role of gender in shaping the research experience. Arendell (1997) argues that in qualitative research involving in-depth interviews, the researcher is the primary research tool, since it is up to the researcher to build rapport with subjects, coax answers from them, and guide and control the interview. Who the researcher is, in terms of race, class, and gender, must necessarily be important to the dynamics of face-to-face interviews.

Other researchers focus on the difficulty female researchers may have gaining respect and deference from subjects. While the researcher is supposed to be in control of an interview, female researchers may find that male subjects attempt to control the process (Green et al. 1993). Male subjects attempted to teach Arendell (1997) how to use her tape recorder and frequently took control of the interview, making it difficult for her to guide them through the set of topics in which she was interested.

Feminist theorists have concentrated primarily on equalizing power relations between researchers and subjects and making the voices of marginalized groups heard in sociological research. Such theories tend to assume that one is interviewing the relatively powerless (Green et al. 1993). However, the subordinate position of women in most cultures implies that they may have less power vis-à-vis male subjects than would be expected given their professional, highly educated status.

Issues of gender and identity are often ignored during the research design process and individual researchers are left to deal with potential problems on their own. For instance, Gill and Maclean (2002) argue that female researchers are more highly scrutinized than male scholars and become acutely aware of their sexual and gender status in the field. Both women conducted research in rural communities in Britain and found that their characters and reputations were the constant subject of discussion and rumor. They had no training on how to respond to such rumors and public attention to their sexuality in the field.

Sociologists rarely consider the distress that researchers may experience due to their research. Gill and Maclean (2002) were completely unprepared for how much their experiences would affect their own self-identities and how defensive they would become over rumors. They argue that these issues are marginalized, and when they emerge during fieldwork researchers are expected to ignore their personal discomfort for the sake of finishing the research.

2.1. *Sexual Harassment, Danger, and Fieldwork*

Certainly some of the most negative encounters researchers may face in the field are intimidation and violence. While danger in the field includes robbery, political intimidation, and natural disasters, among others (Howell 1988, 1990; Peritore 1990), we are primarily concerned with sexual harassment and assault during fieldwork. The research literature to date indicates that this is overwhelmingly a problem faced by female researchers, especially those interviewing male subjects.

Howell (1988, 1990) conducted one of the few large-scale studies of danger in the field under the auspices of the American Anthropological Association. Two percent of all respondents, and 7 percent of women, reported rape or attempted rape of themselves or someone in their research group while in the field. Howell argues that the culture of research, in which individual researchers are supposed to successfully build rapport with those they study, leads some researchers to blame themselves for attacks. Moreno (1995), who was raped by her field assistant, adds that, while sexual harassment and assault may concern women in their "daily lives," concerns about personal safety and sexual advances are not part of the identity of the professional researcher. She argues that female researchers learn to "avoid drawing attention to ourselves as women when we establish our professional identities" (p. 246). In the field, however, female researchers cannot pretend to be genderless.

During interviews with divorced men about their postdivorce parenting experiences, Arendell (1997) reports multiple instances of sexual harassment and intimidation. One man began discussing his ex-wife but soon began to substitute Arendell for her, angrily telling her, "'You [women] have to talk to me. You [women] have to tell me, communicate with me.' By the time he finished speaking, he was shaking his index finger" at her (p. 356). Others touched her inappropriately, and one of her subjects demonstrated how he had choked his ex-wife by grabbing Arendell around the neck, becoming animated and angry. Despite the fact that this interview took place in a public restaurant, Arendell felt very intimidated, and the rest of the interview was strained.

Paterson, Gregory, and Thorne (1999) also experienced a number of threatening incidents during fieldwork. One subject shut and locked the door after the interviewer entered his home and informed her that he had agreed to participate only to get her to come to his home. While she escaped after an hour unharmed, the incident was very frightening and clearly dangerous. Other researchers in the field of health services reported stalking, unwanted sexual advances, and even being held at gunpoint during interviews. Such dangerous incidents are rare during fieldwork, but they do happen. Novice researchers may be especially at risk, as they are often more concerned with their methodology and response rate than ensuring their own safety.

Green et al. (1993) relate their own experiences, as well as the results of interviews with 20 nurses who conducted home-visits with patients. Five of the 20 nurses had experienced threatening situations, and the authors report inappropriate touching and sexual jokes during their own research. It can be difficult to deal with such sexual advances because researchers feel that the subject is doing them a favor by participating. It is also difficult to know when to expect possible harassment or intimidation. They suggest that female researchers interviewing men are always trying to delicately balance their relationship with subjects and their own safety concerns.

3. OUR EXPERIENCES IN THE FIELD

Our interest in the topic of researcher safety and experiences of sexual harassment or intimidation grew out of our own experiences as female graduate students conducting interviews with primarily male subjects. While we had both prepared for the possibility of routine problems encountered during fieldwork, neither of us thought about the possibility of experiencing harassment or intimidation from our subjects.

3.1. *Kremer's Research on Masculinity*

The purpose of my study was to understand how men who are subordinate to hegemonic ideas of masculinity (specifically, self-identified "dorks") talk about their own masculinity. Interviews included questions about leisure activities and friendships, understandings of their own masculinity, and dating and sexual orientation.

I wanted to meet the men in a public place. However, the Institutional Review Board (IRB) at my university did not approve public meetings and instead required that I interview the men alone in a private room. I chose a small office on a quiet floor of a campus building. Some interviews took place on weekends when the building was virtually deserted.

During one interview, the participant made several derogatory comments about women. He then asked me to have drinks with him after the interview. The first time, I simply ignored his comment; the second time I treated it as a joke and laughed; the third time I told him that I could not go out with him because it would violate the confidentiality agreement we had signed.

Because of hostile comments he made about keeping women on "short leashes" and that men should hold power in romantic relationships, I began to worry about my relative isolation in the building. Despite my fear, I continued with the interview out of a sense of obligation to my data. As a young, inexperienced researcher, I felt that it was more important to complete the interview than to address my fears.

In subsequent interviews, I made sure that someone I knew would be in the building for the entirety of the interview, and, after another awkward conversation with a respondent, I had someone call me in the office 45 minutes into each interview to make sure I was safe. Faculty members I spoke to about the incident agreed that this was a good strategy for ensuring my safety, but none of them suggested it to me beforehand or provided any other strategies. Rather, the suggestion arose from conversations with other female graduate students, several of whom had also faced sexual harassment during fieldwork.

3.2. *Sharp's Research in a Rural Setting*

My first experience with fieldwork occurred when I conducted on-farm interviews with dairy farmers during my thesis research. All 27 interviews took place on participants' farms; some occurred in the house, while others took place outside or in the barn. All but two subjects were male, and during most interviews I was alone with the subject or with the subject and male employees. In several cases I stayed in the field for several days before returning home. As a novice researcher, I was very concerned to protect the confidentiality of my subjects and follow IRB policies carefully. As a result, during the days I was doing fieldwork, no one, including my advisor, knew where I was or who I was interviewing.

Three different male participants remarked on my physical appearance and unmarried status. One male subject admitted that he only agreed to participate because he thought I sounded "cute" on the phone. During another interview, the male farmer went to the window and yelled to his employees to come inside and "take a look, we've got a cute girl in here!" One male employee then came in and grinned and stared at me before continuing on with his work. In the final interview in which the subject remarked on my appearance, his unmarried son, about my age, was present during the interview, and I began to suspect that the participant was angling to set us up on a date. The situation became awkward and I was unable to focus fully on the interview because I was trying to think of an appropriate response to the situation.

On another research project, I interviewed ranchers in the Great Plains. Again, most interviews took place on participants' farms, usually with no one else around. Though I had a cell phone, many of the ranches were so remote that there was no signal.

I only encountered serious problems with one participant. He insisted on conducting the interview in the cab of his truck. As the interview progressed, he slowly moved closer to me on the seat. I responded by moving as far away as I could; soon I was huddled against the door, holding my notebook up in front of me as a barrier between us. He then began to casually touch my arm and shoulder as he answered my questions. Eventually he leaned forward, laid his hand on my thigh, and left it there. At that point I abruptly ended the interview, feeling flustered and angry.

Looking back, we are both shocked by how little our own safety entered into our thoughts, given that we were interviewing men alone in very secluded settings. In our nonworking lives, neither of us would have considered entering such a situation. But as researchers, our concerns were for the quality of our data. In our roles as professional sociologists, we were blinded to the fact that we remained female, and therefore open to sexual advances and even violence. Only after we both completed our research and began discussing the issues we encountered did we realize we had begun our projects as though gender dynamics surrounding power and violence were unimportant.

4. STRATEGIES FOR INCREASING SAFETY IN THE FIELD

One consistent factor that emerges across accounts of harassment and violence during fieldwork is that no one prepared these researchers for what they would encounter. Researchers were left on their own to develop safety measures and had no training from their departments or universities on safety during fieldwork.

As a result, female researchers develop their own methods of protecting themselves while interviewing. One of the most common tactics was avoidance of potentially dangerous situations and topics. Whenever possible, researchers suggest meeting subjects in a public place and during the day (Paterson et al. 1999; Green et al. 1993). When this is impossible, researchers should ideally have an initial meeting with participants in a public place before the interview occurs in order to get a sense of how the subject will respond and whether they are clearly hostile, intoxicated, or otherwise potentially dangerous. "Cold call" interviews, with no prior contact with potential participants, are considered to have the highest level of risk. Green et al. (1993) suggest interviewing in pairs whenever possible as a safety measure, while acknowledging that financial and time constraints often make this impossible.

Paterson et al. (1999) and Kenyon and Hawker (1999) stress the need to be knowledgeable of one's surroundings when interviewing. Researchers should know the area well, including major streets and the interiors of buildings in which interviews will take place. An interviewer should be organized and prepared and not overloaded with heavy equipment.

Kenyon and Hawker (1999) suggest avoiding emotional or sexual topics that may lead to unwanted advances or hostility during the interview. Of course, depending on the topic of interest, avoiding emotional or sexual issues may be impossible and would exclude female researchers from many vital areas of social science research. It also ignores the fact that women are gendered beings regardless of the topic of research and cannot simply "de-gender" themselves by limiting their areas of scholarship.

Green et al. (1993) attempted to avoid sexual harassment and unwanted sexual advances by dressing very conservatively, drawing attention away from their femininity and discouraging subjects from viewing them as sexually available. However, when Gill and Maclean (2002) used this approach, they found themselves the targets of rumors that they were lesbians, which potentially jeopardized their research. When they acted in ways that did not downplay their femininity, it led to sexual advances from male respondents. They conclude that female researchers cannot simply "hide" their sexuality from public view.

Paterson et al. (1999) and Kenyon and Hawker (1999) argue that all researchers in the field should have cell phones. Ideally, cell phones should be programmed to a local emergency number, such as

911. Paterson et al. also urge research teams to develop an agreed-upon "danger code" (such as calling the office to cancel a fake appointment) that would be a signal of trouble and that authorities should be contacted. They additionally suggest that all team members on a research project brainstorm about potential situations that may arise and practice responding to them.

Most researchers left sealed envelopes of the names and addresses of those they would be interviewing on a given day with a friend or colleague with instructions to open it and contact the authorities if the interviewer did not call at a stated time (Green et al. 1993; Kenyon and Hawker 1999; Paterson et al. 1999).

Researchers use a number of tactics to defuse sexual harassment during interviews. Paterson et al. (1999) suggest ignoring inappropriate comments or actions. Arendell (1997) gently guided conversations back to the main topic without overtly addressing the sexual advances of her subjects. Green et al. (1993) acknowledge that in some situations, directly reacting to, and rejecting, the behavior may be a better option. However, it may also offend the subject and could endanger the quality of the interview, so researchers should be careful when using this tactic.

Finally, all of the authors stress the need for researchers to trust their instincts in the field. Green et al. (1999) argue that it is essential that all research team members understand that they may end an interview at any time if they feel uncomfortable or endangered. Advisors and research team leaders need to pay more attention to the issue and openly discuss it with their assistants and students. Howell (1990) argues that funding agencies, professors, departments, universities, and professional associations all have a responsibility to ensure the safety of scholars in the field and to create an academic environment that does not place access to subjects or completion of interviews above the safety of interviewers.

While our review of the literature uncovered a number of strategies for dealing with sexual harassment or intimidation in the field, we found a number of them to be unsatisfactory. For instance, while interviewing only in public places might be ideal, those studying sensitive topics or interviewing in rural areas may find this impossible. Avoiding emotional topics is also clearly impossible for many researchers, unless we give up the study of many areas of interest altogether.

After reviewing the existing literature on safety during fieldwork, and considering our own field experiences, we suggest the following strategies and policies as the most realistic:

- All fieldworkers should have a cell phone. Funding for cell phones should be written into grants, and they should be a standard piece of equipment for all interviews.
- When conducting interviews in private, the researcher should have someone call halfway through each interview to ensure that no problems have arisen. They should have an agreed-upon "danger code" the researcher can use to alert the caller to contact authorities.
- Interviewers should leave a sealed itinerary, including names, phone numbers, addresses, and times of interviews, with someone before going into the field. The envelope should only be opened if the researcher does not return or call at an appointed time, thus protecting the confidentiality of participants.
- Research team members should discuss the possibility of sexual harassment or intimidation in the field and think about what types of behavior or situations are most likely to occur.
- Researchers should devise strategies to deal with unwanted sexual advances or intimidation before going into the field. Having pre-planned responses to such situations will help the researcher keep the interview on track.
- All interviewers should understand that they may end an interview if they feel uncomfortable or threatened.

In presenting this paper, we hope to bring the issue of sexual violence to the forefront of qualitative research. Researcher safety should be a priority in any kind of face-to-face interaction with subjects. We encourage social scientists to recognize the need for more attention to fieldwork safety and hope this article provides a starting point for a more in-depth discussion of the extent of the problem and strategies for reducing researchers' exposure to potentially dangerous situations.

REFERENCES

Arendell, Terry. 1997. "Reflections on the Researcher-Researched Relationship: A Woman Interviewing Men." *Qualitative Sociology* 20:341–68.

Coffey, Amanda. 1999. *The Ethnographic Self: Fieldwork and the Representation of Identity*. Gateshead, England: Sage Publications.

Gill, Fiona, and Catherine Maclean. 2002. "Knowing Your Place: Gender and Reflexivity in Two Ethnographies." *Sociologial Research Online* 7 (www.socresonline.org.uk/7/2/gill.html).

Green, Gill, Rosaline S. Barbour, Marina Barnard, and Jenny Kitzinger. 1993. "'Who Wears the Trousers?' Sexual Harassment in Research Settings." *Women's Studies International Forum* 16:627–37.

Howell, Nancy. 1988. "Health and Safety in the Fieldwork of North American Anthropologists." *Current Anthropology* 29:780–87.

———. 1990. *Surviving Fieldwork: A Report of the Advisory Panel on Health and Safety in Fieldwork, American Anthropological Association*. Washington, DC: American Anthropological Association.

Jamieson, Janet. 2000. "Negotiating Danger in Fieldwork on Crime: A Researcher's Tale." Pp. 61–71 in *Danger in the Field: Risk and Ethics in Social Research*, edited by Geraldine Lee-Treweek and Stephanie Linkogle. London: Routledge.

Jankowski, Martin Sanchez. 1991. *Islands in the Street: Gangs in American Urban Society*. Berkeley: University of California Press.

Kenyon, Elizabeth, and Sheila Hawker. 1999. "'Once Would Be Enough': Some Reflections on the Issue of Safety for Lone Researchers." *International Journal of Social Research Methodology* 2:313–27.

Kovats-Bernat, J. Christopher. 2002. "Negotiating Dangerous Fields: Pragmatic Strategies for Fieldwork amid Violence and Terror." *American Anthropologist* 104:208–22.

Logan, Mary Ellen, and Helen Huntley. 2002. "Gender and Power in the Research Process." *Women's Studies International Forum* 24:623–35.

Moreno, Eva. 1995. "Rape in the Field: Reflections from a Survivor." Pp. 219–50 in *Taboo: Sex, Identity and Erotic Subjectivity in Anthropological Fieldwork*, edited by Don Kulick and Margaret Willson. London: Routledge.

Nilan, Pamela. 2002. "'Dangerous Fieldwork' Re-Examined: The Question of Researcher-Subject Position." *Qualitative Research* 2:363–86.

Paterson, Barbara L., David Gregory, and Sally Thorne. 1999. "A Protocol for Researcher Safety." *Qualitative Health Research* 9:259–69.

Peritore, N. Patrick. 1990. "Reflections on Dangerous Fieldwork." *American Sociologist* 21:359–72.

Reinharz, Shulamit. 1992. *Feminist Methods in Social Research*. Oxford, England: Oxford University Press.

NAME INDEX

A

Adalbjarnardottir, S., 260
Adams, R.J., 262
Agresti, A., 174, 175, 178, 180, 190,
    192, 193, 194, 195, 196, 197, 198,
    199, 251n
Albert, R., 114
Allison, P.D., 8, 9, 28, 29, 30, 31n, 156,
    159, 259
Altman, D.G., 179
Alwin, D.F., 65, 78, 79, 80n, 89,
    93, 94
Andersen, R., 238, 241
Anderson, J.A., 5
Arendell, T., 318, 319, 320, 325
Armenia, H.K., 172
Armstrong, B.G., 259
Ato-Garcia, M., 196
Axinn, W.G., 271n, 297

B

Bachman, J.G., 196, 261
Bailey, S.L., 260
Ballarino, G., 8n
Banfield, J.D., 207
Barab·si, A.-L., 114
Barber, J.S., 271n, 297
Barbour, R.S., 319, 321, 324, 325

Barkema, G.T., 106, 140
Barnard, M., 319, 321, 324, 325
Bashir, S.A., 69
Bates, D.M., 272
Bennett, M.E., 261
Berger, R.L., 51
Besag, J., 102, 103, 105, 106
Best, N.G., 58, 59, 59n
Bishop, Y.M.M., 4
Blossfeld, H.-P., 2, 24, 28
Bollen, K.A., 27
Booth, J.G., 198, 199
Bosker, R., 45, 88n
Botvin, G.J., 261
Boudon, R., 28
Box, G.E.P., 62n
Boyle, P., 40, 76, 77
Bracken, M.B., 179
Breen, R., 4, 5, 29, 35
Brennan, R.T., 271n, 295
Breslow, N., 164n
Brooks, C., 5, 24
Browne, W., 62
Bryk, A., 60
Bryk, A.S., 41, 49, 50, 51n, 57, 86, 88,
    89, 89n, 94, 273, 275
Buka, S.L., 271n, 295
Burda, Z., 106

Burns, S., 301
Butts, C.T., 108, 149

C
Caffo, B., 180, 192, 194, 195, 198, 199
Cameron, A. C., 156
Cameron, S. V., 2, 29, 35
Campbell, J.R., 87
Carlin, B.P., 57, 58, 59, 60n
Carlin, J.B., 57, 57n, 60
Casella, G., 51
Catalano, R.F., 260
Chamberlain, G.A., 156
Chang, H.-C., 28
Chassin, L., 260, 261
Cheong, Y.F., 89n, 262, 273, 275
Chmiel, J.S., 172
Chotikapanich, D., 206
Christakis, N.A., 157n
Chung,I.-J., 260
Clayton, D., 77
Cleary, S.D., 261
Colder, C.R., 261
Congdon, R., 89n, 273, 275
Cook, J.M., 101
Cowell, F.A., 202
Cowles, M.K., 58
Cox, C., 259
Cox, D.R., 28
Crombie, I.K., 179
Curran, P.J., 261

D
D'Onofrio, B., 261
Dagum, C., 202, 204, 216
Dasgupta, A., 208
Davies, H.T.O, 179
Davis, J., 304
Davis, J.A., 100
Davis-Kean, P., 304
Deeks, J.J., 179
Detels, R., 172
Diaz, T., 261
DiPrete, T.A., 5
Donnan, P.T., 166

Donnelly, N., 196
Draper, D., 57
Duncan, B., 10, 28
Duncan, O.D., 177, 193
Duncan, S.C., 261
Duncan, T.E., 261

E
Eaves, L., 261
Ekholm, A., 175, 176, 179, 181, 185,
    191
Erikson, R., 5, 24
Esteve, J., 69
Everitt, B.S., 206

F
Featherman, D.L., 2, 28, 34
Federal Interagency Forum, 302, 304
Fienberg, S.E., 4, 6, 45, 46, 76, 77, 83
Finklestein, J, 304
Firebaugh, G., 77, 202, 216
Firth, D., 227, 228n
Fitzgerald, J., 304
Fitzmaurice, G.M., 178, 193
Flewelling, R.L., 260
Fornell, C., 313
Fox, J., 225, 226, 227, 228, 231n, 232,
    234, 241, 253
Fraley, C., 207, 208, 209
Frank, O., 102, 103, 104, 108, 112, 115,
    148
Friedman, J., 226
Fu, W.J., 40, 46, 77, 79

G
Gamoran, A., 29
Gandini, S., 40, 76
Gange, S.J., 172
Gardner, M.J., 77
Gelfand, A.E., 58
Gelman, A., 57, 57n, 60, 61
Geman, D., 108
Geman, S., 108
Gentleman, R., 253
Geyer, C.J., 104

Gill, F., 319, 324
Gini, C., 202
Glenn, N.D., 41, 65, 76, 77, 78, 79, 80n, 89, 93, 94
Glonek, G.F.V., 178, 193
Goldberger, A.S., 7, 27
Goldstein, H., 60, 61, 62, 87n
Goldthorpe, J.H., 5, 24, 29
Goodnight, J.H., 226, 231n
Goodreau, S.M., 108, 149
Gottschalk, P., 210, 304
Gove, W.R., 46, 65, 78–79, 80n, 83, 88, 89, 92–93, 94
Green, G., 319, 321, 324, 325
Greenberg, B.G., 79n
Greene, W.T., 156
Greenland, S., 159, 162, 165, 166, 179
Gregory, D., 320, 324, 325
Griffin, K.W., 261
Griffin, P., 301
Griffiths, W., 206
Guo, X., 57

H
Hagenaars, J.A., 174, 196
Häggströom, O., 106
Halaby, C.N., 156
Hall, W., 196
Hancock, G.R., 313
Handcock, M.S., 105, 106, 108, 109, 114, 115, 126, 148, 149, 150
Hartzel, J., 180, 192, 194, 195
Harvey, W.R., 226, 231n
Hastie, T., 226
Hastie, T.J., 248n, 253
Hauser, R.M., 7, 12, 27, 28, 34
Hauser, R.M.L, 2, 34
Hawker, S., 324, 325
Hawkins, J.D., 260
Heath, A., 238
Heckman, J, 83
Heckman, J.J., 2, 29, 35
Hedges, L.V., 87
Hernan, M.A., 166
Hernandez-Diaz, S., 166

Hill, K.G., 260
Hills, S.E., 58
Hobcraft, J., 46, 77
Hobert, J.P., 198, 199
Hoff, P.D., 102, 150
Hofferth, S.L., 301, 304
Holford, T.R., 77
Holland, P.W., 4, 100, 262
Hombo, C.M., 87
Hops, H., 261
Hout, M., 2, 5, 24, 177, 193
Howell, N., 320, 325
Hox, J.J., 86n
Huisman, M., 108, 128, 136, 149
Hunter, D.R., 108, 126, 149, 150
Hussong, A.M., 261

I
Ihaka, R., 253
Inglehart, R.E.A., 247
Iwashyna, T.J., 157n

J
Jackson, R.J., 159
Jamieson, J., 318
Janis, J.M., 79n
Jankowski, M.S., 318
Johnson, C., 262, 272n, 288, 292, 295
Johnson, V., 261
Johnston, L.D., 196, 261
Jokinen, J., 175, 176, 181, 185, 191
Jonasson, J., 106, 130
Jones, J.H., 115
Jonsson, J.O., 4, 5, 29
Jöreskog, K.G., 7
Jurkiewicz, J., 106
Juster, F.T., 305

K
Karmous, A., 79n
Kaufman, L., 206
Kaufmann, J., 192
Kenny, D.A., 102
Kenyon, E., 324, 325
Khoo, S., 260

King, G., 226
Kitzinger, J., 319, 321, 324, 325
Knight, K., 77
Knorr-Held, L., 69
Kovats-Bernat, J.C., 318
Kreft, I.G., 86N
Krzywicki, A., 106
Kupper, L.L., 79n

L
Laird. N.M., 178, 193
Land, K.C., 40, 41, 42, 44n, 45, 46, 66,
    67, 77, 79
Lang, J. B., 174, 175, 178, 193, 196
Larcker, D.F., 313
Lauderdale, D., 157n
Lazega, E., 117, 134, 139, 144
Lehmann, E.L., 105
Leinhardt, S., 100
Liang, K.Y., 193
Liao, T.F., 210
Lindsey, J.K., 195
Lindsey, P.J., 192
Littell, R.C., 47
Little, R.J.A., 180, 297
Liu, J., 202
Long, J.S., 30, 226, 234, 243
Lord, F.M., 258
Lorenz, M.O., 202
Louis, T.A., 58, 60n
Lucas, S.R., 2, 28
Lunn, D., 59n

M
Maclean, A., 9
Maclean, C., 319, 324
Maclure, M., 159, 166
Magidson, J., 207
Manski, C.F., 29
Manza, J., 5, 24
Maples, J., 271n, 297
Mare, R.D., 6, 10, 12, 23n, 24, 27n, 28,
    29, 30, 35
Margolick, J.B., 172
Marshall, R.J., 159

Mason, K.O., 46, 76, 82, 83
Mason, W.H., 46, 76, 82, 83
Mason, W.M., 45, 46, 76, 77, 79, 83
Mather, N., 303
Mazzeo, J., 87
McCammon, R.J., 65, 78, 79, 80n, 93,
    94
McCrady, B.S., 261
McCullagh, P., 178, 193, 227, 234, 238,
    241
McCulloch, C.E., 68
McDonald, J.W., 174, 175, 176, 181,
    185, 191
McPherson, M., 101
Menken, J., 46, 77
Meyer, K., 166
Milanovic, B., 202
Milliken, G.A., 47, 226, 231n
Mitchell, A.A., 166
Mittleman, M.A., 159
Moffitt, R., 304
Moreno, E., 320
Morenoff, J.D., 263
Morgan, S.L., 29
Morris, C.N., 57n
Morris, M., 108, 149
Mueller, R.O., 313
Murphy, S., 271n, 297
Mussard, S., 202, 204
Muthen, B., 260

N
Natarajan, R., 174, 175, 190, 192, 193
National Center for Educational
    Statistics, 69
Nelder, J.A., 227, 234, 238, 241
Newman, M.E.J., 101, 106, 140
Nilan, P., 318
Novick, M.R., 258
Nowell, A., 87

O
O'Brien, R. M., 77, 83
O'Malley, P.M., 196, 261
Osmond, C., 77

P

Pandina, R.J., 261
Park, J., 106
Paterson, B.L., 320, 324, 325
Pattison, P.E., 104, 105, 107, 108, 116,
   117, 118, 119, 126, 130, 131, 134,
   148, 150
Peritore, N.P., 320
Pinheiro, P.C., 272
Pitts, S.C., 260
Poole, K., 46, 76, 82, 83
Powers, D.A., 234, 243
Powers, W., 164n
Preston, S., 46, 77
Prost, J., 260

R

R Development Core Team, 191,
   253
Rachal. J.V., 260
Racine-Poon, A., 58
Raftery, A.E., 2, 150, 207, 208, 209
Rainer, E., 69
Rao, C.R., 237
Rasbash, J., 61
Raudenbush, S.W., 41, 49, 50, 51n, 57,
   86, 87n, 88, 89, 89n, 94, 262, 263,
   272, 272n, 273, 275, 288,
   292, 295
Reardon, S.F., 271n, 295
Reckase, M., 262
Rijken, S., 35
Rinaldo, C., 172
Robb, R., 83
Robertson, C., 40, 76, 77
Robins, G.L., 105, 107, 116, 117, 118,
   119, 126, 130, 131, 148, 150
Robins, J.M., 159
Robinson, J.P., 305
Rodrigo, M.F., 196
Roeder, K., 209
Rousseuw, P.J., 206
Rubin, D.B., 57, 57n, 60, 180, 297
Rutter, M., 261
Ryder, N.B., 76, 93

S

Sackett, D.L., 179
Sampson, R.J., 262, 263, 272n, 288,
   292, 295
Sandberg, J.F., 301
Schadee, H., 8n
Schaie, K. W., 65
Scheier, L.M., 261
Schifflers, E., 77
Schneeweiss, S., 166
Schneider, M.F., 172
Schulenberg, J, 261
Schwartz, J., 202
Schweinberger, M., 108, 128, 136, 149,
   150
Searle, S.R., 68, 226, 231n
Seltzer, M., 60
Seyte, F., 202, 204
Shavit, Y., 2, 24, 28
Silberg, J., 261
Sinclair, J.C., 179
Singer, J.D., 273
Sinnott, R., 238
Sloan, M., 259
Smith, A.F.M., 58
Smith, H.L., 46, 79, 94
Smith, P.W.F., 174, 175, 176, 181, 185,
   191
Smith-Lovin, L., 101
Smithson, M.J., 219
Snijders, T., 45, 88n
Snijders, T.A.B., 102, 105, 107, 108,
   111, 128, 130, 136, 140, 148, 149,
   150
Snow, C.M., 301
Sobel, M.E., 177, 193
Spady, W., 28
Speed, F.M., 226, 231n
Spiegelhalter, D.J., 59, 59n
Stafford, F.P., 305
Steglich, C.E.G., 108, 128, 136,
   149
Stern, H.S., 57, 57n, 60
Stice, E., 261
Stolzenberg, R.M., 26

Strauss, D., 102, 103, 104, 105, 112, 115, 148
Stroup, W.W., 47
Sturmer, T., 166
Suissa, S., 162, 163, 166
Szelenyi, S., 210

T
Tantrum, J., 150
Tavakoli, M., 179
Terraza, M., 202, 204
Thomas, A., 59n
Thompson, E.A., 104
Thorne, S., 320, 324, 325
Tiao, G.C., 62n
Tibshirani, R., 226
Tibshirani, R.J., 248n
Tierney, L., 108
Tilley, J., 238
Tomz, M., 226
Trivedi, P.K., 156

V
van der Linde, A., 59
van Duijn, M.A.J., 111
Verkuilen, J., 219
Vermunt, J., 207
Vermunt, J.K., 174, 196
Vines, S.K., 58

W
Wadsworth, K.N., 261
Wainer, H., 262
Wang, J., 166
Wang, W.C., 262
Wasserman, L., 209

Wasserman, S., 104, 105, 108, 148
Watts, D.J., 131
Weisberg, S., 226
Werler, M.M., 166
White, H.R., 260
Willett, J.B., 273
Wills, T.A., 261
Wilmoth, J.R., 77
Wilson, J.A., 46, 65, 78–79, 80n, 83, 88, 89, 92–93, 94
Wilson, M.R, 262
Winsborough, H.H., 46, 76, 82, 83
Winship, C., 30, 202
Wise, D.A., 29
Wittenberg, J., 226
Wolfinger, R.D., 47
Wong, W., 60
Woodcock, R., 303
Woolcock, J., 105, 107, 126, 130, 131

X
Xie, Y., 5, 234, 243

Y
Yamaguchi, K., 156
Yang, M.-L., 272, 275
Yang, Y, 40, 41, 42, 44n, 45, 46, 66, 67
Yang, Y., 40, 46, 77, 79
Yao, S., 202
Yitzhaki, S., 202, 204
Yosef, M., 272, 275

Z
Zeger, S.L., 193
Zhang, J., 157n

SUBJECT INDEX

note: t = table; f = figure

A

activity effect, 144

age effects, 64–65, 76. *See also* age-period-cohort analysis

age-period-cohort accounting/multiple classification model. *See* age-period-cohort analysis (APC)

age-period-cohort analysis (APC), 75–94

  development, 76–77

  of finite time period data, 40–41

  GLMM-based models, 68–69

  goal of, 76

  hierarchical (*See* hierarchical age-period-cohort analysis)

  identification problem, 76–77

  mixed models approach, 75–94

  of repeated cross-section surveys, 77

  verbal test scores, 78–82

Akaike's information criteria (AIC), 47, 59, 184–185, 194

alcohol use

  dimensionality, empirical assessment of, 289–295

latent, person-specific estimates of, 276–277

alternating independent two-path distributions, 122–125, 143

alternating *k*-star distribution, 122, 124

  geometric, 113

  graph from, 127–129

  in-*k*-star combinations, 142–143

  mean number of edges and, 128–130

  number of edges and, 128

  out-*k*-star combinations, 142–143

  with parameter λ, 113

alternating *k*-triangle

  alternating independent two-paths and, 122–126

  applications, 137, 138, 140

  edge-plus model, 132–133

  new specifications for, 129–133

  positive effect, 146

  transitive, 143

APC. *See* age-period-cohort analysis

arcs, 142

association model, 181–182

Australian poverty reduction efforts, model of cross-national attitude differences, 247–252

335

autocorrelation plots, 58, 71
avalanche effect, 110, 111

B
Bayesian inference, for hierarchical
    APC models, 55–69
  Gibbs sampling, 55–60
  MCMC estimation, 55–60
  prior sensitivity analysis, 60–63
Bayesian information criterion (BIC),
    208–209
Bayesian information estimates,
    286–287
Bayes-MCMC methods, 56–58
Bayes posterior variance, 285
Bernoulli graphs, 103, 106, 114,
    127–128, 132, 133
BIC (Bayesian information criterion),
    208–209
binary factor, latent, 182, 183
binary logit model, effect displays for,
    228–232
binary response models, 29–30
Britain, political knowledge and party
    choice analysis, 238–242
broken family (BROKEN), 11, 14, 15

C
Canadian occupational prestige, linear
    model of, 232–234
case-crossover method
  description of, 158–161
  vs. case-time-control method,
    167–168
case-time-control method
  description of, 163–166
  with time-varying covariates, 169
  vs. case-crossover method, 167–168
categorical predictors, effect displays
    and, 229, 231n
CCREM (cross-classified random
    effects models), 40, 42–47
CD (conditional dependence), 116,
    119, 121, 126
cell phones, for field work, 324–325

change statistics, 108–110, 113–114,
    121–122
Child Development Supplement, to
    Panel Study of Income Dynamics,
    303–304
class inequality
  definition of, 215–216
  vs. individual inequality, 202,
    215–222
cluster analysis
  model-based (See model-based
    cluster analysis)
  of ordinal data (See clustered
    ordinal data analysis)
  purpose of, 206
clustered ordinal data analysis,
    173–197
  combined marginal, transition and
    random-effects models,
    196
  on government spending opinions,
    180–185
  marginal models, 192–194
  marginal regression, 180
  maximum likelihood estimation,
    190–191
  mean parametrization, 175–178
  null association, 181
  proportional odds, 180
  random-effects models, 194–196
  on teenage marijuana use, 185–190
  transition models, 191–192
CODA (Convergence Diagnostics and
    Output Analysis), 58
cohort effects. See also
    age-period-cohort analysis
  defined, 76
  estimated, 64–65
combined regression and association
    model
  of government spending opinions,
    180–185
  o teenage marijuana use, 185–190
conditional dependence (CD), 116,
    119, 121, 126

conditional maximum likelihood,
    159–160
"conditional severity," 271
conditional univariate probabilities,
    181
Consumer Price Index, 11
continuation ratio model, 271n
Convergence Diagnostics and Output
    Analysis (CODA), 58
core-periphery network structure, 101
couple mortality prediction
    case-crossover method, 167–168
    case-time-control method, 163–168
    nonzero effect of treatment, 168–169
    simulation results, 166–169
covariates
    dichotomous, 182
    effect of, 144, 146
    population-averaged effects, 192
Cox proportional hazards model, 160
Cox regression program, 160
CPS (Current Population Survey),
    March 1973 supplement. *See*
    Occupational Changes in a
    Generation Survey
cross-classified random effects models
    (CCREM), 40, 42–47
Current Population Survey (CPS),
    March 1973 supplement. *See*
    Occupational Changes in a
    Generation Survey

D
decomposition methods, for Gini
    index, 216–217
degeneracy, transitivity models and,
    115–116, 129, 131
degree counts, geometrically weighted,
    112–114
degree-dependent statistics, 125
degree frequencies, 114
degree of node, 103
density of graph, 125
dependence ratios
    joint probability and, 197

in marginal model, 192–193
    for profile probabilities, 180–181
    properties of, 178–180
    second-order, 176, 187, 188
Deviance Information Criterion
    (DIC), 59
DIC (Deviance Information
    Criterion), 59
differential item functioning test (DIF
    test), 262, 289, 292–294
dimensionality, of latent
    characteristics, 288–295
    association of covariates, 289
    correlation matrix, 288
    definition of, 261–262
    differential item functioning, 289
    substance use, empirical assessment
        of, 289–295
directed relations, exponential
    random graph models of,
    141–150
Dirichlet-distributed propensities,
    latent, 182–184
Dirichlet distribution, 182–184
discrete-time hazard model, 29, 271n,
    298
    with Rasch model (*See* partial
        independence item response
        model)
drm, 191
Duncan Socioeconomic Index for
    Occupations, 10–11
dyadic selection processes,
    homophilous, 101
dyads, 142

E
edge-plus-alternating-*k*-triangle model,
    132–133
educational attainment
    of father, 11, 13, 15
    of mother (*See* mother's education)
    OCG survey data, 11–12
    as process in time, 28
    school progression ratios and, 28

educational stratification models, 4–6,
   27–35
educational transitions
   linear probability modeling, 2
   models
logistic response (*See* logistic response
      models)
   multiple factors in, 29
   significance of, 28
   social processes and, 28–29
   unrestricted, 30–31
      OCG survey data, 11–12
      person-transition records and, 6–7
      social background and, 12–14
      socioeconomic background effects, 7
effect displays
   for binary logit model, 228–232
   computation of, 253–254
   estimated population marginal
      means as, 226
   for generalized linear models,
      227–233
   least-squares means as, 226
   for linear model, 232–234
   for multinomial logit model,
      234–241
   for proportional-odds logit models,
      241–252
   purpose of, 226, 253
ERGM. *See* exponential random
      graph model
estimated population marginal means,
      226
exponential random graph model
      (ERGM), 102–108
   alternating independent two paths,
      122–125
   asymptotical distributions, 106
   change statistics, 108–110
   correlation between Lazega's
      lawyers, 134–141
   directed relations, 141–150
   discussion, 147–150
   friendship relation, 144–146
   geometrically weighted degrees and

related functions, 111–115
   Gibbs sampling, 108–110
   independent two-path distributions,
      133–134
   k-stars, 109, 110–111
   modeling transitivity by alternating
      k-triangles, 115–122
   new specifications, possibilities with,
      126–134
   parameter sensitivity, 139–141
   phase transition, 106–107
   of transitivity in networks, 125–126

F
family background, effect on school
      progression, 28
family income (FAMINC), 11, 13, 15
farm background (FARM), 11, 14, 15
father's education (FED), 11, 13, 15
father's occupational status (FASEI),
      10–11, 13, 15
FED (father's education), 11, 13, 15
fieldwork safety, 317–326
   increasing, strategies for, 323–326
   literature review, 317–321
   personal experience, 321–323
filter items, 257
Fisher information, 286
fitted log-linear models, 193
fitting models, to sparse data sets, 197
five-triangle, 118
fixed effects likelihood, for partial
      independence item response
      model, 270–271
fixed effects model, 271
fixed-effects regression methods,
      155–171
   case-crossover, 158–161
   case-time-control design, 163–166
   couple mortality application,
      156–163
   discussion, 169–171
   example, 156–158
   limitations of analyses, 162
   using simulated data, 166–169

four-cycle dependence structure, 123
France, model-based cluster analysis of income inequality in, 209–215, 219–222
friendship modeling, 144–146
fuzzy set theory, 218–219

G
"gate" item, 262–263
gate matrix, 265–268, 290
Gelman-Rubin convergence diagnostic plots test, 58, 70
Generalized Linear Mixed Effects Model (GLMM), 68–69
generalized linear models, effects displays for, 227–233
General Social Survey (GSS), 41, 77
  birth cohorts, 41, 43, 45–46
  verbal ability data, 41–45, 50–55
geometrically weighted degrees
  counts, 112–114
  decreasing distribution assumption, 112
  distributions, 125, 127–129
  in-degrees, 142
  out-degrees, 142, 143
geometric alternating k-star distribution, 113
Gibbs sampling
  change statistics and, 108–110
  conditional distributions, 69
  for hierarchical APC models, 55–60
Gini index (Gini inequality ratio)
  alternative method (*See* model-based cluster analysis)
  between-group differences, 217–221
  decomposition methods, 216–217, 221
  definition of, 203–204
  of distribution with six data points, 204–206
  formulas, 204
  limitations of, 201–203, 222
  Lorenz curve (*See* Lorenz curve)
  mean difference, 204

relative insensitivity of, 205–206
GLMM (Generalized Linear Mixed Effects Model), 68–69
government
  poverty reduction efforts, model of cross-national differences in attitude, 247–252
  spending, opinions on, 180–185
graphs
  from alternating k-star distribution, 127–129
  Bernoulli (*See* Bernoulli graphs)
  definition of, 102
  density of, 125
  exponential random (*See* exponential random graph model)
  k-triangle, 132
  Markov (*See* Markov random graph model)
  nondirected, 109–110, 120, 126
  partial conditional independence model, 116–119
  probability distribution for, 102
  random, 102
  total number of ties and, 107
GSS. *See* General Social Survey

H
Hammersley-Clifford theorem, 103, 117
HAPC. *See* hierarchical age-period-cohort analysis
hazard ratio, 158
hierarchical age-period-cohort analysis (HAPC)
  Bayesian inference for, 55–69
  CCREM, 40, 42–47
  data, 41–42
  development of, 40
  Gibbs sampling, 55–60
  identification problem, 46
  Monte Carlo simulations, 50–55
  REML-EB estimation, 40–41, 47–50
  variables, 41–42
hierarchical linear models (HLM), 77

hierarchical necessary factors,
    186–187, 197
higher-order terms, 227
HLM (hierarchical linear models), 77
Hungary, model-based cluster analysis
    of income inequality in, 209–216,
    219–222

I
income inequality, model-based cluster
    analysis of, 209–215
independent two-path distributions
    alternating, 122–125, 143
    description of, 133–134
inequality
    class, 215–216
    income, model-based cluster analysis
        of, 209–215
    individual *vs.* class, 202, 215–222
    measures of, 201–222
inequality of educational opportunity
    model, 28
interpretation, of dependence ratio, 178
invariance, dependence ratio and, 179
Ising models, 140
item bias, 262
item conditional severity estimates,
    277–280
item structure, for partial independence
    item response model, 265–268

J
joint probability, 197

K
k-independent two-paths, 123–125
k-star
    alternating (*See* alternating *k*-star
        distribution)
    counts, 112
    degree distributions, 112–113
    exponential random graph
        distribution and, 109–111
    Markov graph, 103
k-triangle

alternating (*See* alternating
    k-triangle)
counts, 119, 120
four-cycle dependence structure, 123
higher-order, downweighting of, 122
low-density and higher-density
    graphs, 132
modeling, 111, 117–118
number of, 119–120

L
latent binary factor, 182, 183
latent Dirichlet-distributed
    propensities, 182–184
latent trait models, 260, 262–263,
    295–298
latent variable models, 197, 258
least-squares means, 226
linear model, of Canadian
    occupational prestige, 232–234
logistic response models, 2–4
    advantages/disadvantages, 4–5
    applications, 27
    with partial proportionality
        constraints (*See* LRPPC model)
    with proportionality constraints
        (*See* LRPC model)
    traditional, replication of, 12, 14, 15
logit models
    binary, effect displays for, 228–232
    exponentiation of coefficients in,
        230n
    multinomial, effect displays for,
        234–241
    proportional-odds, effects displays
        for, 241–252
log-linear models, 5
log-multiplicative layer model, 5
log-odds ratio parameters, conditional,
    193
log-transformation, for model-based
    cluster analysis, 213–215, 219, 221
Lorenz curve, 202, 203, 206, 210
LRPC model (logistic response models
    with proportionality constraints)

identification problem, 30, 34–35
restrictions, 33–34
validity, normalizing restrictions
and, 31–33
vs. MIMIC model, 7–8
LRPPC model (logistic response
models with partial
proportionality constraints)
description of, 8–10
of educational transitions, 14, 16–24
identification problem, 30, 34–35
validity, normalizilng restrictions
and, 31–33

M

MAR (missing at random), 180, 191
marginal frequencies, of marijuana use,
185–186
marginal models
for clustered ordinal data, 192–194
with transition and random-effects
models, 196
marginal probabilities, 197
marginal regression model, 180
marginal severity estimates, 277–280
marijuana
dimensionality of use, empirical
assessment of, 289–295
possession arrests, binary logit
model of, 228–231
Markov association model. *See*
Markov random graph model
Markov chain, definition of, 108
Markov chain Monte Carlo (MCMC)
applications, 136–141
directed relations, 145–147
for ERGMs and parameter
estimation, 105
Gibbs sampling and, 55–60
WinBUGS program and, 68
Markovian dependence, 105, 126
Markov random graph model
advantages of, 102–103
change statistic, 109–110
k-triangle, 131

for longitudinal studies, 197
of teenage marijuana use, 187–190
transivity parameters, 115–122, 125
triangles, 132, 133
triangle with negative star
parameters, 130–131
triangle without star parameters,
129–130, 131
Markov structure, 185–186
masculinity research, 321–322
maximum likelihood estimation (ML),
105, 177
binary logit model, 229–230
for clustered ordinal data, 190–191
model-based clustering method, 207
MCLUST software, 209, 210
MCMC. *See* Markov chain Monte
Carlo
mean parameters, 176
mean squared errors (MSE), 67–68
Metropolis-Hastings algorithm, 108,
126, 136
MIMIC (multiple indicator, multiple
cause) model, 7–8, 10, 27
missing at random (MAR), 180, 191
ML. *See* maximum likelihood
estimation
model-based cluster analysis, 202,
206–209
advantages of, 201, 207
basic specifications for, 207
density estimation, 209
of income inequality, 209–215
log-transformation for, 213–215,
219, 221
maximum likelihood form, 207
selection of model, 208–209
uncertainty of classification, 209
Monte Carlo Markov Chain (MCMC),
56–57
Monte Carlo maximum likelihood
estimates, 128
Monte Carlo simulations, 50–55, 67–68
mother's education, 11, 13, 15, 313
MSE (mean squared errors), 67–68

multinomial logit models, effect
    displays for, 234–242
multinomial models, 5
multiple-indicator-multiple cause
    model (MIMIC), 7–8, 10, 27
multiple item analysis, 261–262

N
National Assessment of Educational
    Progress, 69
National Institute of Child Health and
    Human Development (NICHD),
    304
necessary factors, hierarchical,
    186–187, 197
NICHD (National Institute of Child
    Health and Human
    Development), 304
node degrees, functions of, 114–115
node-level-effects, 100–101
nondirected graphs, 109–110,
    120, 126
non-parametric random-effects
    models, 195
nontransitive null model, 100
Norway poverty reduction efforts,
    model of cross-national attitude
    differences, 247–252
null association model, 181–182

O
Occupational Changes in a Generation
    Survey (OCG)
    importance of, 2
    men, 12, 14
    replicating/extending logistic
        response models with, 10–24, 34
    response rate, 10
    school continuation, 12, 14, 15
    second, 28
    social background characteristics,
        10–11, 13
OLS, 58
1-triangles, 120
order of the k-triangle, 118

ordinal data, cluster analysis of. *See*
    clustered ordinal data analysis
ordinal scale, 174

P
Panel Study of Income Dynamics
    (PSID), Child Development
    Supplement, 303–304
parametric random-effects models, 195
parametrization
    definition of, 175–177
    illustration of, 177–178
parents. *See also* mother's education
    father's education, 11, 13, 15
    reading to children (*See* reading to
        children)
parsimonious model, 192
partial conditional independence
    graph models, 116–119
partial independence item response
    model, 257–298
    applications, 259
    background and significance,
        260–263
    computing item and survey
        information, 285–287
    definition of, 258
    development of, 258–259
    dimensionalilty assessment, 288–295
    empirical example, 273–287
    fixed effects likelihood, 270–271
    gate matrix, 265–268
    item conditional severity estimates,
        277–280
    item structure, 265–268
    marginal severity estimates, 277–280
    notation, 268–270
    observed *vs.* predicted item
        conditional and marginal
        probabilities, 280–285
    person-specific item conditional and
        marginal probabilities, 280
    quantities of interest, 258–259
    random effects likelihood, 272–273
    sample and data, 263–265

period effects, 64, 65, 76. *See also*
 age-period-cohort analysis
person-specific item conditional and
 marginal probabilities, 280
PHDCN (Project on Human
 Development in Chicago
 Neighborhoods), 263–265
p* models. *See* exponential random
 graph model
Pochhamer's symbol, 115
political knowledge and party choice
 analysis, in Britain, 238–242
popularity effect, 144
prior density, 57n
probability distribution
 cumulative, 244
 degenerate, 105–106
Project on Human Development in
 Chicago Neighborhoods
 (PHDCN), 263–265
proportionality constraints, 6–10, 29
proportional-odds logit models, effects
 displays for, 241–252
proportional odds model, 180
pseudo-likelihood estimation method,
 103–104, 105, 109
PSID (Panel Study of Income
 Dynamics), Child Development
 Supplement, 303–304

R
random effects likelihood, for partial
 independence item response
 model, 272–273
random-effects models
 for clustered ordinal data, 194–196
 with transition and marginal models,
 196
random graphs, 102
range, of dependence ratio, 179
Rasch model, 263
 alternatives, 295
 fixed effects, 271
 item independence, 285
 risk set for each item, 286n

vs. partial independence item
 response model, 298
reading to children
 analysis plan, 307
 child vocabulary and, 313
 demographic variables,
 measurement of, 306–307
 multivariate analysis, 310–311
 national estimates of, 308–310
 parents and, 301–303
 prediction of verbal achievement
 and, 311–313
 response bias in, 314–315
 school preparation and, 301–302
 stylized questions on, 304–305
 time diaries, 305–306
 time measurement, 312–313
regression coefficients, 192
regression estimates, from
 random-effects models,
 195–196
regression model, without explanatory
 variables, 192
relative risk, 179, 197
REML (restricted maximum
 likelihood), 59, 66, 67
REML-EB (restricted maximum
 likelihood-empirical Bayes),
 40–41, 47–50, 58
researcher-subject interaction
 avoiding dangerous situations, 324
 cell phones and, 324–325
 gender and, 317–318
 professional dress and, 324
 rural interviews and, 322–323
 safety considerations, 324–326
 sexual harassment/intimidation,
 319–320
 violence/intimidation, 319–321
restricted maximum likelihood
 (REML), 59, 66, 67
restricted maximum
 likelihood-empirical Bayes
 (REML-EB), 40–41, 47–50, 58
R language, 209, 210

rural interviews, researcher-subject interaction and, 322–323

S

SAS macro program, 68
SAS PROC LOGISTIC, 165n
SAS PROC MIXED, 58
saturated models, for degree sequence, 111
school
  continuation, social background characteristics and, 2–4, 12, 14, 15
  preparation, reading to children and, 301–302
  transitions (*See* educational transitions)
school progression ratios, 28
self-organization, 101
SES (socioeconomic status), 292n
siblings, number of (SIBS), 11, 13, 15
SIENA program, 128, 132, 133, 136, 137
single-item analysis, 260–261
social background characteristics, 28
  effects on school transitions, in binary response models, 29–30
  school continuation and, 2–4, 12, 14, 15
social inequality analysis, attributes for, 206
social selection, 101
social stratification research, 2
social ties, 101
socioeconomic background factors, 30
Southern birth (SOUTH), 12, 14, 15
S-Plus language, 209
stereotype model, 8
stereotype regression model, 5
stochastic algorithm, 136
stochastic models, 100, 102
stochastic parents, 59n
structural balance effect, 101
stylized questions, on reading to children, 304–305

substance use
  dimensionality, empirical assessment of, 289–295
  marijuana possession arrests, binary logit model of, 228–231
  models for teenage marijuana use, 185–190, 196–197
  partial independence item response model, 273–287
  PHDCN sample and data, 263–265
  single-item analysis, 260–261
Sweden poverty reduction efforts, model of cross-national attitude differences, 247–252

T

teenage marijuana use, models of, 185–190, 196–197
three-triangle, 118, 119
ties, 141
time diaries, 305–306
time-invariant variables, control in case-crossover method, 158–161
Toronto arrests for marijuana possession, binary logit model of, 228–231
transition models
  for clustered ordinal data, 191–192
  educational (*See* educational transitions, models)
  with marginal and random-effects models, 196
transition probability, dependence ratio and, 179–180
transitivity, 100–102
  effect of, 145
  modeling by alternating k-triangles, 115–122
  models, degeneracy and, 115–116, 129, 131
  partial conditional independence and, 107–109

t-ratios, 136–137
triad closure, 100
triad count, 125
triangles, 106
   five-triangle, 118
   k-triangle (*See k*-triangle)
   with negative star parameters,
      130–131
   three-triangle, 118, 119
   1-triangles, 120
   two-triangle, 118
   without star parameters, 129–130,
      131
triangulation, 101
two-star model
two-triangle, 118

U
uniform differences model, 5

V
VEI, 208
verbal ability
   achievement predictions, reading to
      children and, 311–313
   Bayesian model for, 56

W
WinBUGS program, 57, 59, 68

Y
Yule distribution to degree
   distributions, 115